— *Asian Law Series* —

ASIAN LAW CENTER

SCHOOL OF LAW

UNIVERSITY OF WASHINGTON

NUMBER 20

The Asian Law Series was initiated in 1969, with the
cooperation of the University of Washington Press
and the Institute for Comparative and Foreign Area
Studies (now the Henry M. Jackson School of
International Studies). A complete list of the books in the
series appears at the end of this book.

The members of the editorial committee are
Veronica L. Taylor (chair), Susan Whiting,
Saadia Pekkanen, Toshiko Takenaka, and
Dongsheng Zang.

季八供我名叫季文升今年二十八歲是青縣
董京村人父親季幅黄今年七十多歲母親劉
氏我弟兄三人大哥子季文學在總督衙門充
當茶房二哥子季文成他種地都分居度日我
行三我小名叫八兒我女人何氏今年二十九
歲生有兩箇兒子大的叫固兒今年五歲小的
叫喜兒今年兩歲我平日種地為生素與朱家
新莊的王世清認識從十六年三月間我到新
集趕集遇見王世清勸我學好把我叫到他家
留我住了一日一夜他家供著一張紙畫的佛
像也記不真是什麼佛領我燒了香磕了頭教
我學好說是義和門取其和好的意思這義字
我也講不來他教我孝順父母和睦鄉里耳不
聽非聲眼不觀非色鼻不聞顛倒口不說非言
還教我坐功運氣修練鼻眼耳舌說人頭上有
三道橫紋為三道紫金鑷三道紫金箍眉叢中
為人之性臉為三道紫金鑷是氣為鎮運氣冲開頭頂三
道紫金箍本性從顛門出修練真性以修來世

TRUE CRIMES

IN EIGHTEENTH-CENTURY CHINA

TWENTY CASE HISTORIES

Compiled and Translated by Robert E. Hegel

*with contributions by Maram Epstein,
Mark McNicholas, and Joanna Waley-Cohen*

UNIVERSITY OF WASHINGTON PRESS *Seattle and London*

TRUE CRIME IN EIGHTEENTH-CENTURY CHINA IS PUBLISHED WITH THE
ASSISTANCE OF A GRANT FROM WASHINGTON UNIVERSITY IN ST. LOUIS.

© 2009 by the University of Washington Press
Printed in the United States of America
Design by Pamela Canell
14 12 11 10 09 5 4 3 2 1

University of Washington Press, P.O. Box 50096, Seattle, WA 98145 U.S.A.
www.washington.edu / uwpress

Library of Congress Cataloging-in-Publication Data
Hegel, Robert E., 1943–
True crimes in eighteenth-century China : twenty case histories /
compiled and translated by Robert E. Hegel ; with contributions by
Maram Epstein, Mark McNicholas, and Joanna Waley-Cohen.
p. cm. — (Asian law series ; no 20)
Includes bibliographical references and index.
ISBN 978-0-295-98906-8 (hardback : alk. paper)
ISBN 978-0-295-98907-5 (pbk. : alk. paper)
1. Criminal law—China—History. 2. Criminal law—China—History—Cases.
3. Criminal intent—China—History. 4. Crime—China—History. I. Epstein, Maram.
II. McNicholas, Mark. III. Waley-Cohen, Joanna. IV. Title.
KNQ3800.H44 2009   345.51—dc22   2008046287

The paper used in this publication is acid-free and 90 percent recycled from at least 50
percent post-consumer waste. It meets the minimum requirements of American National
Standard for Information Sciences—Permanence of Paper for Printed Library Materials,
ANSI Z39.48–1984. ♾ ♻

Frontispiece: Excerpt from the original text of "Testimony of Ji Ba, 1814" (see pages 197–98).

To the memory of GROSSMUTTER ETTA *(1879–1975)*

and of my parents EARL *(1905–1995) and* OPAL *(1905–2003),*

with unending gratitude for all the stories

they told me through the years.

Contents

Preface and Acknowledgments

Many years ago, Philip Kuhn, the eminent historian of late imperial China, gave a lecture in which he quoted the testimony of a monk who had been accused of a horrendous crime—demonically stealing a young boy's life energy after snipping off the boy's queue. The year was 1768, and China was gripped by political and social uncertainties that produced this widespread "soulstealing" (*jiaohun*) scare. For his part, the monk was one of many thousands of victims of a famine in central China; he had left his monastery to find and bring back food for those who could not travel.

Professor Kuhn's presentation was remarkable for two reasons. The first, of course, is the story told by the material: the overpowering suspicion and the senseless violence committed against innocent strangers by frightened villagers—and local administrators—when gripped by spreading fears of natural disaster and possible supernatural threats to their children. This story merged with the larger political concerns at the heart of Kuhn's subsequent book, *Soulstealers*, tracing the emperor's fears that the sorcery was a diversion meant to hide sedition: any symbolic severing of the hairstyle imposed by the Manchus might, however implausibly, suggest an antigovernment movement. The second, which was even more surprising to me then, is that the monk's testimony had been taken down, apparently, verbatim: his own words were to be found in legal documents preserved in the archives of China's last dynasty, the Qing (1644–1911).

Having taught general courses on China throughout my career, I had always sought to assign readings in primary texts, authentic documents that preserve what people really said, thought, and did. Literature written in Chinese is undoubtedly more voluminous than any other literature in the world; the earliest Chinese poetry dates back three thousand years. But literature in China, as elsewhere, was generally produced by and for members of the social and political elite; the voices of the "common" people were scarcely to be found there, and the artistic conventions of literary forms could circumscribe the expression of great writers as well. It seemed that crime records, through their detailed testimony, could at last provide a view into old Chinese society and allow readers a glance into the lives of people of the past. My original intention for this collection was to present in English the testimony of a number of people who lived in China during the time of the Great Qing Empire.

But texts are frequently not what they seem, and these do not represent common people's lives as directly as I had initially hoped. Historians of China have demonstrated that all testimony in crime reports was carefully edited in order to utilize standard legal language and to meet the expectations of the judicial system; crimes, then as now, had to be described in ways that matched legally established definitions of unacceptable behavior and allowed efficient processing. But even though the texts are phrased in standard terms sanctioned by the imperial government, the real situations that provoked the crimes, the conflicts and clashes of personal desires, are still represented in sufficient specificity to reveal institutional and social realities unavailable in other contemporary sources.

This volume is intended as a window into a society that has often been characterized as having been socially stagnant, as having been uniformly "Confucian," authoritarian, patriarchal, and culturally stultifying. These case reports reveal a society that was anything but uniform, or stagnant—or harmonious. Not surprisingly, common people in late imperial China committed all of the blunders and mistakes to which the human species is prone. Crime reports also show the hopes—and the fears—of specific, named individuals whom we may get to know through re-creations of their words, either in testimony as perpetrators and witnesses or as clerks and officials in the judicial system.

This collection is not intended as a general introduction to Chinese history. Instead, it is meant to be a supplement to more formal textbooks and a new source of information for nonspecialist readers. To that end, the introduction provides only a brief sketch of the complex administrative structures of the Qing period. The cases presented here are categorized to high-light features of the judicial review process relevant only to capital crimes; in each case, early entries are more complete, while later translations are more selective in order to avoid needless repetition. Appendix 3 uses an alternative strategy of grouping cases by types of social conflict. And to make the collection more useful in the classroom, discussion questions are available through a link at the University of Washington Press Web site, www.washington.edu / uwpress. The complete original documents from which these translations were made are available online through the Washington University Digital Library, http://www.digital.wustl.edu.

Despite the limitations of the original texts, this volume provides glimpses of lived experience—both personal and administrative—that would otherwise be lost in time. In this way, it offers a means of complicating the generalizations that broader histories necessarily provide.

At various stages of this project, I have benefited from the questions, comments, and suggestions of numerous colleagues and friends, including William Alford, Cai Zong-qi, Kai-Wing Chow, Marvin Cummins, Du Wenwei, Beata Grant, John Haley, Lane Harris, Stevan Harrell, Wilt L. Idema, the late William C. Jones, Jeffrey C. Kinkley, William C. Kirby, Jerome Packard, Nancy Park, Michael J. Puett, David Rolston, James C. Shih, and Joanna Handlin Smith. In addition to their wise counsel, Maram Epstein, Mark McNicholas, Dian Murray, Janet Theiss, and Joanna Waley-Cohen very generously offered translations or texts, or both, for this project; some of their work is included in *True Crimes in Eighteenth-Century China*. An anonymous reviewer for the University of Washington Press also offered extremely helpful advice. My greatest debt, however, is to Thomas Buoye; by correcting numerous mistakes and misunderstandings, great and small, in both my introduction and the translations, his encyclopedic knowledge of the Qing judicial system and his meticulous historical rigor have very significantly enriched my more literary vision. If this volume has value for historians and legal scholars beyond the China field, it will be because of Tom's guidance through the revision process.

My special thanks to Philip Kuhn, who initially brought these materials to my attention and kindly supplied me with copies of several cases; to Wei Qingyuan of People's University and Ju Deyuan at the First Historical Archives in Beijing, who introduced me to the vast document collections there in 1986; and to Zhu Shuyuan who, along with her very capable staff, supplied me with many more case files during my visit to the archives in 1999. Nicolo Di Cosmo kindly assisted with the Manchu readings for numerous names. China historians Charlotte Beahan and Steven B. Miles raised important questions that led to clarification and corrections in several translations and throughout the introductory material; I am very grateful, too, for Steve's advice on the selection of cases presented here.

For several years, I have assigned selected cases as readings to students in my Chinese Civilization class at Washington University. Katherine Carlitz, able and insightful collaborator on *Writing and Law in Late Imperial China*, has also introduced them to her students at the University of Pittsburgh. Through these classes, I reached a better understanding of what I needed to provide in introducing these judicial records and what could be left to the students to discover. With this project, as with others throughout my career, my numerous students provided keen insights on how to interpret texts. As always, I am extremely grateful for the opportunity to continue my education in large part through their direction. And finally, my thanks to the editors at the University of Washington Press: to Lorri Hagman for her enthusiasm for this project, to Veronica Taylor for including this volume in the distinguished Asian Law Series, and to Marilyn Trueblood and Laura Iwasaki for their painstaking efforts in preparing the text for publication.

Translator's Notes

In recasting these documents into English, there has necessarily been what some literary critics term "slippage," ideas and expressions that do not convert easily from one language into another and either lose (or gain) meaning in translation. I have relied on the standard renditions for original terminology commonly used by China historians writing in English. Some testimony seems to have curious mixtures of formal and common speech. I have tried to convey some of these effects yet resisted the creation of false exoticism, even though I feel strongly that the social relationships so crucial to the individuals involved in these proceedings should be made clear in translation. To that end, I note the pronouns used and identify the degree of self-effacement they suggest. For example, many depositions by men use the pronoun *xiaode*, which I suggest on first use with the phrase "your humble servant"; for subsequent appearances of this conventional pronoun, I use simply "I," "me," and the like. In the original documents, all direct references to the emperor and his official pronouncements are raised above the text; that practice is reflected here with the use of superscript uppercase letters, LIKE THIS. When officials refer to themselves in communications with the emperor, they use the term *chen* (Your subject), and each routine memorial concerning a crime case begins with a formal list of titles held by the submitting official; both "Your subject" and the titles were written in characters that are smaller than those in the rest of the text, and this effect is reproduced here with the use of smaller subscript lowercase letters, like this. Finally, for the convenience of readers unaccustomed to the conventional structure and language of these crime reports—and in particular their redundancy—my own commentaries and summaries, intended to shorten and clarify, are inserted in italic type and are preceded and followed by an extra line space.

Since the early 1980s, when the First Historical Archives in Beijing were opened to scholars from abroad, more and more studies in European languages have relied on documents stored there. A fair number of the studies listed in the bibliography contain translations, or at least summaries, of crime reports.[1] Selected translations appear in documentary histories of imperial China as well. Collections of original archival materials in Chinese generally concentrate on documents having far greater political ramifications than these criminal case reports. Crime reports may be photocopied from such materials at the Beijing Archives, but in limited quantities. Thus, there is no alternative but to spend extended periods of time in the Beijing Archives reading room, among researchers who are illuminating the history of the Great Qing Empire with unprecedented clarity. Virtually all who study there from outside China bring back photocopies; all the translations here were made from such reproductions. I am tremendously grateful to Maram Epstein, Mark McNicholas, and Joanna Waley-Cohen for sharing their copies, translations, and expertise for this volume.

COMMONLY USED TERMS

chi	unit of measurement roughly equivalent to a foot, divided into ten *cun* somewhat longer than an inch, which are in turn divided into ten *fen* .
dan	(sometimes read *shi*) unit of weight used for measuring grains equivalent to about 50 kilograms, or 110 pounds.
jin	unit of weight equivalent to one pound or half a kilogram.
kang	brick platform through which a ventilation route is directed; when a small fire is built in the stove at one side, warm air passes along this circuitous path to the chimney in a far corner, thereby heating the entire platform. In northern China, people slept on the platform at night and, when possible, rolled up the quilts and sat there to work during the daylight hours of winter.
li	unit of distance, roughly one-third of a mile, or half a kilometer.
liang	unit of measurement in weighing silver for monetary transactions, roughly one ounce. The value of a *liang* of silver varied but was

often approximately one thousand *wen* coins. The nineteenth-century English-language translation is "tael."

mu unit of area for measuring land, about one-third of an acre.

sui (years of age) a newborn infant was considered to be one *sui* old, and age was calculated by adding another *sui* at every New Year.

wen ("coppers") standard currency unit made of copper and minted by imperial decree. The value of these coins varied, but their weight, size, and shape (round, with a square hole in the center to allow them to be strung together) had been virtually the same for centuries before the Qing period. They are often referred to as "cash" in nineteenth-century English-language writings.

shi Women's names generally were not to be mentioned in public, hence these official documents regularly refer to a woman by her father's surname or her husband's surname, or both, followed by the title *shi*. When referring to the woman's natal surname, this title has been translated as "Ms." For example, in order to reflect usage in the original documents, translations render Chen Li *shi* as Mrs. Chen Li (meaning Mrs. Chen née Li) and Zhang *shi* as Ms. Zhang.

yamen central administrative compound at county and upper levels of regional administration, comprising the official's courtroom, all relevant governmental offices and storehouses, and his residence.

DATING

In late imperial China, dates were recorded by reference to the reign period of the current emperor, each of whom selected a name for the period during which he would occupy the throne. Although in earlier dynasties, an emperor might change the name of his reign period, during the Ming and Qing dynasties, each emperor elected to have only one. The cases in this volume are from the following reign periods: Kangxi (1662–1722), Yongzheng (1723–1735), Qianlong (1736–1795), and Jiaqing (1796–1820).

When dates occur in the formal sections of these documents, they are given in the traditional Chinese order, with the year of the reign period, the lunar month, and the day (e.g., Qianlong 36.9.15) and are followed by the corresponding dates in the Western calendar. In order to avoid confusing the day with the month, dates in testimony take the form "the fifteenth of the ninth month of Qianlong 36," with the Western equivalent given in brackets when needed for clarification.

Because the months in the Chinese calendar had either twenty-nine or thirty days, the lunar calendar lagged behind the sun's movements. In recognition of these differences, an extra month was added once approximately every three years so that the lunar calendar more closely matched the solar year. These extra, intercalary, months are called *runyue* and are designated by the same number as the month they follow, hence, Jiaqing 8.*run* 2.10 means the tenth day of the *run* second month of Jiaqing 8.

According to traditional time-recording schemes, months were divided into ten-day periods termed *xun*. The day was divided into units equivalent to two hours. During the night, these units were called "watches" (*geng*) and were marked in the larger settlements by the beating of a drum. The watches were marked beginning roughly at sunset and concluded generally around dawn (or cockcrow) and in most areas were probably less than exact. Even so, people referred to the stages of the night at least loosely in these terms: "first watch" (*yigeng*), 7:00–9:00 P.M.; "second watch" (*ergeng*), 9:00–11:00 P.M.; "third watch" (*sangeng*), 11:00 P.M.–1:00 A.M.; "fourth watch" (*sigeng*), 1:00 A.M.–3:00 A.M.; and "fifth watch" (*wugeng*), 3:00 A.M.–5:00 A.M.

PROVINCES OF QING CHINA AND THEIR MODERN EQUIVALENTS

Provinces with a governor:

Qing names	Modern names
Anhui	Anhui
Guangxi	Guangxi
Guizhou	Guizhou
Henan	Henan
Hunan	Hunan
Kirin (Jilin)	Jilin
Jiangsu	Jiangsu
Jiangxi	Jiangxi
Shandong	Shandong
Shaanxi	Shaanxi
Shanxi	Shanxi
Tsitsihar (Qiqiha'er) or Heilongjiang	Heilongjiang
Xinjiang	Xinjiang
Zhejiang	Zhejiang

Provinces without a Governor:

Fengtian or Shengjing	Liaoning
Fujian	Fujian
Gansu	Gansu
Guangdong	Guangdong
Hubei	Hubei
Sichuan	Sichuan
Yunnan	Yunnan
Zhili	Hebei

Multiple-Province Circuits under the Jurisdiction of Governors-General:

Huguang	Hunan, Hubei
Liangguang	Guangdong, Guangxi
Liangjiang	Jiangsu, Jiangxi, Anhui
Dong Sansheng	Liaoning, Jilin, Heilongjiang
Minzhe	Fujian, Zhejiang
Shaangan	Shaanxi, Gansu, Xinjiang
Sichuan	Sichuan
Yungui	Yunnan, Guizhou
Zhili	Hebei

TRANSLATOR'S NOTES

1. See Sommer, *Sex, Law, and Society*, esp. 183, 184, 188, 195, 198, 200–201, 203–4, from cases involving widows; Kuhn, *Soulstealers*; Naquin, *Shantung Rebellion*; and Theiss, *Disgraceful Matters*. For crime reports from other sources, see McKnight and Liu, *Enlightened Judgments*, which presents about half of the cases in *Minggong shupan qingming ji* [Collection of enlightened judgments] (rpt., Beijing: Zhonghua shuju, 1987), a "collection of official documents on local governance and of judicial opinions" (499 n. 1); Bodde and Morris, *Law in Imperial China*, 203–489, from *Xing'an huilan* [Conspectus of penal cases] (Shanghai: Tushu jicheng ju, ca. 1886), the largest collection of Qing period casebooks, covering the years 1736–1885.

True Crimes in Eighteenth-Century China

Introduction

When one first begins to study China, the great length of its history, to say nothing of its geographic and human diversity, seems overwhelming. One may know the dates of major dynasties and the names of physical features and have learned in outline the great philosophical, religious, political, economic, and social changes that have taken place in Chinese-ruled territories yet still have no sense of the real experiences of the billions of people through time who might be considered Chinese. Even the study of literature provides insight into the thoughts, feelings, and artistic endeavors of only a selected segment of society, those men (and far fewer women) who had sufficient education and the motivation to craft poems, prose, or plays. Likewise, traditional paintings seldom represent the lives of common people. Instead, the subjects range through conventional elements of nature to, again, the lives of the culturally most favored members of society. One usually learns about the experience of the bulk of the Chinese population through time only by inference, from passing references to common people in literature, art, and administrative documents. Before the twentieth century and the ready availability of newspapers, photographs, and sound recordings, common people were generally silent and invisible in cultural artifacts.

Judicial records make up one type of artifact that does preserve facets of the lives of China's masses, and these materials have received extensive study only in recent decades. This volume contains several types of documents concerning major criminal cases from the vast archival collections of the Qing period (1644–1911). The selections are intended to reveal interactions among various levels of society and to demonstrate avenues through which the imperial administration dealt directly with the populace. These communications between provincial administrators and the emperor, which include extensive testimony and depositions, offer the opportunity to learn more about the textual representation of individual human experiences, highly mediated as they are. Other recent documentary collections attempt to cover a far broader sweep of Chinese history and include texts of many sorts.[1] They provide general overviews of imperial China. Moreover, historians have recently mined archived crime reports for aggregate data in political, social, and legal studies.[2] By contrast, this collection presents complete or excerpted reports on a few individual acts of violence. Even though this focus precludes generalizations on society as a whole, it does outline the lived experience of individuals—with all its ambiguities and specificities. Through these reports, one gains a better understanding of the Qing administrative system, the values of officials at all levels and of those who committed major crimes (acts of violence and political offenses), and the sources of conflict between individuals at particular places and times. Yet none of these documents represents reality with transparency; all were carefully edited for reasons to be explored below.

All of the cases in this volume date from China's so-called long eighteenth century. Those hundred years, plus a decade or two before and after, saw the Qing empire at the height of its stability, power, and wealth; the period, especially its middle decades, is frequently dubbed the "high Qing" (*sheng Qing*), implying a favorable comparison with that great age of Chinese poetry, the "high Tang," a thousand years before.[3] Commerce had recovered from the dynastic transition, and both the population and the economy grew dramatically.[4] China was the hub of global commerce in both luxury items such as silk and more mundane commodities, primarily tea and porcelains. Except for the inevitable natural disasters, internally the Qing empire was at peace.

By the early decades of the nineteenth century, however, burgeoning trade with European nations—and the disastrous conflicts that arose from commercial competition—would move China in new directions politically and economically and spark the Qing government's sporadic efforts to modernize along Western models. The eighteenth century could be said to mark the end of China's independent development, before the political and military defeats subsequently dubbed "humiliations" by twentieth-century thinkers. The cases presented here reveal some of the conflicts that erupted even during the Qing's finest years.

AN AGE OF INCREASING POLITICAL STABILITY

By the end of the eighteenth century, Manchu rulers, through their efficient military organization and administrative innovations, had extended China's frontiers north and west considerably beyond those of the preceding Ming, effectively doubling China's land area, and the empire became the largest Chinese empire in history (except for the Yuan [1260–1368], when China was part of the larger Mongol empire). The eighteenth century witnessed new heights in literature and art in a land that was generally prosperous and at peace. It was a time of thoughtful reconsideration of received philosophical and ethical teachings on the part of leading intellectuals. Judicial practices, too, were being refined during that period, partly in response to changing conceptions of the role of government as well as to the increased caseloads occasioned by population growth.

A series of able rulers played a role in these developments. The Qing emperors were all members of the Manchu Aisin Gioro clan, descendants of Nurhaci (1559–1626), who is hailed as the founding father of the dynasty although he died well before the Manchu armies swept south across the expanse of China. The "high Qing" began during the reign of the dynasty's second emperor, Xuanye (1654–1722), who ruled from 1662 until his death; he wrested power from his regent to assume direct rule when he was only fourteen. As the Kangxi emperor, he completed the destruction of all remnants of the preceding Ming imperial house, personally led armies into Mongolia and beyond into Central Asia to stabilize the frontiers, and paid great attention to water conservancy. In 1670, he issued a series of moral maxims that were later ordered read aloud to the populace on the first and fifteenth of every month in perpetuity.[5] He also hired a group of European Jesuit scholars to take charge of the Imperial Board of Astronomy in order to produce a more accurate official calendar for the realm. They joined men of a host of Asian ethnicities serving in the Qing administration.

Xuanye's fourth son, Yinzhen (1678–1735), seized the throne to rule as the Yongzheng emperor from 1723 to 1735. He became an efficient consolidator of power, depriving other imperial princes of their authority, ruthlessly purging the official record of documents that commented favorably on them, and, most famously among later generations of readers, causing the financial ruin of the wealthiest commoner family of the realm. A member of that clan, Cao Xueqin (ca. 1715–ca. 1765), was to pen China's greatest novel, known both as *Story of the Stone* (Shitou ji) and *Dream of Red Mansions* (Honglou meng). His saga of the decline of a great house and of Buddhist enlightenment was unfinished at his death.[6]

The Yongzheng emperor began a series of changes in the central government intended to limit the power of his bureaucrats, the outer court (*waichao*). These thousands of administrators served in offices inherited from the Ming and earlier governments and, in accordance with the detailed stipulations of the legal code, managed the everyday business—and paper flow—of governing, including judicial review. Although they all acknowledged in theory that the monarch's power was supreme, they carried out their duties in accordance with the law and relying on consensus, which did not always align with imperial desire. The suspicious Yongzheng emperor established a body of trusted officials to advise him on military matters; as time went on, this group assumed more and more power over the regular functioning of government and served as a buffer between the throne and the bureaucrats. One became the model administrator for the rest of the dynasty.[7]

The fourth Qing monarch, Hongli (1711–1799), reigned as the Qianlong emperor for sixty years, from 1736 to 1796, and then abdicated for filial reasons—to avoid holding power longer than had his grandfather. Even so, he maintained control until his last year of life, making him the longest-reigning ruler in dynastic history. During the 1730s, the advisory bodies inherited from his father became the Grand Council (Junjichu [lit., Council on Military Strategy]). This new body was composed of men who concurrently held important positions in the administration and could use those positions to provide information, and appropriate documentation, to their ruler. Since their positions on the council were supported by neither law nor tradition, they were much more directly responsible to the emperor than was the regular bureaucracy. They could, however, both facilitate and impede communication in both directions.[8]

The Qianlong emperor liked to travel, and his six tours of the Lower Yangzi valley came at outrageous cost, yet he also remitted taxes in areas struck by natural disasters. The imperial treasury remained strong due to the rapid increase in land under cultivation and the growth of the population, which resulted in more tax revenues. By the end of his reign, however, all these surpluses were exhausted, and rebellions in the subsequent Jiaqing reign period (1796–1821) weakened the Qing empire to the extent that China was unable to withstand foreign aggression during the infamous Opium Wars of the nineteenth century.[9]

The Qianlong emperor was a connoisseur of Chinese art; he amassed a huge and very fine collection, much of which is now housed in the National Palace Museum outside Taipei. He wrote poetry and painted (neither very well) and was fascinated by Western art. During his reign, trade with Europeans, especially the British, grew rapidly. Europeans were allowed to live in Beijing, some employed as artists or scholars. Missionary activity was officially forbidden but generally was allowed to proceed without interference, except by zealous local officials. Although the emperor was outstanding in both physique and mental abilities during his maturity, as he aged, he relied ever more on advisers, including the unscrupulous Heshen (1750–1799). By the time Britain's Lord Macartney came to offer the emperor congratulations on his eightieth birthday, signs of military unpreparedness and economic hardship were beginning to appear in the countryside. Imperial China's last "golden age" was winding down to a close.[10]

QING ADMINISTRATIVE SYSTEMS AND PRACTICES

The imperial administrative structure established by China's notorious First Emperor of the Qin, Qin Shihuangdi (r. 247–210 B.C.E.), emphasized strict laws and overlapping responsibilities among bureaucrats. Most subsequent dynasties adapted that structure while officially espousing more humanistic Confucian doctrines of governing. By emphasizing the nurture and education of the empire's subjects, Confucian values thus legitimated paternalistic government; in turn, emperors and their administrations perpetuated the educational system that ensured the orthodoxy of these values.

All educated men (and increasing numbers of elite women) mastered the same basic curriculum. They were also trained to read texts very carefully. They shared the vocabulary and, to a large extent, the values of the core readings; likewise, all prized the terse "classical" style of writing used in formal documents. Students began with basic primers that taught simple ethical standards and proceeded to the Four Books (Sishu) of the Confucian school: *The Analects of Confucius* (Lunyu), *The Great Learning* (Daxue), *The Doctrine of the Mean* (Zhongyong), and *The Works of Mencius* (Mengzi). By the time they had memorized these texts, most would have begun to take the preliminary examinations for the civil service degrees required for any position in the central administration. This would have entailed learning to produce essays in the "contemporary essay" (shiwen) form, also known as the "eight-legged essay" (*bagu wen*) because of its obligatory eight sections. Candidates for the higher degrees would also have committed to memory large segments, if not the entirety, of five more texts (classics) of the Confucian tradition: *Changes* (Yi); *Poetry* (Shi); *Documents* (Shu); *Li*, classical ritual texts; and *The "Spring and Autumn" Annals* (Chunqiu), with commentaries. There were strict limits on how many were allowed to pass each of these upper-level examinations, and many promising young bureaucrats failed to score high enough to qualify even after years of study.[11] But those who did pass the third and highest level of examinations and became *jinshi* ("presented scholars," designating those who had been presented to the emperor) could count on positions in the administration.

By necessity, local and provincial administrators relied heavily on private legal secretaries (termed *xingming* [specialists in penal law] or *muyou* [friends at court]) who had mastered the statutes and all appropriate administrative procedures; magistrates themselves were never trained in laws but instead studied the values appropriate to administration. Most legal professionals came from this same group of highly educated men; they had at least major portions of the same training as the administrators who employed them.[12]

Governing from a Confucian perspective involved maintaining harmony in society by means of a clear hierarchy of merit: those of greater value to society were to receive more of its benefits and were to share the rewards with those of lower status. In theory, thorough training in the histories and the canonical philosophical texts of high antiquity imbued the educated with such high moral standards that they were qualified both to serve as behavioral models for society and to make the best administrative decisions. Confucian concerns among China's bureaucrats, nearly all of whom had achieved advanced degrees in this educational system, took several forms.

First, the family should form the basis of society and provide the model for governing. That is, officials should serve as the parents of the people (institutionalized in the common term *fumu guan*, or "parental officials," used to describe all local and regional administrators) by holding themselves to very high ethical standards. Their need to educate the populace rationalized what amounted to the "preaching" of moral maxims offered by the youthful Kangxi emperor, who, like all Chinese monarchs, was both Son of Heaven (Tianzi) and figurative father to his people. And all of these "family" relationships were to be regulated by proper ritual and etiquette. These virtues were known collectively as the Proper Way (Zheng Dao) or the Sagely Way (Sheng Dao) and were called "Confucianism" by foreigners. As senior members of this extended family, both emperors and their bureaucrats were obligated to treat their subjects fairly and with parental concern for their adequate material support. Thus, an administrator would be called to task if he did not alleviate poverty in the area for which he was responsible. And any flaw in legal judgment could bring public humiliation and financial or even physical punishment in its wake.

Within a conjugal family, male dominance also had political significance: the eldest male was to provide the behavioral model for younger males and all females in the household. All women were theoretically subservient to elder males, despite the crucial economic importance of working-class women and the growth of literacy among female members of the elite by the eighteenth century. This was one factor in what has been termed a "cult of chastity" that developed in the late sixteenth century and culminated in the eighteenth century. Large numbers of elite women had committed suicide in order to avoid rape during the bandit raids that brought down the Ming and during the subsequent Qing conquest. Thereafter, numerous chaste widows were commemorated by memorial arches under Manchu rule. The further commercialization of society and new land rights practices produced an increasingly mobile male population made up of unattached men who traveled frequently to find menial work. Many, termed "rogue rascals" (*guanggun*), got into trouble. Social changes produced a crisis in Confucian thinking that made its way into judicial thought and practice: officials at all levels commented on what they interpreted as a failure in moral leadership on the part of men throughout society, both in the family and in the administration. One response was to draw public attention to the moral heroism of women; another was intense judicial scrutiny of all sexual offenses, and particularly cases of sexual violence, as the state sought to impose a uniform set of standards for gender performance.[13]

Regardless of Confucian niceties, the practical necessities of controlling a vast land with a large population dictated adherence to the rule of law, with harsh punishments for offenders and a complex bureaucracy for their administration; the moral suasion of Confucian teachings was never enough to maintain state power and order in society.[14] Not surprisingly, those who fell into the "net of the law" (*fawang*) through violent crime were most often China's working people; the more privileged members of society generally had access to other means of resolving disputes and relieving frustrations.[15]

Although all authority nominally resided in the emperor himself, routine and even urgent business was usually conducted by the regular bureaucrats at the central and provincial levels of the imperial administration. Complex and even cumbersome as it appears, the judicial system was designed to alleviate the inevitably disastrous effect on an accused person of a prejudiced or insufficiently observant judge or of a false confession given under duress. Because "district magistrates" (zhixian)[16] were responsible for determining both guilt and appropriate punishments, these administrators had to justify their procedures, as well as their verdicts in capital cases, to a series of judicial reviewers stretching upward through the bureaucracy of the "prefecture" (fu), the "province" (sheng), central authorities in Beijing, and ultimately to the emperor himself. Thus, the accused were not the only persons under scrutiny as the case passed through successive levels of review; so, too, were all the lower-level administrators involved in the case. By law and custom, all homicide cases had to be reviewed by (or in the name of) the emperor; only the emperor could authorize execution in cases other than those involving a direct threat to the state, treason, and the like.[17] This is why these reports were preserved: all relevant documents had to be forwarded to the capital for the final levels of review and imperial approval. The far more numerous legal suits over property, misdemeanors, and other such petty crimes were resolved at the county level, where the records normally were retained. It appears that most documents of this sort from the late imperial period no longer exist, except for a few troves recently discovered in Taiwan, Sichuan, and Liaoning.[18]

Secretaries generally drafted all crime reports. Since magistrates were culpable for any shortcoming in them, however, it behooved magistrates to edit carefully all reports that they did not personally write. Effort was clearly expended on discerning all relevant details for the principals in each case and to present their recommendations persuasively. In this sense, then, these cases also reveal the negotiations taking place between Confucian values and administrative expediency in late imperial Chinese society. The local administrator strove to be fair and caring. Such efforts are particularly visible in recommendations of leniency for widows left with small children or offenders who are the sole means of support for aging parents. In the terrible outcomes of transgressing these standards, one sees the devotion appropriate to the bonds of matrimony (even when there is little affection between husband and wife), the social harmony expected at the neighborhood and village levels, and the general understanding of laws and proper standards for conduct assumed to be held by all members of society.[19] One also sees a vindictive state punishing harshly all infractions of the standards the bureaucracy was charged with maintaining.

In some of the following cases, administrators seemingly struggle to define an offense in ways that make it fit one narrow legal description of a transgression—and to select which analogies and substatutes might apply. An apparently safe conclusion was to recommend leniency and, when the offense required the death penalty, to suggest reasons that justified reexamination at the capital. Moreover, the Qing emperors were inclined to recommend reconsideration of the preliminary sentencing at the "autumn assizes" (*qiushen*), an extended review process involving high officials and, finally, the emperor. Longtime legal adviser Wang Huizu (1731–1807), in a section of his manual for legal administration titled "Seek to Preserve Life" (Qiusheng), wrote:

> True enough, if anyone commits a crime for which he must be put to death by law . . . in such a case, the secretary should not find a roundabout way to dismiss it. However, some cases can be regarded as something between trivial and serious, or possibly either way, and the point at issue is focused at no more than a single sentence, the interpretation of which concerns a life-and-death matter. In such cases you have to put yourself in the other's place and search with sincerity for a way of forgiveness. . . . I acted as an assistant in administering punishments for twenty-six years altogether. In that time I entered the names of only six people for capital sentences. . . . In other cases, which I did not enter as "proven," always at the time of making my first report, I examined them, repeatedly, and with caution, with my superior. This is how it came about that after the Autumn Assizes my requests for leniency and mitigation of punishment were always successful. From this we know that the preservation of life is something that sometimes can be sought.[20]

As shown in the following cases, there was ample reason for most offenders to be granted reconsideration of their punishments. Only those who had committed the most grievous crimes were not eligible for this final reconsideration; not surprisingly, some offenses in this category are of political significance.

JUDICIAL REVIEW: PROCESS AND PERSONNEL

The crime reports in this volume demonstrate one of the world's great legal systems at work. Although most of the translations are truncated in order to avoid predictable repetition of legal formalities, several include all of the complex steps involved in a complete investigation, trial, and the successive judicial reviews stipulated for major criminal cases. China's legal codes had been evolving since high antiquity; the last imperial code was revised several times during the Qing, with ever more detailed substatutes designed to accommodate the substantial differences between individual cases in a changing society.[21] The cases offered here document the delicate balancing act the system performed between the seemingly inflexible laws and the paternalistic concern for humane government. Clearly, so many mitigating factors are included, and often repeated, in certain reports because those who drafted them wanted to influence their superiors in deciding how harshly, or even whether, to punish those who had committed the offenses.

The lowest level in the judicial administration during the Qing period was the district magistrate. The magistrate, like his superiors, was appointed directly from the capital in the name of the reigning emperor. His duties were wide-ranging, including virtually all political, economic, police, and military matters at the local level; however, he had authority to make final, binding legal decisions only in civil and minor criminal cases. It was his responsibility to resolve disputes over property and related matters by negotiating settlements or imposing fines.[22] In criminal cases, punishment could not exceed beating or public humiliation in severity; magistrates were authorized to pass judgment only on relatively minor infractions such as attempted assault or petty theft. Investigation of the more serious cases required approval from successively higher levels, where cases were retried as they passed upward through the judicial review system. Each stage produced standardized written reports presenting all the facts and outlining all administrative procedures followed—proving that the process had been conducted properly—and included recommendations as to the appropriate punishment for each individual offender.

Oversight of local magistrates involved frequent inspection tours by judicial review and supervisory officials in addition to the obligatory reconsideration of individual capital cases; any impropriety in procedure or unjustified penalties in any sort of legal action could lead to punishment for the magistrate. The threat of financial and even physical punishment functioned as a strong inducement for magistrates to perform scrupulously and conscientiously as local investigators, mediators, and judges.

There were no attorneys as there are in modern courts of law who might represent their clients by portraying opponents in an unfavorable light; the closest approximations were the private "litigation masters" (*songshi*) who drafted legal complaints for a fee (and were officially disparaged for regularly overstating their clients' grievances). After a magistrate received a complaint at the court, he was obligated to send underlings to investigate at once, and upon hearing their preliminary reports, he then commenced his formal investigation. Magistrates were also required to reach a speedy resolution in every case, as there were time limits established for each stage of the investigation, and late reports brought stiff penalties. His reports then underwent obligatory judicial review; all reviewing officials had to agree that his decision and the punishment he recommended were correct. Careful construction and convincing wording were thus crucial elements of each report.

All major cases originating at the district level were reexamined and even retried by prefectural and provincial administrators before being forwarded to the capital for final consideration. At the provincial level, the "governor" (*xunfu*), the "judicial review commissioner" (*anchashi*) assigned to the governor's court, and the "governor-general" or "military viceroy" (*dudu*) of multiple-province circuits reviewed the cases. Provincial authorities could retry the case together with the judicial commissioner and the circuit intendants; then the case would be referred to the Board of Punishments (Xingbu) in the capital.[23]

Every capital case, regardless of whether the sentence was immediate execution or imprisonment pending reconsideration of punishment, was reexamined by some of the highest central authorities, including the Three Judicial Offices (Sanfasi): the Censorate (Duchayuan), the Board of Punishments, and the Court of Judicial Review (Dali Si). This process of reconsideration, termed the "autumn assizes" for the season in which these officials reported to the emperor, might result in a recommendation for immediate execution, which, with imperial approval, would be carried out expeditiously. It might also culminate in a recommendation for a less severe punishment, further delay (detention pending subsequent reviews), or a pardon.[24] As Article 1 of *The Great Qing Penal Code* (Da Qing lüli) states:

> In all cases of offenses subject to the death penalty, inside or outside the capital, apart from those [offenses] which require execution without delay, the accused must be imprisoned to await the Autumn Assizes or the Court Assizes. The cases are to be distinguished according to [four choices] whether [the case is one in which the] circumstances [of the offense] require the infliction [of capital punishment], [one in which] execution [should take place but may] be delayed, or one in which [the circumstances give rise to] compassion, or where there are doubts.[25]

Assizes led to the regular reduction of sentences in the name of the (paternalistically merciful) emperor, thus demonstrating his leniency toward fallible commoners. Emperors might also issue a blanket amnesty for all convicted criminals; the Qianlong emperor did so eleven times during his sixty-year reign.[26]

Normally, the magistrate and all of the review officials were allowed a total of only six months to reach a final recommendation concerning punishment in an ordinary homicide case. Several factors facilitated communication among the various levels of judicial review. First, the penal code, even though it was large and its details were frequently updated, was of manageable size and complexity. Likewise, every *yamen* had at least one legal assistant who made it his business to be thoroughly conversant with not only the code but all the relevant explanatory handbooks and commentaries on it. The more expert of these specialists were highly paid by the magistrates who employed them and frequently accompanied these officials to successive postings.

Formal government schools did not offer training in the reading and production of legal documents; such schools—and virtually all private and local schools as well—prepared students only for the civil service examinations. Legal advisers learned on the job and through reading on their own. By the Qing period, there were numerous handbooks for *yamen* secretaries and clerks; likewise, numerous retired officials and legal advisers published volumes of advice for their successors, all of which were extremely helpful in familiarizing their readers with standard procedures and providing advice for judging difficult cases.[27]

INVESTIGATIVE PROCEDURES

During the Qing period, the population was loosely organized into groups of households under the supervision of a local warden or headman (their titles varied among regions of the realm). This elderly man was charged with paying attention to possible sources of conflict among his neighbors, and when violence seemed imminent, he was to inform the magistrate. Likewise, when any criminal act was perpetrated, the warden was to be notified first as the intermediary for common subjects. The procedure was informal; the man merely needed to be informed. Subsequently, he might accompany a person more closely linked to the offense, often its victim, to the magistrate's court, where that person would file a formal complaint. This could be done orally, but the court required a written statement providing as many of the particulars as possible, including a complete list of the property lost or damaged and the names of all perpetrators. These complaints might be more hyperbolic than strictly factual and seem not to have been accepted at face value.

Upon receipt of a complaint, the magistrate was obligated to investigate as soon as possible. In a murder case, he was to proceed to the crime scene along with the district "coroner" (*wuzuo*) and a small number of his own assistants; generally, the plaintiff, the accused if already apprehended, and relatives and neighbors of both would be assembled at the scene. At that point, an inquest was held. The coroner examined the body for all signs of injury, reporting orally to the magistrate the location, description, and measurements of each as well as his assessment of whether the wound could have been the cause of death.

The forensic technicians loosely referred to here as "coroners" enjoyed little status or compensation for their efforts. Many were amateur doctors; others were simply court clerks or attendants who had been pressed into this service. From the Song period onward, most relied heavily on a single handbook on forensic medicine, *The Washing Away of Wrongs* (Xiyuan jilu), by Sung Tz'u (Song Ci) (1186–1249). As its author pointed out: "Among criminal matters none is more serious than capital cases; in capital cases nothing is given more weight than the initially collected facts; as to these initially collected facts nothing is more crucial than the holding of inquests. In them is the power to grant life or to take it away, to redress grievances or to further iniquity."[28] Once the coroner had completed his examination of the corpse, the magistrate himself had to check the accuracy of every detail. In addition to corroborating his coroner's report, he was bound to see for himself whether death might have occurred from natural causes in order to determine that in fact a crime had been committed. After ascertaining the condition of the corpse, the magistrate questioned the principals in the case. This procedure put both accused and accuser together in the presence of others, creating a powerful emotional incentive for the perpetrator to confess, thus saving everyone a great deal of time in investigation. All testimony was recorded on the spot by court scribes and rewritten for the record later. Principals and key witnesses were generally kept in the court's custody until a formal hearing could be held—this might last for a month or more while all the necessary permissions were obtained from prefectural and provincial judicial officials. The formal investigation then had to be carried out expeditiously.

Trials at the magistrate's court were generally open to the public. The entrance to the building faced south, and the doors would be wide open while the court was in session. Both accuser and accused, along with all the relevant witnesses, knelt on the stone floor in front of the magistrate's high bench as he observed them from above and questioned each in turn.[29] The magistrate was surrounded by advisers and assistants, including court scribes and his legal secretary, while the principals were carefully monitored by numbers of armed guards, including several equipped with the instruments of punishment and torture, as the interrogation continued. A person who felt he had been wrongly convicted could demand another trial at a higher level, and the magistrate's recommendations could be overturned at any level of review.[30]

JUDICIAL TORTURE AND PUNISHMENTS

Judicial officials were allowed to use torture as a means of obtaining confessions if the accused did not freely admit guilt; witnesses might also be tortured under certain circumstances in order to determine the full "truth" in a case. Some, however, were not allowed to be tortured at all: the old, the very young, the disabled, pregnant women, and members of certain privileged groups.

Acceptable methods of torture included twisting the ears, slapping, beating, or making prisoners kneel on a chain, but the most common method seems to have been squeezing the fingers or ankles with wooden compressors made for this purpose.[31] Men might be subjected to interrogation with "ankle-squeezing blocks" (jiagun). This torture, "interrogation with ankle-squeezing blocks" (jia shen), could be applied only in cases of homicide and robbery, and officials were required to mention its use in their reports to the governor-general and governor. Women, however, could be subjected only to "interrogation with finger-squeezers" (zan shen). In the reports included in this volume, torture was more often threatened than applied, and various administrative handbooks advised against its use altogether. By the end of the Qing, many senior judicial officials had concluded that torture was neither humane nor effective in obtaining accurate information. Even so, Qing judges generally sought the "truth" through clear confessions rather than reached interpretations based on evidence alone.[32]

According to Article 1 of the Qing penal code, five categories of punishments were allowed: (1) Beating with a light bamboo rod, up to fifty strokes; (2) beating with a heavy bamboo rod, up to one hundred strokes (which was generally fatal); (3) penal servitude for periods of one to three years, plus up to one hundred strokes of the heavy bamboo rod; (4) exile to a frontier region, either perpetual or for a fixed term, with or without penal servitude, and either with one's conjugal family or alone; and (5) execution by strangulation, decapitation, or dismemberment—possibly extending to family members for the most serious crimes (multiple murders or crimes against the state). Later revisions of the code stipulated that beatings should be reduced considerably before they were carried out. For example, a sentence of sixty strokes of the heavy rod was to be reduced to twenty, and a sentence of one hundred to forty.[33]

THE DOCUMENTARY SOURCES

All of the documents in this volume are official records of major criminal cases dating from the late seventeenth through the early nineteenth century, or from the late Kangxi through the Yongzheng and Qianlong reign periods and into the Jiaqing reign period. Most are from the Qing administrative records housed at the First Historical Archives in Beijing; others are in the Palace Museum collections in Taipei.[34] The documents are of three types. The majority are "routine memorials" (*tiben*) submitted to the throne about matters of local significance; the cases included here are from subcategories of the "judicial" or "legal" (*falü*) memorials. A second category comprises "depositions appended to memorials" (*lufu zouzhe*) sent directly to the emperor about the groups and individuals involved. The third type of document exemplifies a special avenue of communication: secret memorials from high-ranking officials at all levels of government addressing matters affecting the realm and its government, such as military campaigns and presumed acts of sedition, submitted directly to the emperor via the Grand Council.[35]

All documents in the same category are virtually identical in form. Routine memorials are written in a clear but often workmanlike script on white paper more than a foot in height, with pages folded every four to five inches in accordion style (the format in which Buddhist sutras might be presented), so that the reader could open one or several folds at a time, and the text would remain flat. There are six lines of writing on each folded page; a complete case report might make a pile of folded pages one to four inches or more in height. Memorials that went directly to the emperor were generally inscribed in a better hand, as were their attachments.

As historian Thomas Buoye has noted, given the need for conciseness and clarity in a legal system requiring extensive review of all capital murder decisions throughout a vast empire, these documents generally exhibit a "familiar tenor and rhythm":

> Some cases were brutally complex and others painfully simple, but essentially the body of each report unfolded like a three act play. First, the magistrate set the stage by identifying the source of the dispute that led to violence. Next, he related, in a gory blow by blow description, the confrontation between the killer and victim. Lastly, the denouement, the magistrate recommended sentencing and addressed the aftermath of the killing. The resulting document was a violent, compelling, and concise vignette of a lesser known side of rural society.[36]

Even the small sample of judicial reports presented in this volume reveals both the formulaic structure and the standardized rhetoric such documents required. Offenders are introduced in the first paragraphs in terms that set the tenor of the crime report that follows: the perpetrator may be characterized as utterly immoral or prone to violence, a sign that the villain deserves no mercy.[37] Or the inadvertence of the act of violence may be emphasized in order to alert the judicial reviewer that the accused acted without malice or intent to do harm. Illicit sex is always referred to with the same pejorative term (*jian*) and is frequently described as having been carried out whenever the opportunity arose, with no further indication of the extent or even the nature of the relationship. Witnesses regularly report having arrived too late to intervene in a conflict or having been intimidated by the ferocity of the attacker. Matthew Sommer has observed, and cautioned, that:

> These records are probably as close as we will ever get to the "voice" of the illiterate in late imperial China. But they are not verbatim transcriptions of witnesses' utterances; rather, they are summaries of testimony crafted from witnesses' answers to questions posed during interrogation. The answers were strung together in the form of a monologue in the "voice" of the witness. . . . These statements were shaped by the priorities of the magistrate, and should not be mistaken for purely spontaneous declarations.[38]

Moreover, what these people said in their various languages and dialects was translated to a uniform standard Chinese (Mandarin), or *guanhua* (lit., "the official language"). Their testimony was also edited to remove all vulgarity and local slang and to fit customary prescriptions for the recording of testimony.

After the initial summary of the case, ordinary crime reports outline the procedures followed in the investigation—from the first notice of the crime, to the assembly of all persons likely to have been involved, to an investigation of the corpse. Thereafter the reports include testimony that speaks to the identity of the victim and of the perpetrator and the motivation for the offense. The reports vary in the quantity of testimony included, however; rapid population growth in China during the eighteenth century meant an increase in crime (if not necessarily an increase in its frequency).[39] This placed an extra burden on judicial review officials, who were not employed in greater numbers. Consequently, during the eighteenth century, there were repeated efforts to streamline crime reporting in order to ease this burden, which had the effect of diminishing the amount of testimony included in individual reports and increasing the amount of standard rhetoric used.

Magistrates, judges, and their legal assistants also expended considerable effort on ascertaining motivations and portraying in writing the precise degree of involvement of all persons implicated in a crime. The penal code distinguished between punishments for those who deliberately plotted to commit acts of violence, those who acted rashly or even caused injury by accident, ringleaders, followers, and mere bystanders. Taking another person's life was clearly wrong and inevitably brought punishment, but *how* and *why* the victim died and precisely *who* acted to cause this death, *what* they did and *why*, could dramatically affect the recommended punishment.

In the cases heard by these Qing magistrates, the accused seems to have been convicted by his own and the testimony of others; the magistrate's role was to confirm the accuracy of the original complaint. The defendant's obligation was simply to acknowledge his guilt and then to accept the appropriate punishment. About this seeming prejudgment of crime, historian Brian E. McKnight has observed:

> In traditional China, as in most premodern societies, homicide seems to have come in two basic grades, the obvious and the subtle, which all too often corresponded with the known and the unknown. Most homicides in China, like most in medieval Europe, were the result of sudden violence, of fights or robberies. Except where highwaymen were involved, the identity of the murderer was often common knowledge. Friend assaulted friend; husband murdered wife; an argument, sudden anger, and one of those involved was killed, often in the presence of witnesses. However, in China the problem of subtle

crime seems to have been more appreciated if not more common. Chinese investigators early on became conscious of the set of problems that have remained at the heart of forensic examinations: the distinguishing of accidental from deliberate death, of suicide from murder, or premortem from postmortem wounds, and, in general, of natural death from unnatural.

The forensic problems were compounded not only by those who tried to disguise homicide as accident, but by those who sought to make natural deaths appear unnatural. Murderers and their relatives were apt to hide bodies, dispose of weapons, and attempt to disguise homicide as suicide or even as death from natural causes. Conversely, traditional Chinese investigative works often suggest that making suicide or natural death look like murder, in order to involve enemies with the criminal law and so injure them, was not an uncommon sport, played both by those seeking vengeance and by those practicing extortion.[40]

The cases in this volume are of the simpler, more common variety: most involve people who were familiar with one another—relatives, neighbors, and friends; few reflect the deceptions McKnight mentions above. The more "subtle" crimes were rare in reality, although these were the stock in trade of contemporary "crime-case fiction" (gong'an xiaoshuo) in which mysterious deaths caused by unknown assailants required a sometimes supernaturally insightful investigator to untangle.[41]

These particular cases were chosen—at the risk of giving a highly distorted view of society as a whole—because they include relatively large amounts of testimony from all the principals in a case. As Sommer noted above, however, rather than the words of the condemned and frightened witnesses, depositions are clerical representations of the thoughts, aspirations, and worries of these people rendered into a standard language style; the actions of all persons involved in a crime were similarly standardized so as to fit the degrees of culpability defined by the imperial legal code. Thus, even though these documents are not transparent records of real lives of individual persons, they do present a range of social problems that provoked acts of violence during the period of the Qing empire's greatest military, political, and economic security and at the height of its cultural glory.

THE CRIMES AND THE CRIMINALS

The offenses described in this volume are of several types. Nearly all involve homicide, but one should not infer that Qing period Chinese killed one another with greater frequency compared to people in other societies or of other times.[42] Early modern European societies were similarly violent; contrary to current accepted wisdom, the growth of cities often served to lower the per capita crime rate. Only during the twentieth century did U.S. crime rates, for example, surge above those of previous periods.[43]

Sexual desire, whether requited or spurned, jealousy, and the lust for revenge motivated several of the crimes. A few are products of careful planning with malicious intent. Others are the outcome of mere happenstance—the thoughtless comment that produces a moment's anger, the tool or weapon that falls within the perpetrator's reach as he loses self-control—as intent rises without warning and no one foresees the tragic outcome. Fits of rage over the petty frustrations of daily life lie behind many of these homicides.[44] Others reveal clashes between family members and neighbors that revolve around characteristically Chinese conceptions of proper relations and acts that breached social contracts. Some also reveal the empire's responses to political and religious beliefs of the time. Although these few documents provide a view of late imperial Chinese society that is anything but complete, they do complicate understandings most often derived from the prescriptive statements of Confucian and Daoist thinkers, the idealistic visions of poets and painters, and the generalizations of historians, especially those whose political values motivate them to portray late imperial China in a uniformly negative light.

Viewed from the perspective of the Qing legal system, the crimes may be divided into premeditated or intentional homicide, killing during an affray, and other crimes. Such deliberate killers as Liu Huaiyu (case 2), the rapist Cao Ligong (case 5), Du Huailiang (case 6), the kidnappers (case 9), and the would-be extortionists (case 10) were sentenced to beheading for the crime of "premeditated homicide" (*mousha*) and had little hope of reprieve; their executions were to be carried out after the next autumn assizes. The punishment recommended initially for the leader of the fatal raid on the enemies of his clan, Zhou Fuquan (case 15), was immediate beheading for "intentional homicide" (*gusha*). However, the final recommendation was mitigated to beheading with delay on the charge of "intentional arson" (*gushao*) that caused the deaths of people. Others who committed "homicide during an affray" (*dousha*) (cases 11 and 12) were sentenced to immediate beheading as well, but their sentences were referred back to the Three Judicial Offices by the emperor, and they might not be awarded lesser punishments after reconsideration of the circumstances surrounding the homicides.

Execution by strangulation was recommended in several cases. This was a less horrific sentence: at least the body of the malefactor was left intact, thus not dishonoring the person's progenitors in death.[45] In two of these cases, execution was to be carried out after the autumn assizes (cases 1 and 9), but in others (cases 7 and 14), the sentence was left open for further consideration, with punishment delayed until provincial and capital officials conducted the extensive scrutiny that constituted the assizes. Because the assizes did not address the question of guilt but considered only the appropriateness of the punishment, it is highly likely that these convicts were given significantly reduced sentences. One such recommended penalty for killing during an affray (case 8) was commuted because of an amnesty: clearly, the victim had died by accident rather than by intent on the part of the perpetrator.

The worst penalty levied by Qing judges was "execution by dismemberment" (lingchi). Also known by the lurid term "lingering death," it was further exoticized by some foreigners as the "death of a thousand cuts," as they imagined it might take hours for the writhing victim to be released from his agony.[46] This punishment was carried out extremely rarely, and when it was, it seems to have been much less spectacular—and far less prolonged.[47] Token cuts were made on the body, and then the convict was strangled; thereafter, the corpse was dismembered at the joints and decapitated. The body lying in parts was thus the ultimate sign of the criminal's transgression, not only against the values of the public, but also against the memory of his ancestors. By engaging in a crime of such magnitude, he had shown no respect for the body that was the primary bequest from his parents. The only case bearing this frightful punishment is case 20, in which officials and their underlings conspired to murder a promising young official whom the emperor himself had recently met. Thus, murder became a political crime, and the ruler had no mercy. Dismemberment is the initial recommendation for an adulteress who killed her husband after he caught her in a compromising situation with her father-in-law (case 13), but the document here is inconclusive: the case was sent to another jurisdiction for reinvestigation because of the many illogical elements in its original presentation. It seems highly unlikely that a penalty of this severity would remain unchanged during the assizes.

In a small number of the cases included here, the documents assembled do not indicate the recommended punishment: they are depositions separated from the memorials to which they were originally appended. Case 16 groups testimony of this type from members of various religious sects. In case 17, because Ji Yanghua had by his own admission committed premeditated murder, a death sentence would not be in doubt. Case 19 is translated from a series of memorials sent from a provincial official directly to the emperor. Given the seriousness of the crime, impersonation of an official, the normal judicial review process was simplified, although for the final decision on punishment, the emperor again sought the advice of his senior judicial officials on whether to behead as recommended.

The cases in this volume range from cold-blooded murders to inadvertent acts by victims of circumstance. Destructive violence in eighteenth-century China was generally as banal as it was elsewhere, and as in other cultures, perpetrators and victims usually knew each other, as neighbors or even as relatives. And with each case, we see administrators struggling to identify precisely what the crime was and, on the basis of individual circumstances, what the appropriate punishment should be. Even so, they could rely on higher courts to review their decisions and to find avenues for applying Confucian leniency to nearly all cases. Despite the standardization in these documents, one may still discern clearly enough the gap that separated the lives of these common people from the rulers who held their fates in their hands.

NOTES

1. See Ebrey, *Chinese Civilization*; and Cheng and Lestz, *Search for Modern China*. For a list of some principal events that occurred from the time of the Kangxi emperor's death in 1722 through 1820, see Bartlett, *Monarchs and Ministers*, xviii–xxi.

2. See Buoye, "Economic Change," *Manslaughter, Markets*, and "Suddenly"; Philip Huang, *Civil Justice in China*; Kuhn, *Soulstealers*; Sommer, *Sex, Law, and Society*; and Theiss, *Disgraceful Matters*.

3. Historian Ho Ping-ti originated the term "high Qing" in English, drawing attention to the "long eighteenth century" as a Pax Sinica; see his "Significance." For a systematic survey of the period, see Naquin and Rawski, *Chinese Society*; on this periodization, see ibid., ix–xii. Other general histories are in Mote, *Imperial China*; Ray Huang, *China*; Ebrey, *Cambridge Illustrated History*; and Spence, *Search for Modern China*.

4. Rowe characterizes the middle of the eighteenth century as "the years when things went right" (*Saving the World*, 1). Buoye notes that the population grew from about 185.6 million in 1755 to around 301.4 million in 1790 with no appreciable change in the proportion of urban and rural population distribution. Buoye, "Economic Change," 241, 252. There were significant dislocations of male laborers in the process, however.

5. See Mair, "Language and Ideology."

6. On the Kangxi and Yongzheng emperors, see the following three works by Jonathan Spence: *Emperor of China*, *Ts'ao Yin*, and *Treason by the Book*. The Yongzheng emperor transformed his former palace in Beijing, the Yonghegong, into a Lama temple, which it remains today.

7. Chen Hongmou (1696–1771) was widely admired for his efficient administration. An excellent study of the complex mentality of the period is Rowe, *Saving the World*.

8. For an analysis of the Grand Council's administrative importance, see Bartlett, *Monarch and Ministers*, esp. 1–7, 186–89. The communications in case 20 in this volume were transmitted through this body.

9. See cases 16 and 17 in this volume.

10. On the Qianlong emperor, see Kahn, *Monarchy*. For biographies of the Kangxi, Yongzheng, and Qianlong emperors, see *Eminent Chinese*, 327–31, 915–19, 369–73. Communications exchanged between Macartney and the Qianlong emperor are translated in Cheng and Lestz, *Search for Modern China*, 92–109.

11. The most thorough study of the Chinese examination system is Elman, *Cultural History*.

12. See Macauley, *Social Power*, 48–49. Extensive advice for these essential clerks and their superiors is in Huang Liu-hung, *Complete Book*.

13. Theiss, *Disgraceful Matters*, 8–11, 65–81. Through the Yongzheng and Qianlong reign periods, "chastity" (*jie*) was seen as the female parallel to and metaphor for male "loyalty to the emperor" (*zhong*), thoroughly imbricating personal and political Confucian virtues. Ibid., 25–38.

14. William Rowe, in *Saving the World*, explores the importance during this period of "statecraft" (*jingshi*), or ordering the world: practical approaches to maintaining order and material sufficiency in society regardless of classical values.

15. Sommer, *Sex, Law, and Society*, 15; Buoye, "Economic Change," 242. This is the case in other societies as well; see Zehr, *Crime*, 17.

16. On the magistrate's training and career, see Watt, *District Magistrate*, 45–77. For the magistrate's role in the administration of justice, see Ch'ü, *Local Government*, esp. chapter 7.

17. On the complex role of the emperor in sentencing, see Meijer, "Autumn Assizes."

18. See Ye and Esherick, *Chinese Archives*, 219–20, 279–81, 338–39. For a more detailed explanation of the complicated review process for capital cases in Beijing, see Meijer, "Autumn Assizes."

19. For a general discussion of how legal procedures come to be textualized, and how such texts may be interpreted, see Weisberg and Barricelli, "Literature and the

Law." On the "Confucian" elements, and their limits, in sentencing, see Buoye, "Suddenly," 63–64, 68–70, 80–86.

20. Van der Sprenkel, *Legal Institutions*, 140, quoting Wang Huizu, *Zuozhi yaoyan* [Admonitions on assisting with governance] (1785), in *Siku jinshu* [Proscribed books in all categories] (Beijing: Jinghua chubanshe, 2001), section 16, 6625.

21. Liu, in *Origins of Chinese Law*, traces the development of law through the second century.

22. See Philip Huang, *Civil Justice*, esp. chapters 2, 6, 7, 8.

23. According to Article 411 of *The Great Qing Penal Code* [Da Qing lüli]. See Jones, *Great Qing Code*, 393. Jones translates the basic statutes of the code, without its substatutes, from Xue Yunsheng, *Du li cunyi* [Remaining doubts after reading the substatutes], 1905, reprinted as *"Du li cunyi" chongkanben* [A typeset edition of the *Tu-li ts'un-i*], comp. Huang Tsing-chia (Huang Jingjia), 5 vols. (Taipei: Chungwen, 1970). For a useful survey, see Bodde and Morris, *Law in Imperial China*, chapter 1 (on traditional concepts of law), chapter 2 (on the nature of the Qing penal code), chapter 3 (on the penal system), and chapter 4 (on the judicial review system and its procedures).

24. For a brief history and outline of the assizes, see Meijer, "Autumn Assizes." Buoye notes that sentences of immediate execution were rare, less than 6 percent of his extensive sample of cases from Guangdong, and that leniency was commonly sought in case reports. Buoye, "Suddenly," 62 n. 3, 68–70, 82–86. Extreme punishments are not so rare in the very small sample of cases in this volume.

25. Jones, *Great Qing Code*, 34. See also Buoye, "Suddenly."

26. Buoye, "Economic Change," 244; see Meijer, "Autumn Assizes."

27. Well-known memoirs with advice for magistrates and their assistants are Huang Liu-hung, *Complete Book*; and Lan Dingyuan, "Lan Dingyuan's Casebook," also translated as Lan Ting-yüan, "Lan Lu-chow's Criminal Cases."

28. Sung Tz'u, *Washing Away of Wrongs*, 37. Forensic medicine was an age-old science in China; for a document on procedures and standards of the second century B.C.E, see McLeod and Yates, "Forms of Ch'in Law," esp. 154–55.

29. Huang Liuhong provides various guidelines for effective interrogation; see Huang Liu-hung, *Complete Book*, 268–73. See Conner, "Chinese Confessions," 74–80; and Harrison, "Wrongful Treatment."

30. For descriptions of investigative procedures, see Allee, *Law and Local Society*, chapters 7–9; an introduction to investigative procedures is in Buoye, "Suddenly." For a diagram of the courtroom layout, see Allee, *Law and Local Society*, 221; for the layout of a *yamen*, see van der Sprenkel, *Legal Institutions*, 45. On the magistrate's assistants, see also Reed, *Talons and Teeth*.

31. See Bodde and Morris, *Law in Imperial China*, 98; and Conner, "Chinese Confessions." For illustrations of torture instruments, see Kuhn, *Soulstealers*, 14, 16, 18. About parallel judicial practices in early modern Europe, see de Grazia, "Sanctioning Voice," 294. De Grazia refers to Michel Foucault, *Discipline and Punish: The Birth of the Prison*, trans. Alan Sheridan (New York: Pantheon, 1977), 38–39.

32. Conner, "Chinese Confessions," 88–90, clarifies the need for truth in these procedures.

33. See Jones, *Great Qing Code*, 33–34. The worst of these forms of execution—dismemberment—had been formally removed from the code by 1905, the time of the version translated by Jones, although it was recommended in case 20 in this volume.

34. On the organization of court materials in the First Historical Archives in Beijing and a more detailed outline of the governmental structures and functions, see Park and Antony, "Archival Research"; and Ye and Esherick, *Chinese Archives*, 33–45, 327–30.

35. For descriptions of the Qianlong emperor's secret correspondence during the late eighteenth-century sorcery scare, see Kuhn, *Soulstealers*.

36. Buoye, "Suddenly," 90.

37. I have identified several such phrases (e.g., *wangzhi faji* [utterly lawless], *yishi qifen* [momentarily lost my temper]) in the cases presented in this volume.

38. Sommer, *Sex, Law, and Society*, 26–28. Sommer also notes that all testimony is represented in standard Chinese (Mandarin), or *guanhua*, regardless of the language and dialect in which it was delivered.

39. For a thoughtful discussion of this question, see Buoye, "Economic Change," 252–53.

40. Sung Tz'u, *Washing Away of Wrongs*, 1–2. Truman Capote, in his widely heralded literary narrative of a horrendous crime *In Cold Blood*, notes that even among the murders investigated by a twentieth-century Kansas county sheriff, almost all were similarly "open-and-shut" cases (151).

41. The most famous of these tales involve Lord Bao (Bao Gong) and have little connection to the historical Bao Zheng (*jinshi* degree, 1027); for examples, see Hayden, *Crime and Punishment*. Other insightful fictional detectives include Di Qing, who served as inspiration for Dutch scholar Robert H. van Gulik's famous tales of Judge Dee. Gulik was also among the first to translate early Chinese legal records; see his *T'ang-yin-pi-shih*. For studies of crime-case fiction of this period, see Robert E. Hegel, introduction to Hegel and Carlitz, *Writing and Law*, esp. 11–12; St. André, "Reading Court Cases," in ibid.; Youd, "Beyond *Bao*," in ibid.; and Carlitz, "Genre and Justice," in ibid.

42. Historians of China have found horrific crimes in the record, as could historians of legal traditions in any society. For examples, see Buoye, "Economic Change," 245; and Bodde and Morris, *Law in Imperial China*, 160–73. The idealistic view that tra-

ditional Chinese society was substantially less violent than those of other cultures seems baseless, however; see Buoye, "Economic Change," 244, 258 n. 38.

43. Stone notes that homicide rates in thirteenth-century England were about twice as high as during the sixteenth and seventeenth centuries, which were "some five to ten times higher than those today" ("Interpersonal Violence," 25). King reports the scholarly consensus that "the period from the mid-eighteenth to the mid-nine-teenth century witnessed a fundamental shift in attitudes toward interpersonal vio-lence and a growing sensitivity to, and repugnance of, overt acts of aggression" (*Crime and Law*, 241–42). On this topic, see also Sharpe, *Crime*, 71, 175. Zehr counters the myth that modern societies are generally more violent than those of previous eras: "communalism and harmony of folk society are often less pervasive than com-monly assumed . . . there are many disruptive aspects in rural social life; distrust, sus-picion and social tension, for example, characterize many folk communities" (*Crime and Development*, 18). For recent, anomalous, surges in U.S. crime levels, see Friedman, *Crime and Punishment*, esp. 451–64; for his view that colonial American society was not terribly violent by comparison, however, see ibid., 12–47.

44. In the hundreds of violent land disputes Buoye studied (see "Suddenly," 69) most were defined as "homicides during an affray" (*dousha*), which merited less seri-ous punishments and greater chances of reduced sentences or pardons than did the cases presented in this volume; quite by coincidence, a seemingly disproportionate number of these are identified as premeditated or intentional homicide. Qing admin-istrators were greatly concerned with what they perceived as an unacceptable level of violence in society; see Antony, "Scourges on the People."

45. The first section of *The Classic of Filial Piety* (Xiaojing), a commonly read text at lower levels of a classical education, states: "The Master said, 'Filial piety is the source of all virtue. It is the basis for all our teachings. . . . Filial respect begins when you avoid all risk to your body, limbs, hair, or skin, all of which you received from your father and mother. It is the completion of filial piety that you establish yourself and practice the Way, and that you leave a reputation [for these things] for later gen-erations and thereby bring glory to your parents." (My translation)

46. Europeans seized on this gruesome punishment as typifying negative aspects of Chinese culture during the late nineteenth century. For the deliberate misreading of this punishment, and a thorough account of its uses, see Brook et al., *Death by a Thousand Cuts*.

47. Writing in 1882, Herbert A. Giles comments: "again all evidence tends to prove that though many are condemned, no one is ever subjected to this truly bar-barous process, the very exceptions which might possibly be discovered, forming of course part of the proof. As a matter of fact, there is a great deal more lenity in the *Penal Code* of China than most people are aware of" (*Historic China*, 126).

PART I

JUDICIAL PROCEDURES

Although these cases range from the result of happenstance to deliberate premeditated crimes, the reports in this section are not complicated; they are conventionally straightforward descriptions of acts in which the actors and their motivations are easily identified. They do, however, exemplify administrative procedures followed during the investigation of facts and the interrogation of offenders as well as the documentary forms and standardized language in which these procedures were represented. Several reports in this section are translated in full.

The first case outlines the complicated process of reporting and receiving permission from the various levels of judicial administration at the prefectural and provincial levels before a district magistrate was formally authorized to carry on his investigation of a capital crime. Given the strict time limits imposed on every step of a criminal investigation, from the initial complaint to the memorial to the emperor asking approval of the recommended punishment, communications between levels of government had high priority. On the one hand, when district, prefectural, and provincial offices were located within the same city, this process could have been relatively easy, and the allotted times were shortened accordingly. On the other hand, the considerable distances between some district and prefectural seats and the relevant provincial capital, sometimes through rough territory, meant that clerks at every level were under constant pressure to process communications expeditiously. The last report in this section, case 5, gives some indication of these strictures: because the administrative centers in Zhili were closer than some (only about a hundred miles apart), the normal span allotted for the review process was reduced by several days.

Case 1 is missing its last pages, torn off accidentally and apparently lost at some point over the past three centuries. Case 5 is complete and includes the vital final summary. A boon to researchers, these synopses are written in smaller characters so that they would fit on a single page and provide the emperor with all the relevant details of a case along with the recommended punishment as he reached his final decision.

CASE 1

Xu Si: A Scuffle over a Debt (Jiangsu, 1702)

In addition to a detailed outline of the various levels of judicial review required for a case of this magnitude, this report reveals the work of anxious judicial officers: not only is there no discrepancy between the various summaries of the case, but even the depositions are represented as verbatim renditions of one another, presumably in an effort to eliminate ambiguity about the facts of the case or the guilt of the perpetrator. Regardless of how earlier reports (from the district and prefectural trials) might have read, the last judicial official to edit the record made certain that there would be no confusion about the perpetrator's motivation for the crime. Clarity and consistency in crime reports justified the suggested verdict and demonstrated the conscientiousness of the various judicial reviews. Especially because the death was accidental, it is not surprising that, according to the report's cover, the imperial decision was to send the case back to the Three Judicial Offices for their recommendation at the autumn assizes concerning appropriate punishment.[1]

Your subject Song Luo, Grain Intendant, Provincial Commander in Chief of Military Affairs, Governor of Jiangning and Other Areas, Vice President of the Censorate, Third Additional Grade,[2] respectfully submits this MEMORIAL concerning a capital murder case:

The detailed memorandum submitted by Commissioner Tong Yuxiu of the Jiangsu Provincial Judicial Commission states that he had examined a certain individual named Xu Si, twenty-nine *sui* in age, a native of Chongming District of Suzhou Prefecture. The complaint contends that this Xu Si and the late Zhang Mingfu, whom he beat to death, bore no previous enmity.

It read: "Xu Si is a winemaker by profession. Zhang Mingfu, originally from Tongzhou, together with Jiang Junlong, a native of Jurong District who is presently in custody, lived nearby in New Kaihe Market in Chongming District, where together they opened a wineshop. Previously, Mingfu had purchased wine from Xu Si to sell, but he was in arrears in the amount of 120 coppers. He was billed several times, but he did not repay the debt.

"On Kangxi 40.7.5 [August 8, 1701], Xu Si again went to collect the debt. Mingfu still did not repay the debt, and the two of them fell to arguing. Xu Si smashed pottery bowls in the shop, and Mingfu butted Si with his head. Thereupon, Si wrongfully used his fists to return the blow, injuring Mingfu's ribs on the right side, and he fell to the floor. At that point, Jiang Junlong and others urged them to separate. Zhang Mingfu's injury was serious, and around nightfall he perished."

Zhang Sanyuan, the nephew of the deceased, now in custody, subsequently filed the complaint of capital murder listing Xu Si as the perpetrator, with Jiang Junlong and Li Jingshan as witnesses. The local warden Shen Danwen likewise submitted his report on the matter. These documents were filed at the magistrate's *yamen* on 7.6 [August 9]. Magistrate Wang [Wenyu] of the aforementioned Chongming District, accompanied by a clerk and the coroner, rode by single horse with few followers to the site of the corpse. In the presence of the original parties to the case, he personally conducted an inquest at the scene of the crime.

Coroner Fan Jia reported orally that the deceased Zhang Mingfu was forty-five *sui* in age; his ribs on the right side had a lethal fist wound, purple-red in color, 2.4 *cun* across. There were no other causes of death. When the examination was complete, the corpse was enshrouded and encoffined. The verified report of the coroner's examination was entered into the record to be available before the criminal is brought to court for investigation.

A petition based on the criminal's deposition was then prepared for submission to the various superior offices as is appropriate. Thereafter, I received a rescript from the Suzhou Prefecture authorizing a speedy investigation of the facts concerning the homicide and the proposal of sentencing based on the depositions. Then I awaited rescripts granting authorization from the various superior courts. I received the rescript of authorization from the Suzhou-Songjiang Circuit allowing Suzhou Prefecture to investigate the facts concerning the murder and to propose sentencing in a detailed report. Then I awaited indication of approval by the Censorate and the [Jiangsu Provincial Judicial] Commission. I received a rescript of authorization from the judicial commission allowing Suzhou Prefecture to investigate thoroughly all facts concerning the murder and to submit a statement of consideration with depositions and proposed sentences. Then I awaited indication of the approval of the Censorate and the [Suzhou-Songjiang] Circuit. I received a rescript of authorization from Censor Song, the provincial governor, allowing the judicial commission to investigate thoroughly all facts, to determine penalties, and to submit a report. Then I awaited indication of approval from the Governor-General's Judicial Office. I received a rescript of authorization from [Board of Punishments] senior vice president [buyuan] A, the governor-general, allowing the Jiangsu Provincial Judicial Commission to investigate and to ascertain the facts concerning the capital murder and to submit a report proposing punishments.[3] Then I awaited a rescript of authorization from the provincial governor indicating his approval. The district having received this rescript, Wang Wenyu, Magistrate of Chongming, summoned the criminal and all relevant witnesses to court.

Thereupon, he conducted a strenuous investigation. He interrogated Zhang Sanyuan: "What was your relationship with the deceased Zhang Mingfu? Why was he beaten to death by Xu Si? Ordinarily, was there any enmity between them? Testify."

He testified: "I am from Tongzhou; Zhang Mingfu is my uncle. Together with Jiang Junlong, he sold wine for a living in New Kaihe Market of this district. He had no enmity with Xu Si. My uncle sold wine he bought wholesale from Xu Si, but he owed him 120 coppers for the wine. On the morning of 5.7, Xu Si came to collect the money, but Uncle had none to repay him. Xu Si and Uncle began to quarrel, and he beat Uncle up. At dusk, Uncle died. I wasn't in the shop when they were fighting; Jiang Junlong told me about it, and I filed the complaint. I beg Your Honor to get to the bottom of this!"

Interrogation of Shen Danwen: "You're the local warden? Do you know why Zhang Mingfu was beaten to death by Xu Si? Testify."

He testified: "I am the local warden. That Zhang Mingfu was from Tongzhou. Together with Jiang Junlong, a Jurong man, he opened a wineshop in New Kaihe Market. There, Zhang Mingfu sold wine he bought wholesale from Xu Si, but he owed him 120 coppers for the wine. On the morning of the fifth of the seventh month, Xu Si came to collect the money. When Zhang Mingfu had nothing to repay him, they got into an argument. Xu Si hit Zhang Mingfu and injured him. At dusk, Mingfu died. I live far away from the market town, so at first I didn't know about it. On the sixth, Zhang Sanyuan came and told me about it, and I immediately filed my report."

Interrogation of Jiang Junlong: "Where are you from? Living here with Zhang Mingfu, what did you do for a living? Why was Zhang Mingfu beaten to death by Xu Si? Testify to the facts."

He testified: "I'm from Jurong District. Zhang Mingfu was from Tongzhou. Together, we ran a wineshop in New Kaihe Market in this district. Xu Si's family made wine. Zhang Mingfu bought wine from him wholesale for us to sell. But we owed him 120 coppers for wine. On the morning of the fifth of the seventh month, Xu Si came to collect the money. Zhang Mingfu answered him, 'Come back this afternoon, and I'll pay you,' but Xu Si had his mind made up that he wanted it now. So they got into an argument. Xu Si smashed some of the pottery bowls in our shop, and in the heat of the moment [qingji] Zhang Mingfu butted Xu Si with his head. Xu Si then knocked Zhang Mingfu down with a single punch of his fist. I and a neighbor, Li Jingshan, got them apart, but by dusk Zhang Mingfu was dead."

Interrogation of Li Jingshan: "From your perspective, why did Xu Si beat Zhang Mingfu to death? Testify."

He testified: "I'm the neighbor next door to Zhang Mingfu's wineshop. Zhang Mingfu sold wine that he bought wholesale from Xu Si. But he owed him 120 coppers for the wine. On the morning of the fifth of the seventh month, Xu Si came to collect the money. Zhang Mingfu answered him, 'I won't have it until this afternoon,' but Xu Si had his mind made up that he wanted it now. So they got into an argument. Xu Si smashed some of the pottery bowls in the shop, and Zhang Mingfu butted Xu Si with his head. Then Xu Si gave him one punch with his fist, and Zhang Mingfu fell down on the ground. I and Jiang Junlong got them apart, but by dusk, Zhang Mingfu was dead."

Interrogation of Xu Si: "What enmity was there between you and Zhang Mingfu? Why did you provoke a fight with him and beat him to death? Testify."

He testified: "I make wine for a living. There never was any enmity between me and Zhang Mingfu. He sold wine he bought from me at wholesale, and he owed me 120 coppers for wine. I tried to collect many times, but he was never willing to repay me. On the morning of the fifth of the seventh, I went again to collect the money, but he still wasn't able to repay me. I spoke to him about it, but he cursed me in return. Momentarily I lost my temper [yishi qifen], and I smashed one of the pottery bowls in his shop. Then Zhang Mingfu butted me with his head, and I hit him back once with my fist. I never thought that hitting him in the ribs would make him fall over. By dusk, he was dead. I beg you to be lenient!"

All of the depositions having been recorded in the report, Wang Wenyu, the magistrate of Chongming District, concluded: Xu Si brews wine for a living. He had no prior enmity with Zhang Mingfu, who was beaten to death. Mingfu's place of origin was Tongzhou; he lived with Jiang Junlong of Jurong District, and as partners, they opened a wineshop in New Kaihe Market of this district. Mingfu had previously resold wine purchased wholesale from Xu Si, and he owed him 120 coppers for the wine. He was billed repeatedly but did not make repayment. On Kangxi 40.7.5, Xu Si returned to bill him, but they got into an argument. When Xu Si broke pottery bowls in the wineshop, Mingfu butted Si with his head. Si then raised his fist, struck, and injured Mingfu's ribs on the right side; Mingfu fell to the ground. Jiang Junlong and others separated the two, but Mingfu was seriously injured; at dusk, he expired.

The nephew of the deceased filed a complaint with the district, which examined the wound and submitted a report. Having received rescripts of authorization to conduct an investigation, this office thereupon examined all the true facts concerning the injury; the aforementioned criminal confessed everything without hesitation. Xu Si should be punished in accordance with the law on "killing a person during an affray": the perpetrator "should be sentenced to strangulation after the autumn assizes."[4] Local warden Shen Danwen, having not seen the essential evidence of the affray, has already been released from responsibility. Whether or not this meets with your concurrence, I humbly await instructions from the Prefecture.

The depositions and the facts of the case having been forwarded to the prefecture, the aforementioned Shi Wenzhuo, Prefect of Suzhou, brought forward the criminal for examination. His deposition was identical [to that in the magistrate's report]. I adjudge that in the case of Xu Si beating to death Zhang Mingfu, there was originally no enmity between them. The cause lies in Si's brewing of wine as a profession; previously, Mingfu had purchased wine wholesale from Si for distribution and had accumulated a debt of 120 coppers. On several occasions, he was billed, but he made no repayment. On Kangxi 40.7.5, Xu Si again went to demand payment, and the two argued with each other. When Xu Si smashed one of the pottery bowls in his wineshop, Mingfu butted Si with his head. Si raised his fist and struck him in return, injuring Mingfu's right ribs, and Mingfu fell to the ground. At dusk, he expired. The nephew of the deceased filed a complaint with the district, which filed a brief on its preliminary examination and was authorized to carry on a detailed investigation. The magistrate having forwarded the criminal, this office again carried out a strenuous investigation of the injury along with the depositions. I concur with the magistrate's recommendation that

Xu Si receive the punishment of strangulation. I humbly await the commission's instructions.

The case having been forwarded to the commission, this Commission brought forward the criminal for examination. Interrogation of Zhang Sanyuan: "Was the deceased Zhang Mingfu your uncle? What enmity did he have with Xu Si? What was the source of the conflict over which he beat him to death. Testify."

He testified: "Zhang Mingfu was my uncle. Originally, he was from Tongzhou. Together with Jiang Junlong, a Jurong man, as his partner, he opened a wineshop in New Kaihe Market in Chongming. He had no enmity with Xu Si, but because Uncle bought wine wholesale from Xu Si to sell, he owed him 120 coppers. On the fifth of the seventh month, Xu Si came by to collect, but Uncle was not able to repay him. So Xu Si injured Uncle, and he died. I was not in the wineshop during the fight. Jiang Junlong and Li Jingshan were witnesses.

Interrogation of Jiang Junrong: "You ran a wineshop with Zhang Mingfu. Why was that Zhang Mingfu beaten to death by Xu Si? Testify."

He testified: "I am from Jurong District. Zhang Mingfu is a Tongzhou man. We ran a wineshop together in New Kaihe Market in Chongming. That Xu Si brews wine as a business. Zhang Mingfu bought wine from him wholesale to sell, and he owed him 120 coppers. On the morning of the fifth of the seventh month, Xu Si came to collect the money. Zhang Mingfu said to him, 'Come back this afternoon, and I'll give it to you.' But Xu Si had made up his mind that he wanted it now. An argument broke out, and Xu Si smashed the wineshop's pottery bowls. Zhang Mingfu butted Xu Si with his head, and Xu Si gave him a punch, knocking him down. Li Jingshan and I separated them, but at dusk, Zhang Mingfu died."

Interrogation of Li Jingshan: "From your perspective, what is the real reason that Zhang Mingfu was beaten to death by Xu Si? Testify."

He testified: "I'm the next-door neighbor to Zhang Mingfu's wineshop. Zhang Mingfu bought wine wholesale from Xu Si to sell, and he owed him 120 coppers. On the morning of the fifth of the seventh month, Xu Si came to collect his money. Zhang Mingfu said to him, 'I'll have the money this afternoon.' But Xu Si had made up his mind that he wanted it now. An argument broke out, and Xu Si broke the wineshop's pottery bowls. Zhang Mingfu butted Xu Si with his head, and Xu Si gave him a punch. Zhang Mingfu fell down on the ground. Jiang Junlong and I separated them, but at dusk, Zhang Mingfu died."

Interrogation of Xu Si: "What enmity did you have with Zhang Mingfu? Over what matter did you get into the argument during which you beat him to death? Testify."

He testified: "I brew wine for a living. I never had any enmity with Zhang Mingfu. Zhang Mingfu bought wine from me wholesale to sell, and he owed me 120 coppers. I tried to collect it several times, but he wouldn't pay me. On the morning of the fifth of the seventh month, I went again to collect, but he still wouldn't pay me. I spoke with him, but he cursed me back. In anger, I broke a pottery bowl from his shop, and then Zhang Mingfu butted me with his head. I hit him back just once. I didn't think that hitting him in the ribs would make him fall down. At dusk, he died."

After another summary by the judicial commissioner, the document was forwarded to Beijing as a memorial to the emperor. On the cover is his decision: to remand it to the Three Judicial Offices for their recommendation concerning the appropriate punishment, which was very likely less than strangulation, perhaps a beating and a period of exile as the next most strenuous punishment.

NOTES

Source: *Neige tiben Xingke Xingbu Xingfa* [Grand Secretariat routine memorials, Board of Punishments, Crime and Punishment] 522–113, Kangxi 41 (1702), Suzhou.

1. The Three Judicial Offices (Sanfasi), also known as the Three High Courts of Judicature, are the Court of Judicial Review, the Board of Punishments, and the Censorate—the highest capital officials.

2. Song Luo's many positions are normally held concurrently with that of provincial governor. His awards are ordinary, for regular honorable service. See Brunnert and Hagelstrom, *Present Day Political Organization*, 511. For a biographical sketch of Song Luo, see *Eminent Chinese*, 689–90.

3. Manchu names are often treated as Han names; the first syllable is used as if it were a surname. Because the last pages of the report are missing, the rest of this official's name is not obvious.

4. According to *The Great Qing Penal Code*, Article 290. "Anyone who, during an affray, strikes and kills another, regardless of whether he has struck with the hand, or the feet, or with another object, or with a metal knife, will be punished with strangulation (*with delay*)" (Jones, *Great Qing Code*, 276).

Li Huaiyu: The Missing Brother (Hunan, 1736)

Complications abound in this memorial, sent to the capital in the name of one of the highest imperial princes. The murder had gone undetected for several years, and when the investigation finally began, more deaths occurred: Illness took the life of the magistrate who originally heard the case, and one of the suspects died in prison, ostensibly of an infection, although the care with which the next magistrate conducted the inquest suggests that he was initially unsure whether foul play was involved. In order to make a recommendation of punishment, he had to reexamine the case, and through this process, he learned far more about those involved.

The principals in this case were among the poorest in the region, at the level at which children were sold as indentured servants, and even though the victim was wealthy by comparison, he was indistinguishable in dress and appearance from a roaming beggar. It is hardly surprising that members of the elite serving in public office should have found the stories of these people hard to understand; the family ties so prized by the elite seemed to be less important than personal integrity to these poor folk.[1] Even so, the questioning as recorded here does reveal ever more complex tensions among the people involved, all of whom were related by marriage or birth. The bulk of the memorial is from the magistrates' detailed briefs.

Board of Punishments . . . , and Prince of the Blood of the First Degree, Your subject Yunli respectfully submits this MEMORIAL concerning the report of a fratricide and its investigation. The Board of Punishments' Office of Scrutiny forwards a report from Wu Yingfen, Acting Adjutant for the Huguang Governor and Junior Vice President of the Board of War, concerning a previous matter. Therein, Yuan Chenglong, Commissioner of the Huguang Judicial Commission at Wuchang, reports on his examination of one Liu Xinglong, forty-seven *sui* in age, a resident of Xiangyang District, Xiangyang: the complaint names Xinglong as an utterly lawless [*wangzhi faji*] perpetrator of murder for personal gain [*tucai haiming*]. Previously, Xinglong had lodged at the home of his younger sister's husband Li Huaiming and had maintained warm relations with the deceased Li Huaiyu. On Yongzheng 7.2.8 [March 7, 1729], Xinglong went to Huaiming's house to offer sacrifices at the death of his younger sister. On the way, he encountered Huaiyu and asked him where he was headed. Huaiyu replied that he was buying a water buffalo. Speculating that he must be carrying some silver with him, [Xinglong] determined to obtain that money. Thereupon, he wrongfully initiated an agreement to go with Huaiyu the next day to buy it. Huaiyu believed what he said to be true and returned home. Thereupon, Xinglong went to Huaimin's house to offer sacrifices and rest for the night. Concerned that Huaiyu might back out midway, he then wrongfully went to plot with Zhou Sanming, who died in prison of illness, and invited him to go along. On the following day, secretly bringing along a hatchet from Huaiming's house, Xinglong went to meet Huaiyu. On Back Ridge, he encountered Huaiyu, and together with Sanming they walked to the area of Geng Family Ditch. The time was dusk; while Sanming fell behind, Xinglong then wrongfully struck Huaiyu on the left temporal and occipital areas, including the ear cavity, with the metal hatchet he was carrying. Huaiyu fell to the ground and expired. Sanming fled, but Xinglong searched out the money and then left.

According to the detailed brief concerning this matter submitted by the former magistrate of Xiangyang, Zhang Zhongxiu (who subsequently died of illness):

From the complaint filed by Li Huaiyin on Yongzheng 12.7.30 [August 28, 1734]:

"In the past, my humble self and my elder brother, the two of us, divided our household and lived separately.[2] On Yongzheng 7.2.9 [March 8, 1729], Zhou Sanming and Liu Xinglong made an agreement with my brother Li Huaiyu to go to buy a water buffalo. My brother took the silver from selling land, sixteen *liang*, with him. We never heard from him again. He left behind my sister-in-law Ms. Xiong with two children less than ten *sui* in age. I have made inquiries in all directions, but until now have found no trace of him. On 4.14 of this year [May 16, 1734], Zhou Sanming told me that my brother had been killed by Liu Xinglong and buried on Geng Hongshun's land in the Willow Slope Village [Liuyanji] area. On 7.13 [August 11], Xinglong's own younger brother Liu Yongheng told me that it was his brother together with Zhou Sanming who had plotted to kill my brother. I hereby humbly submit this affidavit begging that you grant me the favor of arresting and questioning them in order to recover the corpse."

Upon receiving this, I immediately began an investigation. Li Huaiyin testified: "During the month of sacrifice [the twelfth month] of Yongzheng 6 [1729], I went into the mountains to collect firewood and returned in the fourth month of Yongzheng 7. When I asked where my elder brother had gone, my mother and sister-in-law said that on the twenty-eighth of the month of sacrifice of last year, he sold some land to Li Shishun's family for sixteen *liang* of silver. On the ninth of the second month of Yongzheng 7, he agreed with Zhou Sanming and Liu Xinglong to go buy a water buffalo, but they never heard from him again. After that, I made inquiries in all directions for several years, but I never found any trace of him at all. Then on the fourteenth of the fourth month of this year, Zhou Sanming said to me, 'Your older brother was killed by Liu Xinglong, and he was buried on Geng Hongshun's land in the Willow Slope Village area.' As soon as I heard this, I went there to check it out. On the thirteenth of the seventh month, I saw Liu Xinglong's brother Liu Yongheng, and I asked him. He said the same thing. I came to make this report only after having checked the truth of it. I beg you to do me the favor of apprehending Zhou Sanming and Liu Yongheng in order to investigate this and right the injustice done to my brother. It will be a great act of mercy on your part."

Thereupon, I had Liu Yongheng apprehended and brought to the court for questioning. Liu Yongheng testified: "Liu Xinglong is my own older brother. When I was five, our father sold me to the Zhu family of Huanglongdang as a servant. I got back home only last year. I had heard people say that Li Huaiyu was killed by my brother. During the fifth month of last year, I went with my nephew Liu Shibang to the Cao Family Temple to watch the plays. As we were walking along, I asked him, 'Did your father kill Li Huaiyu—could such a thing have happened?' My nephew said he didn't know whether it was true or not. Then in the tenth month of last year, I don't remember what day it was, I was warming myself by the stove with my brother Liu Xinglong, and I asked him, 'Did you kill Li Huaiyu—did that happen?' Older Brother said that it did; he had killed him at Geng Family Ditch, and ever since that day, he couldn't get over his regret. This is what my older brother said to me. During the seventh month of this year, Li Huaiyin asked me about it, and I didn't dare to hide it. All of this is true."

On this basis, I commissioned constables to arrest Zhou Sanming and Liu Xinglong secretly. Thereafter, on the twenty-ninth of the eighth month [September 26], Zhou Sanming and Liu Xinglong were arrested and brought to court. Thereupon, I interrogated them.

Zhou Sanming testified: "Li Huaiyu was my wife's maternal uncle. Formerly, I had lived with them. On the ninth of the second month of Yongzheng 7, I ate my midday meal at Li Huaiyu's house and after a while went with him to Liu Xinglong's place to buy a water buffalo. We walked out behind to Pear Tree Ridge, where we ran into Liu Xinglong, and from then on, we all went together for twenty or so *li*. When we got to Geng Family Ditch, it was dark. The two of them were walking up ahead, and I was a little bit behind them. Suddenly, Liu Xinglong took out a hatchet and hacked

Li Huaiyu to death with it. I was scared and ran away. If you want to know how he killed Huaiyu, ask Liu Xinglong."

I questioned him further: "If you saw Liu Xinglong hack at Li Huaiyu with a hatchet, why didn't you cry out for someone to rescue him? And after he was hacked to death, you didn't come forward. Isn't this because you plotted with Liu Xinglong to kill him?"

He testified: "That Geng Family Ditch is a wild place, and it was dark. I didn't dare cry out. And besides, Liu Xinglong is my own uncle on my mother's side—I didn't dare come forward. But I didn't help at all in that business of killing him."

Interrogation of Liu Xinglong. He testified: "Normally, Li Huaiyu and I didn't have any bad feelings between us because my younger sister is Li Huaiming's wife. On the eighth of the second month of Yongzheng 7, my sister passed away, and so I went to burn [sacrificial] paper [money in her memory]. When I got to the ridge behind Li Huaiyu's, I ran into him. I asked him where he was going, and he said he wanted to buy a water buffalo. All at once, I realized that if he was going to buy a water buffalo, he must be carrying some silver at his waist. So I tricked him, saying, 'I've got a water buffalo over at my place. Why don't you come over tomorrow and buy mine?' Then I went to my younger sister's house to burn paper. I stayed the night at her place. The next day, after we ate the midday meal and as I was leaving, I noticed a hatchet there at my sister's house. So I stole it and brought it along with me. When I got up Back Ridge, I ran into Li Huaiyu and his wife's nephew Zhou Sanming. I pretended and asked him, 'Where are you headed?' He said he was headed for my place to buy my water buffalo. So I walked along with them. By the time we got to Geng Family Ditch, it was dark, and he was walking in front. From behind, I hit him in the back of the head with the hatchet, and he fell over. When I hit him again, he died. I gathered up his thirteen hundred coppers. That day, Li Huaiyu was wearing a plain felt hat on his head and a worn-out blue padded cotton jacket and a pair of old worn-out plain short cotton socks.

"Then I turned around and took the hatchet back to my sister's house. Zhou Sanming never planned it with me. Now I've confessed that I plotted to kill Li Huaiyu. If I had been able to find his silver, wouldn't I admit that, too? The fact is, I never saw any of his silver."

Interrogation of Li Huaiming. He testified: "Li Huaiyu was my older clan brother; Liu Xinglong is my wife's brother. He stayed overnight in my house, but whether he took my family's hatchet and killed Li Huaiyu with it, I have no idea. Do me the favor of questioning Liu Xinglong and then you'll know for sure."

Interrogation of Geng Hongshun. He testified: "During the second month of Yongzheng 7, I don't remember what day it was, the constable [*paitou*] Geng Hongyu came to my house and said that somebody had died on the edge of our ditch. I went with him to have a look. The local warden [*paijia*] Zhang Mingjin came to look, and they said it must be some beggar fleeing from a famine. Sergeant Geng Hongyu summoned several men to cover him up with dirt. Those people said the dead man's face was dark and bloated, and they saw two ravens that were pecking at a not very long hole in it. I'm just a foolish sort, but I was afraid to go there to look. I beg you to release me."

Interrogation of Geng Hongyu. He testified: "Geng Hongshun is my older clan brother who lives on the ridge. When I went there to look, all I could see was that the dead man's face was bloated and that there was a place where ravens were pecking it. At that time, snow was falling heavily, and the body was covered with snow. I didn't really look at it closely; I just took it to be some beggar who had died there. That's why we just buried him. I beg you to release me."

Interrogation of Ms. Xiong. She testified: "On the ninth of the second month of Yongzheng 7, when my husband went out with Zhou Sanming, the husband of my sister's child [*waisheng nüxu*], he was wearing a plain felt hat on his head, a blue cotton padded jacket, and a pair of plain cotton socks. Of the sixteen *liang* of silver he had gotten from selling the field, he had with him everything but what he had spent on five pecks of rice. But I don't have any idea who he had paid off. He went out the door and never came back. Even now, I don't know whether my husband is alive or dead. That's the truth."

On the basis of this, I ordered each of the culprits to be held separately in custody and a search to be conducted for the murder weapon. This was a serious case of premeditated homicide, but because years had passed since the incident, the case would be hard to settle, and a punishment in accordance with the appropriate substatute would be hard to determine without a detailed examination of the exhumed remains for the purpose of detecting the traces of wounds on the corpse. Upon receipt of authorization from the two commissions, I sought permission for the examination of the corpse from the relevant prefecture in accordance with the statute on ascertaining the facts in a premeditated homicide, with the instruction that the magistrate's detailed brief should be delayed until it was completed.

Further according to the former magistrate Zhang Zhongxiu's detailed brief: On Yongzheng 12.10.24 [November 19, 1734], I dutifully took clerk and coroner and went in person to that place, where I ordered the culprits, the next of kin of the deceased, and the landowner and others to exhume the remains of the deceased Li Huaiyu. In accordance with the law, Coroner Han Mingcheng examined the remains of the deceased Li Huaiyu and reported that they were 4 *chi* and 5 *cun* long and 7.5 *cun* high at the chest. [He reported] a lethal injury on the left temporal to left occipital area, including the left ear cavity, 2.7 *cun* long and 1.8 *cun* wide, with shattered bone, an injury from a metal instrument. A nonlethal injury 9 *fen* long and 6 *fen* wide on the left side of the jaw, the bone broken, an injury from a metal instrument. Further, the murder weapon was recovered from the home of Li Huaiming; when compared [with the remains], it corresponded with the injuries to the bones. A careful inspection of the entire remains revealed no other causes of death. His examination complete, the next of kin were allowed to examine the remains, and there was no disagreement. Thereupon, the remains were enshrouded and encoffined and entrusted to the local warden for safekeeping. Then interrogations were held at the scene.

The coroner Han Mingcheng testified: "As to the injury to the left side of his head, the left occiput up to the ear cavity, I have made comparisons: it was made by a glancing blow from the side of the hatchet; it was 2.7 *cun* long and 1.8 *cun* wide. That injury on the left jaw was made by the head of the hatchet; it was 9 *fen* long and 6 *fen* wide."

Then Liu Xinglong testified: "At first, I was walking behind. After we crossed the ditch, I was walking ahead of him. I took the hatchet in my right hand and struck sideways with the side of the hatchet to the left side of his head. Then he fell down. Then I used the back of the hatchet to hit him once in the jaw, and that's when he died. It was I who gave him those two injuries."

Interrogation of Zhou Sanming. He testified: "On that day, Liu Xinglong and Li Huaiyu were walking ahead of me, and I was walking behind them. It was already dark by then. All I could see was that Liu Xinglong hit Li Huaiyu with a hatchet. I was scared and ran away. I don't know anything about how many times Liu Xinglong hit him. I really didn't help him in this business of hitting Li Huaiyu."

On the basis of this examination of the remains and the interrogations at that time, in addition to the [initial] report on the facts concerning this case of premeditated murder, I thereby filled in and annotated the list [of injuries] and the [forensic] chart and prepared a report and affixed my seal, to be forwarded as appropriate, and so on. Having received the authorization [from my superiors] to do so, I investigated the facts of the case thoroughly in order to settle on the appropriate sentence to be forwarded for further review.

Subsequently, the next magistrate of Xiangyang District, Shen Mengjian, records that on Yongzheng 13.2.26 [March 20, 1735], the prison warden Li Wenzhu and the guard Long Zepu reported that the imprisoned criminal Zhou Sanming had on 1.9 [February 1] of this year fallen ill with an infection. Thereupon, they reported that a physician had been summoned to treat him, but he did not recover. In the early afternoon of this day, he expired. As appropriate, they thereby reported the matter to their superiors. Consequently, this humble magistrate [Shen] went at once in person with the clerk and the coroner to the jail. There, the corpse was placed on level ground and examined. The deceased Zhou Sanming was a little over thirty *sui* in age. Coroner Han Mingcheng examined him at that site, determining that Zhou Sanming's two hands were lightly clutching his stomach, which was flat, and that his whole body was sallow and lean. Beyond this, there were no visible causes of death. He concluded that death was the result of illness. His examination complete, I made my personal inspection and found no discrepancy. At that time, I donated a coffin and had the body shrouded for burial.

Interrogation of the jail warden Li Wenzhu. He testified: "This Zhou Sanming fell ill on the ninth of the first month. The guard submitted a request, and the physician Zhou Anlin was summoned to treat him. He administered a number of medicines, but to no visible effect. This afternoon, he died of that illness. The guards attending him inflicted no mistreatment whatsoever." I interrogated the guard Long Zepu, whose testimony was the same.

Interrogation of the person jailed next to him, Jin Mingqing. He testified: "In jail, Zhou Sanming fell ill on the ninth of the first month. The physician assigned to us came to treat him. He administered medicines, but none of them had any effect. This afternoon, Zhou Sanming died. There was no mistreatment by the guards. I would not dare give false testimony."

Interrogation of the physician Zou Anlin. He testified: "It was on the ninth of the first month that Zhou Sanming fell ill. I was the physician assigned to treat him; the physician is to go at once to the prison to examine the patient. It was a consumptive illness, on which my medicines had no effect. He died of the disease. This is the truth."

On this basis then, I filled out and annotated the [forensic] chart of the body and prepared a report and affixed my seal. Thereafter, I received the authorization to conduct an investigation to ensure that mistreatment had not been a cause of the prisoner's death and to expedite a judicial examination and penalty to be forwarded for review.

The following was recorded by Shen Mengjian, the acting magistrate of Zaoyang District in charge of Xiangyang Prefecture matters:[3] Magistrate Qiu Yunheng of Xiangyang District, who took office on 4.2 [April 24] of this year, reported: When I had reviewed all of the original documents, I summoned the prison guards and others for a reexamination; I found no evidence of mistreatment in the death of Zhou Sanming. I further summoned all the criminals to court and, at the bench, questioned the landowners Geng Hongshun and Geng Hongyu; their testimony was no different from the first time. I did not question them on other matters.

Li Shishun testified: "Li Huaiyu's land had previously been pawned to me; I gave him twelve *liang* of silver for it. On the twenty-eighth of the month of sacrifice of Yongzheng 6, he sold it to me through Liu Shichao. I gave him four more *liang* of silver as the purchase price. That's the truth."

Li Shichao testified: "It was I who, as middleman, wrote the contract for Li Huaiyu to sell his land to Li Shishun on the twenty-eighth of the twelfth month of Yongzheng 6. His land had been previously pawned and later redeemed. Li Shishun paid Li Huaiyu four more *liang* of silver for it. That's the truth."

Li Huaiyin testified: "My older brother Li Huaiyu sold his own field to Li Shishun during the month of sacrifice of Yongzheng 6. I haven't lived with my brother since childhood. Because he saw that I had no capital, in the first month of the seventh year, he gave me two hundred coppers to go out and buy firewood to sell. When I got back in the fourth month, my sister-in-law Ms. Xiong said that my brother had agreed to go with Zhou Sanming and Liu Xinglong to buy a water buffalo on the ninth of the second month [March 8]. But he still hadn't come back, so she told me to go out to look for him. So I asked Zhou Sanming. Zhou Sanming said that my brother hadn't been able to buy a water buffalo, and he didn't know where he had gone to buy one. I also went to ask Liu Xinglong, but he said the same thing. I went everywhere looking, but I couldn't find him. I thought that my brother always likes to drink, and there's that Black Water River. I was afraid that he had gotten drunk and fallen into the river. But there was no way to tell. I'm just a poor man. All I could do is keep it in mind, and whenever I ran into somebody, I'd ask. But there was no place to go to look for him.

"Then in the fourth month of last year, when I was plowing, Zhou Sanming came up, mad as he could be, and said to me, 'There's a bit of clan business you ought to get in on.' I said, 'If there's some way to make a little money, let me in on it.' He said, 'Your older brother was beaten to death by Liu Xinglong in Geng Family Ditch.' And he told me to go ask him about it, and Liu Xinglong would have to give me some money. He also told me to give him some of it. So I said, 'How would I dare ask him for money?' I just wondered if it was true. So I was even more careful making inquiries. One day, I ran into Liu Xinglong's brother Liu Yongheng. I chatted with him a while, and then I brought up the business of my older brother. He put me off, so I asked him about it again. Then he told me that my brother Huaiyu had in fact been beaten to death by his older brother Liu Xinglong. Seeing that what the two of them said corresponded, only then did I file the complaint. I only beg for justice for my older brother."

Question: "You say that only after Zhou Sanming and Liu Yongheng told you did you believe it and file the complaint. But Zhou Sanming is Liu Xinglong's niece's husband, and Liu Yongheng is his own brother. Why would the two of them be willing to tell you the truth?"

He testified: "It was only when both of them told me that I understood. Even though Zhou Sanxing is Liu Xinglong's niece's husband, I had heard that he had had words with Liu Xinglong for the last several days. But as for Liu Yongheng, it was because my asking him again and again pained him. He's an honest man, and he couldn't help being moved to tell me the truth."

Hoping for more facts, I asked: "That day when your older brother set out, just how much money was he carrying with him?"

He testified: "Because I was not in the house when my brother set out, I don't know how much money he was carrying with him."

Question: "Upon examination, your complaint says that your brother took the sixteen *liang* of silver from the sale of the land with him. Why do you say you don't know how much money he was carrying?"

He testified: "I hadn't seen those sixteen *liang* with my own eyes; that's what my sister-in-law told me. That's why I reported that amount in my complaint."

Interrogation of Liu Yonghong. He testified: "I'm a resident of Xiangyang District, and this year I'm thirty-two *sui* in age. This Liu Xinglong is my own brother. When I was five, I was sold to the Zhu family of Huanglongdang to be a servant. In Yongzheng 11, I finally redeemed myself and went home. While he was plotting to kill Li Huaiyu, I didn't know anything about it. It was only afterward that I heard people say that Li Huaiyu was killed by my brother. Then in the fifth month of Yongzheng 11, when I was on my way to the Cao Family Temple with my nephew Liu Shibang to watch the plays, I asked my nephew, 'Did your father kill Li Huaiyu—did that happen?' My nephew said, 'I have heard that, too, but I don't know whether that's true or false.' During the tenth month, I don't remember the date, I was warming myself at the stove with my older brother Liu Xinglong, and I asked him about it. My brother said that when Li Huaiyu had gone to buy the water buffalo, he had killed him at Geng Family Ditch. Last year in the seventh month, Li Huaiyin asked me about it, saying that his mother had also died and his sister-in-law and his nephew didn't have anything to eat, and he himself was desperate. Nobody knew the whereabouts of his brother. 'I've heard tell that your brother did him in, but I don't know whether it's real or false.' What he said really touched me. So I told him. This is the truth."

Question: "If your brother had beaten Li Huaiyu to death, and suppose that he told you about it, how could you bring yourself to tell his brother Li Huaiyin about it?"

He testified: "There's just the two of us brothers. So at first I didn't want to tell anybody about it. It was only because Li Huaiyin was Li Huaiyu's own brother and he already knew that he'd been killed by my brother. At that time, I was thinking about how my brother really should not have done that. It's hard to ignore your conscience [*liangxin nanmei*]. So I told him the whole truth about the matter."

Question: "You heard somebody say that your brother had killed Li Huaiyu—what was that person's name?"

He testified: "That my brother did it, now that I think of it, it was Zhou Sanming who first brought it up. But everybody knows about it."

Interrogation of Ms. Xiong. She testified: "On the ninth of the twelfth month of Yongzheng 7, Zhou Sanming came to my house to get my husband to go out with him to buy a water buffalo. On the next day, he came again for him. I said, 'He still hasn't come home from that trip out with you yesterday.' Zhou Sanming said that the deal had not gone through with the Liu family buffalo, but he should have come home by now. Then he left. Later, my younger brother-in-law Li Huaiyin came back and searched everywhere for him, but there was never any trace of him. Brother-in-law also went and asked Zhou Sanming and the others. They all said that when the deal fell through with the water buffalo, he'd surely gone somewhere else. I don't have any idea what enmity there was between Liu Xinglong and my husband that he would plot to kill him. I only beg that you question Liu Xinglong and right the wrong done my husband."

Question: "In examining your previous testimony, you said that your husband had sixteen *liang* of silver from selling a field. Could that be true?"

She testified: "I only heard my husband say that he had sold the field for sixteen *liang*; I never saw it with my own eyes. I just know that when we didn't have anything to eat at New Year's, he bought five pecks of rice, half a bundle of salt, and half a piece of paper.[4] Beyond this, I don't know whether or not he had any silver. This is the truth."

Interrogation of Zhang Mingjin. He testified: "During Yongzheng 7, I don't remember the date, Geng Hongyu and Gong Hongshun came over to my house and said that somebody had died on the bank of their ditch. So I went there with them to have a look. That dead man's face was dark and bloated, and there were crows pecking at a hole in it. It was snowing heavily just then, and so I never took a close look at him. I just thought he was a beggar who had died there. That's why we just buried him without making any report. This was my mistake, but I beg you to overlook it."

Interrogation of Li Huaiming. He testified: "I am a resident of this district, and I'm forty-five *sui* old. That Li Huaiyu, now deceased, is my older clan brother. Liu Xinglong is my wife's brother. Whether there were bad feelings between Li Huaiyu and Liu Xinglong, I don't have any idea. As to who might have plotted with him, you already have Liu Xinglong here; do me the favor of asking him."

Question: "The hatchet that Liu Xinglong used to kill Li Huaiyu came from your house. If you weren't in on the plot, why would you be willing to give it to him to kill somebody with? Furthermore, why did he come only to your house to get a hatchet? Why don't you tell the truth?"

He testified: "My wife was Liu Xinglong's younger sister. On the eighth of the second month of Yongzheng 7, Liu Xinglong came to burn paper for my wife. He spent the night there, and on the next day, he left. I don't have any idea whether he took the hatchet with him."

Seeking further facts, I asked: "You say you don't know whether Liu Xinglong took the hatchet. How could it be that nobody in your family saw him do it and asked what he wanted a hatchet for? And afterward, none of you knew about it when he brought the hatchet back? Surely you know more than you're letting on. Tell the whole truth."

He testified: "But in fact no one saw Liu Xinglong either take the hatchet or bring the hatchet back. If he was plotting to kill someone, why would he be willing to wait around for someone to catch him at it? Naturally, he concealed the hatchet on his body both times. And besides, he is my wife's brother—inside or outside, he could go anywhere he wanted to. Who would stop him? Li Huaiyu was my clan brother. If I had known that he had been murdered by Liu Xinglong, why would I have hidden it and not come forward? Do me the favor of examining Liu Xinglong and then you'll find out."

Interrogation of Liu Xinglong: "Where are you from, and how old are you? What was the date and because of what grudge against him did you plot with those two to kill Li Huaiyu? Tell the truth."

He testified: "I am a resident of this district, and this year I am forty-seven *sui* old. This Li Huaiming was the husband of my younger sister. In the past, I stayed at Huaiming's house and then afterward moved back home. That Li Huaiyu is Huaiming's clan brother. I knew him well. On the eighth of the second month of Yongzheng 7, my sister died. It was while I was going to Li Huaiming's house to burn paper that I ran into Li Huaiyu on Pear Tree Ridge behind Li Huaiyu's house. I asked him where he was going, and he said he was on his way to buy a water buffalo. I've always been desperately poor [*qiongzhe de ji de*], and I thought that if he was going to buy a water buffalo, he must be carrying some silver. So I tricked him by saying, 'Tomorrow you should go over to my place; I have a water buffalo to sell you.' Then he stopped and said a few words and then went back home.

"When I got to my sister's house to burn paper, it was dark, so I stayed the night there. But I was afraid that he wouldn't want to go buy it. Zhou Sanming is my wife's nephew, and that night he was at Li Huaiming's house, too. So I said to Zhou Sanming, 'Today, I ran into Li Huaiyu, and when I asked him, he said he wanted to buy a water buffalo. I told him to come to my place tomorrow and buy my water buffalo. After all, if he wants to buy a buffalo, he must have some money that we can get out of him. But I'm afraid that he'll go off by himself to buy one and won't want to come. You're a relative of his. How about you go get him to agree to it?' Zhou Sanming said, 'How are you going to get it out of him?' And I said, 'When the time comes, I'll have a plan.' When Zhou Sanming heard me talk about getting some money for us to spend, he said, 'Sure, I'll get him to agree to it.'

"So the next day, I had already hidden the hatchet from my sister's house on my body, and when I walked up Pear Tree Ridge, I ran into Liu Huaiyu and Zhou Sanming. So I made a point of asking him again where he was going, and he said he was going to my place to buy a water buffalo. So we went along together, but by the time we got to Geng Family Ditch, it was dark. At first, he was ahead and I was behind him. After we crossed the ditch, I was in front of him. Zhou Sanming had fallen behind. I took the hatchet in my right hand and hit him a sidewise blow with it on the left side of the head, his temple, and his ear. Then he fell down. I also hit him with the back of the hatchet on the left side of the jaw, and then he died. By then, Zhou Sanming was so scared that he ran away. He didn't take any part in it. Both of his [Liu Huaiyu's] injuries were my work."

Question: "You first testified that Li Huaiyu was walking ahead, and from behind you took the hatchet and hit him in the back of the head, and then he fell down. Why are you now saying that you were walking ahead of him and hit him on the left side of the head? If you were secretly plotting to attack him, naturally you would hit him from behind. Hurry up and testify."

He testified; "The reason that I first testified that I hit him with the hatchet from behind was that, after so many years, I just made a mistake. Now, sitting in jail, I remembered. At first, Li Huaiyu was walking in front and I was behind him. But that was during the daytime. By the time, we got to Geng Family Ditch and took off our shoes to cross the water, it was already dark. Li Huaiyu was slow in taking off his shoes, so after we crossed the ditch, I was walking in front. At first, I took the hatchet in my right hand, and when he caught up with me, I turned around and hit him a blow across the head. That's why I hit him on the left side of the head, the temple, and the ear as well. If I had hit him from behind, it would still be a crime, so why wouldn't I tell it to you straight?"

Seeking more facts, I asked: "That Zhou Sanming was a relative of his. How could it be that you could tell him you wanted to murder Li Huaiyu— weren't you afraid that he would let Li Huaiyu know about it?"

He testified: "Even though Zhou Sanming was the husband of Li Huaiyu's niece, they never got along very well with each other. When Zhou Sanming heard about getting a little money, all he could think about was money. That's why he went to get [Li Huaiyu] to go along."

Question: "If Zhou Sanming had agreed to go along with you on it, how could it be that he didn't help you hit him? Tell me that."

He testified: "When Zhou Sanming saw that I had knocked Li Huaiyu down, he went a few steps along the stream and then was so scared that he ran away. If he had helped me hit him, why would I confess that I did it alone?"

Question: "Where did Zhou Sanming run to?"

He testified: "First he ran to my place."

Question: "So how much money did you actually find on him?"

He testified: "Actually, all I found was thirteen hundred coppers. I gave five hundred of them to Zhou Sanming, so all I had was eight hundred for myself. That's the truth."

Question: "According to Woman Xiong, her husband took the sixteen *liang* of silver he got from selling the land with him to buy the water buffalo. Why do you say that you only found thirteen hundred coppers? Are you still not telling the truth?"

He testified: "I really found only thirteen hundred coppers on him; I didn't get any silver at all. That Li Shishun who bought the land said that Li Huaiyu's land was first pawned and later redeemed and that all he gave him was the balance of four *liang* of silver. And it was New Year's—how would he not have spent some of it? If I'd gotten some silver from him, it would still be the same crime. Why would I not confess to it?"

Seeking further details, I asked: "Since you discussed with Zhou Sanming getting Li Huaiyu to agree to go and buy your water buffalo so that you could kill him, why did you first and last testify that you had never discussed it with him? Clearly, you see Zhou Sanming's death as a chance to implicate him by dividing the spoils with him."

He testified: "Zhou Sanming was my wife's nephew. He only went to get Li Huaiyu to agree to go along because I asked him to. That's why when I first came to court, I didn't want to drag him into it. This is the truth. But now because Your Honor has examined me so strenuously, I can only tell the whole truth.[5] He was always in on it to share the spoils. I wouldn't dare lie about this."

Question: "If that Zhou Sanming had in fact plotted with you to share the spoils, how could it be that he would tell Li Huaiyin that you had beaten his older brother Li Huaiyu to death so that he could file a complaint against you?"

He testified: "Even though Zhou Sanming is my wife's nephew, he is also Li Huaiyu's niece's husband. If he hadn't been in on it for a share of the loot, not only would he not have been willing to go to Li Huaiyu's house to get him to agree to go so that I could beat Huaiyu to death, but why would he never come forward about it? As for his telling Li Huaiyin, it was all because Sanming was never any too careful about what he said. Ever since he got a little money from plotting a murder, whenever he got drunk, he'd say a couple of words about it, and people came to know about it. Besides, for the last few days, he couldn't take his aunt's scolding, and he was mad because it wasn't fair, so he told Li Huaiyin to scare me into bribing him. But now he's dead. What would be the use of implicating him? What I'm telling you is the truth."

Question: "You took the hatchet from Li Huaiming's house for your plot to kill Li Huaiyu. Was Li Huaiming in on the plot?"

He testified: "It was on the sly that I took his hatchet, and I hid it in my clothes. He never knew. It's a fact that he knew nothing about it and was not in on the plot."

Question: "If you made it so that he didn't see you, when you took the hatchet back, how could it be that not a single person in his family saw you? Plainly, your testimony is an attempt to clear him. Now tell the truth."

He testified: "I waited until I saw that there was no one in the house before I took the hatchet and hid it at my waist. Afterward, when I took it back, I again hid it in my clothes. I was his brother-in-law; I could go anyplace I wanted. That's why no one in his family saw me. It's really not that I'm giving false testimony, so release him."

On the basis of this evidence, I, Qiu Yunheng, Magistrate of Xiangyang District, examined Liu Xinglong for the premeditated murder of Li Huaiyin. To wit:

After the magistrate lays out his summary of the facts of the case, he gives his recommendations for punishment:

Except for Zhou Sanming, who has already expired, thus for whom we need not recommend, we recommend that Liu Xinglong be sentenced to beheading in accordance with the penalty for premeditated homicide for the sake of personal gain, which is the same as for robbers, with no distinction between leaders and followers.[6] I recommend beheading without delay.

The magistrate also suggested penalties for all involved. Even though he did not come forward of his own accord, the murderer's brother Liu Yongheng testified fully and truthfully despite their family relationship; for this reason, he should be cleared of the penalty for being an accessory after the fact, which, for the robbery, would be execution. Instead, as penalty for abetting a murder, his recommended punishment should be a nominal beating of one hundred strokes, reduced to forty. For allowing Liu to steal the murder weapon from his house, Li Huaiming, along with the men who failed to report to the local authorities when they discovered a body, were to be beaten a nominal eighty strokes, reduced to thirty. The others, he concluded, could be released. The eight hundred copper coins Liu Xinglong had taken from his victim should be entrusted to Li Huaiyin. The five hundred copper coins that had been shared with Zhou Sanming were considered lost.

Both the prefect and the provincial judicial commissioner in turn agreed with the magistrate's report and his recommendations. The memorial concludes with another summary of the facts of the case—using virtually the same wording as the magistrate's—which initially reaches the same recommendations for punishment. While the judicial review process was going on, however, a new emperor had ascended the throne. Consequently, a celebratory amnesty was proclaimed, and the final sections of the document debate which principals of the case should be covered by it. All were

pardoned except for the murderer Liu Xinglong. The Three Judicial Offices at the cap-
ital recommended that he be held in custody awaiting execution, but the decision of
the youthful Qianlong emperor was unequivocal: he decreed that Liu be taken to the
place of execution and that the sentence of beheading be carried out immediately.
The others, he ruled, should receive the reduced sentences as recommended by the
lower courts.

NOTES

Source: *Neige tiben Xing* [Grand Secretariat routine memorials, (Bureau of) Punish-
ments] 164, Qianlong 1 (1736).

1. For additional evidence suggesting such class distinctions in values in late
imperial China, see Hegel, "Distinguishing Levels."

2. In this initial complaint, Li Huaiyin refers to himself with the unusual pronoun
yi (lit., "ant[like in insignificance]"). As in other cases, all other male deponents use
the more standard deferential first-person pronoun *xiaode* ([my] humble [self]) in
their testimony.

3. By law, investigations of possible malfeasance of duty were assigned to a magistrate from another district in order to ensure objectivity.

4. Presumably this was red paper, for making conventional New Year's decora-
tions and wishes for good fortune during the coming year.

5. This most likely means that torture was inflicted during interrogation.

6. This refers to Articles 282 (of which the fifth section refers to obtaining property as a result of premeditated murder) and 266 (theft with the use of force) of the
Qing penal code. See Jones, *Great Qing Code*, 268, 246.

CASE 3

Ms. Guo: Accidental Homicide Concealed (Zhili, 1795)

TRANSLATED BY MARAM EPSTEIN

This case is of interest because it implies that a newly married wife did have some
power to resist her husband—at least among the lower gentry. As in other cases, the
deposition of the party of highest status sets the tone and the rhetoric for the entire
case. Note the details that suggest the shrewish potential of the victim: her angry
response to her husband, to the point of hitting him, the mess she leaves on the kang,
and the odd detail that she was naked when their final struggle took place. Atypical

is the number of depositions taken in a minor homicide case; this is likely because of the elite status of both families.

The preceding officials of the Board of Punishments' Office of Scrutiny respectfully copy here the case forwarded by Liang Kentang, the governor-general of Zhili, based on the memorial of the judicial commissioner, Suo-nuomu Zhamuchu, concerning the report forwarded by Yang Junwen, Prefect of Zhengding.

The detailed brief submitted by Xia Wenjiong, Magistrate of Huolu District, states:

On Qianlong 59.4.22 [May 20, 1794], the local warden Zhang Sanzhong reported that on the same day, in Yangling Village east of the Zhengding District seat, *zhiyuan*, Guo Tingyi, personally informed him that his niece, Ms. Guo, had on 4.9 married Zuo Qingxuan, the son of Zuo Yuanrang, of the same village, as a second [primary] wife.[1] On 4.21, he heard that his niece, Ms. Guo, had hanged herself, and he hurried over. He discovered that there was a wound on his niece's chest. Suspicious, he and Zuo Yuanrang subsequently questioned Zuo Qingxuan. He said that he had quarreled with his wife, Ms. Guo, and had stabbed her with a knife, that she had died soon after, and that he had disguised the death as suicide by hanging. [Zhang Sanzhong] personally went to see and had Zuo Qingxuan bound and transported to the court to request an interrogation as appropriate. On this same day, the uncle of the deceased Guo Tingyi filed his complaint by bringing it to the *yamen*.

This humble magistrate [Xia Wenjiong] accordingly proceeded to the place where the corpse lay, accompanied by a clerk and the coroner. In accordance with the law, I conducted an investigation.

In his oral report, the coroner declared: "The deceased, Mrs. Zuo née Guo, was twenty-five *sui* in age. From the front view, her facial color has begun to change. Her eyes are swollen, and her mouth is slightly open; her tongue is pressed against her lower teeth. A lethal wound is beneath her throat; the mark is slightly raised in front, and it extends around to the nape of her neck; the encircling mark is 4 *fen* wide and not quite 1 *fen* deep, of white color. Her two hands are slightly clasped. A lethal wound from a knife lies to the right of her heart, 5 *fen* long and 3 *fen* deep, slightly bloody. There are no other indications. I conclude that she died after being stabbed by a knife. Her death was then disguised as suicide by hanging."

This humble magistrate [Xia] then examined the body to verify that there were no discrepancies. The register of wounds was filled out and annotated.

After questioning, it was established that the oral testimony of the village head Zhang Sanzhong was no different from his written report.

The deposition of Guo Tingyi states: "I am from Yangling Village east of Zhiding District, neighboring the *yamen* here in Song Village. The deceased Ms. Guo is my own niece. Her parents are both deceased, and I raised her myself. On the ninth of the fourth month of Qianlong 59, Ms. Guo was married as a second [primary] wife to Zuo Qingxuan, the son of Zuo Yuanrang of Song Village under your jurisdiction. On the eleventh, because it was the third day, I received the couple in my home and saw that they had harmonious relations.[2] I sent them back home on the fourteenth. On the twenty-first, I heard that my niece had hanged herself. I quickly rushed over and discovered that there was a wound near my niece's heart. I grew suspicious, and Zuo Yuanrang and the others said that the facts surrounding my niece's death were not clear. Everyone asked Zuo Qingxuan [what had happened].

"He said that on the night of the twentieth, my niece said that she wanted to return to my home the next day. He refused her, and she did not give in and argued with him. My niece was angry and then did not speak to him. The two went to bed separately. My niece completely ignored him the entire night. The next morning at dawn, he got up and began to smoke. Since his pipe was broken, he was sitting on the *kang* using a small knife to repair it. Because he saw my niece's clothing strewn about the *kang*, he at first told her off for being lazy. My niece paid no attention and sniped back. He used the pipe and hit her on the back, and my niece cursed him. He grew angry and took his knife to threaten her; undressed, my niece sat up and tried to hit him. He was unable to pull his hand back in time and wounded her in her chest by her heart. She was still for a moment and then died. Afraid, he came up with the idea of disguising it as suicide by hanging. He got her fully dressed and then tied her belt around her neck and carried her corpse over to the rafters behind the door, where he tied her up. He opened the windows and left. There was no other reason. I then notified the local warden and came to the *yamen* to report it. All I ask is that you investigate fully."

The deposition of Mrs. Zuo née Chen states: "Zuo Yuanrang is my nephew; I am also his neighbor. Originally, Zuo Qingxuan was my second grandson; in childhood, he was adopted by Zuo Yuanrang as a son. I have two other grandsons. The deceased is Zuo Qingxuan's second wife. It was only on the ninth of the fourth month that she came into the family. Most days, the couple got along fine. At breakfast time on the twenty-first of the fourth month, I heard Zuo Yuanrang's mother, Mrs. Zuo Zhang, yelling in her house, saying that her granddaughter-in-law, Ms. Guo, had hanged to death. I rushed over and saw that the doors to Ms. Guo's room were closed and that Zuo Qingxuan was not at home. Only Mrs. Zuo Zhang was inside. I saw that the window was open and climbed in through the window, and I saw Ms. Guo hanging by her belt from the rafters behind the door. We, Mrs. Zuo Zhang and I, laid out the body and untied the belt but were unable to revive her. We noticed a wound on her chest near her heart, and it did not look as though she had died from hanging.

"At that time, Ms. Zuo and I opened the door and went out. Afterward, Zuo Yuanrang and Zuo Qingxuan came back separately; Ms. Guo's uncle, Guo Tingyi, also rushed into the house. Everyone asked Zuo Qingxuan what had happened; . . . ."

Her account of Zuo Qingxuan's testimony is identical to Guo Tingyi's, except for the following:

"He was unable to pull his hand back in time and wounded her in her chest near her heart. She fell over onto the *kang*, was still for a moment, and died. . . ."

The deposition of Mrs. Zuo Zhang states: "I am fifty *sui* in age. Zuo Yuanrang is the son of my husband's former wife. Zuo Qingxuan is Zuo Yuanrang's adopted son. Because his former wife, Ms. Fan, died of an illness, on the ninth of the fourth month, Zuo Qingxuan took Ms. Guo, the niece of Guo Tingyi, as a second wife. The couple got along well and had no friction. On the eleventh, because it was the third day, Guo Tingyi received the couple in his house. It was on the fourteenth that he brought them back. At dawn on the twenty-first, my son Zuo Yuanrang went to supervise the work of the laborers in the fields. At breakfast time, I got up, and because I didn't see Zuo Qingxuan or his wife, I opened the door and went to the back courtyard to call them, but they did not respond. I saw that the window was open. I was surprised, and so I entered through the window and saw Ms. Guo hanging by her belt from the rafters behind the door. She was already dead. Zuo Qingxuan was not in the room. I was shocked and began to call out.

"Just at that time Mrs. Zuo Chen, came over to help. . . ."

Again, virtually identical wording, until the concluding statement.

"As to how my grandson argued with Ms. Guo during the night, and how she cursed at him at dawn the next morning, because I live in the front courtyard with a courtyard separating us and my room has no windows in the rear, I did not hear a thing, and that's the truth."

The deposition of Zuo Yuanrang states: "I am from Song Village near the *yamen*. Ms. Zuo Zhang is my father's second wife.[3] Originally, Zuo Qingxuan was my nephew; I adopted him as my son when he was a child. Because his former wife, Ms. Fan, died of illness, he took Ms. Guo as a second wife on the ninth of the fourth month. On the eleventh, her relative Guo Tingyi received my son and daughter-in-law as they returned to her home. On the fourteenth, he brought them back. The couple had harmonious relations.

"At dawn on the twenty-first, I went to supervise the work of the laborers in the fields. When I came back at breakfast time, . . ."

Identical wording until:

". . . and then tied her belt around her neck and carried her corpse to the rafters behind the door where he tied her up to disguise it as suicide by hanging. He opened the window and left, thinking that if he pretended not to know about it, he could avoid prosecution. Little did he think that I and the others would see through it. I can only tell the truth."

Zuo Qingxuan without hesitation made a full confession that he had used a knife to wound his wife, Ms. Guo, and she had died. He then disguised it as suicide by hanging. Zuo Qingxuan was transported under escort to the jail, where he remained in custody. Depositions were recorded, and a report was made.

Having received permission to conduct an investigation and make a detailed report, and having received this dispatch, the accused, Zuo Qingxuan, and all concerned parties were gathered at the *yamen* for detailed interrogation. The testimony of the deceased's uncle and of all others was in agreement with their earlier depositions. There was no need to make further inquiry.

Interrogation of Zuo Qingxuan: "I am from this district and am twenty-three *sui* in age. Mrs. Chen née Zuo is my own grandmother; I also have older and younger brothers. During my childhood, I was adopted as a son by my uncle Zuo Yuanrang. My former wife, Ms. Fan, died of illness. On the ninth of the fourth month of Qianlong 59, I took Ms. Guo of Zhiding District, the niece of the official Guo Tingyi, as a second wife. Our relations were harmonious and there was no friction. . . ."

The murderer repeats information already supplied above. Then he explains:

"On the night of the twentieth, Ms. Guo and I were chatting in our room. My wife said that the next day was the twelfth day and she wanted to return to her natal home. I said that she had just gone home several days earlier and had only just returned. 'What do you want to go back for?' I refused her, but she did not give in. I argued with her for a bit. My wife became angry and would not speak to me. We went to bed separately. During the night, I wanted to have marital relations with my wife (*xing fang*), but she was absolutely unwilling; she ignored me, so I stopped. The next morning at dawn, I got up to smoke. Since my pipe was broken, I was sitting on the edge of the *kang* using a small knife to repair it. At that time, my wife was already awake. When I saw that her clothing was a mess, strewn all over the *kang* and not picked up, I first said she was lazy and told her off a bit. My wife did not heed me and instead sniped back. I then hit her across the back with the pipe. She blocked it with her hands and then started to curse me. I grew angry and took my knife to threaten her, thinking only that it would shut her up. How was I to know that, undressed as she was, she would sit up and start hitting me? I was unable to pull my hand back in time and ended up wounding her in the chest. My wife screamed and fell over onto the *kang*; she was still a moment and then died of the wound.

"I was afraid and didn't dare tell my grandmother, Mrs. Zuo Zhang, or my father Zuo Yuanrang and came up with the idea of disguising it as suicide by hanging in order to cover things up. So I then got my wife fully dressed. I looked for a rope, but when I couldn't find one, I used her waist sash and tied it around her neck and tucked her pants in tightly. My wife's body is small and thin. I carried her corpse over and tied her up to the rafter behind the door. I then opened the windows and went out, pretending I didn't know anything about it. At that time, no one knew anything. I came home after breakfast. My stepfather and wife's uncle started questioning me; I couldn't deny it and had no choice but to tell the truth. I truly had no intention of killing her, and there was no other quarrel. This is the truth."

This is followed by several more layers of summary and repetition of testimony. The final summary, written in smaller characters at the end of the document, reads:

Your subject Agui and others respectfully MEMORIALIZE concerning the case of Zuo Qingxuan, who used a knife to stab his wife, Ms. Guo, killing her, and then disguised it as suicide by hanging. According to the statements reported by Zhili governor-general Liang Kentang, Ms. Fan, the childhood wife of Zuo Qingxuan, had died from an illness. In Qianlong 59.4.9, he remarried, taking Ms. Guo as a second wife. The two had harmonious relations. On the evening of the twentieth, Ms. Guo said that she would return to her mother's home the next day. Zuo Qingxuan refused her; Ms. Guo did not submit, and they began arguing. They then went to bed. In the middle of the night, Zuo Qingxuan tried to take his pleasure with Ms. Guo, but she adamantly refused him, and he stopped. At daybreak on the twenty-first, Zuo Qingxuan was sitting on the *kang*, using a small knife to repair his tobacco pipe. Seeing Ms. Guo's clothing strewn about the *kang*, he told her off, but she did not heed him and talked back. Zuo Qingxuan then struck her across the back with his pipe. Ms. Guo blocked it with her hand and started cursing. Zuo Qingxuan grew angry and used the knife to threaten her. Unexpectedly, although she was not dressed, Ms. Guo struck him. Zuo Qingxuan was unable to pull back his arm in time and stabbed Ms. Guo to the right of her heart. Soon afterward, she died. Zuo Qingxuan was terrified and came up with the idea of disguising it as suicide by hanging. He got Ms. Guo fully dressed and then used her belt to hang her by the neck from the rafters behind the door. He opened the windows and went out. Upon interrogation, he made a full confession, denying nothing. Accordingly, Zuo Qingxuan is provisionally sentenced to strangulation according to the statute.

Thus, as MEMORIALIZED by the said governor-general, Zuo Qingxuan, in accordance with the statute on a husband striking and killing his wife, has been provisionally sentenced to death by strangulation subject to review at the autumn assizes. Your subjects, not daring to arrogate [powers not our own], respectfully submit this MEMORIAL for IMPERIAL APPROVAL·

NOTES

Source: *Neige tiben Xingfa* [Grand Secretariat routine memorials, Crime and Punishment], 2–1949–7, film 60, 6–9.

1. *Zhiyuan* is an honorific term used by lower-degree holders; Guo Tingyi uses it as a first-person pronoun to refer to himself throughout his deposition. A man might have only one primary wife, but if she died, he was encouraged to remarry.

2. Traditionally, a bride visited her natal family on the third day after her wedding.

3. Zuo Yuanrang uses the term *jiansheng*, a purchased title that designates scholars eligible to participate in the metropolitan examinations, as a pronoun here.

Li Cang: Blackmail and Arsenic (Shanxi, 1803)

The following case depicts, with startling precision, the effects of ingesting poison; the point is to leave no ambiguity about the cause of death and no discrepancies between the testimony as recorded and the physical evidence of the case. As with case 3, this translation omits repetitions of identically worded testimony.

Your subject Dong Gao [here follows a long list of titles] respectfully humbly submits this MEMORIAL to explain a case. The Board of Punishments has copied out a case submitted by Bolin, Governor of Shanxi, concerning a past event: According to the report submitted by Zhu Shaozeng, Judicial Review Commissioner [of Shanxi], which forwards the report submitted to his office by Ye Ruzhi, Magistrate of Jiangzhou, in which according to the report submitted to his office by Li Ze, Magistrate of Jishan District, on Jiaqing 7.7.15 [August 12, 1802], local warden Duan Wu reported that according to a petition filed by Li Fu, on 7.13 (August 10), his elder first cousin Li Cang ate steamed dumplings that had been poisoned, suffered great pains in his belly, vomited, and later that night died.

Thereupon, I [Magistrate Li Ze] personally went to ascertain the facts. In order to make my report properly, I went in person to examine the body. At the site, the coroner Yang Shi reported orally that he had examined the corpse of the deceased Li Cang, forty-four *sui* in age; from the frontal aspect, his face was blackened, a fatal condition. On his forehead, a contusion in one place, 1 *cun* wide and 2 *fen* broad, nonfatal; his eyelids were swollen open, the two eyes enlarged and bleeding, a fatal condition; blood from the two ear canals, nonfatal; in addition, blood from both nostrils; darkened gums top and bottom; mouth opened; pustules on the tongue; lips cracked; belly distended; all ten toenails darkened. From the posterior view, all ten fingernails darkened; rectum swollen and protruding. When a silver hairpin inserted into the mouth of the deceased was examined for color, it had turned black and could not be wiped clean, unquestionably a case of death by poison.[1] When his examination was concluded, I personally inspected [the body] and found no discrepancies. I completed the report and entered it into the record.

Warden Duan Wu reported that in response to the complaint, he questioned the neighbors Duan Liang, Duan Shihui, and Li Jinlin; they all testified that before noon on 7.13, Li Jinlin saw Li Cang squatting in his doorway eating steamed dumplings. As they chatted, Li Cang said that the dumplings tasted bad, and he threw the remainder to Li Jinlin's family dog. Li Cang went inside, and before long, the dog died from the dumpling he ate. Hearing that Li Cang had a bellyache and was vomiting, Li Jinlin went in to tell him that the dog had died. Duan Liang and Duan Shihui also went over to have a look. His younger cousin Li Fu tried to save Li Cang, but to no avail; Li Cang died in the middle of that night. Duan Shizhuo had been a regular visitor at Li Cang's house prior to this. Sometimes when Duan Shizhuo went in, Li Cang left, making it look like Duan Shizhuo and Li Cang's wife, Mrs. Li Jia, were having an improper affair. [They affirmed that] this was the truth.

Li Fu, younger cousin of the deceased, testified: "Li Cang was my older first cousin. Around midday on the thirteenth of the seventh month, I heard that my cousin Li Cang had a bellyache and was vomiting, so I went over to see him. Li Cang was rolling around on the *kang* and crying out. I asked him about it, and my cousin said that it was because he had eaten some steamed dumplings. Just then, Li Jinlin came in and said that Li Cang had given his dog the remainder of his dumpling and that the dog had died. I realized that he had been poisoned, and I tried to save him, but it was no good. Around the middle of the night, Li Cang died. Last year, I heard the rumor that Duan Shizhuo and Li Cang's wife, Mrs. Li Jia, were having an improper affair. I mentioned it to Li Cang, but he paid no attention. I beg that you investigate this matter."

Thereupon, I questioned and cross-examined Mrs. Li Jia. In her testimony, without hesitation, she confessed to having illicit sex with Duan Shizhuo and to cooperating with Duan Shizhuo in poisoning her husband Li Cang to death. In his testimony, Duan Shizhuo confessed that he had plotted with Mrs. Li Jia to poison her husband to death. This is the truth. On the basis of this testimony, I arrested Duan Shizhuo and Mrs. Li Jia, recorded their testimony, and filed my reports.

When I received authorization to carry out the investigation, I again assembled all relevant people and evidence, brought out the offenders, and conducted a strenuous investigation. The testimony of the younger cousin of the deceased and the others being in no way different from the preliminary investigation, I do not record it here.

The adulterer Duan Shizhuo testified: "I am a resident of Ma Village, and I am thirty-five *sui* in age.[2] My parents have both passed away. My wife is from the Liu family. I practice medicine to make a living. I live on the same street as Li Cang. During the seventh month of Jiaqing 5, Li Cang developed an ulcer on his back, and he asked me to cure it with medicine. On the afternoon of the twenty-sixth of the eighth month, I went to Li Cang's house and lied to him that the medicine had been made from the finest ginseng and that he owed me ten *liang* of silver in gratitude. Li Cang's wife, Ms. Jia, reported that Li Cang was not at home. So I flirted with Mrs. Li Jia, and we had illicit sex. After that, we had illicit sex whenever it was convenient [*guobian*]; I don't remember how many times. During the ninth month, Mrs. Li Jia said that her husband knew about it and would allow us to continue to get together without interfering. I don't know how much money and clothing I gave Li Cang and his wife on successive occasions after that. During the fourth month of Jiaqing 7, Li Cang asked me to lend him four *liang* of silver, but because my business was only mediocre then, I did not have any silver to lend him. During the fifth month, he again asked me to lend him three thousand coppers, but I didn't have any money to lend him. From that time onward, whenever I saw Li Cang, he would ignore me. Afterward, Mrs. Li Jia said that Li Cang told her he would not allow her to have anything to do with me, and if he caught us together, he'd kill the both of us. So she told me I ought not to come again. I got mad and went home, and I thought that because our illicit sexual relationship was really hot [*qing re*], we couldn't just break it off. I conceived the idea of doing Li Cang in. On the tenth of the sixth month, I went to Mrs. Li Jia and told her that the best thing to do would be to murder Li Cang so that we could be husband and wife forever. But Mrs. Li Jia was scared, and she wouldn't agree. On the third of the seventh month, I took over a packet of arsenic powder [*pixinmo*] left over from making medicine and a packet of crushed croton seeds [*badou*]. Taking advantage of Li Cang being out of the house, again I went to talk to Mrs. Li Jia about poisoning Li Cang. Mrs. Li Jia said, 'How could we poison him?' I took out the arsenic powder and the crushed croton seeds and told Mrs. Li Jia to mix them into steamed dumplings. Wait until Li Cang is going out to sell fruit and then give them to him to eat. If he dies outside . . ."

Here, the case report is missing a page that recorded the end of Duan Shizhuo's testimony and the beginning of the testimony of Li Cang's wife.

[The adulteress Mrs. Li Jia testified:] ". . .that he would not interfere with my getting together with Duan Shizhuo. Duan Shizhuo on many occasions gave me and my husband money and food; I don't remember how many times. During the fourth and fifth months [May and June] of Jiaqing 7, my husband on two occasions asked Duan Shizhuo to lend him money, but Duan Shizhuo didn't lend him any. So then my husband told me that he would not allow me to get together with Duan Shizhuo, and he also said that if he ever came again he would kill the both of us. I secretly told Duan Shizhuo that he'd better not come here any more. On the tenth of the sixth month, Duan Shizhuo came by and said that our illicit sexual relationship was so hot that he couldn't break it off and that the best thing would be to do in my husband so that he and I could be husband and wife forever. I was very scared and would not agree to it. On the third of the seventh month, Duan Shizhuo came again and talked about poisoning my husband. I asked him how we could poison him, and Duan Shizhuo brought out a packet of arsenic powder and a packet of ground croton seeds and told me to mix this into steamed dumplings. We'd wait until my husband went out to sell fruit and then give them to him to eat; if he died outside, then there would be no trouble about it. I agreed and hid them away.

"On the thirteenth, my husband planned to go out to sell peaches. I mixed the arsenic and seeds into the flour and made a poison dumpling. I also made several dumplings that didn't have poison. At noon, I steamed the dumplings and gave my husband one good dumpling and one that had poison in it. My husband wanted to keep an eye on his load of peaches, so he went to eat them outside the door. Afterward, he came back in; he said that eating the dumplings made him feel bad in his heart, and he lay down on the *kang*. In just a little while, his belly began to ache; he rolled around and cried out and vomited on the *kang*. He kept it up until he injured his forehead. I knew it was the poison taking effect. My husband's younger cousin Li Fu came by to see him, and my husband said it was all because he had eaten the steamed dumpling. Li Jinlin also came by and said that his dog had died from eating a piece of leftover dumpling that Li Cang had given to it. Li Fu tried to save my husband, but it was no good. My husband died around the middle of that night. Nobody else knew about it, and no one plotted with us. This is the truth."

I cross-examined them, and they insisted that no one else knew of the matter and no one had plotted together with them.

On the basis of his investigation, the aforementioned Li Ze, Magistrate of Jishan District, recommended that Mrs. Li Jia should be sentenced to immediate beheading in accordance with the substatute that prescribes beheading without delay for adulteresses who plot to kill their own husbands when the husband knows about the affair and allows the wife or concubine to have an adulterous affair with another man.[3] Duan Shizhuo should be sentenced to imprisonment until beheading after the autumn assizes, in accordance with the substatute that adulterers should be beheaded with delay.

This report was transferred to the department, where the aforementioned Ye Ruzhi, Magistrate of Jiangzhou, reexamined the case and found no discrepancies. The report was in turn transferred to the province where the judicial review commissioner reexamined the case.

On Jiaqing 7.10.16 [November 11, 1802], Jin Ruchao, Magistrate of Yangqu District, submitted a report stating that the aforementioned offender, Mrs. Li Jia, had fallen ill, and on 11.8, he subsequently reported that the aforementioned offender had recovered and was transferred.[4] Zhu Shaozeng, the aforementioned judicial commissioner [of Shanxi], examined the case and reached the same conclusions. Thereupon he transferred the case to Your subject. . . .

Hereafter, the memorial presents the summary of the case as determined by the Board of Punishments in the capital, Beijing. The summary generally repeats the wording of the synopsis given at the head of the document, with the following significant changes:

. . . Duan Shizhuo began to flirt with Mrs. Li Jia, which resulted in illicit sexual relations. Thereafter, they had illicit sex whenever it was convenient, not only one time. During the ninth month, Li Cang became aware of it and questioned Mrs. Li Jia. Mrs. Li Jia deceived him about their previous affair, and Li Cang did not express his consent. On several occasions, Duan Shizhuo gave Mrs. Li Jia and Li Cang money and food, without keeping an account of the quantities. . . .

The report also describes their adulterous relationship as "close" (qing mi) rather than "hot." Despite these changes, the Board agreed with the punishments for the lovers recommended by the magistrate, the prefect, and the commissioner. The Board further stipulated that Duan should have the words "vicious criminal" tattooed on his face; Ms. Li was spared that suffering. The Board also noted that Li Cang deserved punishment for abetting his wife in the commission of adultery, but since he was already dead, the matter merited no further discussion. Nor was there any reason to consider the amounts of food and money that Duan had given to the Li family; the identity of the purveyor of the arsenic that killed Li Cang was also not to be sought.[5] This memorial was then returned to the Three Judicial Offices for their review of the recommended sentences; their summary merely repeats that of the Board of Punishments. This body also determined whether every level of judicial review was carried out within the legally defined time limits (all had, except for the acceptable delay when Mrs. Li Jia was ill).[6] After their own extensive examination, summarized in the same terms as at lower levels of review, the Three Judicial Offices endorsed the recommended sentences. The emperor's comment on the cover of the memorial reads:

"Ms. Jia is to be confined until beheading; Duan Shizhuo should be incarcerated as suggested until after the autumn assizes, when he is to be executed. The others as recommended."

NOTES

Source: *Neige tiben Xing* [Grand Secretariat routine memorials, (Board of) Punishments] 73, Jiaqing 8.2.29 (March 22, 1803).

1. This was a common way of determining whether a person had been poisoned in late imperial China; the poison remaining in the mouth would tarnish the silver pin.

2. In the name Macunbao (Ma Village), the term *bao* indicates a walled village in contrast to others that had no such enclosure. Presumably, Ma Village was larger than many and had reason in the past to protect itself against bandits and other external threats by constructing a defensive wall of some sort. This was not a fortification having military value.

3. Article 285 of the Qing penal code prescribes dismemberment as the penalty for a wife who, after adultery, plots to murder her husband. See Jones, *Great Qing Code*, 271.

4. Presumably, she had been incarcerated during her illness; it is likely she fell ill while being transferred from one jurisdiction to another.

5. According to the Qing penal code, knowingly selling poisons to be used against persons was a very serious crime during the Qing period, see, for example, Article 289. See Jones, *Great Qing Code*, 274–75.

6. Those who were ill were exempt from legal action until they recovered.

CASE 5

Cao Ligong: Attempted Rape That Led to Murder (Zhili, 1803)

The memorial on this case is translated here in its entirety. It begins with an exceptional meditation by the magistrate on the probable events surrounding the murder; the testimony he presents thoroughly confirms his "suspicions." The redundancies demonstrate the concurrence of each successive level of administration on the sub-stantial facts of the case and their interpretation. The emperor, however, did not reach a conclusion on whether the murderer should be summarily executed as rec-ommended and as the law stipulated. His decision, written on the cover of the case, was that the Three Judicial Offices should review the sentence and prepare a memo-rial on how and when to punish the murderer.

Bracketed headings have been added to draw attention to the structure of the report, with its several restatements of the basic facts followed by corroborative details and then a summary. The carefully constructed arguments in these reports are reminiscent of the general structure required for civil-service examination essays.[1] The first line, the list of titles held by the author of the memorial written in smaller characters, is not fully legible in this copy.

· · · Secretary of the Board of Punishments, Your subject Yan Jian respectfully submits this MEMORIAL to report a matter. Qing Zhang, the judicial commissioner of the Zhili Provincial Judicial Commission, reports on the submission of Yao Liang, Prefect of Hejian, concerning the detailed brief submitted by Zhao Lun, Acting Magistrate of Dongguang District, that he had investigated a complaint filed on Jiaqing 7.8.12 [September 8, 1802] by Zhu Zhaolong, a local warden in the Cao Family Manor [Caojiazhuang] area under the juris-diction of said district:

[Local warden Zhu Zhaolong's complaint quoted in the magistrate's report:]

"On the morning of this day, a resident of said village, Cao Fugui, came in person to complain that on the afternoon of the eleventh of that month, his wife, Mrs. Cao Wang, had gone to a field north of the village carrying a square basket to pick string beans. By evening, she had not returned, and his search yielded no trace. Early this morning, he discovered his wife, Ms. Wang, lying facedown in Kang Juncheng's field north of the village; a cotton sash was wrapped tightly around her neck as she had been strangled by some person. At that time, he requested that I make a report on this matter; I there-upon confirmed the facts of the complaint and hereby request that you make an investigation of the matter, make arrests, and so on. On this same day, the husband of the deceased, Cao Fugui, brought the matter to my attention, and together we have come here to the district yamen."

[District Magistrate Zhao Lun's review:]

Thereupon, this humble magistrate, together with a clerk and the coro-ner, proceeded to the site. According to the preliminary report prepared at Cao Family Manor, Kang Juncheng's sorghum field is about two li from the village. The body of the aforementioned woman lay facedown in Kang

Juncheng's field with her head toward the east and her feet toward the west. Her hair was disheveled. On her body, she wore one (1) single-layered blue cotton blouse and one (1) pair of single-layered blue cotton pants, ripped at the waist and lacking any sash. Around her neck was wound one (1) cotton sash. According to the oral testimony of the bereaved husband Cao Fugui, the sash with which she had been strangled was the sash from his wife's own pants.

Thereupon, I removed the sash from her neck and measured it; it is 3 *chi* and 5 *cun* long. I also preliminarily ascertained that to the west of Kang Juncheng's field lay a parcel of Cao Zhikang's sorghum field. West of that field is a strip of willow trees. To the south, the field abuts Cao Fugui's field. The sorghum on both sides of that field bears the traces of something having been rolled in it, and there is a trace of blood on the ground in one place there.[2] In addition, one (1) bone hair clasp and one (1) lock of false hair had been abandoned there. I preliminarily ordered the bereaved husband Cao Fugui to identify them, and he acknowledged that in fact they were objects formerly worn by his deceased wife. I examined the spots where the rolling around had taken place, and they were about twenty paces from the location of the corpse of Ms. Wang. The ground bore the traces of pushing and pulling. Moreover, I went to Cao Fugui's field and preliminarily ascertained that some number of string beans had been picked.

The preliminary investigation completed, I returned to the corpse and instructed that the corpse should be moved and laid on a level place for a formal inquest in the presence of the next of kin in accordance with the law. According to the coroner Yang Xing's oral report, he had ascertained that the deceased Mrs. Cao Wang was twenty-four *sui* in age. From the front, the color of her face was purple-red, with her two eyes slightly opened, her nostrils caked with clotted blood, her mouth slightly open, and her tongue pressed against her teeth. A fatal wound was on her throat, the marks of the sash wrapped around it twice, forming one (1) line 9.2 *cun* long, 3 *fen* wide, and 5 *fen* deep, a purple-red color. The two hands were lightly clutching her stomach. Her two cheeks were distended, and the hair around her face was disheveled. A fatal wound was on the back of her cranium, a round laceration. Beyond these, there was no cause of death. When the coroner's report on the cause of death was complete, this humble magistrate conducted a personal examination of the corpse and found no discrepancy. I ordered the cotton sash to be compared with the wound, and it corresponded. At the site, I filled out and annotated the chart and the list [of wounds on the corpse] and entered them into the record along with the testimony of the coroner and the deceased's next of kin. As for the corpse, I ordered it shrouded and given shallow burial outside [the *yamen*] pending further investigation. Warden Zhu Zhaolong's testimony differed not at all from the complaint, leaving no need to question him further.

[Initial interrogation at the inquest in sight of the victim:][3]

Upon questioning, Kang Juncheng testified: "I am a resident of Wu Family Village under Your Honor's jurisdiction. I make my living as a farmer. I live in the same hamlet as Cao Fugui. It has always been recognized that this plot of sorghum field belongs to my family. How anybody could have murdered Cao Fugui's wife, Ms. Wang, who had gone to her own field to pick string beans on the afternoon of the eleventh of the eighth month, in my field at that time I have no idea whatsoever. The next morning, when I heard Cao Fugui shouting, that's the first time I knew anything about it. I hurried out to look, but Mrs. Cao Wang was already dead. With a sash wrapped around her neck, she looked like she'd been murdered. But who could have strangled Ms. Wang to death, I really have no idea. And that's the truth."

Upon questioning, Cao Zhikang testified: "I am a resident of Cao Family Manor under Your Honor's jurisdiction. This year I am forty-six *sui* in age. I make my living as a farmer. The land to the west of Kang Juncheng's sorghum field has always been in my family. South of my land is Cao Fugui's family field. On the eleventh of the eighth month [September 7], Cao Fugui's wife, Ms. Wang, went to her own field to pick string beans. How she was strangled on Kang Juncheng's land, how Ms. Wang's hair clasp and hairpiece came to be left behind on my land, and how a trace of blood was left on the ground there, I really do not know. And that's the truth."

Upon questioning, Cao Fugui testified: "I am a resident of Cao Family Manor under Your Honor's jurisdiction. The dead woman, Ms. Wang, was my wife. She was twenty-four *sui* this year. On the afternoon of the eleventh of the eighth month of this year, my wife walked to our own field to pick string beans carrying one square woven basket. But by the time it got dark, she had not yet returned home. So then I went looking for her, but I could not find her. On the morning of the twelfth, I went to Kang Juncheng's land, where I saw my wife, her hair all disheveled, lying facedown on the ground. The sash from her pants was wound around her throat; she had been strangled by somebody. When I looked, I discovered that the waist of her pants was ripped and her basket was nowhere to be seen.[4] At once, I went to inform the local warden so that he would come and investigate, and then we came into the city to file a complaint at the court. Will Your Honor favor me with your investigation? My wife has truly been strangled by somebody; I beg you to have him arrested and put to rights this evil in order to relieve this injustice [*shenyuan*] to my wife. Please grant us this favor; my family has no neighbors to whom we can turn. And that's the truth."

These were all the available details. Thereupon, I took the sash and other objects with me for storage in the *yamen* repository. At the same time, I offered a reward and selected constables to go separately to arrest the evildoer and to collect any relevant evidence. Then this humble magistrate filled in the picture of the corpse, recorded the [initial] testimony, and submitted the requests. Having received the rescripts of authorization, I began the formal inquiry concerning this case.

At the site where Mrs. Cao Wang had been murdered, I had ascertained that the waist of her pants had been ripped, the sash with which she held them up having previously been removed. This woman being only twenty-four *sui*, I suspect that, given the circumstances, this is an obvious case of murder as a result of attempted but unsuccessful rape. Since the corpse of Ms. Wang was in Kang Juncheng's field, why were the hairpiece and the hair ornament she had worn found in Cao Zhikang's field? We can generally conclude that the primary culprit in this case could not have been some stranger. Likewise, at the time Ms. Wang was murdered, with her life hanging in the balance, she must have cried out loudly, screaming for help. Why did no one working in the fields that day hear her? There must be one among them who is hiding his evil deed. Consequently, I sent out constables to look for evidence and to make arrests. At the same time, I personally went to the aforementioned hamlet to make detailed inquiries.

Thus, on 10.4 [October 30], I ascertained that on the day Mrs. Cao Wang was murdered, Cao Ligong, son of Cao Zhikang of Cao Family Manor, had also gone to work in the fields north of the hamlet. Furthermore, after the aforementioned woman was killed, Cao Ligong hid at home and dared not show himself. Therefore, I ordered the arrest of Cao Zhikang and Cao Ligong and commanded the bereaved husband Cao Fugui to appear in court. I observed that on the back of Cao Ligong's right hand there was one (1) scar of a scratch wound. Thereupon, I questioned them.

Cao Fugui testified that he had heard that on the afternoon of 8.11 of this year, at the time that his wife, Ms. Wang, had gone to the field to pick string beans, Cao Ligong, a distant relative in a younger generation, had also gone to the fields to chop sorghum leaves. No one else had gone to work in those fields on that day. Inevitably, he would have been able to hear as his wife was being strangled. Moreover, Cao Fugui begged for a strenuous investigation of whether or not his wife had been strangled by Cao Ligong. His wife had up to that time never had any friendly relations with Cao Zhikang's family.

Upon questioning, Cao Zhikang testified that he had a son, Cao Ligong, who is twenty-five *sui* this year. Cao Fugui is his distant relative in the same generation, but normally they do not have friendly relations with him. His field adjoins that of Cao Fugui. On the afternoon of 8.11 of this year, his son Cao Ligong had gone to the field north of the village to chop sorghum leaves. He returned around dusk. Whether on that day Cao Fugui's wife had cried out as she was being murdered and whether his son had heard her, he really did not know. But he also said that his son was now in court and could be questioned about the matter.

Thereupon, Cao Ligong was brought before the court for questioning, but the culprit's testimony was confused, and he refused to confess his guilt. This humble magistrate examined him repeatedly until Cao Ligong testified: "All right, I'll tell you the truth. I am a resident of Cao Family Manor under Your Honor's jurisdiction. This year I am twenty-five *sui* in age. Until now, I've always earned my living as a farmer. Cao Zhikang is my father. Cao Fugui is a distant relative in my father's generation, but we've had neither good nor bad relations.

"On the afternoon of the eleventh of the eighth month of Jiaqing 7, I went to our own field north of the hamlet to chop sorghum leaves. At that time, Ms. Wang, Cao Fugui's wife, had brought a square basket and was picking string beans in her own field. I noticed that she was young and was sort of attractive, and all of a sudden I was moved by an evil thought [*yishi dongle xienian*], and I wanted to have illicit sex with her. So I walked into her field and took her left hand in my right hand and asked her to have sex with me. Ms. Wang refused and began to shout and curse at me. Seeing there was no one else around, I conceived the idea of raping her.

"Then I dragged Ms. Wang into our sorghum field and forced her face-down onto the ground, giving her a bloody nose. At that time, I used my left hand to hold her body down while I untied the sash on her pants with my right. Then I turned her over and pulled down on her pants, ripping them at the waist. Mrs. Cao Wang struggled, and she scratched a gash on the back of my right hand. I let go of her, and Mrs. Cao Wang used the chance to hold up her pants with both hands and cry out in a loud voice. I was afraid, and I got up, without having raped her. How could I know that Mrs. Cao Wang would sit up and just keep on yelling. I was afraid that somebody might hear, and I was also afraid that if Ms. Wang went home and told her husband, he'd not forgive me for it.

"All at once, I conceived the idea of strangling her. So I picked up the sash of her pants from the ground, walked around behind her and grabbed her hair with my right hand, and pulled her backward down to the ground, pulling loose her hair clasp and her hairpiece, which fell to the ground. I stepped on her hair with my right foot and wrapped her sash around her throat twice. Ms. Wang was yelling and pulling at the sash with her right hand and struggling to get free with her left. So I tramped down on her left hand with my left foot and quickly made the sash into a slipknot and pulled it tight as hard as I could. After a while, Ms. Wang stopped breathing and died.

"Since Ms. Wang's body was in my field, I was afraid that someone would figure it out. So I dragged the corpse over to Kang Juncheng's field and laid her facedown on the ground. I also hid her basket full of string beans among the willow trees. Then I went home. The next day, I heard that Cao Fugui had found her body and had reported it for investigation. I was scared, so I hid out at home. I never thought that Your Honor would be able to figure it all out. But I haven't given any false testimony. I never succeeded in raping her, nor was anybody else involved. My father didn't know about it or try to hide it. And that's the truth."

Thereupon, I deputed a constable to go to the willow copse west of the culprit's field, where he discovered one (1) square basket, which he delivered to the court for inspection. The basket was filled with string beans; I selected a few pods, and all were dried out. I showed the basket to the bereaved husband Cao Fugui for his inspection, and he affirmed that it was the same basket his wife had been carrying before her death and that the string beans inside it were the product of their field. Thereupon, I immediately provided him with a release to take them and added all these facts to the record.

Thereafter, I remanded Cao Ligong to jail, released his relatives and the others on bail, and continued with my investigation. The [attempted] rape having failed, he conceived the idea to take her life to silence her. The true facts of whether or not the rape had been completed and whether there had been an accomplice should be matters for a separate decision, and I recommended punishment based on confessions and what I have been able to learn from others.

[The formal hearing at the district magistrate's court:]

The culprit having been examined at my humble court, and having recorded that testimony, I requested permission for a formal investigation. Having received the rescript with that authorization, I at once assembled at the *yamen* the people who should be examined along with the jailed Cao Ligong. Subsequently, I questioned and released the local warden Zhu Zhaolong, the neighbor Kang Juncheng, the bereaved husband Cao Fugui, and the father of the culprit Cao Zhikang. Since the testimony of each of them fully corresponded with my original questioning, I did not question them again on any other matters.

Cao Ligong testified: "I am a resident of this district. I am twenty-five *sui* in age this year, and I make my living by farming. Cao Zhikang is my father. Cao Fugui is a distant relative in my father's generation, but we've had neither good relations nor bad.

"On the afternoon of the eleventh of the eighth month of Jiaqing 7, I went to our own field north of the hamlet to chop sorghum leaves. At that time, Ms. Wang, Cao Fugui's wife, was carrying a square basket and picking string beans in her own field. I noticed that she was young and was sort of attractive, and all of a sudden I was moved by the evil thought that I wanted to have illicit sex with her. So I walked into her field and took her left hand in my right hand and asked her to have sex with me. Ms. Wang refused and began to shout and curse at me. Seeing there was no one else around, I conceived the idea of raping her.

"Then I dragged Ms. Wang into our sorghum field and threw her facedown onto the ground, giving her a bloody nose. At that time, I used my left hand to hold her body down while I untied the sash on her pants with my right. Then I turned her over and pulled down on her pants, ripping them at the waist. Mrs. Cao Wang struggled, and she gave me a scratch on the back of my right hand. I let go of her, and she used the chance to hold up her pants with both hands and yell at me in a loud voice. I was afraid, and I got up, without having raped her. How could I know that Ms. Wang would sit up and just keep on yelling and cursing? I was afraid that somebody might hear, and I was also afraid that if she went home and told her husband, he'd not forgive me for it.

"All at once, I conceived the idea of strangling her. So I picked up the sash of her pants from the ground, walked around behind her and grabbed her hair with my right hand, and pulled her backward down to the ground, pulling loose her hairpin and her hairpiece, which fell to the ground. I stepped on her hair with my right foot and wrapped her sash around her throat twice. Ms. Wang was yelling and pulling at the sash with her right hand and struggling to get free with her left. So I tramped down on her left hand with my left foot, quickly made the sash into a slipknot, and pulled it tight as hard as I could. After a while, she stopped breathing and died.

"Since her body was in my field, I was afraid someone would figure it out. So I dragged the corpse over to Kang Juncheng's field and laid her facedown on the ground. I also hid her basket full of string beans among the willow trees. Then I went home. The next day, I heard that Cao Fugui had found his wife's body and had reported it for investigation. I was scared, so I hid out at home. I never thought that Your Honor would be able to figure it all out. But I haven't given any false testimony. I never succeeded in raping her, nor was anybody else involved. My father didn't know about it or try to hide it. And that's the truth."

Through repeated interrogations, the culprit maintained that he had not carried out the rape and that he had no accomplices.

[The magistrate's summary and recommendations:]

In summary, I, Zhao Lun, Acting Magistrate of Dongguang District, have investigated the case of subject Cao Ligong who, because he failed at the attempted rape of Mrs. Cao Wang, on the spur of the moment strangled said woman. To wit:

Cao Ligong is registered as a resident in this district, and he makes his living as a farmer. He resides in the same hamlet as Cao Fugui, his distant relative in his father's generation, but normally they did not have friendly relations with each other. Cao Fugui's family owns a piece of land contiguous with a field owned by Cao Ligong's family. On the afternoon of Jiaqing 7.8.11, Ms. Wang, wife of Cao Fugui, took a square basket with her and went to her land to pick string beans. At that time, Cao Ligong had also gone to his field to chop sorghum leaves. He espied that Ms. Wang was somewhat fair, and there being no one else around, he suddenly conceived an evil thought. At once, he proceeded to Ms. Wang, pulled on her hand, and demanded illicit sex. Ms. Wang did not accede and cried out and cursed him. Overcome by immoral desires, he conceived the idea of raping her. He dragged Ms. Wang over to his own land and threw her facedown onto the ground, thereby causing injury to her nose. Then Cao Ligong held her down with his left hand while he untied the sash of her pants with his right. Turning her over on her back, he pulled on her pants until he ripped them at the waist. Ms. Wang struggled and with her hand scratched the back of Cao Ligong's right hand. Cao Ligong released his grip, and Ms. Wang pulled up the waist of her pants with both hands, shouting loudly. Fearful, Cao Ligong got up without having raped her. Shamed and unwilling to submit, Ms. Wang sat there on the ground, shouting and cursing ever more loudly. Cao Ligong feared that someone might hear her. Likewise, considering that when Ms. Wang returned home and told her husband, her husband would not forgive him, Cao Ligong conceived the idea of taking her life in order to silence her.

Thus, he picked up the sash he had removed, went around behind Ms. Wang, and grabbed her hair with his right hand, pulling her head backward until she fell down. This disheveled her hair, and her hairpiece and bone hair clasp fell to the ground. With his right foot, Cao Ligong tramped down on her hair as he wrapped the sash around her throat. With her right hand, Ms. Wang held the sash, preventing it from being wrapped firmly, while she struggled to get free with her left. Again, Cao Ligong used his left foot to stamp down on her left hand as he tied the sash into a slipknot. Then he pulled hard on the sash to strangle Ms. Wang, and she presently expired. Fearing that he would be easily exposed if Ms. Wang's body were discovered on his land, he dragged the corpse over to Kang Juncheng's land and laid it facedown on the ground. He also hid Ms. Wang's basket of string beans among the willow trees. Then he immediately went home. His father Cao Likang knew nothing of the matter.

Toward evening, because his wife had gone out to the field and had not returned, Cao Fugui went looking for her but did not find a trace. The following morning, he discovered the corpse of his wife in Kang Juncheng's field. He made an outcry to the local warden, who reported it to the district for investigation. Having made inquiries, I deputed a constable to make arrests. I summoned Cao Ligong to court to ascertain the true facts of the case. Moreover, I recovered the square basket and other items. I examined the depositions for all significant details, and having received the rescript of authorization with orders to try the case, I immediately subjected the culprit to successive strenuous interrogations. According to the culprit, he conceived the idea of rape, but when she did not comply, he took her life to silence the victim. He acknowledged the accuracy of each detail of the case without objection and confessed that he had not succeeded in the rape attempt, nor had he any accomplices. I conclude that Cao Ligong, failing in his attempt to rape Mrs. Cao Wang, decided on the spot to strangle her, having been overcome by immoral desires. Because Mrs. Cao Wang is an aunt by marriage to a distant relative, her murder should be considered the same as an ordinary murder.[5] Disregarding the relatively minor offense of moving a corpse, for which he should be forgiven, I recommend that he be punished according to the law concerning the immediate murder of a woman after failing in an attempt to rape her, the penalty for which is beheading without delay.[6] In accordance with the substatute, the culprit should first have the characters "vicious criminal" [xiongfan] tattooed on the left side of his face. Because she had resisted rape even unto her wrongful death, Mrs. Cao Wang was most certainly an exemplar of chastity. Therefore, I recommend that the request be appended that IMPERIAL RECOGNITION be awarded her in order to further public morality.[7]

I have determined that Cao Zhikang had no knowledge of the affair, nor did he attempt to hide any details about it. He ought not to be sentenced; I recommend that he be released without involvement at the provincial level. As for Mrs. Cao Wang's coffin, I ordered the bereaved husband Cao Fugui to take charge of its burial. As for the murder weapon, the cotton sash, after the investigation was concluded, it was returned to the district storeroom to await further examination. Whether or not I have fulfilled my duties, this recommendation together with the criminal I hereby send forward to the prefecture to await further evaluation.

[Review by Yao Liang, Prefect of Hejian Prefecture:]

The magistrate's report having been received at the prefectural *yamen*, I, Yao Liang, Prefect of Hejian, submit that I have again examined the criminal and have no disagreement with the recommended sentence. I hereby send this case, the sentence together with the criminal, forward to await further evaluation, and so on, at the offices of the provincial judicial commission.

[Review by Qing Zhang, Provincial Judicial Commissioner of Zhili:]

The prefect's report having been received at the commission, I, Qing Zhang, Provincial Judicial Commissioner of Zhili, submit that I have again examined the criminal and have no disagreement with the recommended sentence. The sentence together with the criminal I hereby send forward for the personal evaluation and a MEMORIAL.

Furthermore, starting from Jiaqing 7.10.4 [October 30, 1802], the day on which the criminal was arrested, through the date when the relevant district sent forward the criminal through the prefectural to the provincial levels, the route has totaled 327 *li*, which according to the substatute is within the assigned time limitations, six days should be deducted from the time allotted in addition to an additional day for attaching the seal. On Jiaqing 8.*run* 2.10 [April 1, 1803], the limitation was met, according to the clarification, and so on. Because the report having been received by ₍Your subject₎, who has examined it himself and has no disagreements with it, said ₍subject₎ considers that in the case of Cao Ligong, resident of Dongguang District, because he attempted to rape Mrs. Cao Wang but failed and at that time strangled her, to wit:

[Final summary of the facts of the case as corroborated at the provincial level of review:]

Cao Ligong is registered as a resident in Dongguang District, Zhili, and he makes his living as a farmer. He resides in the same hamlet as Cao Fugui, his distant relative in his father's generation, but normally they had no relations with each other. Cao Fugui's family owns a piece of land contiguous with a field owned by Cao Ligong's family. On the afternoon of Jiaqing 7.8.11, Ms. Wang, wife of Cao Fugui, took a square basket with her as she went to her land to pick string beans. At that time, Cao Ligong had also gone to his field to chop sorghum leaves. He espied that Ms. Wang was somewhat fair, and there being no one else around, he suddenly conceived an evil thought. At once, he proceeded to Ms. Wang, pulled on her hand, and demanded sex. Ms. Wang did not comply and cried out and cursed him. Inflamed by immoral desires, he conceived the idea of raping her. He dragged Ms. Wang over to his own land and threw her facedown onto the ground, thereby hitting and causing injury to her nose. Then Cao Ligong held her down with his left hand while he untied the sash of her pants with his right. Turning her over on her back, he pulled on her pants until he ripped them at the waist. Ms. Wang struggled, and with her hand scratched the back of Cao Ligong's right hand. Cao Ligong released his grip, and Ms. Wang pulled up the waist of her pants with both hands, shouting loudly. Fearful, Cao Ligong got up without having raped her. Shamed and unwilling to submit, Ms. Wang sat there on the ground, shouting and cursing. Cao Ligong was fearful that someone might hear her. Likewise, considering that when Ms. Wang returned home and told her husband, her husband would not forgive him, Cao Ligong conceived the idea of taking her life in order to silence her.

Thus he picked up the sash that he had removed, went around behind Ms. Wang, and grabbed her hair with his right hand, pulling her head backward until she fell down. This pulled loose her hair and bone hair clasp, and her hairpiece fell to the ground. With his right foot, Cao Ligong tramped down on her hair as he wrapped the sash around her throat. With her right hand, Ms. Wang held the sash to stop it from being wrapped firmly while she struggled to get free with her left hand. Again, Cao Ligong used his left foot to stamp down on her left hand as he tied the sash into a slipknot. Then he pulled hard on the sash to strangle Ms. Wang, who presently expired. Fearing that he would be easily exposed if her body were discovered on his land, he dragged the corpse over to Kang Juncheng's land and laid it facedown on the ground. He also hid Ms. Wang's basket of string beans among the willow trees. Then he immediately went home. His father Cao Likang knew nothing of the matter.

Toward evening, because his wife had not returned, Cao Fugui went looking for her but could find no trace. The following morning, he looked in Kang Juncheng's field, where he discovered the corpse of his wife. In person, he reported this to the district for investigation. Having made inquiries, [the magistrate] arrested Cao Ligong and brought him to court for repeated examinations. In his confession, he testified that he had not succeeded in the attempted rape, nor did he have any accomplices on the scene.

I conclude that Cao Ligong, failing in his attempt to rape Mrs. Cao Wang, decided on the spot to strangle her, having been overcome by immoral desires. Because Mrs. Cao Wang is an aunt by marriage to a distant relative, her murder should be considered the same as an ordinary homicide. Disregarding the relatively minor offense of moving a corpse, for which he should be forgiven, he should be punished according to the law concerning the immediate murder of a woman after failing in an attempt to rape her, the penalty for which is beheading without delay. In accordance with the sub-statute on beheading without delay, the culprit should first be tattooed with the two characters "vicious criminal" on the left side of his face. Mrs. Cao Wang, because she had resisted Cao Ligong's attempted rape even unto her wrongful death, was most certainly an exemplar of chastity. Therefore, I append my request that IMPERIAL RECOGNITION be awarded her in order to further public morality. As a matter of course, then, I submit this MEMORIAL, humbly begging YOUR IMPERIAL MAJESTY to command the Three Judicial Offices to verify and to carry out a reexamination of this case. Starting from Jiaqing 7.4.11, the date when the criminal was apprehended, excepting the period of transportation and attaining the seal, which should be deducted from the total, this date of Jiaqing 8.*run* 2.10 [March 31, 1803] falls within the statute of limitations, and further deducting the day that Your subject submits this MEMOR-IAL as within the limitation, together with a clear explanation, I respectfully submit this MEMORIAL begging for YOUR EDICT [on the proper punishment].

[The synopsis, written in smaller characters:]

Your subject Yan Jian, Secretary of the Board of War, with simultaneous appointment as Censor of the Right of the Censorate, Governor-General, and so on, respectfully submits this MEMORIAL to report a matter.

Your subject, having evaluated the case of Cao Ligong, resident of Dong-guang District, because he attempted to rape Mrs. Cao Wang and failed and at that time strangled her, to wit: Cao Ligong resides in the same hamlet as Cao Fugui, his distant relative in his father's generation, but normally they had no contact with each other. Cao Fugui's family owns a piece of land contiguous with a field owned by Cao Ligong's family. On the afternoon of Jiaqing 7.8.11, Ms. Wang, wife of Cao Fugui, went to her land to pick string beans, carrying a square basket. At that time, Cao Ligong had also gone to his field to chop sorghum leaves. He espied Ms. Wang and suddenly conceived an evil thought. He approached Ms. Wang, pulled on her hand, and demanded sex. Ms. Wang did not comply and cried out and cursed him. Inflamed by immoral desires, he conceived the idea of raping her. He dragged Ms. Wang over to his own land and threw her facedown onto the ground, thereby hitting and causing injury to Ms. Wang's nose. Then Cao Ligong held her down with his left hand while he untied the sash of her pants with his right. Turning her over on her back, he pulled on her pants until he ripped them at the waist. Ms. Wang struggled, and with her hand inflicted a scratch injury to the back of Cao Ligong's right hand. Cao Ligong released his grip, and Ms. Wang pulled up the waist of her pants with both hands, shouting loudly. Fearful, Cao Ligong got up without having raped her. Ms. Wang sat on the ground, shouting and cursing. Cao Ligong feared that someone might hear her. Likewise, considering that when Ms. Wang returned home and told her husband, her husband would not forgive him, Cao Ligong conceived the idea of taking her life in order to silence her. Thus, he picked up the sash he had removed, grabbed Ms. Wang's hair with his right hand, and pulled her head backward until she fell down. This disheveled her hair, and her bone hair clasp and hairpiece fell to the ground. With his right foot, Cao Ligong tramped down on her hair as he wrapped the sash around her throat. With her right hand, Ms. Wang held the sash to prevent it from being wrapped firmly while she struggled to get free with her left. Again, Cao Ligong used his left foot to stamp down on her left hand as he tied the sash into a slipknot. Then he pulled hard on the sash to strangle Ms. Wang, who presently expired. Then Cao Ligong immediately went home. Toward evening, because his wife had not returned, Cao Fugui. . . .[8] The following morning, he discovered her and reported this to the district for investigation. Cao Ligong was arrested and brought to court for examination; there, he confessed without prevarication. Interrogation revealed that he had not succeeded in the attempted rape, nor did he have any accomplices on the scene. He should be punished according to the law concerning the immediate murder of a woman after failing in an attempt to rape her, the penalty for which is beheading without delay. In accordance with the substatute, the culprit was tattooed. Mrs. Cao Wang, because she had resisted rape even unto her wrongful death, was most certainly an exemplar of chastity. Therefore, Your minister appends my request that IMPERIAL RECOGNITION be awarded her in order to further public morality. I respectfully submit this MEMORIAL begging for YOUR EDICT [on the proper punishment].

NOTES

Source: *Neige tiben Xingfa anjian* [Grand Secretariat routine memorials, Crime and Punishment case records], *juan* 73, "Marriage and Adultery," Jiaqing 8 (1803).

1. For an extensive examination of the system and the essays it required, see Elman, *Cultural History*.

2. Sorghum at that time of the year would have been nearing maturity and would have been taller than an adult person, thus making a convenient hiding place for the intended crime.

3. Huang Liuhong, in his 1694 handbook for magistrates and their legal advisers, strongly endorsed the importance of these initial interrogations. See Huang Liuhung, *Complete Book*, 325. In the presence of the victim (in this case, her corpse) and very soon after the crime was committed, emotions run very high. Consequently, it is much more likely that the perpetrator of the crime will confess on the spot rather than later, in the yamen, after he has had time to make up a story. Likewise, witnesses' memories will never be fresher than at this moment.

4. Her ripped clothing is mentioned repeatedly throughout the report as evidence of attempted rape; for a translation of the standard commentary on the penal code regarding such evidence, see Sommer, *Sex, Law, and Society*, 89.

5. As opposed to a different level of punishment for the murder of a close relative.

6. Several laws in the Qing penal code seem relevant here: Article 316, "Relatives of the Same Surname Who Strike One Another," stipulates that if there is intentional killing, the penalty is beheading. Article 290, on intentional homicide, stipulates that the penalty should be beheading but with delay. See Jones, *Great Qing Code*, 301, 268.

7. For a detailed discussion of the problems created as women who died to maintain their chastity were given imperial recognition, see Theiss, *Disgraceful Matters*.

8. The text is missing a clause here.

INTERROGATION TECHNIQUES

Although clever interrogation formed a central part of the highly romanticized contemporaneous fiction about crime and detection, these case reports represent working magistrates as taking their investigative duties very seriously. As we have seen in the preceding section, some forensic examinations could be extremely detailed and interrogation extensive before all relevant details could be discovered. During the middle of the eighteenth century, pressures to streamline crime reports forced magistrates and their superiors to include only the most essential testimony. Even so, in the cases presented in this section, magistrates sought to establish the culprit's motivations beyond doubt, through repeated interrogation and threats, in order to ascertain the appropriate punishment.

CASE 6

Du Huailiang: Adultery That Brought Disaster
(Shandong, 1696)

In this case, relationships within a household, especially between a grown son and his mother, had been strained beyond the breaking point. A distraught lover (Du Huailiang) killed the husband (Chen Wenxian) of his paramour (Ms. Li) and then his own wife (Ms. Zhang) in the vain hope that with these people out of the way, he and Ms. Li would be free to live together. But the report presents him as so immersed in his own personal feelings that he ignored the role of his mother and even the feelings of his lover. Each level of judicial review carefully preserved an extraordinary amount of oral testimony. Virtually all was originally collected and edited by Magistrate Jin Yingdou of Liaocheng District in Shandong. These depositions are remarkable not only for their air of authenticity but for the active role allotted to the magistrate in examination: here, the magistrate relies on probing questions and apparently only the threat, not the application, of torture to bring out the final admission of guilt and the curious complications of this twisted tale. As a result, the characterization of the principals in the case is also unusually detailed.

[Magistrate Jin initially interrogated Du Huailiang as follows:] "How old are you, and what is your native place?"

Du Huailiang testified: "Your humble servant is twenty-six *sui*, and I am from this district."

Further interrogation: "How did you know that Chen Wenxian was twenty-seven *sui* in age? Why did you kill him and your wife, Ms. Zhang? Tell the truth."

Du further testified: "He and I have been on good terms ever since he moved into my house to live during Kangxi 31 [1692]. That's how I know how old he is. Often, he and my wife Zhang made eyes at each other [*meilai meiqu*]. I was suspicious in my heart, but I didn't have any proof, so I couldn't say anything to him about any 'smelly business' between them. During the fifth month, I told him to get out, and he found a room at Widow Wei's place. He moved out on the seventh of the fifth month of this year [June 18, 1695]. On the fourth of the sixth month [July 14], I took a hatchet with me to sleep in the courtyard to guard the cattle. My wife closed the door and went to sleep inside our room. About the second watch of the night, I heard a sound at the door, like somebody pushing it open and then closing it. Very quietly, I got up, picked up the hatchet, and went over to the door, where I stood for a good long time listening. Inside the room, two people were talking in whispers. I kicked open the door, and there was Chen Wenxian, naked, trying to get away. I blocked the door and chopped at him with my hatchet. He turned back toward the *kang*, where he collapsed on the floor. I caught up with him and gave him a couple more chops, and he died. My wife was sitting on the *kang*. With one chop, I killed her, too. I called the warden and the neighbors to bear witness, and they came along with me to report the matter."

Further interrogation: "According to the complaint filed by Ms. Li, you were suspicious about her husband Chen Wenxian, and you tricked him into coming to your house to drink so that you could kill him. Fearing that you would be found out, you murdered your wife and made it look like illicit sex to deceive us. What do you have to say about that?"

Du further testified: "I never did have any grudge against Chen Wenxian or bad feelings about him. It was just that he came to have illicit sex with my wife, and I happened to catch them at it. So I killed him and my wife as well. It wasn't at all that I was suspicious of him and lured him over to kill him."

Interrogation of Ms. Li: "What's your age? What bad feelings did your husband Chen Wenxian and Du Huailiang have about each other? Why did he trick your husband into coming over so he could kill him? Tell the truth."

She testified: "Your humble servant is twenty-six *sui* this year. In Kangxi 31, my husband Chen Wenxian and I moved into Du Huailiang's house and lived there for three or four years. On the sixth of the fifth month of this year [June 17, 1695], they squabbled with us about the child, and on the seventh, we moved into Widow Wei's house to live. Then on the fourth of the sixth month [July 14], in the evening, my husband went out, saying that he was going to Du Huailiang's house to drink wine with him. When he got to his house, Du Huailiang killed my husband, but I don't know why."

Further interrogation: "According to Du Huailiang's testimony, your husband really went there in order to have illicit sex with his wife. He happened to catch them at it, and he killed them. How can you say that he tricked your husband into going there in order to kill him?"

Ms. Li further testified: "But Du Huailiang did trick my husband into going there in order to kill him. He was afraid that he'd be found out, and he made it look like my husband was having illicit sex with his wife in the hope that he could cover it up. If you'd just question the two neighbors, you'd find out."

Interrogation of Du Weiyuan: "What relation is this Du Huailiang to you? Why did he kill Chen Wenxian and his wife, Ms. Zhang? You're a neighbor— tell the truth."

He testified: "Du Huailiang is a younger member in my father's generation in our lineage. I am his neighbor to the west, but there's a vacant lot between our houses. In the past, Chen Wenxian and Ms. Li lived in the western room of Du Huailiang's house. During the fifth month of this year, Ms. Li got into a squabble with Du Huailiang's mother, and she moved into Widow Wei's house along with her husband Chen Wenxian. Then on the evening of the fourth of the sixth month, around the second watch, I heard Du Wenwu shouting that Du Huailiang had killed somebody. I went over to his house to see, and Du Huailiang said that Chen Wenxian had come to have illicit sex with his wife and he had taken his hatchet and killed both Chen Wenxian and his own wife in their room. I was afraid that he'd run away, so I tried to calm him down. I said, 'Since he came to have illicit sex with your wife and you killed them, there's no problem.[1] We'll just go tomorrow morning and report it to the magistrate.' And at daylight, we did come in to make the report. I don't know why he killed Chen Wenxian and Ms. Zhang."

Further interrogation: "Is it true that Chen Wenxian and Du Huailiang's wife, Ms. Zhang, were having illicit sex?"

He further testified: "As a person, Ms. Zhang was extremely respectable. It was just that her legs were crippled. Chen Wenxian was also an honest man. When he went to work for the Wei house, he often didn't get home at night. I've never ever heard tell that the two of them were having illicit sex."

Further interrogation: "According to Ms. Li's complaint, Du Huailiang had some bad feelings about her husband Chen Wenxian and tricked him into going there in order to kill him. If they had any old suspicions about each other, you're the neighbor, and you would naturally know."

He further testified: "Chen Wenxian lived in Du Huailiang's house for a good many years, and they never squabbled. Only this year, on the sixth of the fifth month, there was a squabble in the house, and on the seventh, Chen Wenxian moved into the Wei house. There were no bad feelings, and that's the truth."

Interrogation of Sun Erchen: "You're a neighbor: Tell me the circumstances behind Du Huailiang's killing of Chen Wenxian and his wife, Ms. Zhang."

He testified: "On the sixth of the fifth month of this year, around noon, Du Huailiang hit his wife because the meal wasn't ready yet. His mother said that Ms. Li had put her up to it, and she said some nasty things about her. Ms. Li heard her, and she got into a squabble with Du Huailiang's mother. My wife made peace between them. But the next morning, Chen Wenxian was all ready to move someplace else. Du Huailiang told me to try to make him stay, but I couldn't talk him out of it, so he moved into Widow Wei's house. About the second watch of the night, on the fourth of the sixth month, I heard Du Wenwu shouting that Du Huailiang had killed somebody. I went to see, and I saw Chen Wenxian dead on the floor and Ms. Zhang dead on the *kang*. Du Huailiang said that Chen Wenxian had come to have illicit sex with his wife, and he had killed the both of them. I don't know why it was that Du Huailiang killed Chen Wenxian and his wife, and I wouldn't dare make something up."

Further interrogation: "Were Chen Wenxian and Du Huailiang's wife having illicit sex—do you know?"

Sun further testified: "Chen Wenxian worked for the Wei family. Most days, he didn't even have a chance to get home. Ms. Zhang was an extremely respectable person. I never ever heard it said that Chen Wenxian was having illicit sex with Ms. Zhang."

Interrogation of Du Huailiang: "In previous interrogations, you said that you were sleeping in the courtyard when Chen Wenxian came to your room to have illicit sex with your wife. You heard someone talking inside, and you went into the room and killed them. If you were sleeping in the courtyard, Chen Wenxian naturally would have seen you when he came in. How did he dare to go into your room to have illicit sex? How did he dare to talk aloud in your room? Clearly, you're just making this up. Tell the truth about why you killed Chen Wenxian, and you can avoid the instruments of torture."

Du further testified: "You don't need to squeeze me—I'll tell the truth, that's for sure! Chen Wenxian and Ms. Li lived with me ever since they moved into my house in Kangxi 31. Later, Chen Wenxian went to work for the Wei family as a farmhand. When he was busy with farmwork, he often didn't come home to sleep. In the eighth month of Kangxi 31 [late September, 1692], during the time for preparing jujubes, I don't remember the date, Chen Wenxian didn't come home.[2] About the first watch of the night, Ms. Li came into my room to get a light from the fire. I saw that there was nobody else around, so I pulled her to me and wanted to have some illicit sex. She went along with it, and we had illicit sex on the *kang* where the jujubes were being prepared. After that, she had illicit sex with me either in her room or in mine. I don't remember how many times we got together.

"This year, my mother figured it out. On the sixth of the fifth month, about noon, I came home from the slope where I'd been cutting wheat, and because my wife didn't have the meal ready, I gave her a couple of slaps. My mother saw me slap my wife, so she came after me and hit me; she said that Ms. Li had put me up to it, and she cursed her, calling her a slut and a bitch. Ms. Li heard her, and she went into the back room and started a squabble with my mother. Sun Erchen's wife and Du Weiyuan came over to make peace between them. When Chen Wenxian came home that evening and heard they'd been squabbling, he beat Ms. Li for a while. Then on the morning of the seventh, Chen Wenxian was getting ready to move out. I told Sun Erchen to try to get him to stay until we had finished cutting the wheat and then he could move, but Ms. Li said she was too ashamed to stay there, so they moved away.

"After they moved, I couldn't get together with her at all, but because I had been having illicit sex with Ms. Li, I thought about her all the time. On the fourth of the sixth month [July 14], I invited Chen Wenxian over to drink wine. He said, 'I don't have any free time in the daytime, but in the evening after I've fed the cattle, I'll come over to your house to have a drink.' That made me think about how I feel about his wife and about how I can't even see her now that they've moved away. The best thing would be to take advantage of his coming over to drink in the evening to say that he was having illicit sex with my wife and then kill him along with my crippled wife so that I could get back together with his wife. When I'd made up my mind, I went home and got a hatchet and put it in my room and waited for him.

About the time of the second watch, Chen Wenxian came over. I showed him into the room; he sat on a plank stool, and I brought out something for him to smoke.[3] When he was good and drunk, I took out my hatchet and aimed a good chop at his head. He cried out once, and then he fell down on the floor. I gave him a few more chops, and then he died. My wife was sleeping on the *kang* there. Then I immediately chopped her to death, too. My mom and the old man both live in the back. I went into the back and shouted for my dad to get up. I told him that the Chen Wenxian who had lived in our house for three or four years and who had moved out for good had come back looking for trouble, so I killed him and my wife as well, and that I wanted to go to the magistrate's court to turn myself in. My old man called Du Weiyuan to come to the house and take a look. I told Du Weiyuan that Chen Wenxian had come to have illicit sex with my wife, and so I had killed him and my wife as well. Du Weiyuan said, 'Since you killed them, there's no problem. You can go report it at the district tomorrow.' After daylight, I went along with the neighbors to turn myself in at the magistrate's court. These are the true facts."

Further interrogation: "Since you had already killed Chen Wenxian, why did you also kill your own wife?"

Du further testified: "Since I'd had illicit sex with Ms. Li, I was afraid there'd be a murder investigation if I killed her husband Chen Wenxian. My wife was crippled, and also homely, so I killed her as well. I hoped that if I killed them while they were committing adultery, I wouldn't be charged with a crime."

Further interrogation: "When you were killing Chen Wenxian, where was your wife that she didn't scream?"

Du further testified: "My wife was on the *kang* all that time. She was about to scream, but I told her, 'If you scream, I'll kill you, too,' so she didn't dare scream. This is the truth."

Further interrogation: "How many times did you strike Chen Wenxian with your hatchet, how many times did you strike Ms. Zhang, and where on their bodies did you strike them? Speak."

Du further testified: "I was in a big hurry at that time, so I chopped once at his head, and after that, I just hit him a few times wherever I could. I can't remember how many times I hit him or where I wounded him. Yesterday when they inspected the corpse, toward the left side of his chin, on the left shoulder blade, on the left side of his back, on the right side of his back—there were ax cuts on all those places. Ms. Zhang had ax cuts on the left side of her throat, on her left upper arm, on her left and right breasts, on her ribs on the left side, and on her left wrist. I made all of those cuts."

Further interrogation: "Since Chen Wenxian came to your house to drink wine and you killed him, how did he come to be naked day before yesterday, when I examined the body?"

Du further testified: "Chen Wenxian was wearing a short jacket and pants when he got there. He took the jacket off himself while he was smoking, and he put it on the stool. The pants—I took them off him myself after I had killed him to make it look like he had come to have illicit sex with my wife."

Further interrogation: "You had illicit sex with Ms. Li for three years. How could it be that Chen Wenxian did not know about it?"

Du further testified: "Chen Wenxian was working for the Wei house, and there were lots of nights when he never came home. He never ever found out about it."

Further interrogation: "Did you discuss killing Chen Wenxian with Ms. Li?"

Du further testified: "Ms. Li moved into the Wei house west of town to live, more than ten houses from here. I never went to her house. And she never came to my house either. I never ever discussed it with her. It was something that I did all by myself. Really, Ms. Li didn't know anything about it."

Further interrogation: "If you did not discuss it with Ms. Li, how did you expect to be able to marry her?"

Du further testified: "Since I killed her husband, if she wanted to get married again, then I'd have a good chance of getting back together with her. That's the truth."

Further interrogation: "In her charges, Ms. Li said that you had some bad feelings about her husband Chen Wenxian and that you had tricked him into going there in order to kill him. You claim to have had illicit sex with Ms. Li—you are obviously trying to frame her."

Du further testified: "If I had had bad feelings toward Chen Wenxian, then how could he have lived in my house for three or four years? Really, it was just because I couldn't even see Ms. Li that I killed Chen Wenxian. I'm not just trying to frame her."

Further interrogation: "Since Chen Wenxian had a squabble with you on the sixth of the fifth month and moved away on the seventh, why was he willing to come to drink wine with you when you invited him over on the fourth of the sixth month?"

Du further testified: "That day, it was Ms. Li who had the squabble with my mother. I had no squabble with Chen Wenxian. Chen Wenxian and I were still on good terms."

Interrogation of Ms. Li: "This Du Huailiang killed your husband all because of his passion for having illicit sex with you. When you moved away, he could no longer have any contact with you, and that's why he killed your husband. Du Huailiang has now confessed to all of this. Now you hurry up and tell the truth."

Li further testified: "If Du Huailiang has already confessed to all of it, then I dare not dispute it. I'll tell the truth, and that will be that. My husband Chen Wenxian and I moved into Du Huailiang's house to live in Kangxi 31. Afterward, my husband went to work for the Wei family west of town, and when he was busy with farmwork, he didn't even come home to sleep. In the eighth month of Kangxi 31 [late September 1692], around the time for preparing jujubes, I don't remember what day it was, one evening, my husband didn't come home. About the first watch of the night, I went to Du Huailiang's room to get some fire. When he saw that nobody else was around, Du Huailiang dragged me in and wanted to have illicit sex. I struggled, but I couldn't get free, and he raped me. Later, we often had illicit sex. I didn't expect that his mother would figure it out.

"On the sixth of the fifth month of this year, Du Huailiang hit his wife a couple of times because she didn't have the meal ready. His mother then said I had put him up to it, and in her room in the back, she cursed me for a slut and a bitch and things like that. When I heard her, I got so mad that I said a few things back until Sun Erchen's wife made peace between us. That evening, when my husband got home and heard we had squabbled, he beat me for a while. I was ashamed to live in their house, so I told my husband to find a house someplace else so that we could move away. My husband found a room at his master's place, and on the morning of the seventh, we moved to the Wei house. On the evening of the fourth of the sixth month, I was sick with malaria and was sleeping. After he fed the cattle, my husband went out, saying that he was going to go drinking at Du Huailiang's house. I went to sleep with the child. I don't know why Du Huailiang killed my husband."

Further interrogation: "You had illicit sex with Du Huailiang for three years, and after you moved away, he then killed your husband. Clearly, you plotted with him to kill your husband because it was no longer convenient for you to see each other. What else do you have to say about that?"

Li further testified: "I don't know anything about how Du Huailiang killed my husband, and I never made any plot with him."

Further interrogation: "According to Du Huailiang, he did it because of his feelings of longing for you. He wanted to be able to be with you. If he hadn't worked it all out with you, how could he kill your husband and then be willing to kill his own wife as well? You say you don't know anything about the circumstances. How can you go on giving false testimony? If you do not speak truthfully, I'll start using the instruments of torture on you."

Li further testified: "On that one day, I lost control, and he raped me. After we moved away to live by ourselves, I felt so ashamed that I could not bear it. How could I willingly get together with him again?! Furthermore, my husband and I had been married for ten years. Seeing that we'd recently had a child, our feelings for each other were very deep. There's no way I would get somebody to kill him. Now I have charged Du Huailiang with killing my husband—I hate that Du Huailiang so much! If I had been in on it with Du Huailiang, how could I not testify to it? I just beg you to get all the facts of the case."

Further interrogation: "If you were not in with Du Huailiang on killing your husband, you should have filed your complaint at the time. Why did you wait two or three days and only then file it?"

Li further testified: "I am a woman left all by myself. And at that time, I also had a fever from malaria. When I finally could get in to file the complaint, Your Honor had gone out to examine the corpses. And because I took the wrong route, I did not meet you along the way. This is why it was only on the third day that I filed the complaint."

Further interrogation: "You were having illicit sex with Du Huailiang. Did your husband know about it or not?"

Li further testified: "My husband often did not return home at night; he never knew anything about it."

Interrogation of Du Wenwu: "Why did your son Du Huailiang kill Chen Wenxian and his own wife, Ms. Zhang? Tell the truth."

Du Wenwu testified: "Your humble servant lives in the back. Du Huailiang lives in the front. On the night of the fourth of the sixth month of this year, about the second watch, Du Huailiang came and got me up, saying that he had killed Chen Wenxian and his wife. I shouted to rouse Du Weiyuan to come and talk to him. When daylight came, we went to report it. I don't have any idea why he killed them."

Further interrogation: "Du Huailiang and Ms. Li were having illicit sex. Did you know about it?"

He further testified: "Originally, Du Huailiang and Chen Wenxian and his wife shared a courtyard in front. Lots of days, Chen Wenxian spent the night at his employer's house and didn't come home. I don't know whether the two of them had illicit sex or not."

Further interrogation: "On the sixth of the fifth month, why was it that your wife got into a squabble with Ms. Li?"

He further testified: "On the sixth of the fifth month, my wife hit Du Huailiang a couple of blows because he had hit his wife. Under her breath, she cursed Ms. Li, so Ms. Li came around to the back, and they bumped heads and got into a squabble. A neighbor made peace between them. The next day, Ms. Li moved away."

This marks the end of the interrogation by Magistrate Jin Yingdou. His summary follows, and then the text outlines the steps taken in the judicial review process, first by Dongchang prefect Hou Juguang and then by the provincial judicial commissioner Su Changchen. Both Hou and Su questioned the principals again, but there was no change in the testimony; their answers were copied verbatim from the magistrate's records, with a few minor variations. When asked again whether he had plotted with Ms. Li to kill her husband, Du Huailiang responded,

"Killing Chen Wenxian was something I did all by myself. Never did I plot together with Ms. Li. She didn't know anything at all about it. O Heaven above—how could I wrong her?!"

Then Ms. Li offered details in her own defense that further reveal her disposition.

". . . One evening, I went over to his house to get a light from the fire. When Du Huailiang saw that there was nobody around, he tried to seduce me into having illicit sex with him. I tried to get away, but I couldn't, and he made me have illicit sex with him. It's true that sometimes we had illicit sex afterward. But I didn't expect that his mother would figure it out. On the sixth of the fifth month of last year, around noon, the two of them got into a fight because his wife didn't have the meal ready. Du Huailiang's mother said it was because I was stirring up trouble. And under her breath, she made some pretty dirty remarks about me. So I quarreled with her for a time. That evening, when my husband came home and found out we'd had a squabble, he beat me for a while. . . . That one time in the past, I wasn't careful and had illicit sex with Du Huailiang. But after I had quarreled with his mother and we moved away, I felt so ashamed that I could not bear it. Even now, I regret it so much—how could I even think of doing that thing with him again?! Talking about feelings—my husband and I were married for more than ten years, and we had a child. How could it be that I had so little feelings for him that I would have been willing to have somebody kill him? If I had any feelings for Du Huailiang, then I would cover up for him. Why would I be willing to file a complaint against him? But I've charged Du Huailiang with killing my husband—I hate that Du Huailiang so much!"

In response to another question about her delay in filing the formal complaint against Du Huailiang, she protested,

"I am a woman left all alone. And at that time, I also had a fever from malaria. And my son is also small. Who could I get to take care of it for me? When I finally could get in to file the complaint, the magistrate had gone out to examine the corpses. And because I took the wrong route, I did not meet him along the way. This is why it was only on the third day that I filed the complaint."

All the officials agreed that the appropriate punishment for Du Huailiang and Ms. Li was execution: beheading for Du for having committed premeditated murder, and strangulation for Li for having been engaged in an illicit sexual relationship that ended in murder.[4] However, judicial review officials in Beijing agreed that Ms. Li was covered by an imperial amnesty and could be pardoned.[5] The emperor concurred. Du, however, was beheaded.

NOTES

Source: *Neige tiben Xingfa lei* [Grand Secretariat routine memorials, Crime and Punishment] 518–46, Kangxi 35.5.17 (June 16, 1696).

1. According to the Qing penal code, Article 285: "Whenever a wife or concubine commits adultery with another, and (*her own husband*) catches the adulterous wife and the adulterer at the place [in the very act of] adultery and immediately kills [both of] them, there is no punishment" (Jones, *Great Qing Code,* 271). (The italicized words

are later clarification by Qing period legal scholars; the bracketed words were supplied by the translator). Clearly, Du Huailiang—and his neighbor—knew of this statute and hoped to use it as justification for the murders.

2. Jujubes are a common fruit in northern China. They can be dried or made into a paste and other confections; it is not clear what "preparing jujubes" (*zuozao*) means in this context.

3. The reference here is ambiguous: *yan* could designate either tobacco or opium. Although its effect on the hapless victim suggests that it might have been the latter, more likely he was exhausted from work and sleepy because of the wine.

4. Du's sentence is in accordance with Article 282, and Li's with Article 285 of the Qing penal code. See Jones, *Great Qing Code*, 268, 271. It is likely that being a widowed mother of the only heir of her husband's family was a factor in this decision for leniency. See Buoye, "Suddenly," 68–70.

5. In his 1694 guide for magistrates, Huang Liuhong notes the important difference between adultery that begins through intimidation or enticement by the man and "those cases in which the parties indulge in carnal knowledge as a result of mutual admiration" (Huang Liu-hung, *Complete Book*, 439–40). Especially because Ms. Li's report on how her adulterous relationship began was repeated several times, with greater detail after the first iteration, one may surmise that the officials involved in this case considered her willing participation to have been a function of her suitor's pressure on her. Ms. Li's life was saved by the Kangxi emperor's announcement of a general amnesty in the twelfth month of the thirty-fourth year of his reign, early in 1695. Because he had committed premeditated murder, Du Huailiang's life was not spared; he was to be executed in accordance with Article 282 of the Qing penal code. See Jones, *Great Qing Code*, 268.

CASE 7

Rui Meisheng: Manslaughter over an Outhouse (Anhui, 1722)

The matter that led to blows here was not merely the foul smell of an open latrine; it also involved crucial matters of respect between neighbors. The family of the defendant saw it as "inappropriate" that Rui Mian's outhouse should face their front door; worse yet, when asked to correct the problem, Rui Mian adamantly refused. Even so, the matter did not escalate to violence until one day when Rui Meisheng had too much to drink. We should not imagine that the two doors were separated by a wide boulevard. Most likely, the alley between them was really quite narrow, perhaps so narrow that it was difficult to pass when the outhouse door swung open.

In the report excerpted here, the essential interrogation is conducted by Jingde District Magistrate Wang. The final pages of the report are missing, including the date that it was forwarded to Beijing for final review. According to the cover, the imperial decision was to send the case back to the Three Judicial Offices for reconsideration of the sentence.

The detailed memorandum submitted by Judicial Commissioner Zhu Zuoding of the Anhui Judicial Commission states that he had examined a certain individual named Rui Meisheng, twenty-nine *sui* in age, of middling height, with pockmarked face and thin whiskers, a native of Jingde District of Ningguo Prefecture in Jiangnan. The complaint contends that this Meisheng, an utterly lawless country bumpkin [*xiangye yumin*], together with Rui Jiu, who has fled, beat in an affray resulting in death the late Rui Mian, a distant relative in an older generation of no recognized degree of mourning who was his near neighbor and against whom he bore no previous enmity.

To wit: when Rui Mian repaired his outhouse, he changed its door to face the outside. Rui Meisheng claimed that it faced the main door of entry and exit from his house and instructed him to return it to its previous orientation. Contrary to expectation, Rui Mian maintained that it was a matter of his own convenience, and he refused to accede to the request.

Late in the day on Kangxi 60.10.2 [November 20, 1721], after drinking, Rui Meisheng happened to go to his front door, where he was struck by a noxious odor. Thereupon, he wrongfully started an argument. Rui Mian was about to strike Meisheng, when Meisheng became enraged and pushed the outhouse over. At that time, Rui Jiu arrived, having heard the commotion; furthermore, he wrongfully took the initiative to injure Rui Mian's nose with his fist. Thereupon, Rui Mian took up a beam from the latrine and was about to strike Meisheng when Meisheng again wrongfully snatched away the beam and struck him. It happened that he injured Rui Mian on the crown and the right temporal lobe; the wound was grievous, and before long he expired. Magistrate Song [Tingzuo] of Nanling District, who was temporarily in charge of Jingde District matters, submitted the following report:

On Kangxi 60.10.3 [November 21, 1721], Constable Rui Fan of the Twenty-second Battalion, Second Section [Ershierdu Ertu Lianbao], submitted his report on this event. His report states that one Rui Renju had filed a complaint that on the second, his father Rui Mian had been beaten, was injured, and had died a violent death at the hands of Rui Meisheng and his brother. A constable thereupon was sent to investigate. These being the true facts, the local warden Wang dared not conceal them, and appropriately he submitted a report on this matter.

The complaint submitted by Rui Renju concerning the murder of his father further states that on 10.2, in a sudden fit of malice (*tu zao xiong 'e*), Rui Meisheng and others by force smashed and destroyed the outhouse over the pit latrine of his household. His father Rui Mian used reasoned words to oppose this force. Tragically, he was with most foul malice struck a blow that gave him a severe injury, and he perished. Witness Rui Bao can provide accurate testimony as to this foul murder of my father. In accordance with the law, I have respectfully filled out the forms and urgently request an examination be held of the injury, with submission of a full report. . . ."

This case came to the previous acting magistrate, but because that acting magistrate had received a commission to escort military provisions, on the fourth, the matter was transferred to my humble district. On the sixth, I took provisional responsibility and rode alone with few followers, taking along a clerk and the coroner; I proceeded in person to the [warden's] station where the corpse lay to inspect it. Relatives of the dead man reported that the deceased Rui Mian was fifty-five *sui* in age. Coroner Fang Qi reported orally that on the anterior of the body, there was broken skin on the forehead toward the right side measuring diagonally 1.4 *cun*, a lethal injury caused by a wooden implement, and a round, red-purple nonlethal injury on the bridge of the nose 2 *cun* across caused by a fist. Beyond this, there were no causes [of death]. I made careful entries of the coroner's findings in the record.

Constables Wang Fa and Yao Ran reported that in the case against Rui Meisheng and others brought by Rui Renju, the criminal Rui Jiu named in the search and arrest warrant given them had fled and has not yet been apprehended. Appropriately, they reported this fact. Accordingly, I separately jailed Rui Meisheng and Rui Bao and ordered an intensive search for Rui Jiu and that he be thoroughly interrogated on the day he is apprehended, with the request for authorization forwarded. Appropriately, I filled out and annotated the register of injuries to the corpse and compiled these documents reporting the procedures already carried out in the case; these I submitted to the offices of the governor-general and provincial governor. I received authorization from Anhui governor censor Li and a rescript of authorization from the judicial commission to arrest Rui Jiu for examination, provisional sentencing, and forwarding of the criminal. I thereupon awaited authorization from the governor-general.

Other procedures, including the passing of memoranda back and forth along the channels for judicial review for the purpose of discussing limitations imposed for the apprehension of the fugitive, and so on, are noted here. With final permission from the prefecture, the investigation was conducted by the new magistrate of Jingde District, Wang Manchuan; the time limit was reckoned from the date he took office, with instructions from his superiors to carry it out expeditiously.

The constables originally assigned to the case report that Rui Jiu has fled without a trace and that they have no leads on where to apprehend him. Thereupon, this humble magistrate examined Rui Meisheng and the others during a strenuous interrogation at my court.

I questioned Rui Renju: "Testify as to why your father was beaten to death by Rui Meisheng and the other man."

He testified: "Our family had an outhouse that was falling down. Last year, our family rebuilt it. That Rui Meisheng and the others said, why should my family make the door open toward their front door? Time and again they asked us to change the direction to what it had been before, but my father paid no attention. This is the truth. Then on the second of the tenth month, to our surprise, Rui Meisheng and the others knocked down my family's outhouse. At first, my father reasoned with them, but unexpectedly they beat my father up. At that time, I was working in the fields. When I heard them shouting, I ran over as fast as I could. I saw my father was already unconscious on the ground. Rui Bao and I carried him home, and then he died. I beg you to make right this injustice!"

Further questioning: "Who gave him the blow on his forehead, and what implement was used? Who gave him the blow on the bridge of his nose?"

Rui Renju testified: "The wound on his forehead was given him by Rui Meisheng when he hit him with a beam. The wound on his nose was made by Rui Jiu, who hit him with his fist."

Further questioning: "If you were working in the fields, how do you know all these details so clearly?"

He further testified: "As far as seeing it, Rui Bao saw it all and told me about it. Just question Rui Bao, and he'll explain it all."

Further questioning: "When you got to your father, what might he have said to you?"

He further testified: "By the time I got there, Father was unconscious on the ground. He couldn't talk anymore."

Further questioning: "How did your father and Rui Meisheng refer to each other in kinship terms?"

He testified: "Rui Meisheng called my father 'uncle,' but they were nine degrees of mourning apart."

Interrogation of Rui Bao: "Who injured Rui Mian and what weapon was used? You witnessed the killing; tell the whole truth about it."

He testified: "I was on my way back from the fields on that day when I heard them shouting. I walked over and saw Rui Meisheng and Rui Jiu, both of them, arguing with Rui Mian. Rui Jiu hit Rui Mian on the bridge of the nose with his fist. I pulled Rui Jiu away, but then Rui Mian picked up a beam from the outhouse and went after Rui Meisheng with it. Meisheng grabbed the beam away from him and hit Rui Mian once on the head with it. When I saw that Rui Mian had been knocked down, I held him in my arms for a while. His son Rui Renju ran up then, and he and I together carried Rui Mian home. I didn't expect that Rui Mian would die."

Further interrogation: "Since you were at the scene of the beating, why didn't you snatch the beam away from Rui Meisheng?"

Further testimony: "At that time, I was holding Rui Jiu back. I didn't expect that Rui Mian would pick up the beam to hit Rui Meisheng with. But Rui Meisheng snatched the beam away from him and hurt him with it."

Interrogation of Rui Meisheng: "How did you and Rui Mian refer to each other in kinship terms? What enmity was there between you before this? Why did you beat him to death? Make a true deposition."

He testified: "Rui Mian was my distant uncle but not within the rules of mourning. Ordinarily, we had no bad relations at all. It was all because the door of his family's outhouse used to open inside, and then, all of a sudden, in the old year, he changed this door to face outward. When it was open, it just about faced the main door of my family's house. Since it wasn't convenient for us when we went in or out, many times I asked him to change the door back to where it had been. But he was stubborn and refused. On the second of the tenth month, after I'd been drinking, I happened to be walking up to our doorway, where I smelled a foul air that hit you hard. So I went over to discuss [lilun] it with him. How could I know that he'd want to hit me? That made me mad, so I pushed his outhouse over. And that's the truth. Then he grabbed that beam and came after me. In haste, I grabbed the beam away from him and hit him once on the head with it. And then he fell down. They carried him home, and he died."

Further interrogation: "Who was it that hit Rui Mian on the nose with his fist?"

Further testimony: "Before I hit him, my brother Rui Jiu heard us arguing and came over and hit Rui Mian in the nose once with his fist. This is the truth."

Further interrogation: "That beam that you hit him with, where is it now?"

Further testimony: "I hit Rui Mian once and saw him fall; then I threw the beam down and ran away. I don't know where it is now."

Further interrogation: "With that one blow, you hit him on a lethal spot on the head. Clearly, you intended to kill him. How can you explain this?"

Further testimony: "Really, it was because he was coming after me. On the spur of the moment, I grabbed that beam and just swung at him. I didn't expect that I'd hit him on the head. And I didn't know that it was a lethal spot. Even though we were distant uncle and nephew, ordinarily we had no bad relations at all. How could I hit and kill him with criminal intent?"

Further interrogation: "Where has your brother Rui Jiu run off to?"

Further testimony: "I've been in jail, and I don't know where he ran off to."

Interrogation of [local warden] Rui Fan: "Tell me the details about how Rui Meisheng and the other man beat Rui Mian to death."

He testified: "I wasn't there when they were hitting each other. On the third, Rui Renju came to make a report to me. He said that Rui Meisheng and his brother had beaten his father to death over an outhouse, so I went to see, and sure enough, Rui Mian was dead. So then I submitted my report [to the district *yamen*]."

All depositions were entered into the record. According to the investigation of the aforementioned magistrate of Jingde District, Wang Manchuan, Rui Meisheng was the distant nephew of Rui Mian, now deceased. . . .

Written here is a clear summary of the facts as revealed above. It concludes:

Without waiting for judicial torture, the aforementioned criminal spilled all the facts of the case without hesitation. Rui Meisheng accords with the statute on cases in which several together strike a person with the result that he dies, and the lethal wound is the most serious, and the one striking the most serious blow should be strangled.[1] I recommend that he be held in jail awaiting strangulation. Since he was at the scene, saw the affray, and attempted unsuccessfully to intervene, Rui Bao's punishment ought not to be beating with the heavy staff. Rui Fan, the local warden who did not deign to testify, ought first to be held accountable (*zhaishi*) for Rui Jiu, who has fled and who should be tried separately upon his apprehension with all the related people taken into custody by the prefectural *yamen*.

The remainder of the report details the review process, during which each successive level of review agreed with the findings of the magistrate's court and added repeated injunctions to speed up the review. In the portion of the report that remains, there is no indication that Rui Jiu was ever apprehended, nor is there any change to the death sentence suggested initially. Because the emperor's decision was to command the Three Judicial Offices to reexamine the case and advise him concerning the sentence, it is likely that Rui Meisheng's execution was commuted, or at least reduced, after the autumn assizes.

NOTE

Source: *Neike tiben Xingke Xingbu Xingfa* [Grand Secretariat routine memorials, Board of Punishments, Office of Scrutiny, Crime and Punishment] 522–102. Because the final pages of the memorial are missing, I am unsure of its precise date.

    1. Citing Article 302 of the Qing penal code. See Jones, *Great Qing Code*, 286–87.

CASE 8

Jia Mingyuan: Accidental Homicide (Fengtian, 1796)

In this case, three generations of close neighbors got into an argument that resulted in the death of one of the oldest among them, perhaps from a stroke, although forensic medicine at that time could not make such a diagnosis. At the beginning of the case, Bolin, a Manchu and the prefect of Fengtian near the modern city of Shenyang, quotes the synopsis offered by Wen Duxun, Department Magistrate of Fuzhou.

On Qianlong 60.6.25 [August 9, 1795], local warden Sun Rong submitted a report, saying "On 6.23 [August 7], Yu Dehai, a laborer hired by the family of Song Shichen, had come to his home to report that toward evening on 6.22, after it had rained, because he was concerned that the grain crops on the marshlands would be harmed, Song Fu instructed Yu to dig a ditch across the cart path alongside our land by which to drain the water. Jia Lun and Jia Mingkui stopped him and started a dispute. Song Fu hit and injured Jia Lun and Jia Mingkui. Jia Lun struck and injured Sun Fu. Then Song Shichen, Song Shizhong, Jia Mingyuan, and others came up. Song Shichen was carrying an iron spear that he handed over to Song Shizhong. Jia Mingyuan snatched it away, causing him to fall, and Song Shizhong was injured. Then they took Song Shizhong to Jia Wenli's house. At sundown, Song Shizhong stopped breathing and died. As appropriate, I have reported it to you for investigation."

The magistrate then proceeded to the location of the corpse to conduct an autopsy. The coroner reported that Song Shizhong was seventy-one sui in age. He had a variety of minor scrapes on his cheeks and elbows, but the only substantial injury was a bruise from a fist on the left side of his forehead. Even so, in the summer heat, blowflies had already attacked the body, which was beginning to swell. He concluded that the elder Mr. Song had died as a result of his fall. He also examined the injuries of other parties in the scuffle, all of which were healing appropriately.

At the site, the magistrate conducted his initial inquiries. The local warden had nothing new to add, but the hired farm laborer Yu Dehai clarified the cause of the dispute and provided more details on what had happened.

". . . Song Fu said that our crops in the marsh field might be damaged by flooding, and that I should take a wooden shovel and an iron mattock and go with him to open a ditch across the cart path that runs along that field in order to drain the water. Then Jia Lun and Jia Mingkui walked up and said that we were cutting off their cart path. And they got into an argument with Song Fu. Jia Lun punched Song Fu in the left eye, and Song Fu hit Jia Lun in the forehead with the iron hammer he had brought along to tighten the handle of the mattock, and he started to bleed. Jia Mingkui came up and Song Fu hit him and injured him in the left ear. Jia Lun grabbed Song Fu's hammer and left with it. Song Fu and Jia Minglun started scuffling on the ground, and I tried to pull them apart. Then, one after the other, Song Shizhong, Jia Wenli, Jia Yile, and Song Shichen carrying an iron spear in his hand all came up. Song Shichen wanted to get into the fight, but Jia Wenli stopped him. All I could hear was Jia Mingyuan yelling that Song Shichen had an iron spear. By that time, Jia Yile and I had just pulled Song Fu and Jia Mingkui apart, and when I turned around to look, I saw Song Shizhong fall down on the ground. Jia Mingyuan ran off toward the west, and Song Shizhong pulled himself up and walked away. But after a few steps, he sat down on the ground. I saw that Song Shizhong had an injury on his head. I asked him about it, and he said that his head and his left elbow hurt. Together with Song Shichen, I steadied him all the way home. By the morning of the twenty-third, Song Shizhong couldn't talk anymore, and Song Fu told me to go inform the local warden about it. When I came back with him, they had already taken Song Shizhong to Jia Wenli's house. About sundown, Song Shizhong died. And that's the truth."

Jia Yile's version corresponded to that of the farmhand, and so the magistrate did not record it. In the following testimony, Song Shichen clarified the relationships among the principals.

Song Shichen testified: "My sons are Song Fu, Song Lian, and Song San. The deceased Song Shizhong is my older first cousin on my father's side. He was seventy-one *sui* this year. In the past, he adopted Song San as his son. He spends his days living with us. We've always been on good terms with Jia Mingyuan and the rest; we've never had any bad relations.

"After it rained on the afternoon of the twenty-second of the sixth month of this year, I had an iron spear and was on the slope east of the village fastening up some nets where the silkworm moths lay their eggs. Toward evening, I heard a commotion in the fields that sounded like a fight.[1] So I hurried over there, and I saw my uncle Song Shizhong standing on the edge of the irrigation ditch looking west. By then, Jia Lun had already left. Jia Mingkui and my son Song Fu were wrestling with each other on the cart path, and they fell to the ground. Yu Dehai was pulling on them, but he couldn't get them apart. I wanted to go over and join in the fight, but Jia Wenli came over and held onto me and said, 'It doesn't matter what those young fellows are fighting about. Not enough that you don't even yell at them to stop, you want to go over and join in the fight as well?' When he said that, I went over and yelled at them to stop and tried to pull them apart.

"Then I heard Jia Mingyuan shouting, 'Song Shichen has an iron spear!' I was afraid that I'd hurt them with it, so I handed the spear over to Song Shizhong. By that time, Jia Yile had already gone up to pull them apart. I saw Jia Mingyuan run up to Song Shizhong and grab onto the spear with both hands. Jia Mingyuan gave it a wrench to the right, and Song Shizhong tripped and fell over to his left onto the ground. But Song Shizhong held onto Jia Mingyuan's clothes with his right hand. Jia Mingyuan struck out behind him with his left hand, struggled free, and ran away. Song Shizhong fell over onto the ground and scraped his right cheek. Yu Dehai and Jia Yile pulled Song Fu and Jia Mingkui apart, and Song Shizhong got up himself and walked away.

"I asked and only then found out that the fight came about because Jia Mingkui stopped Song Fu from digging a ditch to drain the water. After that, Song Shizhong took a couple of steps and then sat down on the ground, saying that his head and his left elbow hurt. Yu Dehai and I held him steady on his way home to rest on the *kang*, but by the morning of the twenty-third, Song Shizhong couldn't talk anymore. Before noon, Song Fu and Song San carried Song Shizhong over to Jia Wenli's house, and about sunset, he died. Sure enough, Song Shizhong died because Jia Mingyuan all by himself snatched away that iron spear, causing him to fall and suffer an injury. There was no other reason. And that's the truth."

Jia Wenli, the patriarch of the Jia family, testified that Jia Lun was his son and that Jia Mingkui and Jia Mingyuan were his grandnephews; they all lived together. He had been walking around his dooryard when he heard the commotion. Arriving on the scene, the first thing he noticed was his son Jia Lun, blood streaming from his head as he hurried home. Before he could shout at the combatants to desist, Song Shichen rushed up as if to join in the affray. He chided Song, as Song had already testified, and observed Jia give Song Shizhong the shove that knocked him to the ground. On the morning of the following day, members of the Song family brought the unconscious Song Shizhong to his house, and by nightfall, the old man was dead.

Song Fu described himself and his pivotal role in the fracas this way:

"Song Shichen is my father; my mother is dead. My brothers are Song Lian and Song San. The deceased Song Shizhong was my paternal uncle; he had adopted Song San as his son. After the rain on the twenty-second of the sixth month of Qianlong 60, I was afraid that our manor's crops would be drowned out by the water, so I told our hired hand Yu Dehai to bring along a wooden spade and an iron mattock; he also brought a little iron hammer so he could tighten the handle of the mattock. We walked over to the cart path beside the field and started digging a ditch across it to drain the water. We hadn't broken through yet when Jia Lun and Jia Mingkui came up and said that we had cut their cart path and wanted to know if we weren't going to let them get their cart through anymore. And they started arguing with me about it.

"Jia Lun ran up and slugged me in the left eye. I was upset, and I picked up my hammer and hit Jia Lun over the head with it. Jia Mingkui also came up to help him, and I hit Jia Mingkui over the left ear. Jia Lun grabbed away my hammer and ran off with it. I wrestled with Jia Mingkui, and we both fell over onto the ground. After that, Yu Dehai and Jia Yile pulled us apart. When we stood up, I saw my father Song Shichen and Jia Wenli standing in front of us. Uncle Song Shizhong had fallen down on the ground, and Jia Mingyuan was running away toward the west. Song Shizhong got up by himself, but he had injuries on his head and on his right cheek. He took a couple of steps, and then he sat down on the ground and said that his head and his left elbow hurt.

Although the rest of Song Fu's testimony matches that of the other deponents nearly word for word, Jia Lun's deposition offers a few more details.

Jia Lun testified: "Jia Wenli is my father; Jia Mingkui and Jia Mingyuan are my nephews. Toward evening on the twenty-second of the sixth month of Qianlong 60, I was returning home from another village with my nephew Jia Mingkui, and when we got to the edge of Song Shichen family's fields, we saw Song Fu along with Yu Dehai digging a ditch across the cart path to let out the water. We told him that they were cutting off our cart path, and asked, 'Won't you let us get our cart across it?' Song Fu said, 'Why don't you mind your own business?' and so I got into an argument with Song Fu. I slugged him in the left eye, and he hit me over the head with his hammer and drew blood. Jia Mingkui came up, and Song Fu hit him and hurt him, too. I grabbed Song Fu's hammer away from him. Jia Mingkui and Song Fu were wrestling when Song Shizhong and Jia Yile came up. My head hurt, so I ran home. The next day, Song Fu and the others carried Song Shizhong over to our house. They said that yesterday my nephew Jia Mingyuan had grabbed the spear away from him, and he stumbled and fell and got hurt. That day about sundown, Song Shizhong died. We reported it to the warden. And that's the truth."

Jia Mingkui's testimony was virtually the same, but when formally interrogated at court, the defendant Jia Mingyuan added details about the families.

Testimony of Jia Mingyuan: "I am a subject of Your Honor. I am twenty-two *sui* in age, and I live in Jia Family Village. My father has passed away, and my mother has remarried. I have an older brother, Jia Mingkui. I have neither sons nor daughters with my wife, Ms. Liu. Jia Wenli is my great-uncle. Jia Lun is my uncle. They all live with me, and we farm for a living. I've always been on good terms with the deceased Song Shizhong, and we've never had any bad relations.

"Toward evening on the twenty-second of the sixth month of Qianlong 60, I was sweeping my courtyard when I heard the sounds of fighting from east of the village. I hurried over and saw that my uncle Jia Lun was running home, bleeding from a wound to his head. I hurried over and saw Song

Shizhong standing on one side and my brother Jia Mingkui wrestling with Sun Fu on the ground. Yu Dehai and Jia Yile had gone up to separate them. Song Shichen had a spear in his hand and seemed like he wanted to join in, but he was stopped by my great-uncle Jia Wenli. I called out, 'Song Shichen is carrying a spear,' but then Song Shichen quickly handed it over to Song Shizhong. I was afraid that he'd use it to help hurt us, so I hurried up and grabbed hold of it. Song Shizhong held onto it with both hands and wouldn't let go, so I grabbed and gave it a twist to the right. Song Shizhong stumbled to his left and sat down on the ground and latched onto my clothes. I gave a shove behind me with my left hand, not thinking that I would hurt him on the head. He fell down again, and I snatched away the spear and ran home with it. Later, when Jia Wenli and Jia Mingkui came home, they told me, and that was the first I knew that the fight was about the trouble Song Fu had caused by digging a ditch across the cart path to drain his field. I didn't think that Song Shizhong would die around sunset on the twenty-third. I didn't intentionally knock him down, and nobody else was involved. And that's the truth."

This ends the testimony in this report. The prefect Bolin summarizes the case at this point, and finds, as had the magistrate, that two laws were relevant to this case.

First, Article 290 of the Qing penal code on homicide committed without premeditation during an affray stipulates that the person causing the death should be sentenced to strangulation with delay for further review of sentencing. Thus, the fate of Jia Mingyuan would seem to have been sealed by this regulation. He and the judicial officials who reviewed the case on its way to the emperor, however, all agreed that circumstances mitigated the case: that Jia Mingyuan snatched away the tool in an effort to preclude further violence rather than to cause injury. His act had involved "neither premeditation, nor intention, nor were there any accomplices who aided him in the deed." Moreover, the injury Jia caused to Song Shizhong was minor, not even breaking the skin. Certainly, the younger man did not deal Song Shizhong a lethal blow; death was presumably caused from the fall the old man took as Jia Mingyuan wrenched the spear from his hands. Since the death did occur during an affray, however, it was clear which law was relevant.

Second, the others involved in fighting—Song Fu, Jia Lun, and Jia Mingkui— would seem to be covered by Article 302, on injuries caused by blows during an affray: all should be caned thirty strokes.[2] However, given the fact that all caused injuries and instigated the fight, the judges agreed that they should be beaten a nominal eighty strokes each, or an obligatory thirty. The provincial governor released all other parties to the case and decreed that the family should be allowed to bury Song

Shizhong's coffined body. Furthermore, Song Shichen was ordered to provide planks as a means for carts to cross over the ditch he had dug to drain water from his field and thereby put an end to the dispute.

The case then went in the form of a memorial to the emperor, who relayed it on to the Three Judicial Offices for their consideration of the sentencing, as usual. Officials from the Three Judicial Offices summarized the case yet more tersely, in relatively elegant language, noting how "regrettable" it was that Song Shizhong had died from a fall caused by accident. At this level, too, mitigating circumstances were duly recorded, but because these events had occurred just before the coronation of a new emperor, the perpetrator would be covered by the imperial amnesty announced in celebration. Jia Mingyuan would go free, upon payment of twenty liang of silver to cover burial expenses for the victim.[3] Should Jia ever become involved in this sort of criminal activity again, however, his punishment would be increased by one degree, probably execution with no chance of mitigation. The Board of Punishments judges agreed that thirty strokes of the cane would be insufficient for the crime of instigating violence and causing injury and that Song Fu, Jia Lun, and Jia Mingkui deserved thirty strokes of the heavy bamboo staff for their roles in the affray. Even so, they, too, were covered by the amnesty and their crimes could be forgiven. This concluded the case, and the final memorial was submitted in the names of twenty-four court officials. As indicated on its cover, the new Jiaqing emperor accepted their findings, and all of the convicts went free.[4]

NOTES

Source: *Neige Xingke tiben Xing* [Grand Secretariat routine memorials, Punishments] 9, dated Jiaqing 1.5.6 (June 10, 1796), submitted by Agui.

1. The term for "fields" here is *tun*, referring to the "military-agricultural colonies" (*tuntian*) established in Manchuria late in the seventeenth century. See Reardon-Anderson, *Reluctant Pioneers*, 24–26.

2. For these two articles, see Jones, *Great Qing Code*, 276, 285. Caning was done with a light bamboo rod and was extremely painful; blows from the heavy bamboo staff caused very serious injury.

3. This monetary repayment to the family who suffered the loss is in accordance with the law on unintentional killing in the Qing penal code, Article 292. See Jones, *Great Qing Code*, 278.

4. Not every criminal penalty could be reduced just because a new ruler came to the throne, as specified in Article 16 of the Qing penal code. For a list of the Great Wrongs and other crimes that could not be pardoned in any way, see Jones, *Great Qing Code*, 34–36, 46–47. Case 6 in this volume falls into this category.

PART III

INTENT AND PREMEDITATED VIOLENCE

In the cases presented in this section, magistrates probe their deponents' testimony for the reasons behind the violence. The inept kidnappers in case 9 are clearly guilty, but the testimony as recorded here seems to open further questions about the relationship between them and the father of the murdered boy. And in order to assign punishment appropriately, the motivation of each participant in the crime must be identified with great precision; even the child of one of the killers is questioned closely about his role in the case. By coincidence, both case 9 and case 10 are from Guangdong, although the crimes took place fifty years apart; they are alike in that the perpetrators of violence in both cases are presented as the victims of grinding poverty.

CASE 9

Luo Zhongyi: Kidnapping (Guangdong, 1728)

The exceptional length of the various oral depositions recorded in this case may reflect the efforts of one or more judicial officials to influence the final reviewers, including the Throne. There can be no misunderstanding, given all of this redundant testimony, about the cold-blooded, self-serving murder at the center of the case. Likewise, several of the judicial officials involved were serving in an acting or temporary capacity, which may have caused them to err on the side of length and repetition in order to strengthen their presentation.

The case reveals a segment of the Chinese population not easily studied otherwise, the early eighteenth-century underworld: a mobile gang of strong-arm enforcers and kidnappers along with their only slightly more socially savory employers, who seem to have wielded a good deal of influence in their community and perhaps with the local administration as well.[1] They could be vicious; as we see here, members of this lowest stratum of society were only too willing to turn on their handlers if doing so seemed to be in their immediate financial interests.[2] The report begins with a detailed initial complaint filed by the father of the murdered boy. The report contains no indication of the fate the kidnappers had in mind for the boy beyond the immediate financial gain of selling him if their plan had succeeded. Presumably, the judicial review officials did not need to be told.

Because several of the principals in the case share the same surname, the report frequently refers to them only by their given names. It begins with an unusually long summary, in effect repeating every relevant fact of the case.

Your subject Deming, Grand Minister of the Deliberative Council, Minister of the Board of Punishments, and so on, Augmented One Degree, Recipient of Seven Citations, respectfully submits this MEMO-RIAL concerning the kidnapping and murder of a male.

The Board of Punishments' Office of Scrutiny copies herein a report from Yang Wenqian, who formerly served as provincial governor of Guangdong, concerning a recent event. In turn, it copies the detailed memorandum from Yinjishan, Acting Manager of Correspondence for the Guangdong Judicial Commission while Detached at Guangzhou Prefecture awaiting promotion, which copies the detailed memorandum from Zhang Xiangqian, the vice prefect [*can zhifu*] of Huizhou, who forwards the report from Zhou Yuren, the assistant magistrate [*xiancheng*] of Shunde in Guangzhou Prefecture temporarily in charge of matters in Xingning District.[3] To wit:

Upon receipt of a complaint, I have examined one Chen Yuanjue, twenty-nine *sui* in age, a native of Xingning District in Huizhou Prefecture. The complaint charges that Chen Yuanjue, stupid and violent by nature and utterly lawless, and Luo Yaosheng, a young boy, previously living, who was kidnapped and subsequently done to death by him, were maternal uncle and nephew of separate residences within the district seat. Previously, there had been no ill will between them. Luo Zongyi, father of Yaosheng and presently in custody, on Yongzheng 5.9.28 [November 11, 1727], sent Yuanjue together with his son Yaosheng to go to collect debts from the Pan family. Along the way, they encountered Chen Caiyu, a kidnapper [*guaigun*] who died of illness after having made his deposition, on his way back to Jiangxi. Caiyu noticed that Yaosheng was clever and consequently said secretly to Yuanjue that a boy like this could be sold for a considerable amount of money. When they finished speaking, they went their separate ways. . . .

The rest of the summary is drawn directly from the testimony below.

I examined all the depositions and the evidence, this office having received the authorization to do so from higher authorities. I, Zhou Yuren, in my acting capacity in this district, hereby submit this provisional report:

On Yongzheng 5.10.11 [November 23, 1727], Luo Zongyi filed a complaint concerning a recent event, which stated:

"I humbly submit that on the fourth of this month [November 16], my second son Luo Yaosheng by misfortune was kidnapped by the kidnappers Chen Caiyu and Chen Yuanjue. Fortunately, I was assisted by my wife's maternal uncle, Chen Tingsheng, in searching for clues. On the fifth, I humbly filed a complaint that they be arrested, and you filed a preliminary report and received permission to proceed with the investigation of Chen Caiyu and the others. They have admitted to the kidnapping and confessed that their gang members were Li Shiguang and others; a time limit was ordered within which to bring the boy back to this court. Unexpectedly, in the middle of the afternoon on the eleventh, Huang Junda reported that there was the body of a child floating near the bank of the river at the Nanji Bridge. I hastened at once to look and recognized that it was my son. I dragged the corpse out and announced it to the local warden Liang Tingren for his examination. He attests that my son was killed, having been alive when he was kidnapped by the kidnappers. This is an evil act that the law cannot tolerate! I beseech the court to investigate this kidnapping and get to the bottom of it, a favor for which I will be eternally grateful."[4]

Here, the report details the initial steps in the inquiry, including another deposition given to the acting district magistrate and to the jail warden Liu Yinchang, and his responses. The steps included the speedy arrest of all members of the gang and the inquest performed on the corpse.

Taking along the coroner and the relatives of the deceased and others, I went in person to the place where the corpse lay and ordered coroner Chen Songsheng to examine the body in accordance with the law. He reported: "I have examined Luo Yaosheng, already deceased: His corpse is 3 *chi* and 3 *cun* long.

He was ten *sui* in age. Anterior view: he is pale in color, with eyes closed and mouth open, blood coming from both nostrils, and blood coming from the right ear. Puffy, white, dry skin on both hands and feet. No sand or dirt in any of the ten fingernails. Skin on the stomach not exceptionally distended. On the anterior side of his throat, injury from a hand squeezing, 5 *cun* around and 6 *fen* across, green-black in color. On the posterior side of his neck, injury from a hand squeezing, 5 *cun* around and 6 *fen* across, green-black in color. On the left lumbar region, a pressure injury from a knee, 1 *cun* across and 1.3 *cun* long, green-black in color. On the back of the ribs on the right, a wound from pressure from a hand, finger marks visible, green-black in color. Beyond these, no further injuries."

Having personally examined the corpse, I found no discrepancies in this report. At the site, I filled out the form and annotated the form and the image of the corpse. I ordered a coffin prepared, that the body be encoffined, and that it be temporarily safeguarded at the warden's station. I also added the coroner's report to the record. Thereupon, I took the relatives of the deceased and the kidnappers back for examination.

Testimony of Luo Zongyi: "That Chen Caiyu is a distant uncle from my wife's father's family; Chen Yuanjue is my wife's distant maternal uncle. Both of them regularly kidnap and sell people. Chen Yuanjue also often came to my house, and so he was familiar to my son Luo Yaosheng. On the afternoon of the fourth, my son Luo Yaosheng went out in the street to play. When he didn't come home, I thought he must have been kidnapped, so I went and told my maternal uncle Chen Tingsheng, and separately we sent people to search the streets all around. I also went along the street banging a gong, looking for him. But we couldn't find a trace of him.

"The next morning, we went together to Chen Caiyu's house to make inquiries, but Caiyu was not at home. His wife told us that yesterday, a child had come there for a while and then gone away with Chen Yuanjue. That's what she said. While we were searching for Chen Caiyu, Chen Yuanjue said that he wanted to help me find my son. When we went back, Your Honor was just going out, so I went along to the warden's station to report, and they arrested Chen Caiyu and Cai Yuanjue, who admitted kidnapping my son Luo Yaosheng together with their fellow gang members Li Shiguang and Chen Sanzi to take him to Jiangxi to sell. That's what they said. I don't know how it happened that they beat my son to death.

"On the eleventh [November 23], Huang Junda came to report to me, saying, 'There's a child's body floating in the river under the Nanji Bridge.' I rushed over there to see and recognized that it was the body of my son

Yaosheng. Now you have favored me with this examination; I beseech you to arrest every member of that gang of kidnappers and get the facts on how they kidnapped my son and beat him to death. Be merciful and make right this great injustice!"

Interrogation of Chen Caiyu, he testified: "I will tell the truth. Because on the twenty-eighth of the ninth month [November 11], when I came back from the Jiangxi area, I ran into my nephew Chen Yuanjue walking along with Luo Yaosheng. I noticed that Yaosheng was a clever and smart lad; if we took him to Jiangxi, we could sell him for several *liang* of silver. On the first of this month [November 13], again I ran into Chen Yuanjue and Li Shiguang sitting together on the foundation outside the west gate. We started talking about how hard it is to be poor. Because I was thinking about how we could kidnap Yaosheng and sell him, I mentioned it to them. I told Yuanjue to work out a plan to kidnap him. On the afternoon of the fourth of the month, Yuanjue came and told me he'd already kidnapped Yaosheng. 'He's outside the west gate with your son Sanzi right now.' Then I went with Yuanjue and took Yaosheng to my house. Halfway there, we ran into Li Shiguang walking along, and so we all went to my house and ate some supper.

"Just as we were about to set off for Jiangxi to sell him, we heard Luo Zongyi and the others all around looking hard for him. We couldn't get him away, but if we let him go home, we were afraid he'd tell our names and his father would file a complaint. I thought wrongly again, and I said to Yuanjue and the others, 'Now we're stuck. The best thing to do would be to wait until dusk and then take him down to the riverbank and kill him to hide our tracks.' They all agreed.

"At dusk, we lied to Luo Yaosheng, telling him we were going to take him home, and we had Shiguang go on ahead with him. The rest of us followed behind, and we went to the bank of the river under Bamboo Grove Ridge. I told my son Chen Sanzi to go up on the hill and look to make sure there was nobody around. Li Shiguang was the first to squeeze Yaosheng's throat with his two hands and force him down onto the ground. Chen Yuanjue knelt down on him with his knee on his waist and used his hand to press down on his ribs on the right. Yaosheng kicked out hard with his two feet, but I held his feet down. Before long, he was dead.

"I used the opportunity to undo the silver necklace Yaosheng wore around his neck and to take off his blue cotton shirt. Li Shiguang quickly carried the body on his back down to the riverbank, where all of us buried him in the mud. Then we all went home separately.

"I weighed the silver necklace, and it weighed 1.06 *liang*. The next morning, I took it to Dalongtian, and in the ruins there, I traded it to somebody I don't know the name of for 760 coppers. I gave that blue shirt to my son Chen Sanzi to take out and sell; he got forty-six coppers for it. I used up all the money myself.

"On the eighth, I was arrested, and Your Lordship put us in jail. That evening, Li Shiguang came to get the news. Thinking about how we were in such a hurry that night when we buried the body by the river, I was afraid it wasn't buried well enough, and somebody might find out about it. So I told Li Shiguang to dig him up and throw him in the water so the body would go off someplace else. That would be a good way to hide our tracks. I never thought that the water wouldn't carry it away and that it would float up to the Nanji Bridge. This is the truth."

The deposition of Chen Yuanjue taken during district-level interrogations agreed totally with that of Chen Caiyu; consequently, his testimony was not recorded. Warrants were prepared for the arrest of Li Shiguang and Li Sanzi, but before they could be interrogated, Chen Caiyu became seriously ill with jaundice. Medical intervention was to no avail, and he died in jail early in the morning of the twelfth of the first month of the new year, Yongzheng 6 (February 21, 1728). The obligatory examination of the body by the magistrate having discovered no other causes of death, the appropriate image and register of marks on the body were prepared and filed along with the other documents of the case. The jailers were not charged with complicity in the prisoner's death. With this matter resolved, and the New Year festivities concluded, the district-level investigation resumed.

Interrogation of Luo Zongyi: "How was it that your son Luo Yaosheng was kidnapped that day by Chen Caiyu and the others who took him out and killed him? How did you know it was Chen Caiyu and the others when you turned in their names to the court? Normally, was there any sort of enmity or grudge between the two of you?"

He testified: "I live on North Street in the district seat. Chen Caiyu is an uncle in my wife's father's family. Chen Yuanjue is a distant uncle in my wife's mother's family. I often send Chen Yuanjue to force people to pay the rent grain they owe me so that I can clean up my ledgers. On the twenty-eighth of the ninth month of last year, I told him to take my son Yaosheng and go collect debts from the Pan family. I treated him well; there was no grievance between us. I don't know why, on the fourth of the tenth month, he kidnapped my son Yaosheng and beat him to death.

"After noon on that day, my son Luo Yaosheng went out in the street to play. When he didn't come home, I was afraid he might have been kidnapped, so I went and told my maternal uncle Chen Tingsheng, and separately we sent people to block off the streets and to search all around. I went along the river banging a gong, looking for him. But there was no trace. Thinking that Chen Caiyu and Chen Yuanjue are generally a bad lot, the next morning, I went with my maternal uncle Chen Tingsheng to Chen Caiyu's house to make inquiries. His wife told us that yesterday a child had come there for a while and then gone away with Chen Yuanjue. That's all she said. While we were searching for Chen Caiyu, we asked Chen Yuanjue, and he misled us and said that he wanted to help me find my son. Then I went to the constable's office to petition that they arrest Chen Caiyu and the others. They admitted kidnapping my son Luo Yaosheng. The other members of their gang are Li Shiguang and Chen Sanzi. The constable gave them a deadline for bringing the boy back. . . .

At this point, Luo Zongyi reiterated his account of hearing the news that his son's body had been discovered floating in the river. The magistrate then questioned Luo about what his child was wearing when he disappeared.

Further question: "About how heavy was this necklace?"

Further testimony: "It weighed a little over a *liang*, but truth to tell, it has been a while, and I don't remember exactly."

Interrogation of Chen Tingsheng: "Luo Yaosheng, the son of Luo Zongyi: Is he your nephew, your sister's son? When he was kidnapped by Chen Caiyu and the others and done to death, how did you and Luo Zongyi know to go to them to find out about it? What relationship is that Chen Caiyu to you? Tell me the facts."

In his testimony, Chen Tingsheng confirmed the facts of the case as presented thus far. He also explained how he and Luo Zongyi had divided up the area in their search for the missing boy. Then he commented:

"Chen Caiyu is a younger clansman of my father's generation. Chen Yuanjue is a clansman of my own generation. Generally, they are the kind who kidnap people and take them away.

"The next morning, I went with my brother-in-law Zongyi to Chen Caiyu's house to make inquiries, but Caiyu wasn't at home. My niece said that yesterday afternoon, a child had come there for a while and then gone away with Chen Yuanjue. Then, while we were asking around for Chen

Caiyu, Chen Yuanjue misled us and agreed to go with us to look for Yaosheng. My brother-in-law then went to the warden's station to petition for their arrest. When Chen Caiyu and Chen Yuanjue were questioned, they both admitted that they had kidnapped my nephew Luo Yaosheng. The warden set a deadline for the return of the boy. I didn't know that they had already killed my nephew or that they had dumped him into the river. On the eleventh, that Huang Junda came to report, and my brother-in-law went to see. He recognized the body and then came to report it to you."

Interrogation of Huang Junda: "Was it you who saw the body of Yaosheng floating in the river at the Nanji Bridge and reported it to Luo Zongyi? On that day, how did you know that this body was Luo Yaosheng and that you should go and report it to his father?"

He testified: "I live near Luo Zongyi on North Street in the district seat. On the eleventh of the tenth month of last year, as I was going over the Nanji Bridge, I heard somebody say that there was the body of a child floating near the riverbank. That's what they said. I knew that Zongyi had lost his son Luo Yaosheng and hadn't found him yet, so I reported it to Zongyi to go look. I never thought that it really was the body of his son Luo Yaosheng. He dragged him out and petitioned for an investigation."

Interrogation of the jail warden Liang Tingren confirmed the discovery of the missing boy's body floating in the river.

Interrogation of Chen Yuanjue: "Where are you from? How old are you this year? How did you kidnap the boy Luo Yaosheng and beat him to death in the tenth month of last year? At that time, who was the first to come up with the idea and work it out? How many in your gang? How did you kidnap him, and where did you hide him? And how did you later take his life? What weapons did you use? Who struck first? Where did you injure him? When? What did you pilfer from the body after he was dead? How much [was it worth]? Who disposed of the body? Answer each one of these questions, one by one, truthfully if you want to avoid the instruments of torture."

He testified: "I live outside the north gate of the district seat. This year, I am twenty-nine *sui*. Luo Zongyi is the husband of a younger clanswoman of my generation. I've never had any enmity or grudge against him. In the past, I've often pressed people to repay the debts they owe him. On the twenty-eighth of the ninth month of last year, Luo Zongyi told me to take his son Luo Yaosheng and go to collect some money owed him by the Pan family outside the west gate. We ran into my nephew Chen Caiyu just as he was getting back from Jiangxi. I asked him how business was, and Nephew said it was only fair. But he saw that Luo Yaosheng was clever and bright, and so he said to me, on the quiet, 'If we had a kid like this, we could sell him for several *liang* of silver.' That's just what he said. Then we all left.

"On the first of the tenth month, I again ran into my nephew Caiyu and Li Shiguang, who I know real well, outside the west gate sitting on the foundations of the city wall, talking about how hard it is to be poor. Nephew Caiyu said, 'Why don't we make a plan to kidnap that Luo Yaosheng who was with you the other day? We could sell him for several *liang* of silver and divide it up among us. It would be a good way to get us through these tough times.' Thinking wrongly, I agreed.

"On the afternoon of the fourth, I was passing Luo Zongyi's alley when I saw Yaosheng standing there. I lied to him, telling him, 'Your father told me to take you along with me to collect money from the Pan family.' That's what I said. Yaosheng went with me to the crossroads, where we ran into Caiyu's son Chen Sanzi, and I asked him if Caiyu was in the city now. I gave Sanzi three coppers to buy some fruit for him and Yaosheng to eat, and I told them to go outside the west gate and wait for me there. I hunted up Caiyu, and we went out of the city together, found Chen Sanzi and Yaosheng, and all went back to Caiyu's house. Halfway there, we also ran into Li Shiguang, so all together we went to Caiyu's house.

"Caiyu kept us to eat a meal, but just as he was about to take Yaosheng and head out for Jiangxi to sell him, we heard Luo Zongyi and his uncle Chen Tingsheng going along the streets banging a gong and looking everywhere and telling people at the mouth of every street to search for him. Then Caiyu said, 'How can we get him out? If we let him go home, maybe he'd tell our names, and that'd be no good at all. Now we've got no choice. The best thing we can do is take him down to the riverbank at dusk and do him in to shut his mouth.' And everybody went along with him.

"Just about dark, Luo Yaosheng started crying and saying he wanted to go home. All of us lied to him and said we'd take him home. Caiyu told Li Shiguang to hang on to Yaosheng's shoulder and go ahead; the rest of us followed along behind. When we got to that deserted place at the foot of Bamboo Grove Ridge, Caiyu told Chen Sanzi to climb the hill to be a lookout and give us a wave of the hand to let us know if there was nobody around. Li Shiguang then squeezed Yaosheng around the neck and throat with both his hands and forced him down onto the ground. I used my knee to press down on the small of his back and my hand to hold him down on the right side of his ribs. Caiyu held his two feet still. Before long, Yaosheng was dead.

"Caiyu used that opportunity to undo the silver necklace Yaosheng wore around his neck and also pilfered the blue cotton shirt he was wearing. Li Shiguang carried the body on his back down to the riverbank. Everybody dug a hole in the soft mud and buried him. Then everybody went home.

"The next morning, Luo Zongyi and the others came to make inquiries, and I pretended I didn't know. 'Let me go find him for you.' That's just what I said. Then Luo Zongyi went to the constable and made a complaint and had me and Chen Caiyu arrested. When they questioned us, we confessed that we had kidnapped him, and the warden set a deadline for bringing Yaosheng back. It was late on the eighth that the warden arrested us and took us in for questioning. Just then, Li Shiguang came by to get the news. Caiyu told him secretly that he was worried that we didn't bury him deep enough because we were in such a hurry on the night we buried him on the riverbank, and it would be no good if somebody found it. So he told Shiguang to dig him up and throw him into the water so that the body would be carried away, and that would hide our tracks. Shiguang dug him up and threw him into the river, but who'd have thought the water wouldn't carry him away and he'd float up to the Nanji Bridge and be recognized by Luo Zongyi?

"The ones who made the plot to kidnap and sell him were Caiyu and me and Li Shiguang, the three of us. Chen Sanzi found out about it only later."

Interrogation of Li Shiguang: "Where are you from, and how old are you? What grudge did you have against Luo Zongyi? For what reason did you kidnap his son Luo Yaosheng and beat him to death in the tenth month of last year? Who was the first to come up with the idea that day? Where did you work out the plan? How many are there altogether in your gang? How did you kidnap him? Where did you hide him? How did it happen that you beat him to death? What weapon did you use? Who acted first? Where did you injure him? When did he die? What clothing and objects did you pilfer from the body? Who disposed of the body? Answer these questions truthfully, one by one."

He testified: "I live outside the north gate of the district seat. This year, I'm twenty-seven *sui*. I never even knew Luo Zongyi before this. I didn't have any grudge against him. On the first of the tenth month of last year, I ran into my good friends Chen Caiyu and Chen Yuanjue outside the west gate sitting on the foundation of the wall. The three of us sat there and talked for a while, and we talked about how hard it is to be poor. . . ."

The rest of his testimony is nearly identical to that of Chen Yuanjue, up to the description of the murder itself.

"We waited until about dark, but Yaosheng started to cry and wanted to go home. Caiyu lied to Yaosheng, telling him he was going to take him home. He told me to take Yaosheng by the shoulder and go ahead and said it would be best if we walked sort of fast. Caiyu and the rest came along behind. When we got to that deserted place at the foot of Bamboo Grove Ridge, Caiyu told Chen Sanzi to climb the hill as a lookout and give us a wave of the hand to let us know if there was nobody around. Then I squeezed Yaosheng around the neck and throat with both of my hands and forced him down on the ground. Chen Yuanjue caught up with us and used his knee to press down on the small of Yaosheng's back and his hand to hold him down on the right side of his ribs. Caiyu held his two feet still. Before long, Yaosheng was dead.

"Caiyu used that opportunity to undo the silver necklace Yaosheng wore around his neck and also pilfered the blue cotton shirt he wore. I carried the body on my back down to the riverbank. Everybody dug a hole in the soft mud and buried him. Then everybody went home.

"Afterward, Luo Zongyi went to the warden and accused Chen Caiyu and the others of kidnapping, and on the eighth, they were arrested and taken away to wait for questioning. When I went to find out the news, Chen Caiyu secretly told me that if they were questioned, they'd admit only to kidnapping. He was just worried that we didn't bury him deep enough because we were in such a hurry when we buried the body that night and that the body might be sticking out and somebody might find out about it. So he told me to go dig him up and throw him into the river so that he'd be carried away by the water, and that would hide our tracks.

"After dark on the tenth, I took a carrying pole and dug up the body and threw it into the river. I never thought the water would be so slow and wouldn't carry him away and that he'd float up under the Nanji Bridge and be recognized by his father."

Interrogation of Chen Sanzi: "Where are you from and how old are you? For what reason did you kidnap Luo Zongyi's son Luo Yaosheng and beat him to death in the tenth month of last year? Who was the first to come up with the idea that day? Where did you work out the plan? How many are there altogether in your gang? How did you kidnap him? Where did you hide him? How did it happen that later you did him to death? What weapon did you use? Who acted first? Where did you injure him? Who disposed of the body? What did you strip off the body? How much [was it worth]? Answer these questions truthfully, one by one."

He testified: "My father Chen Caiyu lives outside the west gate of the district seat. I'm fifteen *sui* in age. How my brother Chen Yuanjue and my father came up with the idea or talked over kidnapping Luo Zongyi's son Luo Yaosheng, I don't know. On the afternoon of the fourth of the tenth month of last year, I went inside the city wall with my father and was playing at the crossroads there when Chen Yuanjue brought along Luo Yaosheng. When he saw me, he asked if my father was in the city, and then he gave me three coppers to buy fruit for Luo Yaosheng to eat and told me to take Luo Yaosheng outside the west gate and wait for him there. I bought two coppers' worth of glutinous rice snacks and a copper's worth of peanuts. I ate them with Yaosheng, and we went out the west gate to wait for him. Afterward, Chen Yuanjue and my father Chen Caiyu came out and took Yaosheng back to our house. . . ."

The rest of this boy's testimony corresponds to that of Chen Yuanjue and Li Shiguang.

Further question: "That night, when your father and the others did Luo Yaosheng to death, since you went along, surely you must have had a hand in it. If you weren't standing beside them, how do you know so clearly who did what and when? Now tell the truth about this."

He testified further: "That night, when we got to Bamboo Grove Ridge, I had planned to lend a hand. But Father was afraid that someone would come along and see us, so he sent me up the ridge as a lookout. Really, I didn't take part in it. The lookout spot was not far from them, and I was high up, so I could see everything they did. I beg you to question Chen Yuanjue and the others, and they'll explain."

Further questioning: "That day when Yaosheng was in your house, he was wearing a silver chain around his neck. Why didn't your father and Chen Yuanjue take it away from him then instead of taking it off only after he was dead? How much were it and the cotton shirt sold for afterward? How did they divide it up? How much did you get?"

Further testimony: "That day when we kidnapped Yaosheng [and brought him] to our house, if they had taken him to Jiangxi, they could have taken that chain off his neck at any time; they had no need to do it right then. And if they had taken away his chain in our house, he might have started crying and scared people, and that would have been bad for us. Later, Father took it off only after he was dead. The next morning, they weighed it at 1.06 *liang.* They took it to the ruins at Dalongtian and sold it there. The fence gave us 760 coppers for it. At first, they said they were going to divide it up to buy rice to eat. My father gave the shirt to me and said that it was all mine. I took it out on the street and sold it to a secondhand clothing shop for forty-six coppers, which I handed over to Father to use. Yuanjue and Shiguang didn't get any share of that. That's the truth."

Further questioning: "Where is that secondhand clothing shop? What's the name of the man there?"

Further testimony: "The secondhand clothing shop is on West Gate Street. I don't know the man's name, but if you take me there in custody, I'd recognize him."

The magistrate then questioned the adult defendants in order to clarify details about the murder and its motivation (robbery or kidnapping for the purpose of selling the child). All agreed (their testimony is recorded as a collective response rather than individual responses) that Chen Caiyu had received and kept all the proceeds from the sale of the child's stolen property. But the investigation did not end there. The youth Chen Sanzi was sent under escort to identify the used-clothing seller; this man, Peng Liangjun, was also brought to court.

He testified: "On the fifth of the tenth month of last year, that Chen Sanzi brought in a blue cotton shirt, which he said was his own, but because he was poor, he had to sell it in order to buy some rice. So I bought it from him for forty-six coppers. The next day I sold it to a passerby for fifty, and that's the truth. You can check my ledger on that. At that time, I did not know that it had been stripped off somebody they had killed. I beg you to forgive me for this!"

The used-clothing seller was released after questioning; this marks the end of the magistrate's report. The strenuous investigation at the prefectural level, in Guangzhou, uncovered no new information. The prefect concluded that the culprits should be punished in accordance with the law on premeditated homicide and that the laws concerning robbery were irrelevant. Specifically, in accordance with Article 282 of the Qing penal code, "Plotting to Kill Another," the principals should be strangled, with delay for reconsideration at the autumn assizes. As an accessory to murder, the young Chen Sanzi should be beaten one hundred strokes and exiled three thousand li from his home. However, given his youth—no more than fourteen at the time of the murder—the recommendation was that his sentence be commuted to a fine. The jailers were found innocent of any wrongdoing in Chen Caiyu's death of illness in prison, as was the acting magistrate under whose jurisdiction the malefactor died. Because he alone had received property stolen during a murder, however, Chen Caiyu was sentenced to beheading.[5] *His debt to Luo Yaosheng's father for the stolen chain and shirt was passed on to the son Chen Sanzi to repay.*

The emperor's decision, written in red on the cover of the file, reads:

"In accordance with the recommendation, Chen Yuanjue and Li Shiguang are to be sentenced to strangulation and imprisoned until execution after the autumn assizes. All others shall be sentenced as recommended."

NOTES

Source: *Neige Xingke tiben* [Grand Secretariat Office of Scrutiny routine memorials] 2–34–2334–7, Yongzheng 6.8.21 (September 24, 1728), Guangdong.

1. Brokaw, in *Commerce in Culture*, traces book trade routes that began in western Fujian and extended in all directions. It would seem that the kidnappers followed a similar route from Guangdong through Fujian to Jiangxi. The activities of these criminals contrast sharply with fanciful tales of heroic outlaws so frequently presented on the stage and in novels such as *Outlaws of the Marsh* (Shuihu zhuan).

2. After a similarly callous multiple murder in Kansas in 1959, a psychiatrist diagnosed the perpetrators as having "schizophrenia, simple type," meaning that the murderers had suffered no delusions while committing acts of violence but had simply divorced their thinking from all feelings. See Capote, *In Cold Blood*, 315.

3. Rowe describes Yinjishan (1696–1771) as a "highly sinified Manchu of minor noble origin" and a favorite of the Yongzheng emperor. A man of many talents, he held numerous important posts. See Rowe, *Saving the World*, esp. 52–53, 55, 61–62, 67–68; and *Eminent Chinese*, 920–21.

4. The complaint here alludes to a line from a text in the civil service curriculum (*The Zuo Chronicles* [Zuo zhuan], Duke Xuan 15), *xian huan jie cao*, "to express gratitude."

5. See Jones, *Great Qing Code*, 268.

CASE 10

Wang Azhen: Murder for Extortion (Guangdong, 1779)

The perpetrators in this case are represented as having committed a brutal murder with neither mercy nor remorse. Instead, they expressed only their own urgent need to find some relief from their constant financial difficulties, even though the case report gives no details to substantiate their claims. In fact, there are very few details of any kind beyond those required by law and ordinary judicial practice. This case does suggest, however, the vulnerability of the handicapped in late imperial China.

The following selection is from the beginning of the report, the initial investigation and testimony the magistrate takes at the inquest. The final memorial was presented by Defu after the provincial judicial review, relaying a report by the governor-general of Liangguang, concurrently acting governor of Guangdong, based on the judicial commissioner Liang Dun's report on the case, which was presented initially by Xu Xian, Magistrate of Chenghai, in Guangdong.

. . . On Qianlong 43.5.13 [June 7, 1778], a petition was filed by Gao Lai, a *jiansheng*, stating that when he arose and opened his door early on the morning of the twelfth of the fifth month of the current year, he discovered a dead body lying on the ground outside his door, covered with blood.[1] He recognized that it was a local man, Lu Ayu [Simpleton Lu]; he had wounds on his right temple, the occipital bone of his skull, the lower neck, and the throat. There were no bloodstains on the ground. He then cried out for the local warden Wang Tingbao to inform the deceased's next of kin Lu Ajiang to come and identify the corpse. He did not know who had killed him but reported the matter as is only right, and he entreated the court to investigate.

That same day, accompanied by Wang Tingbao, the warden of the aforementioned area came to the district court. Together with coroner and constables, I proceeded in person to the place where the corpse lay in order to investigate. Gao Lai's testimony there was identical with his petition.

According to the testimony of Lu Ajiang: "Lu Ayu is my own younger brother, but he is dull-witted. Every night, he goes down to the seashore to catch crabs to sell in order to earn a living. During the second watch of the night of the eleventh of the fifth month of this year, he went out the door carrying a bamboo cage to go down to the shore to catch crabs. But by morning of the twelfth, he had not returned. Thereafter, the local warden Wang Tingbao said that somebody had killed my brother at the *jiansheng* Gao Lai's gate. At once, I rushed over there to examine him, and it was indeed my brother. He had wounds on his right temple, the skull above the temple, his neck, and his throat. I don't know who killed him. I beg you to investigate and find out—that's the thing."

Thereupon, I instructed the coroner to conduct the examination of the corpse in accordance with the law. The coroner called out his report: "I have determined that the deceased Lu Ayu was twenty-five *sui* in age. Facing upward, he has a lethal wound extending laterally from the right temporal to the right frontal area of his head, 2.3 *cun* long, 6 *fen* in breadth, and down to the bone; the bone is damaged to the point that brain fluid exudes from the wound; the edges of the skin are even, curled, and drawn back and stained with blood. A lethal wound laterally across the right temporal bone 2.6 *cun* long, 7 *fen* in breadth, revealing the bone; the bone is damaged to the point that brain fluid exudes from the wound; the edges of the skin are even, curled, and drawn back and stained with blood. Both are knife wounds. A nonlethal wound across the lower neck 3.1 *cun* long, 1 *fen* in breadth; the edges of the skin at the mouth of the wound are even, not drawn back, and have no bloodstains. Incidental lethal wound to the throat 2.5 *cun* long, 8 *fen* in breadth, and 1.2 *cun* in depth, severing both the trachea and the esophagus; the edges of the skin at the mouth of the wound are even, not drawn back, and without blood. These were incidental knife wounds inflicted after death. Beyond these, there were no further causes of death. Indeed, there were wounds inflicted while he was alive, and further cutting wounds inflicted after death." This humble magistrate personally inspected the body and found no discrepancies. Thereupon, I deputed constables to make inquiries and to apprehend the primary culprits.

Thereafter, just as I was filling out my request for permission to proceed with the investigation, my constable Chen Long announced that while making inquiries about the culprits who slew Lu Ayu, he discovered that on the night of the eleventh of the fifth month, Xu Aping, a resident of this village, had seen Wang Azhen and Wang A'ang, the two of them, outside the village, carrying a body and resting under a tree. Furthermore, on this night, Chen Apin heard his dog barking and opened his gate to find Wang A'ang hiding behind the wall of his outhouse with a knife in his hand. Thereupon, I deputed constables to apprehend these two.

On Qianlong 43.5.25 [June 19, 1778], my constables having apprehended Wang Azhen and Wang A'ang, I also summoned Xu Aping and Chen Apin to court for examination.

Xu Aping testified: "Around midnight on the eleventh of the fifth month of this year, I was on my way to the seashore to go fishing. I had just gone out of the village when I ran into two men carrying a corpse who were resting under a tree. I went up to take a look and recognized the two as Wang Azhen and Wang A'ang. Wang Azhen shouted and cursed at me, and I didn't dare go closer. Instead, I went on to the shore. The next day, I heard that the corpse of somebody who had been killed had been left at the gate of the *jiansheng* Gao Lai, and I knew that this was the business that Wang Azhen and

Wang A'ang had been up to. Because they are so vicious, I didn't dare be the first to file a complaint. But later, I ran into the constable and informed him about it."

Chen Apin testified: "I make my living as a farmer. At cockcrow on the eleventh of the fifth month of this year, my dog started barking, and I was afraid there was a thief. So I took a light and opened my gate to look around. I saw Wang A'ang standing beside the wall of my outhouse with a sharp knife in his hand. I called out to him, but he cursed me, saying that I'd better mind my own business. I could see the knife in his hand, and he is so vicious that I was afraid. I closed my gate and went back to bed. The next morning, when I heard that there was a corpse of somebody who'd been killed at Gao Lai's gate, I figured it was Wang A'ang's doing. Because I was afraid he'd drag me into it, I didn't dare make a complaint. But later, when I ran into the constable, I informed him about it."

Wang A'ang testified: "Usually, I pole boats to earn a living. On the afternoon of the tenth of the fifth month of this year, I ran into Wang Azhen, my older distant relative, outside the village. We were enjoying the cool shade under a tree and were talking about how hard it is to bear being poor [*pinku nandu*] when Wang Azhen came up with an idea. He said that two families in the village, Lu and Yao, had pooled their resources and opened a pawnshop. But both are afraid of trouble. 'So why don't we find a corpse and carry it over to scare them and extort some money from them that we can use?' I agreed. On the eleventh, Wang Azhen said he'd looked all around but couldn't find a corpse. 'But that Lu Ayu goes down to the seashore every night to catch crabs, and he's really stupid. Why don't we kill him and carry him over and use him for the extortion?' And I agreed. We decided to make our move that night. At the time we'd agreed on, Wang Azhen came to my house to get me, and together we went down to an out-of-the way place in the Shamu Landing area to wait. That place was along the route Lu Ayu took on his way down to the sea.

"We waited until about midnight, when we saw Lu Ayu walking along with a bamboo cage in his hand. Wang Azhen knocked Lu Ayu to the ground, and I went up and held his feet down. Lu Ayu began to cry out, so Wang Azhen took out the butcher knife he had brought along and gave him a big cut down across the temple and the side of the head. After that, Lu Ayu couldn't make a sound, but when Wang Azhen handed the knife over to me, Lu Ayu began to struggle, so I gave him a cut from his temple across the front of his head. That's when he stopped breathing and died.

"Wang Azhen and I picked up the body to carry it over to the pawnshop run by the Lu and Yao families in order to scare them and extort some money. We had carried him to the edge of the village and were resting under a tree when we ran into Xu Aping walking along. He wanted to come up close and take a look, but Wang Azhen yelled at him and cursed him, and Xu Aping went away. We carried the corpse farther, all the way to Gao Lai's gate, but we were still a long way from the pawnshop when we heard a cock crow. I said, 'It's a waste of strength to carry a corpse; let's cut off his head and take that to scare them into bribing us.' Wang Azhen agreed.

"I was agitated in mind and reckless with my hand; I took the knife and hacked at the base of Lu Ayu's neck on the right side and across his throat. I was just about to cut off his head when I saw a light down the lane and heard somebody's voice. I was afraid we'd be seen, so Wang Azhen and I split up to hide. I hid behind the wall of an outhouse at the end of the lane. I never thought a dog would start barking and that Chen Apin would open up his gate and come out to look around. He hailed me, but I cursed him and told him he'd better mind his own business. Then Chen Apin closed the gate and went inside. By then, it was nearly the fifth watch. I was afraid that the villagers might get up early, so I didn't try to cut off his head anymore. I gave the knife back to Wang Azhen, and each of us went home. It's a fact: we never tried to extort any money from the pawnshop."

Concealing nothing, Wang Azhen confessed to plotting the murder of Lu Ayu with Wang A'ang in order to use the corpse to extort money from a pawnshop, but they failed in this attempt. Thereupon, I had both of the culprits taken to the jail and completed in good order my request to proceed with the investigation. When approval was received, I proceeded with the examination.

The next section is the report of Fang Yingyuan, the prefect of Chaozhou, who records that the trial was delayed in Chenghai District because Wang Azhen had fallen ill in prison on the twenty-first of the seventh month (September 11) and was only sufficiently recovered by the twenty-second of the eighth month (October 13). At the formal trial, the next of kin and the witnesses gave testimony unchanged from that collected at the inquest, as was Wang A'ang's deposition (he adds the fact that he is twenty-nine sui *in age). Since the testimony of Wang Azhen was not recorded on that occasion, it is included at this point.*

Upon interrogation, Wang Azhen testified: "I am a resident of this district, and I am thirty *sui* in age this year. Usually, I slaughter pigs for a living, but my business failed, and I lost my income. On the tenth of the fifth month of

Qianlong 43, I happened to run into my younger distant relative, Wang A'ang, outside the village. We sat under a tree to enjoy the shade. . . ."

The rest of his testimony is identical to that of Wang A'ang. The magistrate and all the judicial reviewers agreed that Wang Azhen, as the ringleader, should be sentenced to decapitation and that, as an accomplice who also participated in the murder, Wang A'ang should be sentenced to strangulation. Both should be incarcerated until after the autumn assizes.[2] The emperor agreed with this sentence, concluding, "Let the sentences be carried out after the autumn assizes," seemingly precluding any reduction of punishment for such a heinous crime.

NOTES

Source: *Neige tiben Xing* [Grand Secretariat routine memorials, (Board of) Punishments] 268, Liangguang, Qianlong 44.5.20 (July 3, 1779).

1. The *jiansheng*, a purchased degree, was generally equivalent to the lowest of the three regular civil service degrees; in total, the Qing sold hundreds of thousands for millions of *liang* of silver. See Ho, *Ladder of Success*, 34. Holders could bypass the preliminary examinations required for the regular *shengyuan* (licentiate), the lowest degree, but they did not have the same status as those who earned their degrees.

2. These sentences are in accordance with Article 282 of the Qing penal code, "Plotting to Kill Another." See Jones, *Great Qing Code*, 268.

PART IV

THE FAILURE OF "CONFUCIAN" FAMILY VALUES

During the eighteenth century, what is generally termed "Confucianism" was a diverse range of values understood and practiced quite differently by people at various social levels and of diverse ethnic or regional backgrounds. Highly educated and philosophically minded men debated the fundamental nature of humanity and of goodness itself: Were human beings intrinsically good, or were they self-centered and destructive? What was the origin of social discord and acts of violence in society? What is the role of education in the formation of a morally upstanding individual? All had studied the same classics of the Confucian tradition, but many thinkers by this time concluded that the real meanings of these teachings had been lost through the ages and so set out to rediscover the original standards through careful philological research on early texts.[1] Even so, the elite generally shared with commoners a concern for family hierarchy and harmony. Brothers should live together or at least cooperate peacefully; men and women should maintain proper distances between each other; wives and their mothers-in-law should work together in harmony.

The cases in this section demonstrate behavior that was far from these ideals and thus a threat to the Confucian orientation of all members of the judicial administration. Minor disputes might lead to civil lawsuits over property, failure to fulfill the terms of contracts, and other matters that sound familiar today.[2] When frustrations reached the boiling point and conflict erupted, these situations could lead to murderous violence.

Li Er and Li San: Two Pecks of Beans (Fengtian, 1738)

In this case, a simple dispute between brothers resulted in a homicide. It seems to have been fully settled when the brothers' mother intervened to beg for leniency from the court. Her pleas were initially successful; after consideration of the family's circumstances, the youthful Qianlong emperor sent the case back to the Three Judicial Offices for their recommendation on sentencing, which most likely deviated from published statutes on the side of mercy. Reasons for doing so are spelled out clearly in the report: having a male to carry on sacrifices to the deceased members of the paternal line was so important that it took precedence over normal punishments even for killing a brother.

The review process for this case differed from standard procedure because both perpetrator and victim were Han bannermen (qiren).[3] Cases involving bannermen went from the local level directly to Beijing, where they were reviewed by officials in the Board of Punishments. The first section of this report is from the local report. It begins with an outline of the facts of the case and the procedures followed when the homicide was initially reported: the magistrate of Ningyuan Department in Fengtian had gone with the coroner to Mayitun (Ant Farm Station) to inspect the body. They discovered a massive gash on the deceased, a cut high on his upper right thigh and lower belly, 3.3 cun long, 1.3 cun wide, and more than 5 cun deep. As soon as they had heard the wife of the deceased crying out, the local wardens had rushed to the scene and apprehended Li San. The following is the testimony of the murdered man's widow.

The testimony of Ms. Bo: "The deceased Li Er was my husband. This year, he was thirty-five *sui* in age. Li San is my husband's own brother. On the fifth of the ninth month of this year [September 28, 1737], we divided households to live separately, but there were two pecks of beans that we didn't divide.[4] They were left in Li San's house. On the twenty-first of the tenth month [December 12] of this year, Li San came to our house.[5] My husband and he sat together on the *kang* drinking, and they brought up the division of those beans. He asked Li San for them, but Li San refused to give him any. It was just then that I went out to look for firewood, so I don't know why the two of them started fighting, but when I got back inside the house, my husband had already been stabbed by Li San and had fallen to the floor. I asked my husband what had happened, but he could no longer speak. I started screaming for the constable from the farm garrison to come and arrest Li San. I never thought that my husband would die early the next afternoon. This is the truth."

The following sections of the report were drafted at the Board of Punishments.

When the documents, principals, and evidence all arrived at the Board, I intensely interrogated Li San: "To which banner do you belong? How old are you this year? For what reason did you and your older brother become such enemies that you would stab him to death? With whom did you plot this affair? Who helped you out? Answer all my questions truthfully."

Accordingly, he testified: "I am thirty-two *sui* this year, and I am a farm-worker [*zhuangding*] of the Plain White Banner under the manor head [*zhuangtou*] Li Fangxu on the Manor of the Fourth Prince of the Blood [Sige Guanling].[6] Li Er, the deceased, was my own older brother. On the fifth of the ninth month, we divided our households to live separately. But there were two pecks of beans left in my house that we did not divide. On the after-noon of the twenty-first of the tenth month, I went to my older brother Li Er's house, and we started drinking together. My brother brought up the beans, and he asked me for them. I told him that our mother had wanted to sell those beans to buy cloth. The beans were already sold, and she had bought several lengths of cloth. Then my brother got mad and started a quarrel, and because I was drunk, I said a couple of things back to him. My brother then pushed me down on the *kang* and began to beat me. In the heat of the moment [*yishi qingji*], I grabbed the little knife my brother wore at his side with my left hand, intending to scare him into letting loose so I could get free and run away. I never thought that I would stab him in the right thigh near the groin and that he'd die on the afternoon of the next day.

"Normally, my brother and I got along well; there was no enmity at all between us. It was all because we had been drinking and he began to beat me that I panicked. I intended only to scare him into letting go; I never thought that I would stab him and that he would die. Squeeze me to death and it'll still be the same story. How could I have had the heart to plot to kill my own brother?! I beg you to look at all the facts. No one plotted with me, and no one helped me. This is the truth." His testimony was unchanged, without variation, even when interrogated under torture.

Just as I was drafting a MEMORIAL suggesting punishment, on Qianlong 2.11.28 [January 17, 1738], Ms. Wang, the mother of Li San, submitted a petition, which read:

"This woman's husband died long ago, leaving me with two sons, Li Er and Li San. I raised these orphans to adulthood, and now I am seventy-two *sui* in age. Li Er is already dead. Li San is all I have left for support, to care for me in old age and to bury me when I am gone. If he were sent to his death and joined his elder brother, then I would have no one to turn to for support and to bury me. That would be most lamentable. Not one drop of our blood have my two sons passed on. If both of my sons were lost, then the sacrifices for my husband's line would be extinguished from that point onward."

Thereupon, on Qianlong 2.12.2 [January 21], the Board transmitted a memorandum to the general at Fengtian, instructing him to ascertain Ms. Wang's age and whether or not she had only two children, the brothers Li Er and Li San, and whether Li Er and Li San had any children. He instructed the neighbors, clan elders, and wardens to file reports, to be corroborated and sealed by the local officials and transmitted to this board. Subsequently, on Qianlong 3.3.18 [May 6, 1738], in accordance with the memorandum submitted by the general at Fengtian based on reports from the deputy commander of Jinzhou stating that Batai, Major Commander of the Middle and Rear Garrisons, had submitted a report stating that he had questioned Li San's clan members and their neighbors in the village, the local corporal, the wardens of their ten-family groups, and others.[7] The report stated that Li San's mother, Ms. Wang, is sixty-one *sui* in age and had in fact only two sons, the brothers Li Er and Li San. Li Er, now deceased, has three sons, the eldest of whom, Gansheng, is fifteen *sui* in age. The second son, Yinger, is five *sui*, and the third, Shou'er, is two *sui*. Li San's son is named Haiqing and is three *sui* in age. These facts are hereby affirmed. During interrogation, Ms. Wang claimed, "I am sixty-one *sui* this year," and all her other details agreed with the reports submitted by her clan members and others.

I have sought out the true facts of the matter in order to make a clear report, and on the basis of my findings from all the facts submitted to this board, Your subject concludes in the case of Li San, a farmhand of the Plain White Banner under the manor head Li Fangxu in the Manor of the Fourth Prince of the Blood, who stabbed to death with a knife his own elder brother Li Er, to wit: Li San and Li Er were normally on good terms with no enmity between them. On Qianlong 2.9.5, they divided their households to live separately, leaving only two pecks of black beans as undivided property stored at Li San's house. On 10.21, Li San went to Li Er's house, and they drank wine together until both reached a state of inebriation. Li Er demanded the stored beans; Li San responded that, in accordance with their mother's instructions, the beans had been sold for cash to buy cloth. Li Er became angry and began to quarrel with him; Li San answered him back. Li Er then forced Li San down onto the *kang* and struck him. Because he was being beaten, Li San panicked and with his left hand drew the small knife Li Er had been wearing on the right side of his body, intending to frighten his elder brother into releasing him so that he might escape. Without intending to, he stabbed Li Er in the right thigh near the lower belly, and it entered into his [brother's] intestines. Li Er was critically wounded, and on the following day, he expired. During interrogation under torture of the aforementioned offender, he adhered to his previous testimony without any alterations.

Upon inspection of the laws, according to the statement that "when younger brothers and sisters injure their own elder brothers or sisters and the result is death, they are to be beheaded without distinction between leaders and followers," Li San is by law sentenced to execution without delay.[8] Upon further consideration, it was found that substatutes under this statute specify that "for those who have fathers and mothers, when a younger brother kills his own elder brother and the family has no other males, the law allows him to be spared in order to care for his relatives. For those persons who have no fathers or mothers, or because of disputes over property, or for some other reason, the family has others who can continue the sacrifices after the death, then the sentence is to be fixed in accordance with the statutes." The substatutes stipulate that the sentence, if there is no dispute over property or other matters, or if, in a moment of struggle during which they are striking each other, the elder brother is done to death, and the father and mother are already deceased and there are no other brothers or other persons to carry on the family sacrifices, then the local officials are to be commanded to ascertain the facts and report on their investigations with the neighbors, clan members, and local warden, with seals from the local officials to attest to the facts of the offense committed by the said offender. Having received such clarification, I submit this MEMORIAL requesting YOUR SAGELY BENEVOLENCE that the aforementioned offender's life might be spared in order to continue the family sacrifices, that his sentence might be reduced to wearing a cangue for three months with an additional forty strokes of the heavy bamboo so that he may continue the family sacrifices. Furthermore, the annotation to the substatute stipulates that "Seventy is considered elderly, and those over sixteen are to be considered adults."[9] At present, Li Er's son is already fifteen, and his mother, Ms. Wang, is only sixty-one *sui*. Having heard these facts, together with those given above, the Board recommends and entreats YOUR MAJESTY'S keen perception to command that the Board's recommended punishment be carried out. Your subject and others dare not unilaterally decide and thus respectfully submit this MEMORIAL requesting YOUR COMMAND.

The memorial is dated Qianlong 3.10.15 (November 26, 1738) and signed by Xideshen as prefect of Fengtian along with five other officials. The Qianlong emperor's decision is written on the cover of the document in red: "Let the Three Judicial Offices review the punishment and submit a memorial with their decision."

NOTES

Source: *Neige tiben Ming'an Douou lei, Bao* [Grand Secretariat routine memorials, Homicides from Affrays, Packet] 106, Qianlong 3.10.15 (November 26, 1738).

1. For introductions to these debates, see Mote, *Imperial China*, 928–35; Theiss, *Disgraceful Matters*, 30–33; and Guy, *Emperor's Four Treasuries*, chapters 2, 3.

2. On civil law and prosecution in late imperial China, see Allee, *Law and Local Society*; Watt, *District Magistrate*; and Bernhard and Huang, *Civil Law*.

3. See appendix 1 for an explanation of the social organizations termed "banners." Han bannermen were tied to the land and could be severely punished if they left.

4. By custom, all brothers received equal portions when the family property was divided. See Wakefield, *Fenjia*.

5. This year had an intercalary ninth month, a *runyue*, hence the relatively long period of time between the dates.

6. For a discussion of the Manchu bannermen's manor system of landholding in Manchuria, see Reardon-Anderson, *Reluctant Pioneers*, 29–34. The "manors" were actually scattered plots of farmland that were allocated to individual families to till; levies on the land were collected for the benefit of Manchu nobles. I am grateful to Steven Miles for this reference.

7. Manchu banner manors were regularly farmed by ten men and their families, one of whom would be designated as the manor head.

8. Article 318 of the Qing penal code is being cited here. See Jones, *Great Qing Code*, 303.

9. These ages are stipulated in Article 22 of the Qing penal code as bases for con-

sidering whether an offender merits special consideration, that is, reduction of sentences; the old and the young might be exempted from punishment altogether for certain offenses. See Jones, *Great Qing Code*, 52–54.

The Hong Brothers: A Quarrel over Manure (Hunan, 1738)

This case involves fraternal violence that resulted in a man's tragic death at the hands of his brother. Perhaps the most remarkable element in the report is the colorful language preserved in the oral depositions collected by the district magistrate. In the Confucian tradition of close reading, the magistrate and his superiors in the judicial process chose their words carefully in representing the depositions and summarizing the facts of the case. Each layer of the combined report makes it clear that the elder brother was the instigator of the dispute and the first to resort to violence. The younger brother is represented as the victim of circumstances, one of which was a much older brother who regularly bullied his younger sibling. Perhaps this is why they had lived some distance apart for many years.

MEMORIAL concerning the beating death of a father [*sic*].[1]

The detailed memorandum submitted by Judicial Commissioner Yan Ruilong of the Hunan Judicial Commission detached to the prefectural city of Changsha states that he had examined a certain individual named Hong Yaozhang, thirty *sui* in age, a native of Ningxiang District in Changsha Prefecture of Hunan. The complaint deposes that Yaozhang and Hong Kunwei, who died from an injury he [Yaozhang] inflicted, were brothers from the same womb. They had lived separately for a long time, but normally there was no dislike or ill will between them.

To wit: [Hong] Yaozhang had accumulated a pile of manure; [Hong] Kunwei had instructed him to leave a few shoulder-pole loads for him. Subsequently, when Yaozhang fertilized his fields, it was insufficient, and he used it all up, leaving none behind. On Qianlong 3.2.7 [March 26, 1738], they encountered each other on a main road. Angry that he had been allotted no manure, Kunwei began to upbraid him [his brother] and was the first to strike using his flat shoulder pole for carrying firewood. Yaozhang ran to get away, but Kunwei pursued him closely, hitting him. Then it happened that they came to a deep ditch, and Yaozhang had no avenue by which to escape. Turning, he snatched away the flat shoulder pole in the hope that he [his brother] would not hit him again. Kunwei further struck him with his fists. Yaozhang then wrongfully used the shoulder pole he had snatched to defend himself, injuring Kunwei on the right side of the head. He [Kunwei] fell to the ground, incurring further scrape wounds on the right side of his ribs in back and on his right buttock in two places. After an interval of four days, he expired. Du Xun, magistrate of Ningxiang, forwarded all confessions, depositions, evidence, and records.

His detailed brief reports: On Qianlong 3.2.12 [March 31, 1738], common subject [*min*] Hong Guangtao and his mother, Ms. Fu, deposed: "My father Hong Kunwei and my uncle Hong Yaozhang, brothers from the same womb, bumped into each other on the road on the seventh of this month and quarreled over some manure. It happened that Uncle injured my father on the side of the head with a flat shoulder pole, and he fell down on the ground. By good fortune, Hong Shize and Hong Wentao heard his calls for help and went forward to carry him to Hong Wentao's house. But the doctor could not heal him, and on the night of the eleventh, his breath ceased. Weeping, we plead that you examine him and report this to the authorities."

This humble office thereupon proceeded at once, riding alone with few followers, taking along a clerk and the coroner, to the place where the corpse lay. In accordance with the law, I conducted an examination. According to the testimony of the widow Fu, the deceased Hong Kunwei was forty-eight *sui* in age. According to the oral report of the coroner Du Meisheng, by his measurement, the body of the deceased was 4 *chi* and 5 *cun* long, and his queue was 1 *chi* long. Examination of the anterior of the body: One lethal wound on the right side of the skull, slanting, 2.8 *cun* long, 3 *fen* wide, and 2 *fen* deep, with broken skin, bleeding, and injury to the bone; this was an injury caused by a blow from the edge of the flat shoulder pole. Posterior of the body: one nonlethal wound to the right lower ribs, round, 3.2 *cun* across, with removal of epidermis. One nonlethal wound to the right buttock, round, 3.5 *cun* across, with removal of epidermis. Both of these are abrasions from falling down. Beyond these, no injuries. This humble magistrate personally made an examination and found no discrepancy. The carrying pole used in the fell act was recovered and compared [with the wound]; it corresponded.

The magistrate then ordered that a coffin be prepared, deputed the local warden and the neighbors to look after it, and then carried out the procedures required for authorization to proceed with a formal investigation.

This humble magistrate summoned the criminal and the witnesses to this court and conducted strenuous interrogations individually.

Interrogation of Ms. Fu: "By what kinship terms did your husband Hong Kunwei and Hong Yaozhang refer to each other? Normally, was there any enmity between them? Why did they get into an argument? How was he beaten to death by Hong Yaozhang? Who witnessed the event? Answer these questions one by one."

She testified: "Hong Yaozhang was my husband's brother from the same womb, but my husband lived in Xiyanzhong and my brother-in-law Hong Yaozhang lives in Pengjiawan; they're several *li* apart. Normally, they were on good terms with each other, and there was no enmity between them. On the seventh of the second month of this year, my husband went to Pengjiawan carrying firewood. When noon passed and he didn't come home, I was about to send someone to look for him, when suddenly I heard that my husband had been injured by my brother-in-law and they had carried him to Hong Wentao's house. I went there just as fast as I could. All I could see was that my husband had a wound on his head and his face was covered with blood. My husband told me, 'Hong Yaozhang had collected a lot of manure in his manure pit, and I had asked him to leave a couple of loads for me. But he used it all up. This made me mad, and I took out my shoulder pole to hit him with it, but he grabbed it away from me. Then I hit him with my fists, but Hong Yaozhang hit me back with the shoulder pole and hurt me here on the right temple. It was Hong Wentao and Hong Shize who carried me here.' Because my husband was injured so badly, the doctor's medicine didn't have any effect, and on the night of the eleventh, he died. Now I only beg that this injustice to my husband be made right!"

Question: "Was that manure pit jointly owned by your husband and Hong Yaozhang?"

She testified: "My husband and brother-in-law had lived separately for many years. That manure pit was Hong Yaozhang's."

Testimony from Hong Guangtao: "I'm still young, and I don't know how to talk. My mother has already testified on all the facts about how my father was beaten to death."

Testimony from Hong Wentao: "About noon on the seventh of the second month of this year, I heard a commotion outside, so I went out to take a look. What I saw was Hong Yaozhang out in front running and his older brother Hong Kunwen chasing after him carrying a shoulder pole. When they got to a ditch that Hong Yaozhang couldn't jump over, he turned around and snatched Hong Kunwen's shoulder pole away from him. Then

Hong Kunwen started hitting him with his fists. Hong Yaozhang struck back with the shoulder pole and happened to hit his older brother on the head. I started yelling, 'Don't fight!' but by the time I got there, Hong Kunwei had already fallen down on the ground. Just then, Hong Shize ran up. We are first cousins, older and younger. When I saw that Kunwei had been hurt, all I could do, together with Hong Shize, was to carry him to the nearest place, which was my house, to give him treatment. I didn't expect that the doctor couldn't help, and on the night of the eleventh, he died."

Question: "Why were the two of them fighting?"

He testified: "I asked him about that. Hong Kunwei said that he told Hong Yaozhang to leave him several loads of manure, and when Yaozhang used it all up, Kunwei got mad, and they came to blows about it. The two brothers had lived separately for many years, but ordinarily they were on the best of terms."

The testimony from Hong Shize was the same as that of Hong Wentao.

Interrogation of Hong Yaozhang: "Where are you from? How old are you this year? What relationship was the deceased Hong Kunwei to you? Ordinarily, what grievance was there between the two of you? Why did you start a fight with him? What weapon did you use to injure him so severely on those several sites that he died? Answer these questions truthfully one by one."

He testified: "I'm from this district, and this year I'm thirty *sui*. Hong Kunwei was my older brother from the same womb. We had lived separately for many years; he lived in Xiyanzhong, and I live in Pengjiawan. They're several *li* apart. Ordinarily, we're on good terms, with no grievance at all between us. It was all because Brother asked me for several loads of manure in the beginning of the second month of this year, and at that time, I agreed to supply him with some. But it turned out that I used up all the manure in the manure pit fertilizing my own fields and still didn't have enough, so I didn't give him any at all.

"On the seventh of the second month, I saw Brother while I was walking along the road. Brother started cursing me, and I said back to him, 'I didn't have enough manure for my own fields. If you still have to have some, I'll make up a couple of loads for you tomorrow, and let that be that.' But Brother wouldn't put up with any explanation from me, and he took the carrying pole out of his load of firewood to hit me with it. I turned around and walked away. But Brother just got madder, and he came chasing after me. By luck [*yuan*], I came up to a deep ditch that I couldn't jump across. There was no path on either side, and no place for me to escape. All I could do was turn around and grab his shoulder pole. At first, I thought that if I took it away from him, he wouldn't hit me anymore. How was I to know that Brother would start hitting me with his fists? I panicked, and I hit him back with the first thing at hand, which was the shoulder pole. I never thought that I would hit Brother on the right temple of his head and that he would fall down on the ground. Just then, Hong Shize and Hong Wentao also ran up, and they carried Brother to the nearest place, which was Hong Wentao's house, to give him treatment. As quick as I could, I got the doctor to come, but his medicines had no effect. Four days later, on the night of the eleventh, Brother died. It was all my fault, and I deserve to die. There's no excuse I can make."

Question: "Your brother also had injuries on the ribs in the back on the right side and on his right buttock. How did you hit him there?"

He testified: "Those injuries on the ribs in the back on the right side and on his right buttock are scrapes he got when he fell on the ground. I never hit him there."

Further questioning: "So whose manure pit was it, after all?"

He testified: "It was my own."

These were the words taken in testimony at my court.

The following summary by Magistrate Du Xun merely restates the facts as revealed in testimony, adding nothing new. He concluded:

This humble magistrate having submitted reports of autopsy and evidence, and having respectfully received the order to examine the case, carried out an investigation at this court. The aforementioned criminal having confessed to all the details above without hesitation, Hong Yaozhang corresponds to the law stipulating that a younger brother who strikes his own elder brother, resulting in death, will be decapitated.[2] Therefore, I recommend that he be sentenced to immediate decapitation. According to substatutes, he should be tattooed.[3] As for Hong Wentao and Hong Shize, who tried to stop the violence but failed, I cannot make a recommendation as to their punishment. I should submit this to the prefecture for its investigation and determination as to whether or not this is appropriate.

At this point, the report records that the Changsha prefect Qian Rubi and the Hunan provincial judicial commissioner Yan Ruilong both reviewed the case, only to reach precisely the same conclusion: that Hong Yaozhong should be beheaded without delay. The case was then submitted to the Censorate, and from there to the Board of Punishments in the capital. No substantial changes were made in wording in summarizing the case; only at the Board were the nephews Hong Wentao and Hong Shize released without punishment for failing in their attempt to prevent the tragedy. The case concludes with the note that all investigations and decisions had been reached within the time limits established by law. The final submission is dated Qianlong 3.10.12 (November 23, 1738) and signed by Zhang Qu, in the Censorate. According to its cover, the imperial decision was to remand the case to the Three Judicial Offices for their investigation and decision concerning punishment. It is possible, then, that Hong Yaozhang was given a reduced sentence; certainly this report provides a sympathetic view of the circumstances and the acts that resulted unintentionally in this devastating family tragedy.

NOTES

Source: *Neige tiben Ming'an Douou lei* [Grand Secretariat routine memorials, Homicides during Affrays], Qianlong 106 *bao*, Qianlong 3.10.12 (November 23, 1738).

1. The case begins by erroneously reporting a "patricide" (*fuming*) rather than a "fratricide" (*xiongming*) by beating.

2. This is in accordance with Article 318 of the Qing penal code. See Jones, *Great Qing Code*, 303.

3. This is Article 317 of the Qing penal code. See Jones, *Great Qing Code*, 301–2.

CASE 13

Ms. Wang: Incest and Violent Homicide (Jilin, 1738)

TRANSLATED BY MARAM EPSTEIN

In this case, the deposition of the accused, a young adulterous woman, is placed first in the record, unlike most cases, in which a respected family or community member establishes the authoritative version of the events.[1] *Perhaps due to the briefness of the clandestine relationship between the father-in-law and daughter-in-law, no outsiders had information worth recording. Many of the questions or pieces of information common to depositions in other homicide cases are absent: there are no comments on the nature of the relationship between the victim and his wife, on when she entered the household, or on the relationship between the victim and his father. In fact, there is no information about the victim at all, such as age or physical size. The wound on Ms. Wang's shoulder is not clearly accounted for, nor was there any attempt to make sense of the brief but garbled testimony given by the victim's mother. Also absent are terms denoting emotional states conventionally used in narrating the motivations for homicide. The nature of the relationship between father-in-law and daughter-in-law is handled somewhat delicately—the woman's reported silence after each incident is to be taken as proof that she did not resist his advances and suggests that the case is to be treated as consensual illicit sex rather than rape. However, the Board of Punishments' Office of Scrutiny (which had authority over the banner administration) was unwilling to allow the father to avoid all culpability and raised probing questions about the testimony of the principals in the case.*

Secretary of the Board of Punishments [and other titles], Your subject Yijishan respectfully submits this MEMORIAL on the case of a woman murdering her own husband forwarded by the general of Ninguta, Jidang'a, and others on Qianlong 2.12.18 [February 6, 1738]. His memorandum is based on the report from the deputy lieutenant general at Baidunuo, Jueluo Qishiwu, concerning a dispatch from Anabu, a platoon commander of the Plain White Banner stationed in the military-agricultural settlements of Wujiazi.

The memorandum reports: Du Yuncheng, who worked as a hired laborer in the household of the manor head Zhang Xun, filed a report that on the twenty-sixth of the intercalary ninth month [November 18, 1737], the son of Zhang Xun, Zhang Zhisheng, was murdered. Thereupon, this office together with the soldier Yi'er Hana and the manor head Feng Ji and others proceeded to the home of Zhang Xun to investigate. The victim, Zhang Zhisheng, had four wounds on his shoulder and one wound on his palm. Next to the corpse on the *kang* were two footprints in the blood; on the floor, there was a vegetable knife with blood on it. The hair of the wife of Zhang Zhisheng, Ms. Wang, had been hacked off with a knife, and there was a stab wound on her shoulder. There was no evidence of anyone entering or leaving through the window or the door. Thereupon, this office ordered Funa, the assistant commandant of the Left Office, to assemble the clerk Cui Alin and the coroner Luo Xiuzhi, who had already conducted an examination of the wounds on the body of the victim Zhang Zhisheng, along with all concerned parties and to transport them to the *yamen* to continue the investigation on the second of the tenth month.

The written report submitted by Funa after he and the others returned states: This office led the clerk Cui Alin and the coroner Luo Xiuzhi [to conduct an inquest in the presence of] the family of the victim. The autopsy revealed that the deceased Zhang Zhisheng had one wound on the right side of his neck, 2 *cun* long, 3 *fen* wide, and 4 *fen* deep; on the left of the neck was a wound 4.2 *cun* long, 3 *fen* wide, and 9 *fen* deep; the windpipe was severed; at the base of the neck was a wound 3.9 *cun* long, 3 *fen* wide, 6 *fen* deep, reaching the bone; on the back of the skull was a wound 4.5 *cun* long, 4 *fen* wide,

1.8 *cun* deep, with injury to the skull. A wound 3 *fen* long partially severed the ear from the head. A wound on the right palm was 2 *cun* long, 2 *fen* wide, and 6 *fen* deep, reaching the bone. On both sides of the corpse were bloodstains; each side had a footprint. An examination of Ms. Wang's wounds revealed that she had a wound on her left upper arm 3 *cun* deep, 2 *fen* wide, and 4 *fen* deep; her hair had been cut off. Beyond these, there were no indications [of injury]. The autopsy report was filled in by the coroner and validated. There was no evidence of anyone having entered or exited by the window. This office then ordered all persons in Zhang Xun's household to remove their socks. It was discovered that Ms. Wang had traces of blood on the soles of her feet. After ordering a comparison, it was discovered that Ms. Wang's feet corresponded with the bloody footprints. This office then ordered Zhang Zhisheng's father Zhang Xun, his mother, Ms. Zhou, his wife, Ms. Wang, and the hired laborer in Zhang Xun's household as well as two neighbors to be taken to the *yamen* for interrogation.

According to the deposition of Ms. Wang: "In the afternoon of the seventeenth of the sixth month [July 14] of this year, my mother-in-law was in her bedroom and I was sitting on the edge of the *kang* in the outer room nursing my child.[2] My father-in-law came over and said he wanted to hold the child. As I was handing him the child, my father-in-law looked at my nipple with a smile. As he picked up the child, he brushed [the child's] leg across my face. I didn't say anything. That same month on the twenty-first [July 18], my father-in-law wanted to ride out to check the fields and asked me for the saddle blanket. As I handed him the blanket, he gave my left hand a squeeze. Again, I didn't say anything. On the evening of the twenty-fifth of the seventh month [August 20], my father-in-law was lying on his back in his bedroom when he called me to bring him his robe and cover him up with it so he could sleep. As I stood there on the floor to hand him his robe, my father-in-law groped my crotch with his foot. Again, I didn't say anything.

"At dusk on the third day of the eighth month [August 28], both my husband and my mother-in-law were out of the house and my father-in-law was by himself in his room. When I came in from outside and went into my room [through her parents-in-law's room], my father-in-law stood up and grabbed my arm and told me that he wanted to have illicit sex. I told him I was afraid someone might come, and my father-in-law said not to worry. He took me and pinned me down on the *kang* and took off my underclothing and had sex one time. On the twenty-first of the eighth month [September 15], my mother-in-law took my son off who knows where and my husband was also out of the house. I was in the inside room doing some housework on the *kang*, when my father-in-law came in and said he wanted to have illicit sex with me. We each took off our pants and had sex one time.

"Late in the day on the twenty-fourth of the ninth month [October 17], I was in the outer room. My father-in-law was holding me and was about to kiss me on the mouth when my husband suddenly came in from outside and saw us. He didn't say anything at all but just continued on into the inner room. My father-in-law was ashamed and left. Later that night, my husband came into our room to sleep. I was too ashamed to look at him and waited until he had fallen asleep to go in to sleep. On the morning of the twenty-fifth, my husband cursed at me, saying, 'Father was holding you and kissing you; it is obvious he has had illicit sex with you.' I said, 'I have not had illicit sex with your father at all. If your father was holding me and kissing me, what could I do about it?' He then stopped cursing and went out.

"At midmorning, my father-in-law came in and took advantage of the opportunity to ask me about what we had done the night before. 'Were we seen by your husband? What did he say to you?' I misled my father-in-law, saying that my husband must not have seen anything since he didn't say anything. That same evening, my husband again cursed at me, saying, 'With you and my father behaving in this way, what's the point of keeping such a shameless woman?' He cursed for a while. I was thinking how shameful it was that I had already been seen by my husband and was being reviled every day so that everyone could hear it. It would be better to kill my husband and pay with my life than to have him yell at me again. If I were somehow lucky enough to get away with it and escape punishment, I would just act as a [widowed] mother raising a child and survive by relying on my father-in-law for support.

"With my mind made up, when my husband went to sleep first on the night of the twenty-sixth, I took my son Liushi'er over to my mother-in-law to sleep with her. I was with the wife of our courtyard neighbor Guo Cheng; we worked in our room until the second watch, when I went out with Guo Cheng's wife. She went home, and as I went back inside, I took the vegetable knife off the stove, wanting to kill him. I was afraid that my parents-in-law might not have fallen asleep, so I hid the knife in the bed. When I went over to where my mother-in-law was to get my child Liushi'er, I saw that my in-laws were already both asleep. As I was picking up the child, my mother-in-law woke up. Afterward, I undressed and nursed the child and dozed off.

"I awoke to the sound of my husband opening the window in order to go outside to urinate.[3] When he came back and lay down, he again reviled me. I couldn't take it and cursed him back. I then took the knife I had hidden, turned around, and stabbed at my husband's forehead, but I missed and slashed the pillow instead. My husband got up and started hitting wildly in my direction; I then butted him with my head and knocked him over. Using all my strength, I pinned him down and covered his mouth with my hand; my right knee pinned down his chest, but he used both hands to grab wildly at me. He seized my hair and wouldn't let go. I wanted to break free, so I used the knife, and with one hack, I cut off my hair and slashed him on the right palm. As he was pulling back his hand, I sat astride him and started cutting at his neck. My husband rolled toward the side, and I again made a cut across the side of his neck. As he rolled onto his front, I got off his body and stood on the edge of the *kang*. I heard him struggling for life and slashed the back of his skull and neck two more times until he died. This is the truth; no one helped me plan it or carry it out."

According to the deposition of Zhang Xun: "This year I am sixty-one *sui* in age. I adopted this Zhang Zhisheng in Kangxi 59 [1720]. He was the son of a fellow manor worker, Liu Guangzi. This year, on afternoon of the seventeenth of the sixth month, . . .

The father-in-law's testimony is identical to that of his daughter-in-law; he corroborates her statement that he initiated their first sexual encounter.

. . . I took off my daughter-in-law's pants and had illicit sex one time. On the twenty-first of the eighth month [September 15, 1737], I walked into the room from outside and saw my daughter-in-law sitting by herself on the edge of the *kang* in the inner room doing some housework. I said "Let's have illicit sex." We then each took off our pants and had sex one time.

"On the twenty-fourth of the ninth month [October 16], as I was holding and kissing my daughter-in-law in the outer room, my son Zhang Zhisheng suddenly walked in from outside and saw us kissing. He didn't say anything and walked into the inner rooms. I was ashamed and left the room. On the morning of the twenty-fifth, I took advantage of the fact that no one was home to ask my daughter-in-law, 'Did your husband see what the two of us were doing yesterday? Did he say anything to you about it?' My daughter-in-law said, 'My husband must not have seen anything; he didn't say anything at all.' That my daughter-in-law and I had illicit sex is the truth; as to how she killed her husband, I know nothing at all."

According to the deposition of Ms. Zhou: "At the second watch of the twenty-sixth day of the intercalary ninth month [November 18], I was suddenly awakened by noise from the inner apartment.[4] I felt around for my grandson Liushi'er and called for my daughter-in-law two or three times. My daughter-in-law suddenly opened the door and came out, saying that somebody had killed Liushi'er. I got up and lit the lantern, and when I went into the inner room to look, I saw that it was my son Zhang Zhisheng who had been killed. As to whether my husband and my daughter-in-law had sexual relations and killed my son, I know nothing about it."

According to the deposition of Ms. Xie, the wife of farm laborer Guo Cheng, Zhang Xun's courtyard neighbor: "On the twentieth of the intercalary ninth month, my husband had gone into town to deliver the tax grain and was not at home. I did housework with Ms. Wang in the inner apartment every night. Each night, I would do some chores in the inside room with Ms. Wang. On the evening of the twenty-sixth, I was doing some work with Ms. Wang. Ms. Wang's husband Zhang Zhisheng, Zhang Xun, and his wife had all gone to bed. Ms. Wang and I worked until the second watch, when we headed out. As to how Ms. Wang killed her husband, I was fast asleep and know nothing."

In addition to entrusting the corpse of the deceased Zhang Zhisheng to his mother, Ms. Zhou, and the manor head Feng Xiu, I recorded all depositions and took Ms. Wang and Zhang Xun into custody. Since Zhang Xun's wife Ms. Zhou and the others knew nothing of the facts, there was no need to interrogate them in detail. At the *yamen*, I carried out a strenuous interrogation of Zhang Xun and Ms. Wang, but there was no difference between their depositions and what they confessed to the deputy lieutenant general of Baidunu.

Funa then summarizes the testimony above with neither interpretation nor addition. He concludes:

According to the law, a wife or concubine who commits adultery and plots to murder her own husband is subject to dismemberment; the penalty for the adulterer is beheading. Also according to the law, however, when the adulterous woman kills her husband but her lover knows nothing about it, his sentence takes only the crime of adultery into account. To wit: Ms. Wang and her father-in-law had illicit sexual relations, and afterward, because her husband Zhang Zhisheng discovered it, she then got the idea to take a knife secretly at night and kill her husband. At no point did she inform or consult with Zhang Xun. Not considering Ms. Wang's lesser crime of adultery, she should be judged according to the statute concerning a wife or concubine who commits adultery and kills her husband and should be provisionally sentenced to dismemberment.[5] On this, I await the consideration of the Board for appropriate action.

Zhang Zhisheng was the adoptive son of Zhang Xun of a different surname. Ms. Wang killed her husband Zhang Zhisheng. Although Zhang Xun was unaware of these facts, he nonetheless had an illicit sexual relationship with Ms. Wang. By analogy, Zhang Xun, who had illicit sexual relations with the wife of an adoptive son, should be judged according to the statute on [a man] who has illicit sexual relations with the daughter of his wife's previous husband and should be sentenced according to the crime of having illicit sexual relations with the daughter of one's wife's previous husband and beaten one hundred strokes with the heavy bamboo and exiled to penal servitude for three years. The law states that the sentence should be one hundred strokes of the heavy bamboo and three years penal servitude; however, under the substitute statute concerning manor farmworkers who are bannermen, there is a question of whether it is appropriate to commute the sentence to forty days of wearing the cangue and one hundred strokes of the light bamboo.[6] On this, I await the consideration of the Board, following precedent.

Interrogation of Zhang Xun's wife, Ms. Zhou, revealed that she knew nothing of these events. After interrogating all the neighbors [names deleted here], it was determined that they were not involved and there is no need to report in detail. As for the corpse of the deceased Zhang Zhisheng, the deputy lieutenant general of Baibunuo should entrust his adoptive mother, Ms. Zhou, to bury him.

Forwarded to the Board [of Punishments] on Qianlong 3.3.11 [April 29, 1738].

The officials of the Court of Judicature and Revision, having reviewed the case concerning the manor head Zhang Xun under the command of Anabu, Platoon Captain of the Plain White Banner, who had illicit sexual relations with Ms. Wang, the wife of his adopted son, in which Ms. Wang killed her husband Zhang Zhisheng. The memorandum submitted by Jidang'a, the general of Ningguda, reports the following:

According to the deposition of Ms. Wang: "I am nineteen *sui* this year. My father-in-law Zhang Xun frequently flirted [*tiaoxi*] with me, but I said nothing. At dusk on the third of the eighth month [August 28, 1737], my husband Zhang Zhisheng and mother-in-law, Ms. Zhou, were both out of the house. My father-in-law was sitting by himself in the bedroom. When I was about to enter my own room, my father-in-law Zhang Xun stood up and grabbed my arm and wanted to have illicit sex. I consented, and we had sex one time. On the twenty-first, my mother-in-law and husband were both out, and I was sitting in the inner room on the *kang* doing some housework, when my father-in-law came in and had sex with me one time.

The rest of her deposition on this occasion is identical to her previous testimony.

According to the deposition of Zhang Xun: "This Zhang Zhisheng was the son of a farmer from my manor, Liu Guangzi. In Kangxi 59, I adopted him as a son. It is true that I had illicit sexual relations several times with my daughter-in-law. But I know no details as to how she killed her husband." His testimony accorded with that of Ms. Wang.

According to the deposition of Ms. Zhou: "During the second watch of the night of the twenty-sixth of the intercalary ninth month, I was suddenly awakened. I heard banging sounds inside the room. I called my daughter-in-law two or three times; my daughter-in-law opened the door, and I got up and lit the lantern. When I went inside the room to look, I saw that my son Zhang Zhisheng had already been killed. As to whether my husband and daughter-in-law had illicit sexual relations and my daughter-in-law killed my son, I know nothing at all."

After several interrogations, they confessed everything without exception. According to the statute concerning a wife or concubine who commits adultery and plots to murder her own husband, Ms. Wang should be provisionally sentenced to dismemberment. Zhang Xun should be provisionally sentenced according to the statute concerning a woman who commits adultery and murders her own husband while her paramour knows nothing; his sentence takes into account only the crime of adultery. A man who has illicit sexual relations with the wife of his adopted son, by analogy, should be provisionally sentenced according to the statute concerning a man who has illicit sexual relations with the daughter of his wife's previous husband, to the appropriate degree of wearing the cangue, penal servitude, and beating with the light bamboo as communicated in the dispatch.

A more abbreviated summary of the facts of the case as drawn from the depositions follows.

. . . We note that when Ms. Wang killed her husband, if there was no one who abetted her, when Ms. Wang was holding the knife but had not yet managed to slash her husband and he got up and was hitting her, how was it that a woman could pin him down? Zhang Zhisheng was a man in the prime of his life who was already on his feet and knew that this was a matter of life and death. How could he not have fought with all his strength and called out for help? How could he have tolerated her pinning him down and taking his life?

Furthermore, according to the testimony of Ms. Wang, "I straddled his body and slashed at his neck and then the base of his skull," and so on. We note that there was a wound on Zhang Zhisheng's neck that went down to the bone, that his windpipe had been severed, and that the wound at the base of his skull also went to the bone. If Zhang Zhisheng was being pinned down on his back so that his neck was sliced and his windpipe severed, there is no way he could have rolled his body over. How could he have been stabbed to the bone at the base of his skull? Consider the number of wounds—how could one young woman have been able to cause them by herself? Moreover, there is only one wall separating the bedrooms of Zhang Xun and Zhang Zhisheng. How could [Zhang Xun] not have heard anything? Furthermore, his son had discovered Zhang Xun and Ms. Wang embracing and kissing. Would [Zhang Xun] not have been thinking about this and watching their actions morning and night? Given their close proximity, how could he not have heard the noise coming from the room? Zhang Xun must have been nervous that Zhang Zhisheng would kill his daughter-in-law and perhaps himself as well. How could he have had the peace of mind to sleep so deeply that he did not get up to look?

Given the details of this case, there must have been an accomplice in the plotting and murder of Zhang Zhisheng. The office of the general did not investigate thoroughly enough. The accused have fabricated evidence in order to escape punishment. Because this is a serious case involving adultery and premeditated homicide, the general should try the case with greater diligence and establish the true facts and then resubmit a report. At that time, this Board will deliberate the case.

Upon deliberation, the here named officials of the Board of Punishments respectfully submit this MEMORIAL requesting YOUR COMMAND.

The cover has the terse imperial decision: "As recommended." The case was thus retried in an effort to discover whether Ms. Wang was covering up for her father-in-law.

NOTES

Source: *Xingke tiben* [(Board of Punishments) Office of Scrutiny routine memorials] 2/80/9, dated Qianlong 3.6.17 (July 19, 1738).

1. Theiss concludes that when confronted with the murder of an elder male who had raped his daughter-in-law, the highest authorities during the Qing regularly overlooked his sexual predation and punished his killers, often the son or other male relatives, with the harshest penalties for their crimes against the patriarchy (*Disgraceful Matters*, 116–17). For the commentary on Article 366 of the Qing penal code that outlines the requirements for evidence of rape, see Sommer, *Sex, Law, and Society*, 89. Sommer notes that punishments for rape grew in severity over time and reached a new level during the Qing (*Sex, Law, and Society*, 70–71).

2. She uses the northern pronoun *wo* rather than some more deferential form.

3. He goes out the window in order to avoid going through his parents' room, which lies between the couple's room and the outer door.

4. She also uses the general northern pronoun *wo*.

5. Reference is made here to Article 285 of the Qing penal code. See Jones, *Great Qing Code*, 271.

6. References are to Articles 368 and 9 of the Qing penal code. See Jones, *Great Qing Code*, 349, 42. This is a clear example of preferential treatment under the law for bannermen.

CASE 14

Ms. Ma: Disguised Poisoning (Shandong, 1795)

TRANSLATED BY MARAM EPSTEIN

Of interest in this case are the details that designate the victim a shrew. The emplotment in the summary constructs Ms. Ma as the primary agent in the events—it is her resentment of her husband's poverty that sets the conflict in motion. Her husband, who admits to premeditated homicide, is presented as a secondary character and a victim of her shrewish behavior. The real issues in their marital conflict seem to be Ms. Ma's resistance to her marital family and her close relationship with her mother. Her mother was willing to shelter her from an unhappy marriage and supported her for long periods of time. Her mother's deposition repeats none of the details about her daughter playing the shrew. She only provides the dates of how frequently and how long her daughter ran "home." Even though daughters were said to be temporary residents of their natal homes, this case illustrates that a young wife might resist the expectation that she transfer her filial loyalties to her husband's family.

Several other facts are of particular interest here. For one, it never occurs to Wang You that he could divorce his wife and send her back to her parents as a way of light-

ening his burden. Likewise, no one seems interested in pursuing the degree of Wang Deshun's knowledge of what happened that night (popular understanding of poisoning by arsenic is that it is extremely painful, so it is unlikely that Wang You's father did not hear any moans). Finally, the more serious crime of premeditated poisoning is elided into a less serious charge of homicide as a result of a husband striking his wife (even though the punishment remained the same for husbands who struck their wives with intention to kill).[1] As can be seen from Wang You's final explanation of what he did with the arsenic that poisoned his wife, the possession of compounds that could be used as poison was tightly regulated by the state.

Your subject Agui [here follows a long list of titles in very small characters] respectfully submits this MEMORIAL to clarify a matter.

Jiang Lan, former recording secretary for the governor of Shandong now serving as judicial commissioner, records a matter according to the memorandum submitted by Acting Judicial Commissioner Cedan based on documents first processed under the previous judicial commissioner and transferred over to him. This report states that Wang You of Putai District poisoned his wife, Ms. Ma, and disguised it as suicide by hanging. According to the detailed report submitted by Prefect Xiang Lin of Wuding Prefecture, Liu Fushan, the magistrate of Putai District, reported:

On Qianlong 59.4.9 [May 7, 1794], the local warden Lu Haoshun reported that the villager Wang You had reported that his wife, Ms. Ma, had hanged herself on the evening of the eighth. When [Lu] inspected the corpse, he saw that she had already been laid out but there were no markings on her neck. As appropriate, he reported this for investigation. I [Magistrate Liu Fushan] then proceeded to where the corpse lay and in accordance with the law conducted an investigation.

In his oral report, the coroner declared: "According to the questioning, the deceased, Mrs. Wang née Ma, was nineteen *sui* in age. From the front, her complexion is dark, and blood is coming from her nostrils; her upper and lower lips are contorted and purplish black. Her mouth is open, and her tongue has contracted and is showing pustules. Her ten fingernails are all cracked and blackened. Her torso, chest, and abdomen are all black in color. There are no other injuries. Indeed, she was poisoned while still alive. Unquestionably, her death could not have been caused by suicide by hanging."

I [Magistrate Liu] personally examined the body and found no discrepancies. The testimony of the local warden Lu Haoshun corresponded with the written plaint.

The deposition made by Mrs. Ma née Lin states: "The deceased Mrs. Wang Ma was my daughter.[2] She was married to Wang You for more than two years. Because Wang You's family was bitterly poor, my daughter was not willing to live with him. She ran away and came home twice last year, but I sent her back. This year, over the New Year [around February 1, 1794], my daughter again ran back home and stayed for more than two months until I sent her back on the seventeenth of the third month [April 16]. Early on the ninth of the fourth month, my son-in-law went to say that my daughter had hanged herself and died. When I hurried to see, her body had already been taken down, but there were no marks on her neck. Today, after this examination, it is clear she was poisoned. I beseech you to investigate this injustice thoroughly."

Wang Deshun's deposition states: "I am sixty-eight *sui* in age. My wife died young, and I have only one son, Wang You. The deceased Ms. Ma was my daughter-in-law and entered our house two years ago. Ms. Ma resented the bitter poverty of my family and frequently yelled about not being willing to live in my household. Last year, she ran home twice; each time, her mother sent her back. This year, over the New Year, she again ran home and stayed there for more than two months. It was not until the seventeenth of the third month that her mother sent her back. Ms. Ma frequently fought with my son. I was unable to discipline her. On the eighth of the fourth month, when Ms. Ma was about to run away again, I saw her and prevented it. Ms. Ma had a fit, crying and screaming (*sapo kunao*); my son hurried over to beat her, but I told him to leave her alone. At dusk, when my son came home, my daughter-in-law was lying on the *kang* and was not willing to make supper, so my son made supper for me by himself. Then I went to sleep. On the morning of the ninth, I got up and saw that Ms. Ma was dead on the *kang*. I questioned my son in detail, and he informed me that he had mixed left-over arsenic with the rice and had left it for Ms. Ma. She ate it and died from the poison. I was afraid my son would be charged with a crime, so I told him to claim that Ms. Ma had hanged herself to death in the hope that we could cover it up. Now, after the inquest, it's not possible to cover it up; I have no choice but to confess the truth. In fact, I only learned of it after the fact and did not conspire to kill her. That is the truth."

Wang You made full oral confession of his plotting to poison his wife Ms. Ma and of disguising it as hanging. On this basis, I jailed Wang You, recorded the depositions, and filed my report. Having received authorization to carry out a full investigation, I proceeded to interrogate strenuously all related parties. The statements were in agreement with the previous depositions.

Wang You's deposition states: "I am eighteen *sui* in age. My father Wang Deshun is sixty-eight *sui*, and my mother died early. I have no brothers. The deceased Ms. Ma was my wife; she married into my family two years ago. We had no children. Ms. Ma resented my family's bitter poverty and was unwilling to live with me. She often quarreled with me. In Qianlong 58, she twice ran home; each time, my mother-in-law personally sent her back. During the first month of Qianlong 59, she ran away again. Only on the seventeenth of the third month did my mother-in-law send her back. Ms. Ma frequently quarreled with me; my father tried to discipline her, but she wouldn't obey.

"On the afternoon of the eighth of the fourth month, my wife again tried to run away, but my father prevented her, and she had a fit, crying and screaming. I hurried over to beat her, but my father shouted at me to leave her alone. About dark, I came home, and my wife was lying on the *kang* and hadn't even made supper. I made supper myself and ate together with my father. Because I was thinking that I would have to put up with a lifetime of my wife being a shrewish woman (*pohan*), I came up with the idea of finishing her off. I remembered that there was some arsenic left over from wheat planting last year. I took advantage of my father being asleep and found the arsenic and mixed it in with the leftover rice and placed it on the stove beside the pot. I was thinking that my wife would eat up the rice when she got hungry; it would then poison her, and I'd be rid of my troubles. I lay down in an outer room and pretended to be fast asleep. After a while, I made out the sound of my wife getting up and eating the rice. She slept until the middle of the night on the *kang* and then called out for some water to drink. I didn't give her any. My wife vomited for a while, and then she stopped breathing and died. The next morning, my father got up and asked me all about what had happened. I told him the truth. My father was worried that I would be charged with a crime and told me to claim that my wife had hanged herself and to report it to the warden. Now that the wounds on the corpse have been discovered by the examination, I can't blame anyone else and have no choice but to confess the truth. I came up with the idea of poisoning my wife all by myself; my father knew nothing about it.

"As for that arsenic, I bought it last year from the stall of a dry-goods vendor whose name I do not know. The rice bowl in which I mixed the arsenic has already been washed. That's the truth."

The magistrate of Putai District, Liu Fushan, investigated and judged Wang You according to the statute for a husband who hit and killed his wife, provisionally sentencing him to strangulation. Since it was intentional homicide, the laws on strangulation stipulate a sentence of strangulation subject to review at the autumn assizes.[3]

The documents were transferred to the prefectural *yamen*. A further detailed investigation was made, and there were no discrepancies in the findings. . . .

The facts, depositions, and provisional sentence are repeated from investigations at the prefectural and provincial levels. The imperial decision on the cover of the memorial confirms the sentence of strangulation with delay. Because Wang You was the only son of an aging widower, his life might have been spared.

NOTES

Source: *Xingke tiben* [(Board of Punishments) Office of Scrutiny routine memorials] 2/1941/7, dated Qianlong 60.2.13 (1795).

1. This is Article 315 of the Qing penal code. See Jones, *Great Qing Code*, 300.

2. She uses the deferential pronoun *xiao furen*.

3. This apparently refers to Article 315 of the Qing penal code. See Jones, *Great Qing Code*, 300. Article 290, on intentionally killing another, prescribes beheading with delay. See ibid., 276.

PART V

CONTROL OF POLITICALLY MARGINAL
GROUPS AND INDIVIDUALS

The Manchus established the Qing empire by the same means that all their Chinese predecessors had used, military conquest. Fighting continued sporadically for decades, first with local rebels and the armed remnants supporting Ming pretenders in Taiwan and southwestern China, next with breakaway commanderies in the south, and later with Central Asian peoples, the Mongols and their Turkic neighbors farther west, where fighting continued until 1784. Even long after the conquest was complete in China proper, the barest shred of evidence might provoke imperial fears of plots and uprisings, such as the "soulstealing" scare of the 1770s. Such fears provoked the empire's lack of tolerance for any religious movements not recognized by the state (see, for example Kuhn 1990). The following cases highlight official responses to marginal peoples, Zhuang at the frontiers of the empire and followers of the White Lotus Teachings (Bailian Jiao) at the fringes of Han society. Neither could have presented any real threat to the state at this time, although in nineteenth-century China, the Qing was nearly overthrown by a combination of the two: a marginalized ethnic group, the Hakka, led by a new type of religious leader, Hong Xiuquan (1814–1864), and his Christian Taiping Heavenly Kingdom (see Spence 1996).

A Village Vendetta and Han Intercession (Guangxi, 1728)

Conflicts over property rights became much more common during the eighteenth century as population growth, commercial development, and new production relationships in agriculture forced increases in the price of land. During the middle Qing, landowning was no longer seen as the inalienable right of the long-term occupants. Instead, real estate could be bought, sold, or, in this case, taken away from one group of people and assigned to another by local government; it could even be appropriated for public use.[1] This trend was particularly common throughout southern China during the eighteenth century.

In this case from 1728, two clans of the Zhuang people, the Zhou and the Tan, were feuding over the control of land and fields around a village that had changed hands several times within living memory.[2] Their long-simmering conflict resulted in a retaliatory raid on the village by the Zhous that incidentally left many Tans dead and which, in turn, brought further reprisals. After quoting the two original complaints in the case, the compilers of this report relied on unusually close cross-examination in order to trace the rivalry and its consequences in great detail. Judicial officials at all levels looked past the skein of reprisals in an effort to address the problem of land control. All proclaim that the deponents described the events in such detail that it was "as clear as a picture" (lili ruhui).

This case is remarkable for the use and threats of torture, especially the assertions of its efficacy in getting beyond claims and exaggerated counterclaims and arriving at facts on which all could agree. This extensive interrogation represents deliberate and self-conscious efforts to produce contrasting yet coherent and convincing narratives of chaotic events and conflicting motivations. Here, the Han investigators seek to apply terms that are familiar to them, rather than highlighting distinctly different Zhuang values. Apparently, they respect their traditional need to avenge the murder of one's father but generally distrust the validity of all Zhuang testimony. They also question the Zhuang code of honor that allows a leader to take all the blame and to claim ignorance that would allow others to escape, presumably never to be apprehended. Note, too, that judges ordered that financial compensation be paid only by family members of those who directly caused so much loss for the Tans—and not by the Zhou clan as a whole. In the final resolution of the dispute, both clans would be deprived of access to the land, many of the Zhous were banished, and the property in question would be used by the state to produce relief grain *for local emergencies.[3] See especially the provincial governor's summary, in which all pieces are neatly woven into a single narrative line.*

Your subject Deming, Grand Minister of the Deliberative Council, Minister of the Board of Punishments and other offices, with Additional Second Rank, Six Times Lauded, and so on, respectfully submits this MEMORIAL of explanation.

The Board of Punishments' Office of Scrutiny hereby copies a case submitted by Jin Hong, Governor of Guangxi, concerning a past event. According to a report submitted by Judicial Commissioner Yuan Zhancheng on an investigation of one Zhou Fuquan, age twenty-one *sui*, a Zhuang villager from Yishan District, the complaint reads:

"[Zhou] Fuquan is stupid by nature and ignorant of all rules and regulations. Because the criminal condemned to beheading Tan Hongfa—who escaped from prison after having been sentenced, fled, was recaptured, but fell ill and died between trials—had seized by force the farmland around the old stockade village [*zhaijiucun*] in Kangxi 56 [1717], burning to death Fuquan's own father Zhou Fengyang, his maternal uncle Zhou Fengzao, and Zhou Fenggui, the father of Zhou Wenqiang, who has been apprehended for examination but who died of illness on the way, and his own elder brother Zhou Diju, they all hated [Tan Hongfa] in their hearts.[4]

"On Yongzheng 6.1.3 [February 12, 1728], Wenqiang wrongfully plotted to get revenge. He wished to capture Tan Hongren so that he could take his life in repayment for the life of his father and to take control of the fields and houses in the stockade village. At first, he plotted with Fuquan, but Fuquan would not agree to comply. Zhou Wenqiang thereupon banded together with Zhou Fujiang, Zhou Fugun, Zhou Fuyang, Zhou Fuju, Lan Fujie, Zhou Fuhong, Meng Lao'er, Meng Laosan, Meng Laoliu, and Meng Laoqi (all of whom remain at large) as well as Zhou Shanhe (who has already been captured) and Zhou Fushou, Zhou Fuhai, and others (who had previously fled but were killed by Tan Zongsheng, who also fled). All of them wrongfully agreed to participate, and they set the night of 2.2 [March 12] of that year to make their move.

"When the date arrived, the whole band—fifteen in all—armed with spears or blades, gathered first at Cow Horn Pass. During the second watch, they went together to Hongren's residence in the stockade village to wait for the second cockcrow of the morning. During the fifth watch on the third, they cut through the bamboo palisade to the west of the village. Zhou Shanhe, Fuhong, Fushou, Fuhai, the four of them armed with machetes (*huandao*), stood guard outside, while Fuquan together with Zhou Wenqiang, Zhou Fujiang, Zhou Fugun, Zhou Fuyang, Zhou Fuju, Lan Fujie, Meng Lao'er, Meng Laosan, Meng Laoliu, and Meng Laoqi, eleven of them, entered the stockade. Because he did not know the whereabouts of Hongren, Wenqiang again wrongfully conceived the notion of leading his gang to set fire to the houses in order to capture him. Fuquan and the others again wrongfully went along with Wenqiang and set fires to burn down the houses. As a consequence, the old and young, men and women, if they were lying sick in bed or if they were sound asleep and did not awake, could not get out of their houses. Thus, Wei Hai, Tan Fudan, (Ms. Lu) Tai Nen, Tan Fuben, Tai Fumi, Luo Misong, Mrs. Tan Tai Xiang, Tan Fuli, and Tan Fuliang all died in the fire, together with Tan Liangfu who died from a fall—twelve lives in total were lost.

"At that time, Tan Fengtai and Wei Fengli rushed out of their houses. Again wrongfully, Wenqiang took them to be his enemies and slashed Wei Fengli across the right breast with his machete. Seeing that Tan Fengtai was carrying a club, Fuquan also wrongfully stabbed Fengtai in the midsection on the left side with his spear. Both expired."

Thereafter, Tan Hongren, a resident of Yongtai Hamlet, filed a complaint at the district magistrate's office. Yishan District reports that his petition concerned this great robbery and the killings, appealing to Heaven to exterminate the culprits in order to still the ghosts and settle the matter. Dated Yongzheng 6.2.11 [March 21, 1728], Yongtai Hamlet resident Tan Hongren's complaint reads as follows:

"Originally the stockade village of Lagao was the property of the Tan lineage. The previous district magistrate clearly granted my humble person the right to enter the village and to till and plant there in perpetuity, making no transgression thereby. We did not foresee that on 3.2 of this year, in the fifth watch of the morning, that we should run into the persons of Zhou Wenqiang, Zhou Fuhui, Fushou, Zhou Wenrong, Zhou Wenyi, Lan Guanggong, Wei Wenxiang, and Wei Fuzhong, who had tricked Wei Hanjing and Hanchen and others into maliciously setting fires, besieging us, killing fourteen, and injuring seven more who died. We did not expect that they would steal one horse, eighteen draft oxen, and thirteen storehouses of various food grains. By their own admission, Zhou Wenqiu and [Zhou] Wenzhuang had told them to do this; their leaders were clearly Wei Mingtai, Tan Zongsheng, and Tan Mingqiang. Just count our dead and wounded. In this peaceful and tranquil world, how can one allow such major criminals to go on a rampage, killing and injuring people in all directions, to belittle the laws of the land, and to disparage the ghosts of the people? Weeping with emotion,

I submit this complaint for your action. Capture and punish all the guilty parties; our fates are in your hands!"

Likewise, the magistrate [xunjian] of Desheng Market Subdistrict, Meng Jian, reported on these events to the district, and on the same day, Tan Fuxu, together with [Tan] Liangbi, Fuying, Fuxiao, and Funuan, reported on the murder of their innocent father, a most miserable affair: "Our father Tan Liangfu, on the night of the second of the first month of this year, took shelter for the night in the stockade village of Lagao. Unexpectedly, Zhou Wenqiang and others, leading a group of local barbarians, encircled the village and set fires there, killing countless people within. Our father and his manservant Wei Fuman were both among those killed. At present, the bodies are scattered and exposed; indeed it is a most grievous affair! The injustice of it all simply cannot be borne! We beg that you take charge of rectifying this matter."

When all of these matters had been reported to the district, Magistrate Zhang Mengbai secretly had Zhou Wenqiu imprisoned awaiting investigation and set out at once to the scene of the attack, accompanied by a coroner. There, he held a formal inquest on the bodies of the fourteen victims. Wei Fengli had been killed by a single deep cut from a dagger a few inches below his left nipple; Tan Fengtai had died from a stab wound just below his left kidney. The rest all burned to death; most were women and children. After giving the next of kin permission to prepare the bodies for burial and to encoffin them, the magistrate examined those who had been injured during the attack. These seven people all had suffered burns and abrasions fleeing from the conflagration. In addition, the fire had consumed seventeen houses and thirteen granaries; seven head of cattle had also died. The magistrate began his interrogations at the scene of the crime by asking Lagao village leader Tan Hongren:

"In your complaint, you said that Zhou Wenqiang and others told you that Zhou Wenqiu and Zhou Wenzhuang had ordered them to come here to do this. Precisely what was their reason for attacking you?"

[Tan Hongren] testified: "Our village was assigned to our Tan clan by your esteemed office. Likewise, your esteemed predecessors at the district and prefectural levels granted us the right to till this land in peace and to enjoy the grain we produce on it. Now Zhou Wenqiu, Zhou Wenzhuang, and the others told Zhou Wenqiang and the others to come kill us and burn us out to get revenge. I beg you to adjudicate this matter and to right this wrong."

Question: "If you were attacked at the fifth watch on the third of the month, then why did you wait until the eleventh to come file your complaint?"

[Tan Hongren] testified: "The bandits chased me, and I fell and hurt my leg. That's why I was late in filing."

I also questioned Tan Fuhu, Tan Fuchang, Tan Fubian, Tan Fuyou, Tan Fuhua, Luo Fudi, and others: "Why did Zhou Wenqiang and the others come to attack you that day? Who was it who set the fires to burn down your houses?"

They testified: "We were all hired by Tan Hongren to come here to work the fields. We've heard Tan Hongren say that this manor was granted to us by the government. He hired us to plant and to harvest. At the fifth watch on the third of this month, a fire suddenly broke out in the village, and there was shouting, 'Kill Tan Hongren!' We were startled awake, and we got up and fled for our lives. We beg you to take care of this matter."

I asked: "Was this a fire set outside that burned itself in, or was it a fire that accidentally spread from inside?"

They all testified: "We were all asleep, and we don't know where the fire started."

I asked: "At that time, did you see the village head Tan Hongren?"

They all testified: "We didn't see him ourselves; all we could think about was running for our lives."

I asked: "How many houses were burned down? How many bandits were there? Why were these several people not able to escape and so all burned to death?"

They all testified: "There were seventeen houses in the village, and they all burned down. Those who ran fast got out, but the sick folks, the women, and the children who were asleep when the fires burned down their houses, they couldn't get out. We heard somebody yelling 'Attack!' but we couldn't tell how many; maybe there were ten or twenty of them."

Later, the magistrate questioned Zhou Wenqiu, who was in custody and who had filed a countercomplaint concerning the reasons behind the attack. It states:

"In my grandfather's generation, we bought the fields around the two old stockade villages of Weirong and Lagao for twenty-six *liang*. Without warning, in Kangxi 22 [1683], we suffered the unprovoked occupation of our villages and fields by Tan Mingquan and Hongren, father and son. At that time, Zhou Jinhan, Zhou Guizheng, and others sued and got a settlement whereby the fields were returned to our ancestors, and we were given a certificate of authorization [from higher authorities]. Then, in Kangxi 34 [1695], we again suffered occupation by Tan Hongfa and others. We filed another complaint with all the details, and we were given the right to farm the fields in peace. We did not expect that in the ninth month of [Kangxi] 56 [October 1717], Tan Hongfa and others would suddenly round up a gang to attack and rob our village, killing four altogether. The case was investigated, and the evildoers were sentenced to death, but they escaped from prison. Now my clansmen Zhou Wenqiang and the others led a group of men to return to the village and seize the fields, but in the fight, many were killed. It was on the eleventh of this month that I went to town and was just walking past the district *yamen* when I was arrested. This is the first I heard of any details about getting revenge. Furthermore, on the day of the revenge attack, on the third of the month, I had gone to the district *yamen* to file a new registration [*na xinbian*]; all the clerks there will know that this has nothing to do with me. All you need to do is examine the facts; I fervently beg you to adjudicate this matter properly."

The magistrate then ordered troops out to find and apprehend all members of the Zhou gang and reported to his superior on the feud between the "Zhuang barbarian" (Zhuang Man) clans. At the prefectural level, by Yongzheng 6.3.1 [April 9, 1728], only Tan Wenzhuang had been captured, and he adamantly refused to admit to any knowledge of the affair. Working in cooperation with the district magistrate, the prefect secretly sent more constables to arrest more members of the gang. Then, on April 23, Zhou Wenqiang was apprehended and brought to the district yamen for questioning. He testified:

"Tan Hongren and Hongfa had in the past killed my and Zhou Fuquan's father and mother, the whole family, and had taken over our fields. We suffered destruction of our house and the loss of lives. We had to beg outside in order to eat. I felt such hatred in my heart that I wanted to get revenge. In the first month of this year, I came back to our house from Nandanchang and stayed in the village. On the thirtieth of the first month, Tan Hongren's hired farmhands Wei Fuquan and Wei Fuyan, the two of them, came to my house. They said, 'That Old Tan the Sixth from Nanxiang (i.e., Tan Liangfu) hired our six families to come to the village to plow and plant. And we helped him out. But now he wants to drive us away, a state of affairs that is hard to bear. We'd be willing to lend you a hand from inside.' So we talked it over, and some of them were willing to go with me to catch Tan Hongren and the others and take them to court to get justice. Originally, I said that I'd give eighty *liang* of silver to them if they could catch Tan Hongren, but they wanted half in advance. So that day, I personally gave them forty *liang* of silver, and on the second of the second month [March 12], we went to the temple to drink blood wine.[5]

"At that time, my clansmen from Si'en District, Zhou Fugun and Zhou Fujiang, the two of them, had come to see me. I made the agreement with Zhou Fuquan, Zhou Fujiang, and Zhou Fugun, the three of them and I made four, that on the night of the second, we would go to the stockade village along with Wei Fujuan and the others. Fu'en went into the village first; Fujuan and Fuyan then went in after him. We were still afraid to go in, but when we saw fires starting up on all sides and the attack going on everywhere, only then did we go into the village, and we killed two people at random. By that time, Tan Hongren and the others had got away, and we couldn't catch them. All of the ones who were injured were from those newly hired six families of farmworkers. Of the people from there, one was not wounded; he was burned by the fire we set. The fire spread and killed several sick people, and some kids as well."

Question: "Tan Hongren's complaint states that you had recruited a number of people, some named Lan and some named Wei. Why are you testifying that there were only four of you?"

[Zhou Wenqiang] testified: "Tan Hongren exaggerated in his complaint. Since I came forth to be questioned about this crime, as I ought to do, if there were people from the Lan and Wei clans, why would I not report this openly? At the time that Wei Fujuan and the others came to my house to discuss taking action together, I agreed to go into the village with Zhou Fuquan and the others, the three of them. If we had any hope of success, we certainly could not use many people. And that is the truth."

Question: "You called people together to capture Tan Hongren, and yet you dragged in the plowmen from his village to serve as your accomplices to work on the inside. Clearly, this is an attempt to trump up some way of avoiding punishment for the crime yourself. What proof do you have that they were your accomplices?"

[Zhou Wenqiang] testified: "Originally, when Wei Fujuan and the others came to discuss being our accomplices, they said that if they captured Tan Hongren, I should give them eighty *liang* of silver. If they hadn't acted as our accomplices, given how tightly fortified that village is, how would we ever have gotten in? Government soldiers and officials have all seen how that village is. I beg you to arrest Wei Fuquan and the others and question them. They'll explain."

I asked: "Were Zhou Wenqiu and Zhou Wenzhuang working with you at the scene of the crime?"

[Zhou Wenqiang] testified: "They live outside the wall of the prefectural city; they were never at the scene."

I asked: "If they were never at the scene, why did the Tan family accuse them?

[Zhou Wenqiang] testified: "Some years ago, when Tan Hongfa, Tan Hongren, and Tan Hongzhao raided us, it was Zhou Wenqiu and his brother who came forward to lay the complaint against them. That is why he named Wenqiu in the complaint. The day of the incident, Zhou Wenqiu and Zhou Wenzhuang knew nothing at all about it. And that's the truth."

At this point, the magistrate summoned the plaintiff Tan Hongren to court for interrogation, but Tan refused to comply and went into hiding. Only on Yongzheng 6.6.26 (August 1) did he appear in court to testify. Since there was no way to proceed without a plaintiff, deadlines for the resolution of the case were repeatedly extended, involving all judicial officials up to and including the provincial governor. Magistrate Zhang's interrogation follows.

Interrogation of Tan Hongren: "Where are you from, what is your age, and what is the reason you repeatedly refused our summons to appear in court?"

[Tan Hongren] testified: "I am a Zhuang from Yongtai Hamlet, and I am seventy *sui* in age. I've been very ill in my old age. When the Zhou clan was chasing after me to kill me, I fell and hurt my back. I have been recuperating at the Lenggang area in Yongshun Subdistrict. I was also afraid that the Zhou clan would be looking for me in order to kill me. This is why I have been secretly hiding and would not come out for interrogation. This is the truth."

Question: "Altogether, how many houses are there in the stockade village where you live?"

[Tan Hongren] testified: "Altogether, the stockade village has seventeen houses."

Question: On the eleventh of the second month of this year, you filed a complaint stating that at cockcrow in the fifth watch of the morning of the third of the second month, Zhou Wenqiang and [eleven other names are listed here] came to the stockade village of Lagao, where they burned and killed Tan Fengtai and [all the other victims are named], altogether fourteen lives, along with one horse, eighteen head of cattle, and thirteen granaries. According to this district's investigation, Tan Fengtai died of a spear wound, and Wei Fengli was killed by a knife wound. Wei Hai and the other eleven people were all burned to death. Tan Liangfu fell all by himself and died as a result. At that time, the district magistrate granted your request to enshroud Liangfu without inspection. Why does your complaint state that fourteen were killed?"

[Tan Hongren] testified: "Even though Wei Hai and the other eleven were burned to death and even though Tan Liangfu fell and died from it, all of them were burned to death or died from a fall only because they set fire to our houses. That's why I complained that they had killed all of them."

Question: "Did you have any previous grudge against the Zhou clan?"

[Tan Hongren] testified: "We did have a grudge against the Zhou clan; that is true. The thirty-seven *mu* of fields around the stockade village of Lagao worth fifteen *liang* of silver originally belonged to our ancestors.[6] But the Zhou family took control of them. Later, in Kangxi 56 [1717], when my clansman Tan Hongfa took some men to recover our property, they burned and killed several members of their Zhou lineage. This year, on the third of the second month during the fifth watch of the morning, we were again attacked by Zhou Wenqiang and the others; Tan Fengtai and the others died of wounds, burns, or falls, fourteen of them altogether. Your Lordship has examined all of this. They also stole a horse, eighteen head of cattle, and thirteen granaries of grain. This is the truth."

Question: "In his previous testimony, Zhou Wenqiang testified that your field hands Wei Fujuan and Wei Fuyan, the two of them, were accomplices who led them into the village. Is this really true?"

[Tan Hongren] testified: "This is Zhou Wenqiang's evil plan to absolve himself of guilt in this crime by implicating them. If in fact they had been in on it, I would certainly have included them in my complaint. Why would I be willing to stand up for them? That "Wei Fuyan" is really Wei Fuge, and that "Wei Fujuan" is really Wei Yingchun. That was nothing but Zhou Fuqiang's attempt to cover up his own crime by implicating them."

Question: "How do you know that Wei Yingchun and the other man were not accomplices in these crimes?"

[Tan Hongren] testified: "Wei Yingchun and the others lived next door to me, so all of their possessions were burned up and their livestock was stolen, too. And the Wei Fengli who was killed was Wei Fuge's uncle. He had just that night gone to their house to pass the night, and yet he was killed. How could they have been talked into burning up their own property and killing their own uncle? I beg you to get to the bottom of this."

Question: "If they had no accomplices to let them in, how did they get into your stockade that night?"

[Tan Hongren] testified: "That was the night we country people have our annual festival, and we were all drunk. They got in by digging a hole through the bamboo palisade on the west side."

Question: "What time did the fire start that night? Did they kill people first or set fires first? How many voices did you hear from Zhou Wenqiang and the others? How many did you see with your own eyes? Did you recognize any of them? Tell the truth."

[Tan Hongren] testified: "The cocks had just crowed the second time in the fifth watch that night when I heard shouts to attack. I was startled awake, and I went to the door of my house, and I saw that houses were on fire. At that time, I quickly ran out of the stockade. Whether they set the fires first or killed people first, I don't know. And as for how many people there were, I was not able to see."

Question: "Since you didn't see, why did you initially file a complaint against Zhou Fuhui and so many others?"

[Tan Hongren] testified: "The people I listed all had a grudge against me. Now if somebody comes to kill me, how could it be anybody but that gang of people?"

Question: "How did you know that Zhou Wenqiang was their leader?"

[Tan Hongren] testified: "He often told people that he wanted to come and kill us. That's how I know he was the leader."

Question: "You said it was Tan Hongfa who led people to recover your property. Why is it you who are living in the stockade village?"

[Tan Hongren] testified: "Tan Hongfa is my brother. The previous magistrate Zhang called me in to manage the receipt of money and grain, and he let me live here as a reward."

Question: "What proof do you have of that?"

[Tan Hongren] testified: "Originally, I had a deed [*paipiao*], but now it's burned up."

Question: "Tan Fuhua and the others who were injured, have they all recovered?"

[Tan Hongren] testified: "They have already recovered."

Magistrate Zhang then interrogated Tan Fuxu about the death of his father Tan Liangfu, who had been visiting the village on the night of the attack. His father had already been encoffined by the time he arrived, Fuxu testified, and he had no oppor-

tunity to see any wound that might have caused his parent's death. Then the magistrate turned his questioning to the ringleader of the Zhou gang.

Question to Zhou Wenqiang: "Where are you from, how old are you, and do you have a wife and children?"

[Zhou Wenqiang] testified: "I am thirty *sui* this year, and I have no wife or children. I am a Zhuang from Yongtai Hamlet."

Question: "Tan Hongren and the others have filed a complaint that during the fifth watch on the morning of the third of the second month of Yongzheng 6, you led a group of men to the stockade village of Lagao, where you killed or burned to death fourteen of their men and women and stole a horse, eighteen head of cattle, and thirteen granaries of grain. Is it true that you were the leader?"

[Zhou Wenqiang] testified: "I was the one who first had the idea to go there to do it, that's true."

Question: "Why did you want to go kill so many people?"

[Zhou Wenqiang] testified: "The fields around the stockade village were originally the property of our Zhou ancestors. During the ninth month of Kangxi 56, Tan Hongfa, Tan Hongren, and the others led their brothers, their sons, and their nephews—several tens of those brigands—to attack the village and to burn to death my father Zhou Fenggui and my older brother Zhou Di and to occupy our village and our fields. His Lordship the IMPERIAL commissioner investigated Tan Hongfa on the blood feud [*diming*], but later Tan Hongfa again escaped from prison and fled. So I took a group of men to take revenge."

Question: "How many men did you take? What were their names?"

[Zhou Wenqiang] testified: "One was Zhou Fuquan. His father Zhou Fengyang and his maternal uncle Zhou Fengchao were both burned to death by Tan Hongfa that year. There was also Zhou Fugun, Zhou Fujiang, Zhou Fuyang, Zhou Fuju, Lan Fujie, Zhou Shanhe, Zhou Fuhong, Zhou Fushou, and Zhou Fuhai. They were all living in the stockade village at the time the Tan clan occupied it. That's why I made an agreement with the ten of them. I also recruited Meng Lao'er, Meng Laosan, Meng Laoliu, and Meng Laoqi. Including me, we made fifteen in total. Fujiang, Fugun, Fuyang, Fuju: I sent Lan Fujie to go recruit them. Fuhong, Fuxhou, Fuhai: I sent Zhou Shanhe to go recruit them. I sent a letter to the four brothers of the Meng family; they agreed to join only after I promised them fields to work if they came back to live in the village."

Question: "Fujiang and Fugun, along with Meng Lao'er and the others, thirteen in all—where are they from? Where have they gone now? Tell me about them, one by one."

Zhou Wenqiang lists all their places of residence and concludes:

"I don't know where they have gone by now. Being locked up here in prison, I don't know their whereabouts."

Question: "Where did you assemble that night? What time was it when you went to the stockade village? How did you get into the village?"

[Zhou Wenqiang] testified: "We had accomplices inside the village, Wei Yingchun and Wei Fuge, who agreed to let us in. On that night, we were outside listening while they set a fire inside as a signal that they were opening the main gate, and only then could we get in."

Question: "Once you got in, how did you set fires and kill people?"

[Zhou Wenqiang] testified: "It was our accomplices who set the fires that burned people; only after that did they open the gate and let us in."

Question: "Previously, you testified that your accomplices were Wei Fujuan and Wei Fuyan, two of them. Why do you now give two men's names that don't correspond?"

He testified: "Wei Fujuan is really Wei Yingchun; Wei Fuyan is the same as Wei Fuge. There were only two of them; that's the truth."

Question: "So according to you, what sort of men are Wei Yingchun and Wei Fuge—why would they want to act as accomplices for you?"

He testified: "Originally, they were recruited by Tan Hongren to work the fields in the stockade village of Lagao. Then he recruited others who fought with them over land to cultivate. They knew that there was a blood feud between me and Tan Hongren, and so they came and asked me for silver. They said that they wanted to be my accomplices. So I promised that I would certainly give them forty *liang* of silver if they would capture Tan Hongren and turn him over to me so that I could get revenge for my father's death. They took my silver and became my accomplices."

Question: "How many times did you give them silver?"

[Zhou Wenqiang] testified: "Only on the second of the second month."

Question: "According to your previous testimony, on the second of the second month, when you gave them the silver and drank blood wine with them, [Zhou] Fugun and [Zhou] Fujiang came to see you, and so you told them to go off together. Why do you now say that you had summoned Fugun and the others to come?"

He testified: "Originally, I had made an agreement that they should come; that's the truth."

Question: "According to what you've said, Wei Fuge and Wei Yingchun, the two of them, were your accomplices. Could it be that they set fires and killed people with you as well?"

[Zhou Wenqiang] testified: "It was the accomplices who first set fires and killed people. Only then did we enter the village."

Question: "Wei Yingchun and Wei Fuge were natives of that stockade village. How could it be that they would set fires and kill people themselves and only then open the gate to let you in? Weren't they afraid that the people of the stockade would see them? Furthermore, according to what you've said, originally you agreed for them only to capture Tan Hongren alive. So later, why did they not capture Hongren and instead kill and burn to death so many bystanders? Clearly you're trying to shift the blame. If you don't confess truthfully, I'll have to squeeze you."

He testified: "The truth is that the two of them were our accomplices. They set fires and killed people. It was nearly daylight when we got into the stockade."

Question: "Since you will not testify truthfully, I'll begin the squeezing."

During torture, [Zhou Wenqiang] testified: "Truly it was our accomplices who first set the fires and killed people. Only then did we get in."

Question: "If you persist in refusing to speak truthfully, I'll squeeze the truth out of you."

He testified: "I beg you to release the instruments; I'll speak truthfully. On the third of the first month of this year, I made the agreement with Zhou Fuquan at his house. On the twenty-eighth of the first month, I set the date with him to be the second of the second month, the day of our local holiday festival. We assumed Tan Hongren would surely be in the stockade getting drunk, and it would be easy to make our move and catch him. I also agreed with Zhou Fujiang and the rest of the fourteen that we would get together on the second of the second month at Cow Horn Pass, behind the Lali Temple, ten miles from the stockade. Afterward, Zhou Fuquan and the others, one after the other, did arrive there. At the second watch, we all went to the stockade village, where we could hear that people inside were still drinking and singing songs. We didn't dare make our move. Then finally, at the fifth watch, we dug through the bamboo palisade on the west of the stockade and got in. All of us set fires and burned houses. And by accident, we burned to death several people. That's the truth."

Question: "Who was it that dug through the bamboo palisade? After you dug through, who went into the stockade first?"

[Zhou Wenqiang] testified: "Everybody dug at it, but when we got through, I was the one who went in first. Meng Lao'er together with Zhou Fuquan, Zhou Fujiang, Zhou Fugun, and the others all went in with me. We left only Zhou Shanhe, Zhou Fuhong, Zhou Fushou, and Zhou Fuhai, the four of them, to keep watch outside."

Question: "What weapons did each of you take into the stockade?"

He testified: "I carried a spear and a dagger. Fuquan carried a spear and a knife. Fujiang, Fugun, Fuyang, Fuju, and Lan Fujie all carried firearms.[7] Zhou Shanhe, Zhou Fuhong, Zhou Fushou, and Zhou Fuhai all carried machetes. Meng Lao'er, Meng Laosan, Meng Laoliu, and Meng Laoqi all carried spears."

Question: "Tan Hongren's complaint states that a large number of you went along. Why do you testify that there were only fifteen of you?"

He testified: "That's true, that's true: there were only fifteen of us who went with me. There was no one else at all."

Question: "The complaint of Tan Hongren and the others states that Zhou Fuhui, Zhou Wenrong, Zhou Wenyi, Lan Guangtai, Wei Wenxiang, Wei Fuzhong, Wei Hanjing, and Wei Hanchen set fires and attacked the village. When you got into the village, you shouted that Zhou Wenqiu and Zhou Wenzhuang and others had told you to do it. Why haven't you testified about even one of them?"

[Zhou Wenqiang] testified: "Of those people named in the complaint, Zhou Fuhui—who is really Zhou Fuhai—and Zhou Fushou, the two of them, went along with me. Of the others—Zhou Wenrong, Zhou Wenyi, Lan Guangtai, Wei Wenxiang, Wei Fuzhong, Wei Hanjing, Wei Hanchen, Zhou Wenqiu, Zhou Wenzhuang, and the rest—not a one of them knew anything about it. None of them went with us. We never said that Zhou Wenqiu and Zhou Wenzhuang told us to do it. I don't dare to make up a false story."

Question: "What relation are that Zhou Wenqiu and Zhou Wenzhuang to you?"

[Zhou Wenqiang] testified: "Both Wenqiu and Wenzhuang are my clan brothers."

Question: "Why did the two of them originally discuss getting revenge with you?"

He testified: "The two of them never discussed it with me. I never let them know about it. The plan to go to avenge my father was all my own. It had nothing to do with them."

Question: "All the complaints filed by your Zhou clan through the years were in the names of Zhou Wenqiu and Zhou Wenzhuang. Now, when you go to get revenge, it's not at all their idea. How could you dare go and do this without informing them?"

He testified: "Because Wenqiu and Wenzhuang are my clan brothers, they also have grudges against the Tan family. But in spite of all the complaints they've filed through the years, they've never succeeded in winning back our village and our fields. Instead they just wasted money. I can't stop laughing at them. I've had fights with them and can't stay on good terms with them. That's why each of us minds his own business. I never discussed it with them, and that's the truth."

Question: "Later, of the people you went to do this with, with whom did you discuss it first?"

[Zhou Wenqiang] testified: "During the first month of this year, I started discussing it with Zhou Fuquan. It was only afterward that I sent Lan Fujie to go and get Zhou Fujiang and Zhou Fugun to discuss it with them. Only after all three of them agreed did I enlist Zhou Fuyang, Zhou Fuju, and the rest of them."

Question: "In what terms did you discuss it with Zhou Fuquan, Zhou Fujiang, and Zhou Fugun?"

He testified: "It was always a matter of getting revenge, and that was that."

Question: "Although it was a matter of getting revenge, what man did you want to go kill?"

He testified: "Our original plan was to take Tan Hongren alive and make him pay for my father's life with his own. The others we just wanted to chase out and not let them live in the village."

Question: "If all you wanted to do was to take Hongren alive, then why did you set fires, burn houses, kill and burn to death so many bystanders?"

He testified: "Once we got into the stockade, we didn't know where Hongren lived, and there was no way of catching him, so I told Zhou Fuquan and the others to set fires and burn houses and wait for him to run out so that it would be easy to catch him and tie him up. I never thought when I was setting fires that some of the people in this stockade would not be able to escape and that they'd be burned to death. That had nothing to do with us."

Question: "At first, how did you get fire? What did you use to set the fires? Who started setting fires first?"

He testified: "For torches, we just grabbed some straw from the piles beside the stockade. I set them on fire with some igniting paper; that was it."

Question: "Did you start the fires wanting to burn people to death?"

[Zhou Wenqiang] testified: "All we wanted to do was burn the houses so that Hongren and the others would all run out. We never intended to burn people to death. It was just because some of them couldn't get themselves out that they burned to death."

Question: "Was setting fires something you personally thought up as a way to burn the houses?"

He testified: "Originally, we never wanted to start fires or burn houses. That's something I thought up on the spot when we got into the stockade and couldn't find [Tan] Hongren."

Question: "Originally, your father was burned to death when Tan Hongfa set fires. How did you expect to get revenge by capturing Hongren?"

He testified: "Even though the ringleader who originally killed my father and my uncle was Tan Hongfa, Hongren was on the inside, helping him to kill them."

Question: "I've examined the original [1717] case report, and Hongren's name does not appear in it. Why do you now say that Hongren played a part in killing your father?"

He testified: "Hongren is Hongfa's younger brother. If he hadn't played a part from the beginning in killing and stealing, then how could he come to occupy our stockade village and our farms afterward?"

Question: "According to your testimony, at first Hongren ganged up with Hongfa to burn your father to death. Why were neither of your names mentioned in the original complaint?"

[Zhou Wenqiang]: "At that time, I was still very young and didn't put my name on the complaint. I beg you to interrogate Zhou Fenggui. It was my father; if [Tan Hongren] wasn't involved, then he [Zhou Fenggui] would know."

Question: "I have consulted the earlier case report of Kangxi 56 [1717], which states that Tan Hongfa led a gang to burn and kill your clan. It had been submitted to the IMPERIAL commissioner, who investigated and transferred the houses and fields to Tan Hongfa. How could you say that he had occupied them by force?"

[Zhou Wenqiang]: "This was our ancestral property. It was taken away and given to the Tan family; we'd resist that to the death."

Question: "How many did you kill that night in Tan Hongfa's stockade? Who started the killing?"

He testified: "We never killed anybody; they all burned to death in the fire."

Question: "At the time of the [original] district magistrate's investigation, besides Tan Liangfu—who had died from a fall and whose family had already enshrouded him in order to avoid an inquest—Wei Hai, and the others, eleven lives in all were lost in the fire; this is true. But there's still Tan Fengji, who died of stab wounds from a spear. And Wei Fengli was hacked to death with a knife. Why do you still testify that you never killed anyone? If you don't tell the truth, I will start squeezing you again!"

[Zhou Wenqiang]: "I can't deceive you on this; let me tell you the truth. At that time, we ran into a man who suddenly came out of a door and caught sight of us. We were afraid he would resist us, so we hacked him just once with a knife, and he fell down on the ground. And there was another man, who was carrying a wooden club and rushed out from a house; Zhou Fuquan stabbed him with his spear, and he fell down. This is also the truth."

Question: "The magistrate's examination showed that the one who was hacked to death, Wei Fengli, was slashed below the right nipple. The one who was stabbed to death, Tan Fengtai, was stabbed in the left kidney region. Did both of them have a feud with you?"

[Zhou Wenqiang]: "Normally, we wouldn't have even recognized each other; there was no feud between us."

Question: "If you had no grudge against them, why did you kill them?"

He testified: "At that time, they rushed out of their houses, one after the other. We were scared that they were coming to kill us; that's the only reason that we attacked and killed them."

Question: "As for Wei Hai and the others who were burned to death, they all lived in the same village. Could it be that you had a feud with them, too?"

[Zhou Wenqiang]: "As for those people who burned to death, I never even knew who they were; there was no feud."

Question: "Did Wei Hai and the others have a feud with Zhou Fuquan and the others?"

[Zhou Wenqiang]: "Zhou Fuquan and the others never had any feud with Wei Hai and those people."

Question: "This was just your doing on your own account to get revenge! Why do you slander Wei Yingchun and Wei Fuge by calling them your accomplices inside the stockade?"

[Zhou Wenqiang]: "The two of them now occupy our village and farms. I hate them so much I couldn't help dragging them into it. That's the truth."

Question: "So in fact those two were not your accomplices?"

[Zhou Wenqiang]: "It's true that those two were not our accomplices."

Question: "How many livestock and how much grain did you pillage there?"

[Zhou Wenqiang]: "We never took away any of their livestock, but I saw that eight head of cattle were burned to death. The grain was also destroyed by the fire. Later, when I went to look, I saw that they were all empty granaries that had never had any grain in them, so we never got anything from them. That's the truth."

Question: "In Tan Hongren's complaint, he said that you had stolen one horse and eighteen cattle as well as the grain from thirteen granaries. Why do you testify that there were only seven or eight cattle burned to death and that the granaries were all burned up?"

[Zhou Wenqiang]: "This is all a story made up by Tan Hongren."

After this extended questioning of one of the principals in the case, Magistrate Zhang tried to corroborate the details through further interrogations.

Interrogation of Zhou Fuquan: "Where are you from, how old are you, and have you a wife and children?"

[Zhou Fuquan]: "I am a Zhuang from Yongtai Hamlet. I'm twenty *sui* and have neither wife nor child."

Question: "In the beginning, how did you come to discuss going to burn out and kill the Tan family? Whose idea was it?"

[Zhou Fuquan]: "In Kangxi 56, Tan Hongren occupied our village and farms and killed my father Zhou Fengyang and my uncle Zhou Fengchao. Zhou Wenqiang knew that I always hated them in my heart. On the third of the first month of Yongzheng 6, Zhou Wenqiang came to my house to discuss taking revenge. I said we didn't have anybody to help. But Wenqiang said, 'If you are willing to go with me, then of course I'll go get some others to help us.' When I heard that we would have help, then I agreed. Then on the twenty-eighth of the first month, Wenqiang came again and told me that he had set the night of the second of the second month as the date for us to act and that we were to meet at Cow Horn Pass. Then, on the second, I went to Cow Horn Pass, and sure enough, I saw that Zhou Wenqiang was already there, and Zhou Fujiang and the others showed up one after another. When the second watch came around, we all went to the front of the stockade village. Since we could hear that there were still people awake and drinking inside, none of us made a move. It was only at cockcrow that we dug a way through the bamboo palisade and everybody went inside. Since we couldn't get Hongren to come out, Wenqiang said that if we set fires and burned the houses, we should not worry that he wouldn't come out. So each of us went to get some straw and set fires to burn the houses. I never thought that we wouldn't catch Hongren after all and that so many of the people sleeping in the houses would be burned to death. This was all Zhou Wenqiang's idea."

Question: "Originally, the one who burned your father and uncle to death was Tan Hongfa. Why do you say that Tan Hongren killed your father and uncle?"

[Zhou Fuquan]: "I was only nine *sui* old when my father and uncle were killed, and so I didn't know. It was only because Wenqiang told me that Hongren had helped Hongfa kill my father that I went along with him to get revenge."

The magistrate then sought to ascertain the number and composition of the Zhou raiding party. Zhou Fuquan confirmed Zhou Wenqiang's account; Fuquan also confirmed who had recruited the others.

Question: "And why were these people all willing to go along with you to get revenge?"

[Zhou Fuquan]: "Zhou Fujiang and the others originally lived with us in the stockade village. And all of them had been robbed by the Tan family. Meng Lao'er and those four came along only because Wenqiang had promised to give them land to work if we got our village and fields back."

Question: "Tan Hongren's complaint mentioned Zhou Fuhui and others. Why didn't you mention them?"

[Zhou Fuquan]: "Of the people he names in his complaint, only Zhou Fushou and Zhou Fuhui, who is Zhou Fuhai, went along. The rest of them didn't."

Question: "How did Zhou Wenqiu and Zhou Wenzhuang discuss this with you at first?"

[Zhou Fuquan]: "This happened because Zhou Wenqiang and I wanted to get revenge. Wenqiu and Wenzhuang had filed complaints lately, but nothing came of it. So we didn't get them involved. That's why they didn't know anything about it."

Question: "Then there were Wei Yingjuan and Wei Fuge, who took your forty *liang* of silver to be your spies inside. Why didn't you testify about them?"

[Zhou Fuquan]: "It was Zhou Wenqiang who said that. I never saw that; it never happened."

Magistrate Zhang then asked about weapons carried by the raiders and each person's separate role in the attack. Zhou Fuquan concludes:

"I set fires, too. That's the truth."

Question: "How many people did you kill and wound? Who among your gang killed and wounded people?"

[Zhou Fuquan]: "That night, only Zhou Wenqiang ran into a man, and he hacked him down with his sword. I saw a man carrying a wooden club rush out of a house; I stabbed him once with my spear, and he fell down. I didn't kill or wound anybody else."

[Question]: "The spear and the knife you carried then—where are they now?"

[Zhou Fuquan]: "I still carry the spear. I lost the knife, but I don't know where."

Question: "When you were first discussing it, which person did you want to kill to get revenge?"

[Zhou Fuquan]: "The original plan was to capture Tan Hongren alive and take him to court to make him pay for my father's life and to get our stockade back. But when we got inside the stockade, we didn't know where Hongren lived. That's why Wenqiang told us to set houses on fire and wait for him to come out so we could catch him. These are the true facts."

In response to a question about why so many bystanders were killed, Zhou Fuquan replied:

"The rest of them died because they couldn't get out and were burned to death by the fire. Nobody wanted to burn them to death. Nobody knew how Tan Hongren could have escaped without our catching him. That's the truth."

Question: "Zhou Fujiang and the other ten or so people—where are they now?"

[Zhou Fuquan]: "I don't know where they've all gotten to now."

Magistrate Zhang next interrogated the alleged Zhou accomplices within the stockade.

Interrogation of Wei Yingchun (who is Wei Fujuan): "Where are you from, and how old are you? Where have you been living? What do you do for a living?"

[Wei Yingchun]: "I am from Da'an Village in the Luoxi area; this year I am thirty-eight *sui*. In Yongzheng 2, Tan Hongren hired me to come to the stockade village to live and to work the fields with him."

Question: "Since you were hired by Tan Hongren to farm, and if, as Zhou Wenqiang testified, you served as accomplices, why did you let Zhou Wenqiang and the rest in to raid the village?"

[Wei Yingchun]: "Zhou Wenqiang is just falsely accusing me. Now I farm Tan Hongren's fields, and I live in Tan Hongren's house. Why should I let Zhou Wenqiang in to raid my own village?"

Question: "He said that, because you had argued over the farmwork, you and Wei Fuge were willing to serve as accomplices and that you had received his forty *liang* of silver as down payment. Will you still not confess? Must I make use of the instruments of torture before you will confess?"

[Wei Fuquan]: "If I had received silver from him—even if I had received four *qian*, much less forty *liang* of silver—we would still need to have a witness. I beg you to ask him where it was that he gave me the silver and who acted as the witness. I am willing to risk a death penalty on this."

Question: "He did not make empty accusations [*fengying*] about people from other families, and so they have not been implicated. Why should he implicate you two? If you don't confess, I will squeeze you."

[Wei Fuquan]: "He hates us. We farm the fields with Tan Hongren, and we live in the stockade village. He wasn't able to kill us that night, so he's trying to do us in by this means—it's just a part of his original plan."

Question: "Your stockade was so tight—if there had been no accomplices to let them in, how could they get inside?"

[Wei Fuquan]: "We in the stockade deserved defeat [*gai bai*]. Everybody was drunk on festival wine that night, and I don't know how they broke through our bamboo palisade to get inside. By the fifth watch, they had set fires on all sides, burning houses. Tan Liangfu died from a fall, and Tan Fengtai and Wei Fengli were killed. And another eleven men and women, young and old, were burned to death. My wife and I were fortunate; we were startled awake early and fled for our lives, but all of our property and things were burned up. If we had acted as accomplices, why would Tan Hongren let us off? I beg you to consider the details."

The magistrate clarified other details about Wei's movements during the confusion, and what he saw happening, and then asked about Tan losses in cattle and grain.

[Wei Fuquan]: "Truly, altogether we lost eighteen head of cattle and one horse, but afterward, one by one, we found most of them. Only eight cattle were burned to death. And of our thirteen thatch-roofed granaries, three were filled with lime and had no grain. Of the other ten, some held three *dan*, some two *dan*, and some one *dan*. In total, about forty *dan* of grain were burned up. That's the truth."

Question: "In the whole stockade, how many houses were burned up?"

[Wei Fuquan]: "There were only seventeen in the whole stockade. All of our thatched houses were burned down by Zhou Wenqiang and the others."

Thereafter, Magistrate Zhang interrogated Wei Fuge [Wei Fuyan] and got virtually the same responses to similar questions. Fuge was from the same village as Wei Fuchun, but was forty-four sui, a little older. He, too, insisted that Zhou Wenqiang had tried to implicate him because he was working for Zhou's enemy. Wei Fengli, one of those who had been killed during the raid, was Wei Fuge's uncle, who had come to the village the previous day to treat eye diseases there. He, too, explained the success of the raid as the result of everyone's drunkenness in the stockade; the previous day had been the local earth festival, and everyone participated in the celebration. He himself had only barely escaped the flames. He and his wife had fled to the south along with Tan Hongren. He confirmed the losses to the village that Wei Fuchun had identified.

Thereafter, the magistrate questioned the two Zhou clan elders about their role in the raid.

Interrogation of Zhou Wenqiu: "Where are you from, where have you been living, and what is your age?"

[Zhou Wenqiu]: "I am fifty-three *sui* this year, and originally I am from the stockade village in the Yongtai area. It was only in Kangxi 61 that I came to live in First Village in the Luoying area.

Question: "In their complaint, Tan Hongren, Tan Fuxu, and the others claim that you and Zhou Wenzhuang masterminded the raid on their stockade led by Zhou Wenqiang on the second of the second month of this year. What was your original plan? You must tell the truth; otherwise I will apply the instruments of torture."

[Zhou Wenqiu]: "Because Tan Hongren had occupied our homes and farms, Zhou Wenzhuang and I time after time filed complaints against him. But later, because none of our complaints were ever resolved, we moved to First Village near the city wall. Even though Zhou Wenqiang is of the same clan, we have not been on good terms of late, and for the last two years, we've had nothing to do with each other. On the day he went to take revenge, I was still in the city paying my land taxes and knew nothing at all about what he was doing. This is all because Tan Hongren and I are enemies to the death. He knew that because I live outside the city, I could not be falsely accused of anything else, so he accused the two of us of being the masterminds in order to do us in."

Question: "By your own account, you time after time filed complaints against him—of course you are the masterminds. If you don't confess, I will squeeze you."

[Zhou Wenqiu]: "Both of them wanted to get revenge in order to avenge their fathers' deaths. This was not at all my idea. I beg you to look into the details."

Question: "You and Zhou Wenqiang are members of the same clan. And you're both enemies to the death of Tan Hongren. Supposing it was not your idea originally, surely they must have come to inform you before they took action?"

[Zhou Wenqiu]: "He never informed me at all. In truth, I knew nothing about it. I beg you to ask Zhou Wenqiang and Zhou Fuquan, and then you'll understand."

The magistrate's interrogation of Zhou Wenzhuang followed a similar line of questioning. This elder was fifty sui in age, and he lived with Zhou Wenqiu. The magistrate did apply torture to him, but he, too, swore that he had not even been consulted in advance about the raid.

At this, the magistrate returned to questioning their accuser Tan Hongren, pressing him on why he had reported that so many others were involved in the raiding party.

". . . How could you create such lies as that Zhou Wenqiu and others told them to carry this out?"

[Tan Hongren]; "In fact, that first list I drew up was based on speculation. I didn't see them all with my own eyes. Nor did I hear them call out names with my own ears. That's the truth. Since Zhou Wenqiang has admitted that he was the leader, I beg you to get to the bottom of it with him, and that will be that."

The magistrate then proceeded to question Tan's initial claims about the extent of the losses in the village, noting that Zhou Wenqiang and the others all testified that it was never their intention to steal cattle or grain from the village. He also reiterated the testimony of Tan's own employees that most of the cattle had subsequently been found, having strayed during the confusion attending the fire. For his part, Tan immediately backed down from his earlier claims, asking instead only that the village be compensated for its real losses. Then the magistrate asked whether those who died in the raid had been involved in Tan Hongfa's earlier raid when the Zhou clan occupied the village.

[Tan Hongren]: "Wei Hai and the rest of those eleven who burned to death—I had recently hired them all to come and work at the stockade. Tan Fentai, Wei Fengli, and Tan Liangfu, who were stabbed, slashed, or knocked down to their deaths, had all just recently come to our village to stay for short periods. Tan Fengtai and Tan Liangfu had come to see me, and Wei Fengli had come to treat eye problems here. None of them had been involved in the raid on the Zhou family, nor were they enemies of the Zhous."

Tan Hongren also admitted that many other people named in the original complaint as having suffered were seasonal workers, hired for plowing and planting, who had moved on to work elsewhere before this raid.

In his report, Magistrate Zhang Mengbai recorded in more detail the history of the land dispute, all of which is summarized in the provincial governor's report below, concluding:

From this time onward, they struggled constantly for control, with unending blood feuds [*zhengzhan wuchang, chousha buyi*].

After consideration of all the relevant facts, Magistrate Zhang concluded that because Tan Hongren had not been named in the case that sentenced his brother to death for killing their fathers, Zhou Wenqiang and Zhou Fuquan could not use the excuse of avenging their fathers as rationale for their murderous attack on the stockade. The attack had been a function of the "wild, violent nature [yexing xiongcan] of the Miao and the Zhuang," and all involved should be sentenced to decapitation. Even though the motivation was revenge and not robbery, he recommended that the Zhous be ordered to compensate the residents of the stockade fully for their lost houses, granaries, grain, and cattle.[8]

The investigation having been completed at the district level, it was sent upward for review by the prefect of Si'en Prefecture. But while en route, Zhou Wenqiang died of acute appendicitis, and the case was sent back to Yishan District for retrial. There, the magistrate's questions—and his reliance on torture—followed the same pattern as before: he was still unconvinced that the younger Zhous had acted without even the knowledge of their clan elders. But as the elders declared,

"You can squeeze us to death, but it will still be a false accusation! Even though we struggled with Tang Hongren for years over control of the land, and have sued him several times in court, we moved to the outskirts of the city and gave up the lawsuits because we never succeeded. Zhou Wenqiang and the others scorned us for that. We got into arguments with them, and we've been on bad terms since. That's why, when they went to take revenge, they did not even come to inform us. And that's the truth."

On Yongzheng 6.9.11 (October 13, 1728), the Tan clan took its revenge: five of their men shot to death two of the men who had participated in the raid on the stockade, Zhou Fushou and Zhou Fuhai. Both were killed by one musket ball each in the abdomen, and each had been struck on the back of the head by a heavy bladed weapon. Zhou Fuhai was twenty-five sui, according to his widow, Ms. Lan; Fushou was thirty. A few days later, another member of the Zhou raiding party, Zhou Shanhe, was captured and questioned extensively; he confirmed the details of the motivations and actions ascertained earlier. He had lost his machete as he was flee- ing and had no idea where the other fugitives might be hiding.

Then Tan Hongren died of dysentery (on October 17), as did one of his under- lings, Wei Fuge, just ten days later. After checking to ascertain that there was no foul play behind their deaths, Magistrate Zhang made his final report and again advanced the case to the prefectural level. There, the innocence of the Zhou clan elders was finally accepted, and full blame was assigned to the younger Zhous who had led the raid. Beheading should have been their penalty, but Zhou Shanhe, who had only stood guard for the raiders, was sentenced to a beating and three years of exile. His wife was to accompany him into exile, and the beating was reduced, as was common, from the nominal one hundred blows to forty. The warrants remained open for the arrest of the other Zhou clan partisans, and the five Tans who killed two Zhous were tried in a separate case.

The summary report by the provincial governor follows:

. . . Originally, the stockade village in the aforementioned district had thirty- seven *mu* of land that had previously been the ancestral property of Wei Fu'e, who mortgaged it to Zhou Bangyuan to cultivate. Subsequently, when Bangyuan's son Zhou Guisheng fell into arrears in his tax payments, it was given to a family named Wei, whose farm manager Wei Guangding took the value of the grain owed by the Zhou family, fifteen *liang*, as the value of the land and for this amount transferred ownership and management to Tan Hongfa's father Tan Mingquan. Then in Kangxi 31, Zhou Fengyang sued in district court, claiming that the clan possessed documents of ownership for the thirty-seven *mu* being cultivated by the Tan clan, sealed by a previous magistrate. Zhou Fengyang was given control of the land's cultivation, and from that time onward, contention over its occupation never ceased.

In Kangxi 56, seeking to snatch back his property, Tan Hongfa led his sons and nephews, all of them armed, on a raid on the aforementioned village, burning to death Wenqiang's father Zhou Fenggui, his brother Zhou Di, and also the father of Zhou Fuquan, Zhou Fengyang, and their uncle Zhou Fengchao, taking four lives in total. The IMPERIAL commissioner sent to Guangdong to examine the matter sentenced Tan Hongfa to beheading, with delay until after the assizes, and determined that the land and its dwellings should revert to Hongfa. Then in Kangxi 61, Hongfa escaped from prison and fled, and because his father's death had not been avenged, Zhou Wenqiang harbored bitter hatred in his heart.

Seeing Hongfa's elder brother Hongren still in occupation of the stockade, he transferred his hatred to Hongren. Thinking that Zhou Fuquan's father and uncle had also been killed, and that he, too, carried on the enmity, in the first month of Yongzheng 6, he discussed with Fuquan his desire to capture Hongren so as to avenge his father's death. Fuquan agreed [to participate]. Wenqian also recruited Zhou Fujiang [and the others, all listed by name], fifteen in all, to help. He set the night of the second of the second month of Yongzheng 6 for their action. . . .

The rest of the report summarizes the testimony recorded above, noting details of timing, weaponry, and the circumstances under which the fires were started as well as their outcome. The report praises the clarity and consistency of the testimony elicited by the magistrate Zhang Mengbai; the governor concurs on the recommended penalties for the Zhou party based on the prescribed punishments for intentional homicide and intentional arson. He also had the words "vicious criminal" tattooed on their faces. He declared that the current market value of the lost property—oxen, houses, granaries, and grain—should be repaid by the families of the eleven who entered the stockade and set the fires. After confirming that the elders of the Zhou clan and others who had been cleared of all wrongdoing should be released, he concludes:

Upon reconsideration, surely the revenge sought by the aforementioned criminals that resulted in the loss of fourteen lives may be seen as constituting an evil act [xiong'e]. The persons themselves and the families of Zhou Wenqiang, who died of illness, Zhou Fuquan, now sentenced to beheading, and Zhou Shanhe, who is sentenced to exile, should all be relocated to some lands at a distance greater than six hundred li under the supervision of an exile official. The lands of the stockade village were originally the property of the Wei lineage, and the transfer back and forth between Zhou and Tan lineages is not clear. If possession is adjudged reverting to the Zhou lineage, then the Tan lineage will not agree; if possession is transferred to the Tan lineage, then the Zhou lineage will not agree. Clearly, the blood feud stemmed entirely from this land. . . . In truth, there would be no benefit in transferring possession only to one lineage and simply creating a cause for further feuding. As the prefect and magistrate recommended above, it should become government property, and strong young men from the countryside should be recruited to cultivate it, with the grain set aside as disaster relief for the area. . . .

The emperor's decision was to confirm the sentences for Zhou Fuquan, beheading with delay until after the autumn assizes, and the others as recommended, presumably including the disposition of the disputed land.

NOTES

Source: *Xingke tiben* [(Board of Punishments) Office of Scrutiny routine memorials] 2–24–2342–1, Yongzheng 6 (1728).

1. In *Manslaughter, Markets*, Buoye describes the rapid increase in homicides stemming from such disputes, particularly in Guangdong. In other parts of China where this transition had occurred earlier, fewer violent clashes erupted during this period. See also Buoye, "Economic Change." Min, in "Theory of Political Feudalism," traces the debates over how much social control to allow local elites and how much to reserve for central officials that apparently lie behind the historical decisions that fomented this vendetta.

2. According to one Qing period historian, the Zhuang were a "clan" (*zu*) of the Man peoples, non-Han "Others" who originally lived, probably as hunter-gatherers, in the mountains of southern China. Naquin and Rawski refer to them as "Tai" (*Chinese Society*, 177). The Zhuang reputedly used poisoned darts against their enemies, making them greatly feared. Yet as seen from this report, by the eighteenth century, the Zhuang people were sedentary farmers, no longer the slash-and-burn agricul-

turalists they had been for hundreds of years. By the twentieth century, they were living in Guangxi as well as in Hunan.

3. On the practice of "civilizing the barbarians" during the Qing, see Harrell, *Cultural Encounters*; and Herman, "Empire in the Southwest." This case exemplifies the spread of "cosmopolitan" culture and Han values to this marginal region and the negotiations necessitated between central power structures and local traditions in imposing punishments for infringements of central values. On the Yongzheng emperor's policy for assimilating these aborigines, see Naquin and Rawski, *Chinese Society*, 177. Will, in *Bureaucracy and Famine*, sees the empire's widespread development of relief granaries as a response to its need to prevent famine—and to keep the rapidly expanding populace from migrating in times of natural disaster.

4. When Chinese settlers, most of them Hakkas, moved into the area, they, too, built highly fortified residential structures. For a Hakka structure, see Naquin and Rawski, *Chinese Society*, 174–75.

5. He means wine mixed with a few drops of blood from all who swear brotherhood in the gang; the cup of blood wine was shared by all who took the oath. Usually, such a ceremony was held in a local temple, with oaths of fidelity sworn before the statue of the temple deity, who would serve as a divine guarantor for their commitment.

6. This is not a large plot of land, only slightly more than ten acres.

7. These firearms were probably long-barreled fowling pieces but may have been muskets (they did not have spiral grooves cut into the bores and hence were not rifles, strictly speaking).

8. By reference to the Qing penal code, Article 383, which stipulates that those who set fatal fires should be punished in accordance with the punishment for intentional homicide, and Article 290 on homicide. See Jones, *Great Qing Code*, 358, 276. The order that the Zhou clan compensate its victims financially for all lost property is also in accordance with Article 383.

CASE 16

Rebellious Religious Sectarians (North China, 1791–1814)

The following selections are from depositions made by members of several religious groups affiliated—or thought to be—with the White Lotus Teachings (Bailian Jiao). The White Lotus movement was generally Buddhist in orientation; it originated in the fourteenth century during the fall of the Mongol Yuan dynasty and contributed significantly to the founding of the Ming in 1368. Thereafter, White Lotus sects were associated with the Ming cause, which made them obvious enemies to the Qing after the Manchus took power in 1644.

The Eight Trigrams Teachings (Bagua Jiao) first became powerful early in the nineteenth century, and as several of the following depositions attest, the rebels attacked the capital of Beijing and even broke into the Imperial Palace in 1813. Several palace eunuchs were involved in the conspiracy, but the raid was foiled by other eunuchs who remained loyal to the emperor. (The emperor was not in Beijing at the time.) The Manchu prince who later became the Daoguang emperor played an important role in defeating these rebels.[1] Military officials interrogated anyone suspected of being involved in an armed insurrection and then often executed the subject. Information gleaned from these depositions was forwarded to the emperor via direct memorials.

The first text records the astonishing tale of Liu Zhaokui, a poor man who crisscrossed the country several times as a message carrier for leaders of his sect. His interrogator was initially incredulous, but soon realized that Liu was really quite smart and had somehow learned to read during his many years on the road. In his testimony, Sun Guozhu reveals the core teachings of his group in an apparent effort to demonstrate that he has nothing to hide—his group had no political aspirations and had not been involved in either local uprisings or the attack on Beijing. Two other deponents, Qin Li and Xu Anguo, refer to many of the same figures in the movement that attacked Beijing in 1813. One leader of the insurrection, Lin Qing, reappears in their testimony; eighty thousand lives were lost in their rebellion.[2] Through his comments, Xu outlines his life story; he also hints at his personal commitments and the individual tragedies involved in the government's suppression of these sectarian movements. Ms. Xing records the special abuses women faced even if they joined the movement unwittingly, as in her case, by marriage. Each of these documents offers unmistakable evidence of the importance of ritual and personal loyalties that were central to Chinese sectarian movements.

The depositions reveal something of the lives and the beliefs that society members held in common, such as shared concepts of the relationship between Heaven and earthly authority, the importance of hierarchical and family relationships in society, and personal ethics. Taken together, they constitute a revealing portrait of popular religious beliefs and groupings of the time. These depositions date from 1791, late in the Qianlong period, to 1814, into the Jiaqing period. By then, the "high Qing" was over.

"I am thirty-seven *sui* in age, and I am from Pingxin Market in Weinan District. My father Liu Xuefang passed away long ago. My mother, Ms. Zu, was remarried to a man named Yang. My older brother Liu Zhaogui left home to beg; I haven't seen him for many years. My one younger sister married a Yang. I don't have any paternal uncles, nor do I have a wife or children. I've been poor ever since I was a child, and I had no one to turn to. When I was eight, I went with Niu Bing in Weinan District to learn magic tricks [*xifa*].[3] In Qianlong 35 [1770], we left and went our separate ways to earn a living. At first, I wandered through various places in Sichuan, Guizhou, and Yunnan for twelve or thirteen years. In Qianlong 48 [1783], I went to Taiping, Liuzhou, and various other places in Guangxi looking for work.

"In the fourth month of 49, I went to the Yangli Department area and stayed in the shop of a military exile, Liu Shufang. When I asked, he told me he was exiled there because of the Eight Trigrams Teachings case in Shan District, Shandong. So I asked him, 'What good points does this school have to offer?' He said, 'Once you join this school, you can eliminate calamities and avoid disasters. Not only can you garner good luck in this life, but in your next, you will surely be reborn in a better place.' I was converted at that moment, and on the first of the fifth month of that year, I vowed to follow Liu Shufang as my master and joined the school. Because I didn't know how to read, he lectured me on all the principles of the Eight Trigrams Teachings. I still remember each and every one of them.

"On the sixth of the first month of 50 [February 14, 1785], Liu Shufang gave me four *liang* of silver and two thousand coppers and told me to go to his home area of Shan District in Shandong to deliver a letter to his family. So then I set out from Yangli, and on the fifteenth of the fourth month [May 23] of that year, I got to his home and delivered the letter. I stayed there until the end of the tenth month [December 1], when his wife, Ms. Li, gave me a letter and some pongee pants and told me to take them back to Yangli.

"During the first month of 51 [February 1786], I returned to Yangli and delivered the letter and the thing. I also told Liu Shufang what I had heard at Ms. Li's house, that fellow school members who had been exiled to Guangdong—Li Dazhi, Wei Rong, and Li Shu—had all fallen sick and died at the exile stations in Guangning and Heshan Districts. Liu Shufang said that Li

Dazhi and the others were all his friends in the [Eight Trigrams] Teachings. Since they had all died at the exile stations, if somebody could transport their remains back home, it would be a work of great merit in our sect. At first, I wasn't willing, but when I saw how earnestly he talked, I felt generous and agreed to do it. Just before I set out, Liu Shufang gave me ten *liang* for my travel expenses and gave me a letter and twenty-five *liang* to give to his wife, Ms. Li. He also told me to go to Deqing Department in Guangdong to make inquiries about another man who also had been exiled in this case, Bu Wenbin.

"Because I didn't have enough money for travel expenses, I first went to various places in Guangdong where I did magic and saved up more than thirty ounces. Only in the summer of 53 [May–June 1788] could I get to Guangning and Heshan and have the coffins of Li Dazhi and the others cremated. Then, carrying their remains with me, I went on to Shandong. My road went through Deqing Department, where I found Bu Wenbin and informed him about how Liu Shufang had accepted me as his disciple and had told me to make inquiries about him along the way and to escort the remains of their fellow school members home. He kept me there with him more than ten days. Because I was totally committed to the Dao, he recognized me as his foster son. He wrote a letter and told me to take it to his wife, Ms. Xiao. He also taught me more of the principles, all about "acknowledging the ancestor and returning to the root" [*renzu guigen*]. I remember each and every one of them, too.

"In the eleventh month of 53 [December 1788], I arrived in Shandong and, having delivered the letter, the silver, and the remains to the various places, I lived at the house of Ms. Xiao, Mrs. Bu, and helped with the farming. I didn't go out at all to do magic tricks. At the end of the winter of 54 [late January 1790], Ms. Xiao gave me five hundred coppers and told me to take them to the Mrs. Wang Yuan at Yuan Family Village in the north of Heze District. She said that when Mrs. Wang Yuan's husband Wang Zhongyuan, Administrative King of the Eastern Zhen [Trigram], died, the people all put forward her son, Wang Zizhong, as administrator for the school.[4] The one who was exiled beyond the Great Wall the year before last was Bu Wenbin's wife's brother's son. When I got to Mrs. Wang Yuan's house, I saw that Yang Wu, Guo Xin, and a fellow named Liu, all from Pei District in Jiangnan, had brought two pecks of rice, a cask of wine, and twelve *liang* of silver to give to Mrs. Wang Yuan. I asked Mrs. Wang Yuan, and she said that when Wang was alive, he had given permission for them to propagate the Gen Trigram

School [Gengua Jiao]. After I made acquaintance with them, we all went our separate ways.

"In the first month of 55 [mid-February 1790], I went with Mrs. Bu Xiao to Mrs. Wang Yuan's house to celebrate the New Year. Mrs. Wang Yuan said her son Wang Zizhong had been sentenced to exile beyond the Great Wall and she had not heard anything from him. Because I was a man of righteousness, she wanted to send me beyond the Wall to see Wang Zizhong. And since Wang Zizhong was the administrator of the Eastern Zhen, I was willing to take a letter to him for her. Mrs. Wang Yuan gave me twenty-four *liang* of silver, and on the nineteenth of the second month of 55 [April 3, 1790], I set out from Shandong. In the fourth month, I arrived at my hometown in Weinan District. I stayed at the home of my clan aunt Mrs. Liu Li for two days, and then I went outside the Wall.

"Only after I got outside the Wall did I learn that Wang Zizhong had been exiled to Kashgar [in Xinjiang]. I made inquiries all along the way, and when I got to Kucha, I saw my fellow in the [Eight Trigrams] Teachings Mao Youlun, who had been sent there for punishment. At Akhsu, I saw Zhou Facai and Zhou Jin, and at Ye'erqiang, I saw Qu Jinhe, Shen Wencheng, Song Ming, and others. The six of them all told me to let Wang Zizhong know that they were still firm in their faith when I saw him. They wanted me to ask Wang Zizhong for titles for them. I was delayed along the way, and so it was only on the sixteenth of the tenth month [November 22] that I finally arrived in Kashgar. I found Wang Zizhong and gave him the news of his family and relayed to him the message from Qu Jinhe and the others requesting titles.

"Wang Zizhong kept me there for a month, explaining to me everything about the teachings in detail. He also said that there were just eight levels of titles in the teachings. After joining the school, with good conduct, you will have the first title of Pastoral Officer [Chuanshi]. From Pastoral Officer, one may be promoted to Officer of Totality [Quanshi]. From Officer of Totality, one may be promoted to Igniter [Dianhuo], and afterward Navigator [Liushui], then General Navigator [Zong Liushui], Defender Perfected Man [Danglai Zhenren], Pathbreaking Perfected Man [Kailu Zhenren], and Trailblazing Perfected Man [Zhilu Zhenren]. After patiently working one's way up to Officer of Totality, you may transmit the teachings to your disciples. From Navigator [levels] and above, you are allowed to keep the accounts. After you've reached the Perfected Man level, you may manage the funds. He said that because I had escorted the remains of my fellows in the teachings to Guangdong and had traveled beyond the Wall to deliver a letter, I had earned great merit in the teachings. He appointed me directly to Pathbreaking Perfected Man of the Most Virtuous Conduct, Eastern Zhen Trigram [Dong Zhen Zhixing Kailu Zhenren], and he told me to return to Shandong.

"If the original teachings could be revived, I was commanded to administer all the internal affairs of the school there. He gave me twelve *liang* of silver and a horse and sent me off, instructing me to go back to Ye'erqiang, Akhsu, and Kucha and to see Qu Jinhe and the others. They are to be granted the titles Officer of Totality and others, and they must keep the teachings always in their hearts. He also told me to go to Shandong and to tell everything about the school to his nephew La Yuaner so that he could easily revive the original teachings. He also gave me two letters that I should first take to Liujiazhuang in Pei District, Jiangnan, where I should find Yang Wu, Guo Xin, and Liu Xing and tell them to figure out some way to take care of the school's business there. Then I was to go to Deqing Prefecture in Guangdong, where I should award Bu Wenbin the title Trailblazing Perfected Man, and so on. When I had finished with business matters, I was to bring a letter back to him in Kashgar and he would give me a scarlet sword with jade inlaid in brass. With that, I would have the authority to decide matters of life and death. Then I picked up the letters to the families of Wang Zizhong and the others and set out from Kashgar.

"Just as I was about to leave Zhan Qingzhen and others, exiles from the Guangdong Heaven and Earth Society [Tiandi Hui] case, entrusted me with letters for their families as well. At first, I was not willing, but Zhan Qingzhen gave me two strips of paper and said that when I deliver his letter to Guangdong, if I bring out the strips of paper and show them to the members of their families, I will surely be heavily rewarded. So, scheming for some payment, I took their letters along. Afterward, I returned to Ye'erqiang, Akhsu, and Kucha and told Qu Jinhe and the others about the Officers of Totality titles Wang Zizhong had awarded them. I also took out the family letters for all of them, and those people altogether presented me with more than thirty *liang* of silver for my travel expenses. Then I set out on my return journey.

"On the eighteenth of the sixth month [July 18, 1791], I returned to my old home in Weinan and borrowed a place to stay at my clan nephew Liu Shibing's house. I had originally planned on resting a few days before going to the other places to deliver the letters. I didn't expect that the local warden would report me to the district magistrate there and that I'd be arrested for questioning. My only purpose in joining the Eight Trigrams School was to eliminate catastrophes and to obtain good fortune. I never had in mind any other reason or to do anything illegal. Nor did I ever take any disciples. I've wandered ever since I was a child; certainly I had never preached any of the teachings here in my home, Weinan. My title in the [Eight Trigrams] Teachings was just announced orally; there was never any written certificate. This is the truth."

Question: "Liu Zhaokui, you found Liu Shufang, Bu Wenbin, Wang Zizhong, and the others, and even though the places to which they had been sent were very far away from one another, they were able to exchange letters. I can see how you were able to share information in your teachings. That Duan Wenjing was an important criminal in the Zhen Trigram School; surely he, too, sent letters back and forth. You must have carried letters for him as well. Where is Duan Wenjing hiding out now? There's no way you could not know! Yang Wu and the others in Pei District have long been in league with Wang Zizhong in establishing the Gen Trigram School. Where are they practicing the teachings now? Who's in charge? How many members are there in the teachings now? Surely you know all about that. Zhan Qingzhen was exiled because of the Heaven and Earth Society case in Guangdong. Surely what was written on the paper strips he gave you were the society's secret passwords. Why would he give them to you without any concern if you hadn't become a member of their society? And when he gave them to you, he must have explained the meaning of what was written on them. Hurry up and tell the truth about them, and tell me how you interpret every line from those letters you were to deliver." He was questioned repeatedly; likewise, heavy torture by squeezing was applied during interrogation.

Further testimony of Liu Zhaokui: "After I joined the school, I never saw Liu Shufang again. Bu Wenbin and Duan Wenjing exchanged letters. As for the letters I carried for Wang Zizhong and the others, I inspected what was in all of them, and none mentioned Duan Wenjing. I could tell that none of them had secret information in them. Only once, at the end of the winter of 54 [early 1790], I was in the house of Mrs. Wang Yuan and I saw Wang Zizhong's nephew La Yuaner. He was originally a constable for Heze District. He had a bill that he showed to Yang Wu, Guo Xin, and the man Liu from Pei District, and he said that it was an arrest warrant for Duan Wenjing issued by the magistrate there. Yang Wu and the others wanted to know how he could dare to hide out here if the chances for his arrest were this high. They had heard that he had some disciples around Dengzhou, and so maybe he had fled to the coast. Who those disciples were or where Duan Wenjing is hiding out now, I truly have no idea.

"I saw Yang Wu and the others only once, in Mrs. Wang Yuan's house. I asked her and then found out that they are in the Gen Trigram School. I never had any dealings with them. Whether they are practicing the teachings there and how many there are in the school, again, I truly have no idea. I got to know Zhan Qingzhen, that exile from Guangdong, only in Kashgar. I never joined their school. I wrongfully listened to what Zhan Qingzhen said about taking those strips of paper only because I hoped to get a few extra gifts of gratitude for delivering the letters. Whatever those strips of paper said, I just couldn't figure out the characters, and I didn't ask him for an explanation.[5]

"The letter from Wang Zizhong to Bu Wenbin said, 'My elder brother Yuanfu: As for the duties of the position I formerly held in Guangdong, I rely on you, elder brother, to assist me in managing them.' What he meant by that was that before Bu Wenbin was convicted, he had originally been a Trailblazing Perfected Man. Later, after the case was exposed and he was convicted, he was not able to manage the affairs of the teachings, and the position was left empty. Now that Bu Wenbin has taken me as his foster son to carry on the duties of the teachings, Wang Zizhong has been restored to his original position of Trailblazing Perfected Man. This means that when Guangdong men from our teachings are exiled, the title each one will be awarded depends on Bu Wenbin's recommendation. Likewise, the letter from Wang Zizhong to Yan, Guo, and Liu said, 'Travel expenses for everyone exiled along the western frontier would be grain from the Southeastern Gen Trigram. In my heart, I foresee that with these provisions, members of our school will reform their humanity and return home.' What that means is that when he was exiled to Xinjiang, Yang Wu, Guo Xin, and Liu of the Gen Trigram provided for his travel expenses all along the way. 'Even now my gratitude overflows for the provisions of your school' means that he calls on practitioners in the Gen Trigram school to continue to offer provisions.

"And Mr. Qu said to Zhou Youxin'na, 'Uncle Bu has bestowed upon us, Qu and Zhou, a single Path. We now entrust to Zhou's own grandson a humble contribution to Du Sanyuan. We three thus entreat you for a signal by which to transmit a command to the society's leaders to move the imperial accounts expeditiously. Each utterance is grounded in our loyal hearts and filial thoughts.' Mr. Qu is Qu Jinhe. Because I succeeded him as Bu Wenbin's foster son, he called me 'Uncle Bu.' When I got to Kashgar, I asked Wang Zizhong for titles for Qu Jinhe and the others. So he said I 'bestowed upon them, Qu and Zhou, a single Path.' Qu Jinhe wrote a letter telling Zhou Yousun to make a contribution to Du Sanyuan. The 'signal' he requested were these titles. So what Zhou Jin gave to his grandfather Zhou Youxin'na was the same thing. The 'command to the leaders' means the people in the teachings who have titles. 'Quickly move the imperial accounts for loyal hearts and filial minds' tells them to rely on their consciences and quickly raise money, either to send to Mrs. Wang Yuan for her use or to send beyond the Great Wall for Wang Zizhong to use as travel expenses.

"This is all true. Because I wrongly listened to what Liu Shufang said and became a member of the teachings, I was truly so muddle-headed that I should die for it. Beyond this, I did nothing else, no illegal activities. Nor did I ever accept any disciples or proselytize the teachings. I beg for a lenient punishment."

TESTIMONY OF SUN GUOZHU, 1810

"I am from inside the east gate of the Xuyi District seat in Anhui, and I am forty-three *sui* in age. My father Sun Yuwen and my mother, Ms. Hou, have already passed away. My elder brother Sun Guobin opened a rice and noodles shop in order to make a living. My wife is Ms. Fu; we have three sons. The oldest is Yongchang, the second is Yongning, and the third is Yongpu. Formerly, I was a financial section scribe [*hufang tiexie*] for the district, but later I went out to work selling my writing skills.

"On the eighth of the fourth month of Jiaqing 10 [May 6, 1805], in Longshan Temple outside the east gate, I was invited to join the Heavenly Principle Society [Tianli Hui] by the butcher Zhou Yongtai, the salt monopoly clerk Guo Tai, the Sizhou constable Ren Tai, the district constables Jin Kui, Fan Rong, and Wu Jie, and the boatman Ji Yougong. We all swore brotherhood. Zhou Yongtai had appointed himself the Loyal and Filial King [Zhongxiao Wang] and head of it; he taught us all the mantras. I have heard that this teaching was transmitted by Lin Sheng, the head of the Eastern Peak [Dongyue] Daoist Monastery who lived at Wang Family Garden on Shencuihua Alley in this district. All of them originally were Sword-Carrying Society [Yedao Hui] members.[6]

"During the fifth month of 13 [June 1808], I returned home and went to the house of Zhou Yongtai, where he had a paper man. Zhou Yongtai said that he could change it into a person. He said that because there had been year after year of famine, the dynasty was doomed and that we should take advantage of this opportunity to make our move. He told me to go out and find places where there was turmoil, where we could stage our uprising. When I had some facts, I was to return and report to him, and in the future, when our enterprise was successful, he would appoint me his prime minister. That year, I left and went all over Jiangnan selling my writing skills; I got back in the fourth month of the following year [May 1809]. Zhou Yongtai said that we would stage our uprising in less than a year and a half, and he told me to go back out and gather information. He wanted to set out for Henan and Zhili after the Dragon Boat Festival [Duanwujie] this year [June 6, 1810] and made an agreement to meet me at the end of the eighth month in Zhengding Prefecture.[7] So I set out in the sixth month, making my way selling my writing skills as before, gathering information in the Shandong, Henan, Zhili region.

"On the third of the ninth month [October 1] of this year, I arrived in Zhengding Prefecture and went to look for Zhou Yongtai. At that time, Gao Yongkui, Du Wenli, and Zhang Rujiu of Daming Prefecture and Wang Xizeng, Wu Shikui, and Du Qiheng of Guide Prefecture were all there. Zhou Yongtai said they were all brothers in our teachings, and he wanted to meet outside the east gate of Zhangde Prefecture to recruit men. If we couldn't recruit men there, he wanted to go back to Xuyi District and invite Guo Tai, Ren Tai, and the others to make our move. He told me to go to Shanxi to find a route that we could take with both men and horses. He agreed that on the twentieth of the tenth month [November 16, 1810], I should hurry to Zhangde for a conference. Then I passed through Zhengding, Xinle, Fuping, and other districts and through the Longquan Barrier to Wutai District, traveling through Yingzhou, Datong, and Fengzhenting. I went beyond the [Great] Wall to Ningyuan, Guihui, and Twenty Families and reentered the Wall at Shahukou Pass. From Zuoyun and Guangwu, I traveled to Daizhou. I was spying out how many soldiers there were when I was arrested and taken into custody by military police.

"Nowhere on my route to Shanxi had I seen anyone from our society. Only at Twenty Families I saw Yang Qizi and Zhou Wuzi, the two of them. They had the marks of incense burns on the backs of their left hands as a sign, so I knew that they were members of our society. Only after I talked to them did I learn that they were Du Wenli's men. So I told them that Du Wenli was in Zhengding Prefecture. 'Why haven't you gone there yet?' And they agreed to go. As for the main leaders in our school, I heard Zhou Yongtai say that Wang Daolong was from Qingyuan District in Zhili and that he was with Lin Qing. Wang Daolong, Wu Yi, and Han Zhang are all very good men. They all agreed to start their uprising around the fifteenth of the ninth month [October 13].

"Wang Daolong is over fifty *sui* in age, with a dark face, pockmarks, and a big beard. And Yu Kejing (also known as Yu Kejiang and Yu Diqi) is a Daming Prefecture man; I've never seen him with my own eyes. Zhou Yongtai said that Li Wencheng was from Hejian District and is fifty-four. He has three lines on his forehead, a high-bridged nose, high cheekbones, brown sideburns, and lots of abilities. I saw him at Zhou Yongtai's house. I also saw Wang Tizhi and Liu Chengzhang from Guide Prefecture and Cheng Wenkui from Weihui Prefecture at Zhou Yongtai's house. Every one of the main leaders of the Heavenly Principle Society had from several hundred to more than a thousand men under his command. The heads in Zhili are Wang Daolong and Lin Qing. Zhou Yongtai from Pengde Prefecture in Henan should also be counted among them. Li Wencheng, Wang Tizhi, Liu Chengzhang, and Cheng Wenkui are all leaders. I've heard that there are eighty or ninety leaders altogether. We have members in Zhili, Shandong, Henan, Anhui, and Hubei.

"Our names are Heavenly Principle Society, Teachings of the Great Accomplishment [Dacheng Jiao], White Lotus Teachings, and White Ocean Teachings [Baiyang Jiao], but all members of these schools share the spirit of helping one another. Zhou Yongtai has scriptures from our school at his house; I've seen them. He taught me the mantra, but I can recite only seven lines. Zhou Yongtai gave me this Dashun period coin last year to wear as a mark.[8] Zhou Yongtai dug that coin up from under the pagoda beside Lake Huze in 14; altogether there were more than eighty of them, but I can't remember clearly which people he handed them out to. Zhou Yongtai said that after our uprising was successful, we would call our state Dashun. People in our school carry cow's horn boxes, or they have a 2- or 3-*cun*-long strip of red cloth in their felt hats, or they have a little strip of red cloth on the lapel of their robes. These, and the incense burns on the backs of our left hands, are our marks. As for those who went to the capital to make mischief, I didn't recognize any of them at all. I don't know how many there were or where they had stayed. This is the truth."

TESTIMONY OF XU ANGUO, 1814

"I am a resident of Chen Family Manor [Chenjiazhuang] in Changdan District, Zhili. I am thirty-nine *sui* in age. My father Jincheng has already passed away. My mother, Ms. Zhao, who belonged to the wife of Xiaolong, Ms. Li, has also passed away.[9] My elder brother is Anbang; my younger brothers are Anfu and Anming. My son Xiaowu is nine *sui* this year. My own nephew is Xu Xian. I am a member of the Zhen Trigram. In Jiaqing 14 [1809], Wang

Xueyi led us in paying our respects to Liu Guoming of Hua District as our master, and we joined the Dui Trigram. At Dingtao, the Cao District seat, and in Wudan District and Jinxiang, one place after another, I recruited followers, both men and women, old and young, 113 families. In total, there were about six or seven hundred people, and all were major disciples. Zhu Chengfang took charge of them and registered them in a ledger.

"During the eighth month of this year [September 1810], Lin Qing came to Hua District, and he and Li Wencheng settled on the fifteenth of the ninth month [October 13] as the date for the uprising. At that time, I was in Hujiaji in Cao District, at the house of Zhu Chengfang. Liu Guoming wrote a letter to inform me. I went home to hear it [read]. Later, at Jinxiang District, they arrested my disciples Cui Shijun, Sun Zhanbiao, Lü Huarong, Zhang Wenming, Yang Yujin, Li Ronghui, and others. At Cao District, they arrested Zhu Chengfang's brother Zhu Chengzhen, but the bulk of our disciples did not submit and took Zhu Chengfang as their head. In the dark of night on the ninth of the ninth month [October 7], they killed the master [taiye, i.e., the magistrate] of Cao District and burned down the jail. On the seventeenth [October 15], Zhu Chengfang and others brought their disciples all together in a group, about fifteen hundred of them all told, to Chen Family Manor, where they put me forward to be their head.

"On the twentieth of the ninth month [October 18], I led the whole band off toward Hua District; we first killed our enemies the two military licentiates and three people in the Xu Tongjia family, robbing and killing along the way. On the twenty-eighth of the ninth month [October 26], we arrived in the Hua District seat. The Hua District magistrate had already been killed on the seventh of the month. There, I met with Li Wencheng, Liu Guoming, Song Yuancheng, Song Kejun, Wang Xiuzhi, Yin Chengde, Shou Guangde, Wang Daolong, Feng Laosan, Liu Zongxun, and Niu Liangchen. Zhu Wencheng appointed me and Zhu Chengfang barons of the Dui Palace, which he wrote on a large, white, pointed pennant. We had been there for seven or eight days when Li Wencheng told me to take the fifteen hundred people I had brought and, with the more than seven thousand brought by Wang Xiuzhi, Song Kejun, Wang Daolong, and Feng Laosan, to occupy Daokou.[10] We fought several battles west of the [Yellow] River.

"On the twenty-sixth and twenty-seventh of the tenth month [November 22, 23], we encountered government troops led by Commander Yang of Shaanxi. Our people were defeated, and all retreated into the Hua District seat and sealed up the city gates with rocks and earth, leaving the north gate open.[11] The government troops advanced and made their camp outside the west gate. Li Wencheng said he wanted to flee toward Beijing, to Lin Qing, but he was not able to ride a horse because his legs had been broken by torture, so at the end of the tenth month, he fled in a carriage through the north gate, protected by three hundred men led by Liu Guoming, Song Kejun, and Wang Xiuzhi. Later, one of Song Kejun's disciples named Zhao came from Taoyuan to Huacheng, where he scaled the wall with a rope to say that Li Wencheng and the others had a force of two to three thousand in the Taoyuan-Nanhu area. They stayed in Nanhu for two days and then headed toward the Fenqiu region. After Li Wencheng left, Song Yuancheng became the commander in chief, and Niu Liangchen, Yin Chengde, and I secured the area from the north gate to the east gate. On the fourth and fifth of the eleventh month [November 30, December 1], the government troops completely surrounded the district seat. From the wall, we fired muskets and beat gongs and kept watch.

"On the second of the twelfth month [December 27], the government troops set off land mines at the east gate at both outer and inner gates, but they weren't destroyed. The government troops also dug a tunnel under the southwestern corner of the wall, and on the tenth they set off a mine under the southwestern corner, which blew a big hole in the wall, and the government troops swarmed in. Our people were all wearing plain cotton sashes, so whenever the government troops saw plain sashes, they opened fire with muskets and arrows. We could not hold out, and I was wounded and fell. My older brother Xu Anbang and my nephew Xu Xian dragged me into a family's house, where they dug a pit in the ground. Taking a sword, my brother, my nephew, and I all got down into it, and Wang Xiuzhi's brother Wang Xiuren covered us with a polished plate over our heads and piled dirt on top to hide it.

"When the government troops entered the house, one of the scouts noticed that the dirt covering us was wet and opened up our pit. Seeing that the situation was bad, I took care of my brother and nephew and was about to slit my own throat when I was stopped and held fast by soldiers under Commander Ge.

"Zhu Chengfang had registered all of our disciples, male and female, old and young, without distinction in his ledger. But Zhu Chengfang had already burned up all those ledgers by the time he was captured. I can remember that, in addition to Cui Shijun and the others, there were among the major disciples Zhang Yi, Feng Ju, Cai Tingyuan, Xue Ziyou, Liu Guohan, Hu Chengde, Zhao Bingren, Zhang Shijin, Li Huayi, Zhao Mingjie, and Liang

Duozhu; all of them had come to Hua District with me. But whether they're alive or dead now, I really do not know. And the others, the minor disciples, I really cannot remember. Song Kejun told his disciples Zhu Zhigui and An Huaipu to take men and go to Chen Family Manor and move my family members to Hua District. I don't know if they are dead or alive now.

"During the battle, I used a lance. In the Hua District seat, we had eleven cannons at the four gates. Large fowling guns and saltpeter are produced in Hua District, where we dug six hundred *jin* out of the mines. We hadn't used it up yet. We got our lead by melting tin utensils from pawnshops.

"You asked me whether Liu Chengxiang, Liu Diwu, and Zhu Xianzhi had given us financial support: none had come to Hua District. Nor did they manage the business of the children from the Song [imperial] Zhao family descendants. This is the truth."

TESTIMONY OF MS. XING, WIFE OF ZHU BINGREN, 1814

She testified: "I am a resident of Wang Family Manor in Wanping District; I am twenty-four *sui* old. My father is Xing Wenbin, and my mother is Ms. Cui. When I was nineteen, I was betrothed to Zhu Bingren, son of Zhu Xian of Sangfa, as his wife.[12] We have one daughter. When I married into their family, I had no idea that Zhu Xian's family was in the Heavenly Principle Society. After I was married, I heard it said that at first Zhu Xian's family was not in the society, but when my stepmother-in-law, Ms. Long, was taken into the family, she was already a member, and my senior mother-in-law, Ms. Xu, converted. From that time onward, the whole family took up Song Jinhui's teachings. They said it was none too convenient that I wasn't in the society, and they told me to pay my respects to Chen Shuang as my teacher. He taught me the eight-word [mantra]: Primordial Father and Mother of the True Vacuity Land [Zhenkong Jiaxiang Wusheng Fumu]. From then onward, they didn't keep anything from me.

"Zhu Xian and Lin Qing were on good terms, and he often sent Lin Qing money. When Lin Qing came to our house, everyone called him 'Old Master' [Lao Yezi]. Either they would tell my stepmother-in-law to sleep with him, or they'd tell me to sleep with him. Neither of us would dare to object. When my husband Zhu Bingren went to Lin Qing's house, he always had illicit sex with Lin Qing's women as well. They thought nothing of it among believers.

"There were more than thirty under Zhu Xian's command. Zhu Zhen, Li Fengquan, and Wang Shiyou were the short-term hands in our house; Young

Wang (also known as Wang Qixing) was the long-term help. Aside from them, Li Fengyin, Li Chengzong, Li Ming, Gong Shu, Chen Wenkui, Liu Xi'er, and others were people Zhu Xian had converted. I can't remember the rest of them.

"During the seventh and eighth months of last year [1813], they discussed entering the city [Beijing] to start a rebellion, and early in the ninth, they all went off in plain clothing [baibu]. Zhu Xian also knew that the chances were not good, and he said that this enterprise was like riding a tiger—you can't get off. He spoke to us with tears streaming down his face, and we all cried. Zhu Xian had a soft heart, and he went to Lin Qing's house to withdraw from attacking the city. Lin Qing inspired him by saying that being desirous of one's wife and enamored of one's children was not the way of the real man [haohan], and Zhu Xian took heart. On the thirteenth, just before he set off [for Beijing], he said to us that if it were fated, we'd meet again, but if it were not, this would be our last time. All of us wept bitterly and then said farewell. Zhu Xian was riding a red horse with a long jade-colored blaze, and Young Wang went with him, riding a red horse with a curved white blaze.

"Ever since the sixteenth of the eighth month, my husband Zhu Bingren had been at Lin Qing's headquarters and had not come home. At the second watch on the fifteenth of the ninth month [the day of the attack on Beijing], Liu Pei'er, Yang Laoshi, and Li Shiwang returned to our village to report, and our village was thrown into confusion. Just at sunset on the sixteenth, Liu Xi'er came to our house to say that everyone who had entered the city had been killed by the government troops.[13] Zhu Xian was hiding on the old levee. He had sent him [Liu Xi'er] to come here and give us the news and also sent Young Wang to go to Lin Qing's place to get horses so they could escape together.

"We were all in a panic, and when we heard on the eighteenth that the government troops were arresting people, we all fled in a hurry. My senior mother-in-law, my stepmother-in-law, and their three maids all became separated on the road. I abandoned my daughter, not even a year old, by the roadside and just ran aimlessly for two days. My immediate plan was to find my way to Wang Family Manor, where I'd look for my mother and father. But when I got to Wang Family Manor, I saw they were arresting people there. I thought that if I went home and was arrested, it would just be my death. But how would that not implicate my parents? Better I should turn myself in.

"So I found the local constable Sun Erlong and made my statement. Sun Erlong kept me for twenty days. A local constable under his jurisdiction reported me to the magistrate of the Lugou Subdistrict, His Lordship Chen [Chen Shaoyong], who said he had to go south and that he'd interrogate me when he returned. The next day, His Lordship Chen returned, but before he interrogated me, my mother heard about it and hastened over and asked his people to beg his man Yu Tingfu to say that a woman would not dare to rebel, and it would be best if he'd release me for a little money. He demanded fifty strings of coppers from my mother, so my mother sold some food grain and paid Yu Tingfu twenty-four strings, and he promised to release me and let me go home. Later, he also said that if he released me, I'd probably just be arrested somewhere else, so it would be better to hide me for a while in His Lordship Chen's court. That day, he took me to the *yamen* where I lived with Her Ladyship [Chen's wife].

"While on his way back, His Lordship got the message that he had been dismissed from office, so he returned to the court and spent half the night writing a petition. He entered the city [Beijing] at dawn the next day. During the tenth month, I heard that the prefect from Xilu was coming to the subdistrict *yamen* to make an investigation. Her Ladyship was frightened and took me to a powder shop in the capital and rented a room on Liuli Street for me to live in. But just as I was moving in, I heard that they were searching very carefully for people in the capital. Her Ladyship was frightened and sent me to stay at the house of a matchmaker, Ms. Cao.

"At the beginning of the eleventh month, His Lordship Chen was released by the Board of Punishments and sent Her Ladyship back to Lugou Bridge. He told a runner of the court, Huang Er, to take me back to his residence. That night, he had illicit sex with me there. The next day, he sent me to the Zhao family in Dry Noodles Hutong and falsely claimed that I was the wife of his uncle Chang's family. Chang had escorted a coffin back south for burial, and because he no longer had an official position, he couldn't take care of me and so was entrusting me to them. When Chang returned from the south, he would claim me. The Zhao family consented to have me stay there.

"I stayed at the Zhao house for three months. Because His Lordship Chen had taught the children in their family and because he had been an official, they believed what he said was true and never asked me anything about it. Only when you officials heard about me did the Zhao family turn me in."

The rest of the document is in the voice of arresting officials in the gendarmerie.

"Your subjects interrogated her strenuously concerning the whereabouts of Zhu Xian. She responded, saying, 'After the sixteenth of the ninth month, when

Liu Xier brought the message, he never again returned home.' On the twenty-second, she went to the *yamen* of the subdistrict magistrate, after which she never again saw anyone from her village or from her sect. 'Truly I don't know where Zhu Xian fled to.' As for his becoming a monk, she testified that two years previously, he had twice gone with his mother to the Tanzhe Monastery [west of Beijing] to burn incense. After he returned, he said that it was so quiet in the mountains that he would be happy if he could practice meditation in this place. But this was something he said two years ago, and as he was about to set out, he said nothing about becoming a monk.

Your subjects questioned her about which relatives or friends Zhu Xian was particularly close to in their daily contacts, who might be helping to hide him now; we instructed her to tell the truth. According to the criminal woman, there were several among Zhu Xian's in-laws, his relatives on both sides, and his friends with whom his contacts were closest. Among them were five families who had joined the society and were believers in its teachings. The others among Zhu Xian's closest friends had never joined the society. Even after strenuous questioning, she stuck to her story."

The interrogating officials from the Beijing Office of the Gendarmerie (Bujun Tongling Yamen) recommended that she be turned over to the Board of Punishments for sentencing and that Yu Tingfu, the servant of the already cashiered Magistrate Chen Shaoyong, who had taken bribes, and Chen, who had hidden a fugitive and had illicit sex with a prisoner and thus "has no sense of shame" (wu lianchi), should both be arrested and interrogated. They also recommended that all who had close relations with Zhu Xian, whether members of the White Lotus or other sects, should be carefully interrogated about his whereabouts.

TESTIMONY OF QIN LI (ALSO KNOWN AS QIN XUEZENG), 1814

"I am thirty-three *sui* old. I have no parents, brothers, wife, or children. I am a resident of Jun District. In the past, I served as a corvée laborer working for the Hua and Jun District governments.[14] Ever since my grandfather, we have practiced the White Lotus teachings. All people in Hua and Jun Counties are followers of the same Zhen Trigram of the Teachings of the Former Heaven [Xian Tian Jiao nei Zhenzi yigua]. Only the Later Heaven [Hou Tian] was divided into the teachings of the Eight Trigrams. Our masters transmitted the teachings from the Grand Eunuch [Taijian] Wei Ziyi during the Shunzhi reign [1644–61] to Li Letian in Shandong, who changed the name.

Liu Fengtian transmitted them to a person named Gao in the south, who transmitted them to a person named Qin in Qingfeng District, and he transmitted them to a person named Wang in Cao District. Both of them were arrested and executed as criminals.

"Now what our scriptures say is that there is an Old Lord of the Former Heaven, an Old Lord of the Later Heaven, and an Old Lord King of the Zhen Trigram Palace. This Old Lord of the Former Heaven is Liu Fengtian. This man named Wang is Old Lord Wang of the Zhen Trigram Palace. The scripture that we used to read is *The Three Buddhas' Response to Calamities* [San Fo ying jie]. Niu Liangchen fled in Jiaqing 7 [1802] because of the criminal charge against him, and in Jiaqing 14 [1809], he brought Lin Qing with him to Hua District. He said that Lin Qing was Liu Fengtian who had reincarnated to become an Old Lord of the Later Heaven; he is the head of the whole Eight Trigrams Teachings. He also said that Feng Keshan was the head of the Yang Trigram. Wang Xiang of Jining Department in Shandong is the head of the Wu Trigram. He said that Li Wencheng was the incarnation of Li Zicheng as King of Heaven;[15] Yu Kejing, who is Yu Diqi, would be King of Earth; and Feng Xueli would be King of Humanity: all of them manage the Eight Trigrams. Each one of the trigrams divisions has a trigram head. That of the Li Trigram is Wang Daolong; of the Gen Trigram, Li Zongxun; of the Zhen Trigram, Song Kejun; of the Qian Trigram, Shou Guangde; of the Kun Trigram, Feng Xianglin; of the Xun Trigram, Wang Xiuzhi; of the Dui Trigram, Liu Guoming; of the Kan Trigram, at first Yin Decheng, but after he died, it's now his son Yin Zhen. All of them recognize Lin Qing as their sage.

"Every year, I collected funds for Li Wencheng's use. Sometimes, I gave them to Li Wencheng's foster children Liu Chengzhang or Song Yuancheng or turned them over directly to members of Lin Qing's house for their use. Sometimes, Lin Qing came in person to take them away. During the seventh month of this year, I went with Liu Chengzhang to take five hundred *liang* of silver to Lin Qing's household. I know that among his adopted sons is Zhu Xian, the son of Zhu Xianzhi, of the Bordered Blue Banner, and Chen Wenkui of the same banner.[16] Both were Lin Qing's adopted sons. He also took me to a shop south of the mouth of Vegetable Market Road, where we stayed for two days. There, I saw a man he said was Old Li Five from Xiong District wearing a mandarin's red hat with a peacock feather down the back and also one he said was a son of Cao Lun, I don't know his name, who was wearing a white mandarin's hat. Even more, the Grand Eunuchs Liu Jin, Liu Decai, Wang Fulu, and Gao Zhen all came to the shop and gave them deepest respect.[17] They also gave them carriages and silver.

"In the past, when Liu Chengzhang was in the Board of Punishments prison, he saw another inmate who was an old member of the White Lotus Teachings from the Zhen Trigram, Jiao Chengfang.

"In the secret text that Lin Qing let me read, it said that we would make our move on the fifteenth of the ninth month of this year [October 8, 1813]. Altogether, there would be four provinces, eight prefectures, and sixty-four counties. Li Wencheng is the True Ruler. He still had to go to Hua District and Shandong to see the people in the Teachings and explain the schedule for making our move. In the twenties of the eighth month, he came to the Hua District seat. After that, I took my leave and went home. By the time I got home, Lin Qing had already gone with Feng Keshan to Shandong and had returned to the capital. I never expected that Inspector Liu [Xunyan] of Lao'an Village would report us to the magistrate because we were making weapons. On the third, the magistrate's runners arrested Li Wencheng, Niu Liangchen, and others and took them to the Hua District *yamen*. The magistrate had Li Wencheng beaten several hundred strokes and broke both his legs. Li Wencheng confessed to all the facts about the White Lotus Teachings' plans for rebellion. We discussed it together with other school members, and very early on the seventh, we broke into the city, killed the magistrate, and rescued Li Wencheng. Then we occupied the city.

"Li Wencheng was the True Ruler, Niu Liangchen was his prime minister, and Song Yuancheng was his commander in chief. I was Vanguard for Recruiting and Training Infantry and Cavalry. All the heads of the Eight Trigrams were Kings of Palaces. Every palace had eight barons, but I can't remember the names. Afterward, because Jinan Prefecture in Shandong had arrested Cui Shijun, then Zhu Chengfang and his younger brother Zhu Xing (Zhu Ying), Xu Anguo, Dong Jiwen, and the others made their move. They defeated and pacified Taocao District. In Changhuan District, in Zhili, there are school members Zhao Fu (Zhao Delong) and Zhao Lu (Zhao Defeng). Because their own magistrate was himself investigating and making arrests, Zhao Fu and the others in their shop killed the magistrate and made their move. All of them in turn brought men to Hua District, Daokou, and Taoyuan and made their camp at Daokou.

"After they were defeated, Liu Guoming, Song Kejun, Niu Liangchen's son Niu Wencheng, Wang Xiuzhi, Wang Xueyi, Lü Juntai, Luo Guowang, Zhu Chengfang, Zhu Ying, Zhao Lu, and others went into the mountains, protecting Li Wencheng with more than four thousand men. So for a while, I heard nothing from them. I didn't expect that the government troops would catch up with them and wipe out so many of them, time after time. Even when Hou Zhaochuan occupied the official stockade, he was surrounded by government troops. Li Wencheng had no way out and at first decided to commit suicide. Only then did the lot of them start fires, with each one committing suicide by himself.

"I personally was a member of the school that my grandfather had taught, and I have read the books of the school. I have also seen the secret ledgers of Lin Qing, which tell of a Liu Si who lives in a village, I don't know its name, twelve *li* outside the west gate of Dongchang Prefecture. He lets his hair grow, and he wears a gold hoop on his head. He carries a three-ringed iron meditation staff [*chan zhang*] over his shoulder and wears Daoist robes.[18] He protects a man called Big Head Zhang from East of the Pass [Guandong] who is sixteen or seventeen *sui* old, has a big head and long ear lobes and hands that hang down below his knees. They say he is an extraordinary man.[19] They are generally active in the Nanyang Prefecture area. There are herbalists in Kaifeng Prefecture, Wang Rizhong and Wang Riyu, who know his whereabouts.

"If you're willing to let me go into the [Hua District] city, I will bring Niu Liangchen and Song Laozhan out in fetters for you. As for Xu Anguo, only Jin Zhongzhao could capture and kill him. Of the leaders in our school, the head of the Wu Trigram, Wang Xiang of Jining, already died of disease in the fourth month. The King of Earth in Hua District, Yu Kejing, was captured by the government troops in the mountains, at Ruifu Hill, and was killed. Zhao Fu (Zhao Delong) was killed by government troops outside the north gate of Hua District. The King of Heaven Li Wencheng and the King of Humanity Feng Xueli, head of the Li Trigram Wang Xiuzhi, Liu Guoming, Song Kejun, and Wang Xueyi all burned themselves to death at the official stockade. Wang Xuecheng and Niu Liangchen's son Niu Wencheng, Han Yishu, Zhao Lu (Zhao Defeng), Zhu Xing (Zhu Ying) all died from the beatings administered by government forces outside the stockade. I, Shen Wenxian, and Song Laozhan's son Song Linmei were arrested and kept at Lintong. Zhao Deyi was the baron of the Li Trigram Palace; now he's in the city. Of our leaders still in the city, there are only Niu Liangchen and Song Yuancheng (Song Laozhan), Xu Anguo from Shandong, the trigram heads Yin Zhen, Wang Daolong, Shou Guangde, Liu Zongshun, and Feng Xianglin. All the rest are lower level, and I can't remember their names clearly. This is the truth."

He further testified: "Even though Li Wencheng was a false ruler, he had no talent. Everything was controlled by Lin Qing. His foster child Liu Chengzhang was very smart and a really capable administrator. Li Wencheng did not take charge of anything; everything was in Liu Chengzhang's hands. When Li Wencheng died, it should have been Liu Chengzhang who became ruler. But Lin Qing said that he could be so only after rebirth and that he had no successor. When Yu Kejing and Feng Xueli died, they had no successors either. Lin Qing maintained that Li Wencheng was the son of wood. He also said that Niu [combined with] *ba* was the surname Zhu, and that *shuangkou* [two mouths] was the surname Lü. *Zou* [combined with] *xiao* was the Zhao character. All of these were foretold in our scripture, but the people in our school could not interpret them."[20]

Qin Li's interrogators clearly wanted more information about other members of the organization. They began to ask specific questions; the responses are only summarized here.

He further testified: "Nearby to the east of Lin Qing's house in Song Family Manor [Songjiazhuang] was a Ji Jincai, who was Lin Qing's sister's son. And he was in the [Eight Trigrams] School, too. Chen Dilao is Chen Dakui's father, and he's in the school as well. His house is on the west side of Song Family Manor, but I don't know the name of the place. And then there was Liu Yuanlong who also lived near and on the east of Lin Qing in the manor. They were all later converts."

He further testified: "In Shandong, there's a Dong Jiwen. If he's not from Dingtao, then he's from Cao District. He's also in the school, but he's not at all one of Lin Qing's adopted sons. Only the Cao who is Lin Qing's nephew is an adopted son. I don't know his given name. I don't know who Dong Tuanwang is.

He further testified: "There's a Zhang Youyong in Longping District of Zhili; he's also known as Zhang Xiaohou [Little Monkey Zhang]. And in Qufu, in Shandong, there's a Kong Fubiao. They are followers of another tradition of teachings. In the past, they invited Lin Qing to join them, but he wasn't willing to follow their teachings, and he got into an argument with them."

He also testified: "As for how Li Wencheng died, I think surely somebody at the district seat will know. If they get news of it, then surely they'll have a public discussion about what course to follow; they won't necessarily be willing to surrender. If I go and give them the order to do so, then they would disband."

The following seem to be responses to yet more specific questions.

Response to questioning: "Liu Chengzhang's family, including his younger brother Liu Xianzhang, were all in the Hua District seat. After Liu Wencheng was captured, I don't know where Liu Chengzhang went."

Response to questioning: "On the eighth of the ninth month, Feng Keshan was at Daokou. He was carrying five *liang* of silver with orders to go to Dezhou to roust out the members of our teachings. I never saw him return."

Response to questioning: "Liu Chengxiang was Lin Qing's landlord. He lived in the same courtyard as Lin Qing, and was head of the Kan Trigram. He made his living as a farmer."

Response to questioning: "Lin Qing recognized his sister's son as his foster child. His name was Dong Guotai. He had a paternal uncle, but I'm not sure whether he was Dong Tuanwang.

Response to questioning: "Zhu Xian, also known as Zhu Xian,[21] was a garrison solder of the Blue Banner, but he had never been sent out on a mission [for the school]. He lived about ten *li* southwest of Song Family Manor; I don't know the name of the village."

Response to questioning: "Chen Wenkui was also a bannerman. He lived in the same manor as Zhu Xian. He made a living as a carter. He came to the Hua District seat with Lin Qing in the eighth month of this year."

Response to questioning: "I saw the man who was wearing a red hat with a peacock feather in the southern shop at the mouth of Vegetable Market Road in the capital. Once I asked Lin Qing about him, and he said that he was Li Laowu from Xiong District."

Response to questioning: "During the fourth month of this year, Yu Kejing and Song Yuancheng came back from the capital with a letter for Jiao Chengfang and 150 *liang* of silver. In the seventh month, Liu Wencheng handed 500 *liang* over to me, along with an additional 150 *liang*. Together with Lü Juntai and Liu Chengzhang, he went to Lin Qing's house and delivered 500 *liang* to Lin Qing. That 150 *liang* was what Lin Qing, Liu Chengzhang, and Zhu Xian had taken to the Board of Punishments prison to give to Jiao Chengfang. But because the gate guards at the Board of Punishments wouldn't let them in, they brought the original sum back. Whether or not they ever delivered it, I don't know."

Response to questioning: "Liu Jin was originally a military-degree holder from Caozhou. I don't know why he had himself castrated to become a Grand Eunuch. I did see this man once, in the capital."

Response to questioning: "The four provinces that Lin Qing mentioned [as prepared to rise in rebellion against the Qing government] were Zhili,

Shandong, Shanxi, and Henan. As for the [eight] prefectures and [sixty-four] counties, he didn't say what places they were, and I didn't dare to ask him."

Response to questioning: "It was only when we were plotting to rise in rebellion that Lin Qing said he was the True Ruler."

Response to questioning: "Dong Jiwen was killed by the government troops when he came out of the official stockade to do battle."

Response to questioning: "Song Yuancheng was from Niedu in Rui District. He was in the Gen Trigram. Now he's at the Hua District seat.

Response to questioning: "Chen Dilao was Chen Wenkui's father. He was a bannerman, but he had never been sent out on missions."

TESTIMONY OF JI BA, 1814

He testified: "My name is Ji Wensheng, and this year I am twenty-eight *sui*. I'm a resident of Dongjing Village in Qing District. My father Ji Fuhuang is more than seventy this year; my mother is Ms. Liu. There are three of us brothers. My oldest brother Ji Wenxue manages the tea stall in the *yamen* of the governor-general. My second-older brother Ji Wencheng farms. We divided up the family and all live separately. I'm the third in my generation, and my childhood name was Ba'er [Little Eighth]. My wife is Ms. He; this year she is twenty-nine. We have two sons. The older is called Tun'er, and he's five *sui* this year. The little one is called Xi'er, and he's two *sui* this year. I've always worked as a farmer for my living.

"I've always known Wang Shiqing of New Zhu Family Manor. During the third month of [Jiaqing] 16 [March–April 1811], I went to Xinji to market, and there I ran into Wang Shiqing, who converted me. He told me to go to his house, where he kept me for a day and a night. He had a painting of a Buddha on paper that he had up in his house, but I honestly don't remember what Buddha it was. He told me to burn incense and *ketou*, and he taught me to say nicely that it was the Righteous Harmony Sect [Yihemen], based on the idea of harmony.[22] I can't rightly explain that 'righteousness' idea. He taught me to be filial to my parents and to forge good relations in my neighborhood. My ears should not listen to wrong sounds, my eyes should not look at wrong things, my nose should not turn smells around, and my mouth should not say wrong words. He also taught me to sit in meditation and to move my *qi* and to cultivate my nose, eyes, ears, and tongue.[23] He said that there were three lines across people's foreheads that are three gold locks and three gold hoops. A person's basic nature [*xing*] is between his eyebrows, and his face is the key to it. The *qi* is a great bell. If you move your *qi*, you can wash open the three gold hoops around the top of your head, and your nature can come out through the front of your forehead. You cultivate your true nature in order to cultivate your next life. There's nothing more to it. This is what he taught me. Afterward, I went to his house from time to time, and I saw that he had scriptures in his house. But because I can't read, I couldn't read those scriptures.

"In the fall of 16 [1811], I was going back and forth to Keniu Village, taking livestock and peddling firewood. I converted Wang Kuan, and in Wang Kuan's house, I converted Hao Mingyuan and Li Xing. In Li Xing's house, I converted Li Xing's brother Li Wei (also known as Li Er). From time to time, I went to market at Li Village, and I converted Li Fa (known as Li Er). At Li Fa's house, I converted Yue Fu. At Yue Fu's house, I converted Dai Zhenxian and Li Ba (also known as Li Shenghua). Li Ba is about forty *sui* old, and he shaves heads for a living. In the twelfth month of 16 [early 1812], in Dai Er's house, I converted Dai San, but because his nose was stuffed up, Tang Shijiu couldn't move his *qi*, and so I didn't teach him how. All of this happened over the last two years, and I don't remember precisely when. And then in the ninth month of last year, in Dai Zhenxian's house, I converted Liu Huichang. That night, I taught him the practice of moving his *qi*. I used ashes to draw a man's face and showed him how moving your *qi* could wash your forehead clean, that I did.

"Beyond these people, I haven't preached to anybody. And I never said to Dai Zhenxian that he could bring in several hundred people at a time. Truly, I never converted Wang Sangangzi or Wang Sigangzi or Gu Xiang. As for Young Dai Er, I was in his house only that one evening, but he was never converted. As for that rebel bandit at the capital Lin Qing or those rebel bandits who made trouble in Henan, I really don't know even a one of them. We are the Righteous Harmony Sect, not at all one of those 'teachings.' Ever since last month, when I heard about the announcement that this wasn't a good thing, I've been scared and have wanted to repent. And this is the truth."

NOTES

Sources: For Liu Zhaokui testimony, *Lufu zouzhe* microfilm 3.166.8800.2, dated Qianlong 56.7.13 [August 12, 1791]; Liu was interrogated by Shaanxi governor Qin Cheng'en. For Sun Guozhu testimony, *Lufu zouzhe* microfilm 3.166.8811.37, undated (apparently Jiaqing 15 [1810]). For Xu Anguo, *Lufu zouzhe* microfilm 3.166.8809.1 dated Jiaqing 18.12.26 (also designated 3.2390.1 in the "Peasant Uprising" [Nongmin qiyi] category). For Ms. Xing, wife of Zhu Bingren, testimony, *Gongzhongdang* 017364, dated

Jiaqing 19.2.26 (March 17, 1814), a memorial submitted by Yinghe, Xilabu, and Ying-shou. For Qin Li (also known as Qin Xuezeng) testimony, *Lufu zouzhe* microfilm 3.166.8810.9, dated Jiaqing 19.11.14 (December 25, 1814). For Ji Ba testimony, *Lufu zouzhe* microfilm 3.166.8797.22, dated Jiaqing 18.12.10 (January 1, 1814).

1. The Heaven and Earth Society (Tiandi Hui), began in Guangdong and Sichuan. The White Lotus and Eight Trigrams sects described here were northern Chinese phenomena, in Shandong, Zhili, and Henan, starting in the sixteenth century. A succinct description of White Lotus teachings appears in Naquin and Rawski, *Chinese Society*, 135–37. Murray, in *Origins of the Tiandihui*, concludes that all of these groups arose as a consequence of economic need in China's countryside.

2. For a detailed study of the Eight Trigrams movement, see Naquin, *Millenarian Rebellion*. For the career of Lin Qing, see ibid., 72–117, 146–76, 184–88.

3. *Xifa* here means sleight of hand as entertainment and has nothing to do with religious beliefs or practices.

4. The Eight Trigrams (Bagua) of *The Book of Changes*, the ancient collection of auguries and philosophical meditations, were organizational groups within the White Lotus Teachings and other movements. See Naquin, *Millenarian Rebellion*.

5. Presumably, these were composite characters of the sort used in protective amulets even today.

6. Neither the Sword-Carrying Society nor the Heavenly Principle Society were significant movements in national terms.

7. The Dragon Boat Festival falls on the fifth day of the fifth lunar month and commemorates the fourth-century b.c.e. statesman Qu Yuan, who committed suicide because his king refused to listen to his good advice and instead followed the urgings of sycophants. As a consequence, the state fell to the machinations of a rival. Boat races are traditionally held in Qu Yuan's honor on that date.

8. Dashun is the reign period of one of the Ming pretenders after the Manchus took Beijing. By carrying the coin, members demonstrated that they were rebels against the Qing.

9. Presumably, she "belonged" to Ms. Li as a bondservant.

10. On the crucial Daokou meeting, see Naquin, *Millenarian Rebellion*, 110–17. On Xu Anguo's role in the rebellion, see ibid., 104–5, 115, and elsewhere.

11. For a description of the horrendous situation in Hua based on other depositions from participants, see ibid., 197–202, 210–12. For the rebels' strategy, with reference to the leaders named here, see ibid., 211–19. For a reproduction of a wanted list from *Gongzhongdang 16763*, *Fupian* Jiaqing 19.10.20 [December 1, 1815], with the names of Liu Chengxiang, Zhu Xian, Zhi Jincai, and Liu Chengzhang, see Naquin, "True Confessions," 14, fig. 7.

12. Zhu Xian's name is represented with two different characters (see the glos-

sary). For a discussion of Zhu Xian's role in the Eight Trigrams rebellion, see Naquin, *Millenarian Rebellion*, 158–60. Portions of this deposition are also translated in Naquin, "True Confessions," 2–4.

13. For an account of the disastrous attack on the Imperial Palace, see Naquin, *Millenarian Rebellion*, 176–84. On the capture and execution of Lin Qing, see ibid., 184–88.

14. Corvée service was regularly required of residents in many jurisdictions; they worked on roads or irrigation projects or, like Qin Li, as menials for a magistrate or prefect.

15. Li Zicheng was one of the most notorious rebels of the late Ming period. He took the capital of Beijing in 1644, leading to the suicide of the last Ming emperor and providing a rationale for the Manchu armies to advance into northern China to "restore order." See Wakeman, *Great Enterprise*, esp. 225–318.

16. On the banner organization, see appendix 1 in this volume. To have recruited bannermen to their cause demonstrated the range of the Eight Trigrams Teachings appeal.

17. Literally, gave them their *ketou*, the series of prostrations and touching the head to the ground properly reserved for the emperor. To do so before anyone but one's senior relatives indicated heretical political allegiance and could be considered an act of treason by Qing administrators.

18. The meditation staff is a padded staff with which drowsy meditators are prodded back to wakefulness. Here, it indicates his mastery of meditation techniques: he wields the staff instead of needing its prompting.

19. These characteristics were often attributed to True Rulers, those fit to be dynasty founders.

20. Such cryptic phrases were considered prophetic in children's songs or in revealed texts requiring at least modest reading skills; they seemed to refer to the names of individuals already living or yet to be born. The meaning works on visual puns: the character *zou* (walk) plus the character 肖 *xiao* (resemble) make up the character for the surname Zhao 趙; the surname Lü 呂 is made up of two *kou* 口, or mouth elements; the character for the surname Niu 牛 and the character *ba* 八 (eight) make up the surname Zhu 朱, and the character for the surname Li 李 may be deconstructed to form *mu* 木 (wood) and *zi* 子 (son). Li was the imperial family of the Tang dynasty, Zhao of the Song, and Zhu of the Ming. Empress Lü was the controlling power behind the throne during the early Han dynasty. The prophecies here all indicate a new ruling dynasty that would supplant the Qing and were treasonous ideas at the time.

21. The text gives the two characters by which Ms. Xing's father-in-law was known.

22. Here, *ketou* probably means only prostrating oneself before the image.

23. *Qi* means breath as well as one's spritual essence.

CASE 17

Ji Yanghua: Secret Society Member (Shanxi, 1814)

This early nineteenth-century deposition from North China suggests that members of some secret organizations lived at the margins of society, in a kind of underworld of violence and immediate gratification beyond laws or normal social ties. Although most adherents of these religious movements were farmers who had been driven from their lands by natural disasters and high taxes, others were apparently callous criminals. Portraying all the naive rebels as wandering riffraff fit the government's policy of discrediting them and thereby justified the harsh treatment they received. There is, however, a clear distinction between the self-centered lawlessness of Ji Yanghua and the ways in which other religious sectarians defended their political aspirations in the previous cases. Ji Yanghua was a religious charlatan; Ji Ba and others were sincere in their proselytizing.

Testimony of Ji Yanghua (also known as Ji Xuezhu): "I am a native of Yue Village of Yongle Market, Yongji District, in Puzhou Prefecture of Shanxi. I am forty-seven *sui* in age, and my parents have passed away. Of the four brothers in my family, my oldest brother Ji Xuezhong is fifty-seven, but his wife, my sister-in-law Yang, has passed away. Some time ago, my oldest brother moved to Mount Meng Fork [Mengshancha] in Jingning Department. My second-older brother Ji Xuezhi is already dead. The fourth of us, my younger brother Ji Xuerong, is now twenty-five *sui*. He never married, but he went west beyond the [Great] Wall. I'm third in my family. I have never been married. We brothers divided the household long ago, and we all live separately. Usually, I make my living as a hired laborer; I have no trade.

"In Jiaqing 16 [1811], I went to work for Chen Yongfa's family in Bahewan in Xianyang District of Shaanxi. Because her husband was away, his nephew's wife and I started to mess around, we started having illicit sex, and we had a child. Then her husband came home, and he wouldn't forgive her, so the woman hanged herself. I was scared and ran away and took a job working in Yang Zhifa's wineshop in Dengzhou in Henan, where I got acquainted with Li Mao, a native of Weinan District in Shaanxi.

"In the eighth month of Jiaqing 17 (1812), Li Mao wanted to go home. Since I wasn't making any money, I took my leave of the wineshop keeper and went along with Li Mao. We found a place to stay in the Taibai Temple in Yiyang District, Henan.¹ It didn't even have an abbot, but we discovered that there were two monks and a twelve- or thirteen-*sui* boy staying there. So we moved into the temple, too. Li Mao noticed that their baggage looked pretty heavy, and so he conceived the idea of plotting to kill the three of them. He told me to help him.

"That night, when they were sleeping soundly, Li Mao and I strangled the two monks with a rope. Later, we strangled the boy, too. Li Mao broke open their cases, and there were 110 *liang* of silver in them. We divided it, and when morning came, we carried the three bodies on our backs and dumped them into the Wei River. Then we fled to the Yaozhou area, where we shaved off our hair and queues, changed into the robes and hats of the two monks we had strangled, and traveled along the road, begging for alms.

"In the tenth month, we came to Mountain Blessings wineshop on Gou Family Mountain [Guojiashan] in Wulangting to beg for alms. Four men were already drinking there. One among them asked me where I was from, and we introduced ourselves. He said his wife was sick and was seeing spirits and ghosts. 'Do you two have some way to help her?'

"'I have some charms and spells that might cure her,' I answered him, and he arranged for us to go to his house to write charms and recite spells for his wife. Afterward, she got better, so he kept us at his house for a good long time. Then, one day, he said to the other three, 'I can tell that these are great guys, and they have some real talent [*benshi*]; wherever they've been, they've been able to pull things off. If they are willing to follow our teachings, everything will be fine between us from now on. What would you guys think of that?' And they said, 'If you recommend them, Great King, of course we will go along with you.'

"Hearing this, we were really surprised and wondered what they meant. We asked them, and only then did we learn that the fellow who had invited us to cure his wife was none other than Liu Tiangui, the Great King of Heavenly Peace [Tianping Dawang]. Of those three men who were drinking with him, one was Zuo Fengxian, the Great Instructor of the Bright Portal. One was Jiao Tingyan, and the other was Jiao Jinxian; they were both Generals of the Palace of Suppression. We were confused, and without thinking, we agreed, and he appointed us Great Chan Masters Who Protect the Troops.

"With Li Mao, I went to Jiao Jinxian's house on Gou Family Mountain some twenty *li* from Wulangting, where we lived for three months. We saw that under the floorboards of a room in his eastern wing, there was a cave in the earth with more than thirty dirt steps that finally opened to a very broad space big enough for seven or eight hundred men. At that time, there were already seventy or eighty men there with many spears and swords as well as [sleeping] mats and stores of food.

"In the first month of this year, Liu Tiangui said that the day before, Liu Chengyu (the King Who Follows Heaven), Wang Fuyu (who is Big Head Wang), Niu Bangting, Li Tiancheng, and others from the Kan Trigram mark in Weihui Prefecture in Henan had sent Liu Chengxiang with a message saying that they had more than ten thousand men and were about to fight their way from there into Zhili and wanted to arrange for us to join forces with them. 'Because we are short of troops, we cannot rise with them, and only after we get more men will we make our move. I've already sent a response.' Because he was short of men, Li Tiangui could not make his move, so on the twenty-sixth of the first month [February 26, 1813], he told Guan Xiaoxian, Du Kongxian, Li Mao, and me to go out and find men to join our teachings. We were to give every man a wood-block print of the Great King of Heavenly Peace and a four-line password. He gave us thirty or forty *liang* of silver, depending on the person, and sent us along different routes. 'If you use up the silver, I'll send Wang Chengxian to bring travel money to you there on the winter solstice.'

"Wang Chengxian is forty-two *sui* old and a native of Chenggu District in Hanzhong Prefecture. He's of middling height and has a bare face with thin whiskers. Guan Xiaoxian is forty-two and is from Baoding Prefecture. He's of middling height and has a bare face with thin sideburns. He went along the road to Huguang. Du Kongxian is something more than thirty *sui*; he's from Linjin District in Shanxi. He's tall and has a bare face with sideburns. He went along the Sichuan border road. Li Mao is forty-six; he's a native of Weinan District in Shaanxi. He's of middling height, has a bare face with sideburns, and is dressed like a monk. He went along the Changwu-Yongshou and northward route, to Yulin and Dingbian. I went through Xingping, Fufeng, Wugong, Qingshui, Qinzhou, Fuqiang, and Gongchang.

"At the end of the tenth month [around November 20], I arrived in Qingshui District, where I ran into Jiang Desheng and Jiang Deli, two brothers I used to know. They asked me when I had taken my monk's vows and where I lived now. So I told them about entering the teachings, and when I told them the good points about it, the two of them were willing to enter the school. There were also Yang Ji of Qinzhou and his son, and Liu Yu of Gaoju, and others who entered the teachings. I gave every one of them two lots of silver. Each lot was worth seven or eight coppers; they varied. I also taught them the four-line password: 'Heaven and Earth are as they are; The Jade Vapor has spread around; So many kinds of Mysterious Space, Brown [Earth] and Bright [Heaven] are the Great Mystery.'[2] I gave them each a block-printed card and told them to go to Gou Family Mountain. I never thought that I'd be rounded up by government runners when I got to Gongchang.

"As for Liu Wuxun, I don't know him, nor have I heard anyone mention him.[3] So surely I can't tell you where he is. This is the truth."

NOTES

Source: *Lufu zouzhe* 3.166.8807.50, dated Jiaqing 18.12.12 (January 3, 1814).

1. The temple is dedicated to the memory of the great Tang period poet Li Bai (701–762), whose name is sometimes romanized as Li Po.

2. "Tian Di ziran, Yuqi fen san; Zhongzhong xuanxu, Huang lang Taixuan." This is more a spell or mantra than a statement of fundamental beliefs.

3. Liu was apparently another secret society leader whom the authorities were seeking in this region.

PART VI

SOCIAL MOBILITY AND CRIME

W idespread economic and demographic changes during the Qing period produced a fairly large number of dislocated people who often traveled long distances to find work. Several are featured in part V. The two cases in this section feature a family and its probably unwanted follower—precisely the sort of unattached and wandering unskilled laborer that became so common during the eighteenth century as to constitute a worry for central bureaucrats—and an imposter whose successful assumption of false identities depended on the extensive travel generally required for official service. China's transportation routes were undoubtedly crowded with all sorts of people—merchants, religious seekers, criminals, and fugitives as well as those driven by more personal needs.

CASE 18

Jin San: A Spurned Lover (Sichuan, 1728)

In this case, desire changed to hatred, and an outraged lover killed his paramour because she ended the relationship. The recorded testimony is rich in the many voices enlisted to corroborate the facts and the detail with which the judges explored the motivations behind the crime. The case also exemplifies the internal migrations of the poor who journeyed from one region of China to another in the hope of finding work; some of the neighbors as well as the principals of the case had moved there from Hunan.

Your subject Xiande, provincial Governor of Sichuan, Territorial Military Superintendent, and Right Assistant Censor-in-Chief of the Censorate, and other offices, respectfully submits this MEMORIAL to report on a matter:

Hereafter, the report submitted by You Qing, acting assistant judicial commissioner serving on the Sichuan Transport and Salt Control Circuit, on Yongzheng 6.9.26 [October 28, 1728], concerning his investigation of one Jin San, twenty-six *sui*, originally of Longyang District, Changde Prefecture, in Huguang, currently a resident of Suining District [Sichuan]. The complaint acknowledges that this Jin San is by nature violent and depraved [*fuxing xiongyin*] and utterly lawless. To wit: Both he and the former Ms. Zhang, murdered by Jin San, were residents of Chu.[1] When her husband Luo Er, previously but not currently in custody, came to Sichuan in search of his father, Jin San then established an illicit relationship with this woman. By Yongzheng 5, the mother of Luo Er, who has never been in custody, together with his elder brother Luo Da, brought the woman to Suiyi and lived in the village with his father. Luo Er supported himself by selling incense. Soon thereafter, he again moved the woman to a separate residence in his shop. Because Jin San could not forget his feelings for her, he also followed her soon afterward to Suining, ostensibly in order to carry on their affair.

At that time, they resumed their former relationship, but Luo Er knew nothing of it. It happened that his father Luo Qisheng, previously but not currently in custody, got wind of it first and twice confronted Jin San in his residence. Consequently, he was angry and cursed his son. Knowing that the affair had been discovered, the woman resolutely rejected his attentions, but Jin San was bewitched by desire. Then on Yongzheng 6.4.22 [May 30, 1728], he discovered that Luo Er had gone away to market. That night, he pushed open the woman's back door, but the woman cried out and awakened the neighbors to drive him away. Consequently, Jin San nourished hatred in his breast. The following day after breakfast, wrongfully carrying a concealed dagger, he entered the front door and went directly to the woman's chamber, where he accused her of rejecting him, and he questioned her about the reason for her calling out the previous night. When the woman sat there paying no attention to him, he became even more enraged and yet more wrongfully drew out the knife he was carrying. With it, he savagely hacked at Ms. Zhang's throat and neck. She instantly expired. Jin San then fled through the back door. Because the woman's child was outside crying, Yang Shangda, the young nephew of a neighbor, Yang Gongyi, previously but not currently in custody, picked him up and carried him home, where he discovered the woman murdered in her bed. He called the local warden and the neighbors to go see. They then proceeded to the district *yamen* to report. The criminal Jin San likewise of his own volition turned himself in at the jail.[2]

Having reviewed the said district's examination of wound form and his complete report, I forwarded the brief to request authorization to investigate the case here at this court. On Yongzheng 6.5.16 [June 23, 1728], I received the authorization to proceed from the appropriate Censorate office.

Hereafter the detailed report of Xu Ren, Magistrate of Suining. On Yongzheng 6.4.23 [May 31, 1728], local warden Chen Yaosheng submitted a report, which reads:

"The neighbor to the east Zhang Yuanbin and the neighbor to the west Hu Gongshan reported an event that had recently transpired. They reported the details as follows:

"'Yesterday afternoon, Luo Er left his home to go to today's market in Ximei. This morning, after breakfast, Luo Er's child was in the street crying. Yang Shangda, the young nephew of the neighbor one door over, Yang Gongyi, picked him up and carried him home. Finding the front door tightly fastened, he took him in through the back door. Upon entering, he saw Luo Er's wife, Ms. Zhang, fallen over onto the bed; blood covered the mat. He cried out. Neighbor Hu Gongshan heard him and went to the back door to look. He then called the neighbors along the street and opened the front door. Thus, they all saw Luo Er's wife murdered on her bed, her body covered in blood, but they did not know by whom she had been killed.' I report this to Your Honor that you might carry on the investigation."

Accordingly, in my humble capacity [as district magistrate], as I was ordering the arrest of the criminal, the jailer brought in Jin San and reported, "Just now as I was on duty in the jail, this Jin San, all nervous and flustered, came to the door, yelling for me to open up, saying he wanted to turn himself in. I didn't dare take responsibility for this myself, and so I brought him here to report and to ask you to question him."

Thereupon, I interrogated Jin San. "Where are you from? For what reason have you come to turn yourself in at the jail?"

He testified: "I am from Huguang. Previously, in Huguang, I had an illicit sexual relationship with Ms. Zhang, the wife of Luo Er. Last year during the intercalary third month, Luo Er's elder brother and his mother brought Ms. Zhang to Sichuan because his father and younger brother Luo Er were already here. I set out in the fourth month [May 1728] and arrived here myself on the twenty-eighth of the eleventh month [December 28]. Then I went to her house, and we often had illicit sex as before.

"But lately, this woman has turned her back on me. Last night, because her husband wasn't at home, I went to her back door and pushed it open. At that, Ms. Zhang started screaming about there being a thief. She woke up the neighbor Hu Gongshan, and he got up and came to chase me away. So I left; I never even went in. Today, after I ate breakfast, I went into her house through the front door. The only other person I saw was Hu Gongshan standing at the door of his own shop. After I went in, I fastened the front door tight and went into her room. There was nobody else there; all I saw was Zhang sitting on the bed, making shoes.[3] So I said, 'Last night, you knew very well it was me—why'd you start screaming that there was a thief so Hu Gongshan would get up and chase me away? What's the matter—are you turning your back on me? Did you take up with somebody else?' When she wouldn't confess, I momentarily went berserk [*yishi qimi le*]. With my right hand, I took out the dagger I was carrying by my side and cut her a couple of times on the left side of her neck, across the collar line. Then she fell back on the bed, and I could see she was dead. So I wiped the blood off my knife onto her quilt, put it back at my side, and went out the back door. When I got home, I stuck the knife into the eaves on the upper floor. I was afraid that I'd implicate somebody else, so I came to turn myself in at the jail."

On this basis, I at once ordered that the knife be found and, at the same time, escorted the criminal, the local warden, the neighbors, and the coroner, riding alone and with few assistants, to the place of the corpse. I summoned the father-in-law of the deceased to carry Ms. Zhang's corpse out to a level spot. There, I personally examined it in accordance with law.

Hereafter the oral report delivered on the spot by the coroner Zheng Lun: "I have examined the corpse of Ms. Zhang, deceased. On her [upper] body, she is wearing one plain old cotton unlined blouse; below, she is wearing one pair of blue cotton unlined pants; on her feet, she is wearing blue cotton wraps and a pair of black cotton shoes. Her clothing is orderly. The father-in-law of the deceased Luo Qisheng reports that Ms. Zhang is twenty-four *sui* in age and that she is a native of Longyang District in Changde Prefecture, Huguang. I observe that her hair bun is orderly. Her body is 4 *chi*, 2 *cun* tall, she measures 4.5 *cun* through the chest, and she is 9 *cun* across the shoulders. One wound on the left side of the throat, slanting, length 2.1 *cun* long, width 4 *fen*, a knife wound, lethal. She is pregnant. One wound at the neckline, toward the right side, length 2.2 *cun*, width 4 *fen*, a knife wound, non-lethal; I conclude that she was alive when the lethal wound was inflicted.

Nowhere else on her body are there any other causes of death." Furthermore, I sent an aide to bring the recovered weapon, one knife, to the inquiry, to compare it with the wound; it corresponded. Then, on the spot, he filled out the inquest report and I received it. Coroner Zheng Lun has not concealed any wound; I entered his report into the record. I had a coffin prepared and the corpse enshrouded, ordering the local warden and the neighbors to safeguard it.

Later that afternoon, the husband of the deceased Luo Er arrived at the court. Subsequently, I interrogated him. "Luo Er, where were you today that you should return only now? Did you know that your wife has been murdered by Jin San? For what reason did he murder her? Answer with all of the facts."

He testified: "Today, I was in Ximei for the market.[4] It was yesterday afternoon that I went there. Today, a person came to the marketplace to tell me that somebody had murdered my wife, so I hurried back. It's a long way—that's why it took until now for me to get here. When I got inside the wall, I heard people say that Jin San had confessed. I don't know what the reason could have been for him to murder her. I think he must have tried to rape her and my wife wouldn't go along with him, so he murdered her."

Further interrogation: "Jin San just now confessed to having had an illicit sexual relationship with your woman for a long time. How could you not know about it?"

He testified, "I've never seen them, and that's a fact. My poor wife—she had a baby in her belly and we wanted to have it, but now she's been murdered by Jin San. I beg you to right this wrong!" This and other testimony were disclosed before my court.

On these grounds, I authorized the criminal Jin San to be taken to the district jail for incarceration while I carry out further interrogation.

Magistrate Xu then completed the legal procedures required at this stage of the review process. He proceeded with his formal investigation on Yongzheng 6.9.5 [October 7, 1728], having received authorization from the provincial judicial commissioner, in the presence of the warden, relatives of the murdered woman, her neighbors, and the murderer, who had been fetched from the jail.

Interrogation of Luo Qicheng: "Where are you from? The murdered Ms. Zhang—which of your daughters-in-law was she? Did you share a residence or did you reside separately? Might you know the reason why Jin San murdered your daughter-in-law? Testify."

He testified: "I am from Longyang District of Changde Prefecture in Huguang. The murdered Ms. Zhang was my second daughter-in-law. I live separately from my son Luo Er. During Kangxi 59 [1720], I came here by myself from Huguang to rent fields to farm. My wife, along with my sons and daughters-in-law, all stayed in Huguang and didn't come. The year before last, my son Luo Er came here to find me. I had heard that Ms. Zhang had had some dealings with Jin San in Huguang that smelled bad. So I sent my son Luo Er back, and I instructed him, 'Your woman's getting a bad reputation. You had better go back and look into it.' In the second month of last year, my son Luo Er came back again all by himself. It was only on the fourth of the intercalary third month that my older son moved my wife here along with this second daughter-in-law. They didn't get here until the first of the seventh month. In the eighth month, my second son rented a store in town and opened an incense shop.[5] At that time, daughter-in-law Zhang moved into the shop to live, and I live outside the city wall with my wife and my older son. But I often go into town to spend some time with them.

"In the twelfth month of last year, I didn't expect to bump into Jin San in my son's house. So then I scolded my son: 'How can you let that kind of person hang around, even sit down in your house and talk?' My son said, 'He came to get some money because I owe him some. But I'll pay him off and not let him come again, and that will be that.' In the first month of this year, I ran into Jin San again sitting in my son's house. I lost my temper and cursed him a good one. After that, I never saw him come again. On the twenty-second of the fourth month, my son went to the Ximei market. Only the daughter-in-law and a three-*sui*-old grandson were at home. It was on the twenty-third that Yang Shangda came to me, screaming that my daughter-in-law had been murdered. I hurried inside the city to where the corpse was. I took my grandson and went to see with my own eyes. Earlier that day, Jin San had come to turn himself in at the jail and had already been questioned. On the spot, he had confessed straight out that he was the one who did the killing. And now, I can only beg you to right the wrong done to my daughter-in-law!"

Further interrogation: "Do you know why Jin San murdered your daughter-in-law Zhang?"

He testified: "I really have no idea why she was murdered. I beg you to question Jin San severely, and then you'll find out."

Interrogation of Luo Er: "Where are you from? Where did you go on the twenty-third of the fourth month? Why was your Ms. Zhang murdered by Jin San? Do you know whether or not they regularly carried on an illicit sexual relationship? Tell the truth now."

In his formal testimony, Luo Er repeated all that he had initially told the magistrate, using nearly the same words. As before, he speculated that Jin San had tried to rape his wife, and mentioned that she was pregnant.

Further interrogation: "According to what your father said, your Ms. Zhang had a sexual relationship with Jin San in Huguang, and he told you to keep an eye on her. After you came here, you should not have let her have any more contact with him. How could you let him come and go all the time, even to the point that he murdered your wife?"

[Luo Er] testified: "My father told me about it, but I really never had seen with my own eyes my Ms. having any such kind of smelly business with him. This Jin San came to my house because I borrowed some money from him when we were in Huguang. Two times when he came to collect, Father bumped into him and cursed him—this did happen. Later, I gave him a straw hat, some shoes, some incense, and some tobacco leaves, so I figured he was paid back. I said to him that the money was all paid back and told him never to come again. I never thought that he would come back again on the twenty-third of the fourth month and murder my wife. I beg you to interrogate Jin San strenuously [*yanxun*] and get to the bottom of it."[6]

Interrogation of the local warden Chen Yaosheng: "You are the local warden. What is the reason that Ms. Zhang was murdered by this Jin San? Did you or did you not know that he was regularly carrying on an illicit sexual relationship with Ms. Zhang? Testify."

He testified: "I am the warden for this area, but I live a long way from Ms. Zhang's house. That day, I had eaten breakfast and was in my house when I heard somebody in the street screaming about how Luo Er's woman Ms. Zhang had been murdered. At once, I went out and saw a group of people in Luo Er's house looking. I went in and discovered that in fact Ms. Zhang had been murdered in her bed. At that time, I did not know who it was that killed her. At once, I came with the neighbors to report. Afterward, Jin San came to turn himself in at the jail and was interrogated. Only then did I find out that he was the one who killed her. But I don't have any idea why he murdered her. As for whether or not he was regularly carrying on illicit sex with Ms. Zhang, I don't know. I beg you to interrogate Jin San, and then you'll find out."

Further interrogation: "On that day when Jin San murdered Ms. Zhang, how could there have been not even one person at home?"

He testified: "Her mother-in-law lives outside the city wall. Her husband Luo Er had gone to the market in Ximei. The only person left was a three-*sui*-old child, nobody else at all. That's a fact."

Interrogation of the neighbor on the right, Hu Gongshan: "You are Ms. Zhang's neighbor to the west. Surely you know the reason why this Jin San murdered Ms. Zhang. Tell the court the facts."

He testified: "I am Ms. Zhang's neighbor to the right. At first, that Ms. Zhang and her husband Luo Er lived outside the city wall with his parents. In the eighth month of last year, Luo Er came next door and opened an incense shop, and that's when he moved Ms. Zhang here to live with him. Later, Jin San, who said he was a relative, often came to her house to hang around. This is a fact. On the twenty-third of the fourth month of this year, Luo Er went to the market in Ximei Town, and he didn't come back. When it got dark, I went to sleep. Suddenly, I heard Ms. Zhang screaming, saying there was a thief at her back door. When I heard that, I got up quick, and I hurried to her back door, taking a shoulder pole with me for self-protection. But the thief had already left; I could see that there was nobody outside her back door. I cursed the thief a couple of times, and then I went back inside and went to sleep.

"The next day, just after breakfast, I was standing in front of my shop when I saw Jin San go into Ms. Zhang's house. Because he came and went so often, I didn't pay any particular attention. Just then, somebody came to buy some fruit and things, so I went to wait on him. When he murdered Ms. Zhang, I didn't hear any scream. In fact, I didn't even know about it. Afterward, it was Yang Gongyi's nephew Yang Shangda who saw Ms. Zhang's baby walking down the street crying, and he picked him up and took him home. He pushed at her front door, but it wouldn't open, so he took the baby in through the back. Suddenly, I heard him yelling, saying Auntie Luo Er was murdered in her bed. I hurried over and saw that in fact Ms. Zhang had been murdered. The bed mat had blood all over it. All I knew was that if there was breath, we might save her. So I went up and touched her neck, but the skin was all cut open. I quickly backed away and cried out. The neighbors from down the street, Zhang Yuanbin and the rest of them, came and pushed in the front door and came in to have a look. Then, all of us went to report it. I didn't have any idea that she had been murdered by Jin San. Afterward, Jin San turned himself in at the jail and confessed that he had murdered Ms. Zhang, and he brought up the murder weapon. Only then did I know that Jin San had killed her. I hadn't known the details until then. That's a fact."

Further interrogation: "Previously, Jin San testified that he had had an illicit sexual relationship with Ms. Zhang. Did he?"

He testified: "Whether Jin San had illicit sex with Ms. Zhang or not, I never saw. But I regularly heard Luo Er's father Luo Qisheng cursing about how that daughter-in-law of his had no sense of shame—that did happen."

Interrogation of the neighbor to the left, Zhang Yuanbin: "For what reason was this Ms. Zhang murdered by Jin San? You're a neighbor. Tell the court the facts about the cause."

He testified: "I am Ms. Zhang's neighbor to the left, but I'm separated from her house by a big alley. After breakfast on that day when Ms. Zhang was killed, I didn't know anything about it. When I heard the neighbor to the right Hu Gongshan shouting, I went outside, and all of us went to see. That's when I found out that Ms. Zhang had been murdered in her bed. So we all went to report it. It was only afterward, when Jin San came to turn himself in at the jail, that I learned that he committed the murder. But I don't know anything about the details."

Further interrogation: "The night before, when Ms. Zhang screamed and Hu Gongshan chased away the thief, you must have heard that, didn't you?"

He testified: "That night when Ms. Zhang screamed and Hu Gongshan chased away the thief, I was worn out because I had cut tobacco all day, and I went right to sleep. In my tired-out dreams, I heard somebody scream, and it woke me up. But I didn't hear anything going on, so I didn't get out of bed. This is the truth."

Interrogation of neighbor down the street Yang Gongyi: "How far are you from the place where Ms. Zhang lived? On the twenty-third of the fourth month, whom did you see go into Ms. Zhang's house? For what reason did somebody murder Ms. Zhang? Why didn't you even try to save her? Tell the court the facts in detail."

He testified: "The place where I live on this street is two houses away from Ms. Zhang. Because I'm getting old, I sit quietly in my house and don't go out into the street much. On the twenty-third of the fourth month, I didn't see anybody go toward Ms. Zhang's house. I don't know why it was that somebody murdered her. It was just because my nephew Yang Shangda saw Ms. Zhang's child walking along the street crying. . . ."

The rest of his testimony repeats what others had said about his nephew's discovery of the murder. He continued:

"Since Luo Er had gone away, I told the nephew Yang Shangda to go and tell her father-in-law Luo Qisheng to come. At that time, I had no idea who had killed her—so you tell me how I could have gone to save her?!"

Interrogation: "Might you have known that Jin San was having an adulterous affair with Ms. Zhang?"

He testified: "I never saw it with my own eyes. In the past, I heard Luo Er's father Luo Qisheng cursing that his daughter-in-law was apparently having a secret affair of this sort. That is a fact."

Interrogation of Yang Shangda: "How old are you this year? On the twenty-third of the fourth month, you screamed to Hu Gongshan that Ms. Zhang had been murdered. How did you know that?"

He testified: "I am just fourteen *sui* this year. I'm Yang Gongyi's nephew. We are originally from the same place as the Luo family. That day, I didn't know anything about Ms. Zhang being murdered. It was because I saw her baby on the street crying, and I saw he was so young, and his father Luo Er had gone to Ximei Market and wasn't back yet, so I went and picked up the baby and took him home. I saw that the front door of her house was fastened tight, and I couldn't push it open, so I went around to the back door to drop him off. I saw Ms. Zhang had fallen over on the bed, and the bed was covered with blood. I got scared, and I yelled to the next-door neighbor Hu Gongshan that Auntie Luo Er had been murdered in her bed. When Hu Gongshan came to see, then I ran home to tell my uncle Yang Gongyi. He told me to go tell Luo Qisheng."

Further interrogation: "When you entered the room, did you see anyone else in the house?"

He testified: "At the time when I went in, there was nobody else at all in her house. All I saw was Ms. Zhang dead on the bed. This is a fact."

Interrogation of Jin San: "Where are you from? How old are you this year? On the twenty-third of the fourth month, for what reason and how did you conceive the notion and with what sort of weapon did you murder Ms. Zhang? Did you or did you not have an accomplice? Tell the court all the facts."

He testified: "I'm from Longyang District in Changde Prefecture of Huguang. I'm twenty-six *sui* this year. When I was still at home in Huguang, I lived in the same place and on the same street as Luo Er, the husband of Ms. Zhang. During the eighth month of Yongzheng 4, Luo Er came to Sichuan, and that Ms. Zhang had nothing to eat. I often lent her things, and that's how I started having illicit sex with her. Luo Er returned in the twelfth month, but he didn't know anything about it. Then in the first month of last year, he came back to Sichuan. And again, this Ms. Zhang borrowed quite a lot of money from me in order to get by. In the intercalary third month, Luo Er's mother wanted to come to Sichuan because his father was in Suining.

Luo Er's older brother and his mother then brought Ms. Zhang with them. Ms. Zhang had already made promises to me before that. Seeing as how I had spent a lot of money on her, she made a secret agreement with me that I should follow her to Sichuan.

"So I set out in the fourth month for Sichuan, but once I got on the road, I didn't have any money to pay my traveling expenses. So I worked as a day laborer along the way to earn a little. I finally arrived here on the twenty-eighth of the eleventh month, and I found a place to live not far from Ms. Zhang, inside the east gate at the foot of Stone Slab Tower. When I went to Ms. Zhang's house to collect some money, her husband Luo Er brought out a straw hat, shoes, incense, and tobacco leaves and added it up for me. But it wasn't enough to pay me off, so I often went to her house to collect some money and to talk. Once, I ran into Luo Er's father, who cursed at me. Later, I found out that Luo Er went to market on every third, sixth, and ninth day.[7] When he wasn't at home, I went over to Ms. Zhang's house and had illicit sex with her like before, and Ms. Zhang had no objection at all. Luo Er didn't know anything about it either. I never thought that on the nineteenth of the first month of this year, I'd be at Ms. Zhang's room, talking with her, when Luo Er's father happened to come in again. He got real mad and really cursed at me and wouldn't let me go to her house again. Afterward, when I saw that there was nobody home, I quietly went back in to scout it out. Then Ms. Zhang told me, 'My father-in-law made a big fuss because of you. Don't you ever come back again. If you do come back again, I will certainly scream and call people to arrest you. Now get out of here.' There was nothing for it but for me to leave.

"On the night of the twenty-second of the fourth month, I knew that Luo Er wouldn't be home, so I went to his house to have illicit sex with Ms. Zhang.

His narrative of the rebuff he had received the night before and the events of the day of the homicide corresponded precisely with the first account he gave when he turned himself in, except for the details of the crime.

"But she wouldn't confess anything. I momentarily lost my temper [*yishi qifen*], and I went up to her and, with my left hand, pulled on her skein of thread, but she turned her head to the right. With my right hand, I took out my knife and cut her once on the left side of her neck. She dropped her head, and I cut her again across the neckline. Then she fell over. I pushed her back up, but she fell faceup on the bed. I could tell she was dead. I wiped the blood off my knife onto her quilt, put it back at my side, and went out through the back door. Not a single person knew about it. When I got home, I took the knife and stuck it in the eaves upstairs. But I was afraid that I'd involve somebody else, so right then, I came to turn myself in at the jail. These are the true facts."

Further interrogation: "That day when you went in, might there not have been someone who saw you? At the time that you killed her, why did Ms. Zhang not scream? How was it that the neighbors didn't know anything about it? Furthermore, Ms. Zhang was pregnant—how could you have killed her?"

He testified: "That day when I went in, the only person I saw was Hu Gongshan standing in the doorway of his own shop; I don't know if he saw me or not. At the time when I killed Ms. Zhang, there was nobody else at home. I killed her because I was so mad—what did it matter to me whether she was pregnant or not? All it took was two cuts and she was dead—how could she scream after that? So none of the neighbors knew about it. This is something I did all by myself. I confessed on my own; nobody else had anything to do with it."

Further interrogation: "Is this the knife you used to kill Ms. Zhang?"

He testified: "That is the knife I killed her with."

Further interrogation of Luo Er: "The facts concerning the murder of your woman by this Jin San have already been established by this court, as you have heard. Do you wish to be remanded to the upper courts to hear the investigation there?"

He testified: "I have a three-*sui*-old child at home, and my parents are old. I don't want to be dragged into this; I beg you to be merciful and release me from custody."

Here follows Magistrate Xu Ren's generally predictable summary of the facts of the case. His interpretation in several places is worth noting, however:

. . . Because during the eighth month of Yongzheng 4, her spouse Luo Er came to Sichuan in search of his father, leaving Ms. Zhang to pass her days in poverty, Jin San made loans to her, and in their communications, they established a sexual relationship of great emotional depth. . . . Contrary to expectation, Jin San was reluctant to part from her and thus, on the eleventh month of that year, likewise came to Suiyi and, using the pretense of collecting on her debt, had frequent interactions with her. . . . Seeing that the

affair had been discovered, Ms. Zhang tried to break it off, without success. . . . Jin San harbored resentment in his heart. On the following day, the
twenty-third, after breakfast, armed with a knife . . . [s]eeing Ms. Zhang on
her bed making shoes and, upon inspection, seeing no one else, he asked her
why she had screamed on the previous night and chased him away. In addition, he accused her of fickle feelings and of turning her back on their previous vows. Because Ms. Zhang paid no attention to him, he conceived a
murderous plan. Thus, he took up the knife at his side. . . .

The magistrate concluded with his recommendation:

Jin San fits the category of intentional homicide and should be beheaded.[8]
He is to be held in prison in accordance with the regulations; his execution
is to be delayed and not carried out until after the autumn assizes. In such
serious matters, the law allows little leniency for the criminal. Consequently,
I request that, in accordance with regulations, he be tattooed, that the local
warden Cheng Yaosheng and the neighbors Hu Gongshan, Zhang Yuanbin,
Yang Gongyi, and Yang Shangda, who have been interrogated but who know
nothing of the matter, should all be released. In accordance with precedent,
they have already been released at the provincial level.

   Father-in-law of the deceased Luo Qisheng and spouse of the deceased
Luo Er wish not to proceed in person as this investigation goes forward. In
accordance with regulations, I have dismissed them. I have commanded the
husband of the deceased, Luo Er, to take custody of the coffin and to bury
it. The weapon with which the crime was committed, one knife, has been
forwarded with the investigation; whether or not it is relevant, I dare not
decide on my own. Together with the person and the documents, I await
your judicial review at the prefectural level.

*Other summaries followed as the case moved up through the judicial review process.
All agreed that Jin San was of the category of criminal that "cannot be pardoned"
(nan kuanyou) whose crime should be tattooed on his cheek. Jin San was held in
prison at the capital. By Yongzheng 6.10.20 (November 21, 1728), the case report had
been submitted to the Throne in the form of a memorial requesting that the Three
Judicial Offices give one final review and confirm the death sentence as recommended
initially by the investigating magistrate. The emperor's conclusion, written on the
cover of the report in red ink, directed the Three Judicial Offices to indicate the appropriate sentence in a further memorial.*

Source: *Neige tiben Xingfa lei* [Grand Secretariat routine memorials, Crime and Punishment] 2–34–2335–5, Yongzheng 6.10.20 (1728).

1. The ancient state of Chu was in modern Hunan; Hunan and present-day Hubei were called Huguang during the early Qing.

2. According to Article 25 of the Qing penal code, an offender who turns himself in and makes a confession before he is caught avoids punishment if the crime is minor. For major crimes such as homicide, however, he will still be punished in accordance with the relevant law for the original crime. See Jones, *Great Qing Code*, 56–58.

3. Presumably, she was sewing them out of cloth.

4. Most such market towns held periodic markets, every ten days or more frequently; as Jin San reveals below, the market was held here every three days.

5. Presumably meaning cheap incense to be used in religious rituals.

6. *Yanxun*, meaning "interrogate strenuously," is a formal term, suggesting interrogation using torture.

7. By this, he means on the third, sixth, and ninth day of every ten-day period, or *xun*, that is, the thirteenth, sixteenth, nineteenth, and so on.

8. This is in accordance with Article 282 of the Qing penal code, with no allowance for the murderer's voluntary confession. See Jones, *Great Qing Code*, 268.

CASE 19

Luo Fenpeng: A Phony Scholar-Official (Jiangxi, 1763)

TRANSLATED BY MARK McNICHOLAS

During the Qing period, a serious crime did not necessarily include an act of violence. The following two documents relate the exploits of a poor but resourceful scholar on the margins of elite society who impersonated an official during the middle years of the Qianlong period.[1] *Luo Fenpeng was an unsuccessful teacher from Jiangxi, in south-central China. Teaching does not seem to have supported his financial needs, for he was twice punished for theft by the local magistrate before he set off on his new adventures.*

Luo Fenpeng's experiences while posing as a man of higher status and finer prospects who had fallen on hard times demonstrate the importance and usefulness of native-place solidarity and classical education in late imperial China. In planning his appeals for aid, Luo carefully targeted fellow natives of his home province. He also made good use of his education, combining the facility in writing required of any civil-service examination candidate with a widely understood political symbol—a hat ornament indicating official rank—in weaving tales of hard luck that enabled him to obtain free food, clothing, and lodging. His experiences also reveal how position brought with it the ability to influence others in the administration: because of his supposed connections, Luo was asked to intervene in a lawsuit, which ultimately resulted in his undoing. This case exemplifies the daily struggle for food and shelter that took place at the margins of society. It also reveals an ideal of traditional social harmony: people helping a stranger in distress.

DOCUMENT I. LUO FENPENG'S CONFESSION

This confession is quoted in the initial report submitted to the Throne by the Jiangxi provincial governor Tang Pin on May 1, 1763.

"I am from Luling District in Ji'an Prefecture. I was originally surnamed Luo, and my name is Fenpeng; Li Rongzong is an assumed name. This year, I am thirty-eight *sui* old. My father is Luo Junzheng, and my younger brother is Luo Yunpeng. I have taken a wife surnamed Li, who gave birth to a son, Xunguan, only eight *sui* old. In Qianlong 24 [1759], I left home and went from Hunan to Hubei, working as a scribe along the way to get by. I did not falsely pretend to have official rank. In Qianlong 25 and 26 [1760 and 1761], I went to various places in Henan, selling calligraphy, and committed no acts of banditry or swindling.

"In the eleventh month of Qianlong 26 [late November and December 1761], I heard that THE EMPEROR was touring the south, and I wanted to go and see. After the twentieth [December 15], I arrived at Yangzhou and first stayed at the Jiangxi native Shan Zixian's needle shop on Coppersmith Street. As I saw that Yangzhou was bustling, I conceived the idea of pretending to be an official in order to swindle. So I invented the name Ouyang Zhang and said I was a vice prefect by purchase.[2] Then, I met Li Huancai, who had a tailor shop on Peppertree Alley and was also from Jiangxi. I told him that I was Ouyang Zhang of Anfu [also in Jiangxi, and close to Luo's home] and that because of a boating accident when crossing the Yellow River, my baggage had been swept away and lost. He believed it and borrowed sixteen *liang* on my behalf. I also borrowed a total of eighty *liang* from Shu Wen and Zeng Er, who were on a Ji'an tribute boat. I had clothing made, hired servants, and, wearing a crystal-buttoned official's hat, used the name Ouyang Zhang and went to visit the Nanchang *jiansheng* Lu Xuan.[3] I met him several times and also went to visit the Yangzhou subprefectural magistrate Xie Tao. He, too, is from Ji'an, and I thought he would give me some traveling money, but he had gone off on business, and I never got to see him. There was also the Zhenjiang Transport Command company commander Ouyang Weiguo, escorting [grain boats] to Yangzhou, and his brother Ouyang Zhiping and the fellow provincial lumber merchant Xiong Wenjin. I went to see all of them. Ouyang Weiguo had already departed, and I did not swindle any money from him.

"As I had stayed at Yangzhou for a long time and feared discovery, on the nineteenth of the second month [March 14, 1762], I threw the hat button away and, taking the remaining two or three *liang*, fled across the [Yangzi] River. On the twenty-third [March 18], I reached Suzhou and, on the second of the third month [March 26], reached Hangzhou, where I amused myself for a few days on West Lake. As my traveling money was exhausted, I again thought of swindling, whereupon I bought a dark blue rank button at a stall.[4] Fearing that someone from Yangzhou would come searching, I dared not keep using the name Ouyang Zhang and changed my name to Li Chunguan. Saying I was a Ji'an native and a prefect by purchase, I went to visit the Hangzhou prefect Zeng Yueli, who was also from Jiangxi, but was not received. There was also the Chuzhou brigade commander Zeng Jieji, at Hangzhou on a horse-buying mission. He was a Jiangxi native, and I went to visit him, hoping he would give me some traveling expenses, but I did not meet him either. I had no money to spend, so I worked as a scribe to make a living.

"Later, I traveled on foot to Jiangning. Seeing that there were many Jiangxi lumber merchants there, I again wore the blue-buttoned hat and, using the name Li Chunguan, went to visit them. I wrote some calligraphy samples and gave them to the lumber merchants Chen Lüxiang and Huang Canxian, earning more than thirty *liang*.

"In the fifth month [late May to late June 1762], I set out from Jiangning, going north of the [Yangzi] River to the Shouzhou area [in Anhui] and, as before, getting through the days by working as a scribe. On the twentieth of the first month of this year [March 4, 1763], I arrived at Nine Temple Mountain in Tongshan District, Hubei, and stayed at Jiuyi Temple. The Daoist priest, Liu Jingting, was also a Jiangxi native, and he invited me to eat. But I had no money to donate.

Recalling that there was a fellow provincial, Li Xuan, [who] had served as district magistrate of Yuanrang [in Hunan], I wrongfully used his name to write the calligraphy for two door tablets. Moreover, I wrote the words: "Rewarding the regular metropolitan graduate, Board of Revenue office director, and Grand Master for Governance of Shaowu Prefecture, Fujian, who accompanied the IMPERIAL CARRIAGE on a southern tour, IMPERIALLY FAVORED with conferral of a court necklace, satchel, and advancement by one class." I meant only to show off to him.

Unexpectedly, when I went to stay at an inn outside the Tongshan District walls on the twenty-third [March 7], someone surnamed Yu was gambling for high stakes there with some others; they were arrested by constables, and I was taken with them for questioning. In the heat of the moment, I put on my official's cap and said I was Li Xuan and was awaiting an appointment as prefect. The Tongshan magistrate questioned me for a while and handed me over to underlings to keep in custody for further investigation. I seized an opportunity to escape.[5] On the sixth of the second month [March 20], I reached the Shankou area in Wuning District and spent the night at the home of one Hong Nanyang. On the seventh, the dismissed stipend student [*linsheng*] Ye Guangjia, seeing that I wore a rank button, took me to his home.[6] I lied that I had served as prefect of Zhangzhou, Fujian. Because his relative Nie Xianmo was in the midst of a lawsuit over the compilation of a clan genealogy, Ye Guangjia promised me eighty *liang* if I would intercede with the district magistrate on his behalf. We went to the district seat together. Considering my own false position, I dared not go to meet the district magistrate and seized an opportunity to flee. I reached the Shatian area but on the fourteenth [March 28] was caught by magistrate's runners from the two counties of Wuning and Tongshan and brought to this court. I did not receive money from either Ye Guangjia or Nie Xianmo and except for [what I have related in this confession] have not done anything illegal. Even in my home of Luling, I merely made a living by instructing the young."

Luo's testimony was confirmed by depositions from all the persons he named, each of whom was summoned to the court for interrogation.

DOCUMENT 2. GOVERNOR TANG'S FINAL REPORT

The following is an extract from the Jiangxi governor's final report on the case, retelling the story with added details acquired during the course of his investigation.

Governor of Jiangxi and concurrent provincial military commander, Your subject Tang Pin respectfully submits this MEMORIAL on the matter of apprehending, trying, and passing sentence on a false official.

_{Your subject} ventures to report on the case of the Wuning District magistrate apprehending Luo Fenpeng, also known as Li Rongzong, who pretended to be an official. I immediately forwarded the criminal and evidence to the provincial capital. I also immediately ordered the Nanchang and Jiujiang prefects to conduct investigations on the details of the depositions. _{Your subject} further led commissioners and intendants one by one in rigorously investigating all the particulars. On 3.19 [May 1, 1763], I respectfully memorialized for YOUR MAJESTY'S information, at the same time speedily sending communications to the governors-general and governors of Jiangnan and Zhejiang to make clear through investigation whether Li Huancai and others were in fact defrauded and moreover to obtain the truthful, personal depositions of Zeng Yueli, Zeng Jieji, and other civil and military officials and moreover requested investigation into the details of the crimes at Tongshan District, Hubei, so as to compile evidence. Now the various provinces have one after another responded. Beginning on the twenty-fourth of the fourth month [June 5], _{Your subject} led Provincial Administration Commissioner Fuming and Anhui provincial judicial commissioner Yan Xishen in personally bringing Luo Fenpeng to my court in order to interrogate him with torture and, layer by layer, get to the root of the matter.

The said criminal is a native of Luling District [in Ji'an Prefecture, Jiangxi]. Never content with his lot in life, he twice committed theft and was punished by the district magistrate, as is on record. Then, in Qianlong 24 [1759], he left home and worked his way to the Hubei-Henan area via Liling District [Hunan], working as a scribe along the way and every day obtaining twenty or thirty coppers for his living. In the eleventh month of Qianlong 26 [December 1761], he arrived at Yangzhou [in Jiangsu] and saw that the place was thriving, whereupon he conceived the idea of swindling. He bought a hat bearing the crystal rank button and invented the name Ouyang Zhang. Learning that the Jiangxi native Shan Zixian operated a needle shop in Yangzhou, and that the brothers Li Jingting and Li Huancai had a tailoring business there, the criminal first went to Shan Zixian's needle shop and spent the night. The next day, he went to Li Huancai's home and falsely claimed that he was a vice prefect by purchase whose boat had been damaged and luggage swept away on the Yellow River and that now he was sending a letter home to press for money to be sent to him. Li Huancai, long knowing of the great Ouyang clan, believed it and took him to the Quelling Monsters Temple [Fumomiao] next door to stay. From beginning to end, he lent the criminal sixteen *liang*.[7]

The criminal bought clothing and hired Xiao Shun and other servants to accompany him. He asked Li Jingting to act as guarantor and borrowed a total of eighty *liang* from the Ji'an [his home prefecture] traveling boat merchants Shu Wen and Zeng Er. He also borrowed three *liang* and six coppers from Xiao Shun's father, Xiao Yu. Then, he asked Li Huancai to advance twelve *liang* for him as security on boots and hats and, further, claiming to be purchasing a concubine, asked Chen Laosan to act as matchmaker, make a match with a Miss Zou, and give two *liang* in betrothal money as well as earrings, rings, and so on. Moreover, he borrowed silver from the temple monk Jie'an and asked Jie'an to act as guarantor to borrow eight thousand coppers from a squad commander [*bazong*] Xu, who was also staying at the temple.[8] Jie'an, seeing that he lived there for some time with no sign of the [expected] letter from home, inquired about it morning and night. The criminal feared that he would be exposed, and on the nineteenth of the second month of Qianlong 27 [March 14, 1762], he used the pretext of an excursion to flee. Squad Commander Xu demanded his money from the monk. Jie'an, together with Li Huancai, sold the bedding the criminal had left behind for five *liang*, two coppers. Jie'an further pawned his own clothing to raise enough to pay off [the debts]. The amounts that Jie'an had lent and spent [on Luo Fenpeng's behalf], including rent, added up to a total of fifteen *liang*. Li Huancai drew up an agreement pledging to repay it.

The criminal took his remaining silver and, during the second and third months, wandered along the road from Suzhou to Hangzhou. In the fifth month, he arrived at Jiangning. With his traveling money exhausted, he again conceived the plan to swindle, bought a dark blue hat button, invented the name Li Chunguan, and claimed he was a prefect by purchase whose servant had absconded with his baggage, leaving him stranded. He walked to the Twisting Dragon Monastery at Shangxin River [in western Jiangning Prefecture] in search of lodging and encountered the Jiangxi raft-maker Zeng Wenmao. They talked about their longing for home, and Zeng Wenmao let him stay at the monastery, on various occasions lending him silver and cash and giving him food, spending a total of twenty-some *liang*. The criminal also wrote calligraphy samples and gave them to [Jiangxi] lumber merchants conducting trade at Jiangning; of these, Chen Lüxiang gave him a *liang* and two coppers and Huang Canxian gave eight coppers. By the eighth month, Zeng Wenmao had spent much money and told him to borrow elsewhere. The criminal falsely claimed that although he had several friends in this place, it would be difficult to go call on them without [proper] clothing and headwear. Zeng Wenmao then had clothes and a hat made for him. The criminal again feared exposure, and on the tenth of the eighth month [September 27, 1762], he left the temple, hid the blue hat button, and escaped, going north of the Yangzi River toward the Shouzhou area and again working as a scribe along the way.

On twentieth of the first month of this year [March 4, 1763], he arrived at Jiuyi Temple in Tongshan District, Hubei, cheating the Daoist priest Liu Jingting out of food by writing calligraphy for a door tablet. Recalling that his fellow provincial Li Xuan had been magistrate of Yuanrang District, he assumed his name and wrote the words "accompanied the IMPERIAL CARRIAGE on the southern tour, IMPERIALLY FAVORED with conferral of a court necklace, satchel, and advancement by one class" and gave it to the Daoist priest to store. On the twenty-third, he went to a restaurant outside the walls of the Tongshan District seat, wearing the blue-buttoned hat and falsely claiming to be a prefect. When the owner Yan Guoxiang informed patrolling runners that there happened to be one Yu Lijiu and others gambling heavily at the restaurant, they were all taken to the magistrate for interrogation. In the deposition that the Tongshan District magistrate immediately had him write, [Luo] claimed that twice, at Jiangning and at Huai'an, he had received the EMPEROR, and that moreover Junior Vice-Minister [of the Board of Personnel] Cheng Yan and Grand Secretariat [Neige] Academician Shuangqing had presented him at audience, and again that he had, accompanying the EMPEROR, arrived at the capital on the fourth of the fifth month [June 14] and received the IMPERIAL benevolent conferral of a promotion by one class and so on. The Tongshan magistrate handed him over to underlings to guard, but the criminal escaped.

On the sixth of the second month [March 20], he fled to the Shankou area of Wuning District. The dismissed stipend student Ye Guangjia detained him at his home, promising to give him eighty *liang* if he would go to the district magistrate and intercede in the matter of his relative Nie Xianmo's lawsuit over the compilation of a clan genealogy. The criminal, considering his own false position, escaped to Shatian. On the fourteenth, Wuning District learned [of his whereabouts] and sent underlings to apprehend him. It happened that Tongshan District runners also arrived in Wuning, and they collaborated in his apprehension. This is the true tale of the said criminal repeatedly pretending to be an official and lying and swindling in various localities.

The governor concluded his report by noting that Luo Fenpeng's confession was as clear as a picture in every detail and recommended that Luo be beheaded after the autumn assizes in accordance with the law on impersonation of an official. The doc-

ument ends with the emperor's decision in red: "Let the Three Judicial Offices make a recommendation and memorialize accordingly." Presumably, Luo was executed.

NOTES

Source: For document 1, Guoli Gugong bowuyuan [National Palace Museum], ed., *Gongzhongdang Qianlongchao zouzhe* [Secret palace memorials of the Qianlong reign] (Taipei: Guoli Gugong bowuyuan, 1982–89), vol. 17: 243–46, memorial dated Qianlong 28/3/19. For document 2, ibid., 566–70, memorial dated Qianlong 28/4/27.

1. In accordance with Article 360 of the Qing penal code, punishments for impersonating an official ranged from beheading with delay to beating with the heavy staff. See Jones, *Great Qing Code*, 343–44.

2. At various times throughout the Qing period, the government sold official ranks (and sometimes even posts) as a temporary revenue-gathering expedient. Even a purely honorary rank enhanced the purchaser's social status.

3. In the Qing period, the button at the top of one's hat designated official rank. The colors assigned to each rank were, from highest (rank one) to lowest (rank nine), ruby, red coral, transparent blue, dark blue, crystal (transparent), opaque white, golden, gilded, and silvered. Thus, Luo's hat button indicated the fifth rank. Brunnert and Hagelstrom, *Present Day Political Organization*, 507–8. The *jiansheng*, a purchased degree, was generally equivalent to the lowest of the three regular civil-service degrees.

4. Dark blue is the color for the fourth-rank button.

5. Article 389 of the Qing penal code stipulates increased penalties for those who escape from jail; Article 392 outlines punishments for jail guards who fail to prevent such escapes. See Jones, *Great Qing Code*, 362, 366.

6. A stipend student attended a government school, received a stipend, and was certified to take the provincial civil service examination. Hucker, *Dictionary of Official Titles*, 313.

7. The temple was dedicated to Guan Gong, patron deity of merchants and warriors. Lord Guan was the historical general Guan Yu of Shu Han who lived during the Three Kingdoms period (third century).

8. During the Qing period, the squad commander led ten soldiers in charge of protecting a fortification. These minor military officers were also charged with protecting transports along the imperial waterways. See Hucker, *Dictionary of Official Titles*, 360–61.

PART VII

IMPERIAL INTERVENTION

For cases involving "normal" acts of violence, the tragedies recorded in the routine memorials that recorded investigative reporting by magistrates at the local level and by their superiors further up the chain of judicial review, the emperor might have been only nominally involved. Executions were carried out in his name, and central government officials required his approval before they could proceed. In some cases, however, the emperor participated directly. The communications in the following report were found in a chronologically arranged collection of imperial edicts and the memorials they inspired.

CASE 20

Li Yuchang: A Magistrate Murdered for His Integrity (Jiangsu, 1809)

TRANSLATED WITH THE ASSISTANCE OF JOANNA WALEY-COHEN

Li Yuchang was a newly minted jinshi, a holder of the highest degree in the civil-service examination system, and was about to take his first position as district magistrate of Shanyang, in Jiangsu, when a natural disaster intervened. In 1809, there was a flood in parts of that province, and he was reassigned as one of the ten commissioners who were to oversee the distribution of disaster relief funds in the area. Soon after he arrived, however, he was invited to join an embezzlement scheme: a number of local officials planned to exaggerate the population statistics in order to collect more government relief funds (paid in silver) and pocket the difference. Li not only refused to participate but even threatened to file formal complaints against those who did. Before long, he was dead, the victim of greedy underlings and several utterly unscrupulous colleagues.

The official record of this homicide and its outcome appears in memorials and edicts that passed nearly daily back and forth between the Jiaqing emperor and the senior members of his Grand Council during late summer of 1809, from 6.21(August 2) to 7.24 (September 3).[1] It would appear that some of the officials involved were initially skeptical about whether such an outrageous offense could really have taken place. When everyone was convinced, the emperor demanded the highest penalties for all involved—not only because they had committed murder but also because of their concerted effort to defraud the relief system of the realm, a cornerstone of responsible Confucian government.

As if it were not enough that the highest officials of the Qing empire were outraged by these crimes, the natural order itself became unbalanced. According to witnesses, the spirit of the dead man returned to take possession of the minds of the living in order to articulate his mournful complaints of injustice. Surely it was to propitiate this restless spirit—and to deter further embezzlement of relief funds—that the emperor took the extraordinary step of ordering that the murderers be dismembered and that executions be carried out at the murdered man's tomb.

Because he was to be the next magistrate of Shanyang District, Li Yuchang is often referred to as Magistrate Li, even though he never served in that capacity.

Your subject, Grand Councilor Tie [Bao], Governor-general of the provinces of Liang Jiang, on Jiaqing 14.6.21 [August 2, 1809], having respectfully received YOUR HIGHNESS'S INSTRUCTION concerning the unclear matter of the death of Li Yuchang: At this time, when Shandong deputed several personnel to open his coffin and to inspect the corpse of Li Yuchang, they discovered numerous dark spots on the bones of his joints, above and below, which must in fact be evidence that he was hanged after he had been poisoned. When there are further facts, I will submit a MEMORIAL accordingly.

Further, I have heard that on the twenty-second of the first month of this year [March 7, 1809], Jing Chongfa, Li Yuchang's old friend, all of a sudden became wild and confused; he fell to the ground and declared, "I am Li Yuchang, returned from Shanyang, where I died most bitterly!" And he wept without stopping. A few moments later, Jing Chongfa ceased breathing.

We have taken into custody and have delivered to the capital for investigation a group of felons, to be interrogated by members of the Grand Council and the Board of Punishments. They will be examined so strenuously that not a shred of evidence can be concealed. Previously, when this case was first examined at Jiangsu, officials seemingly could find no reason for which the magistrate and the prefect should poison the administrator, now deceased, and for them to carry out such a thorough cover-up. Furthermore, the higher of those two administrators gave evidence intended to mislead when he declared that the late magistrate had of his own accord taken poison and then hanged himself. When he was enshrouded and encoffined, why should there be yellow paper spells on the body along with a small mirror? Moreover, lime had been daubed at various places around his face and body to obscure the marks there. Obviously, the relevant governor-general had failed in his duty to observe carefully and had been deceived.

Although we have already broken this case in general, [I,] Tie Bao, will further depute a clever and reliable person to investigate personally and determine how Li Yuchang was poisoned that day, whose plan this was, and who was involved. . . .[2]

From a memorial of two days later, 14.6.23 (August 4):

Yesterday, Your subjects met and personally brought in Ma Liansheng for intense and detailed examination. He testified:

"During the ninth month of last year, I accompanied my master Li Yuchang on his trip to the various townships of Shanyang District to inspect the relief efforts. On the twenty-eighth of the tenth month [December 15, 1808], we returned to the city of Huai'an. On the sixth, Lord Wang [Shenhan] of Shanyang [then magistrate of Shanyang District] invited my master to drink wine, and my master proceeded to the great gate of the *yamen*. But as it happened, Lord Wang had official business and had gone out and was not able to entertain us. Instead, Lord Wang's younger brother and his legal secretary named Li, along with deputy inspectors of the relief effort named Lin and Gong, had wine with us. By the second watch, the party broke up, but just then Lord Wang returned to the *yamen* and instructed his household staff to detain us a bit longer. All the guests had another round of tea. After my master drank his tea, I felt his words had become somewhat confused: he asked me whether I had brought along my blanket to the district court. Everyone found his words absentminded. Thereafter, my master returned to rest at the place where we were staying, the Virtuous Rewards Abbey. There, he said to us, 'In the district, they have no record of my family; probably we'll have to go to Suzhou.' Li Xiang and I comforted him a bit, and Gu Xiang poured our master a cup of the tea that he had made previously and set it on the table. My master drank it and sat for a while, and then he went to bed to sleep. He told us to be up early the following morning so that he could make his report at Huai'an, rent a boat, and return home for a new assignment. Then, he told us to take away the lamp and close the door of his room. We, too, took off our clothes and went to sleep.

"We three were staying in the eastern room of the southern wing, and each went to sleep separately. The next morning, Li Xiang got up first and went to our master's room. Suddenly, he began shouting, saying that our master had been hanged. All of us went in, to discover that he was no longer breathing. Thereupon, we went to the Shanyang District *yamen* to report. Before long, [the administrative heads of] Huai'an Prefecture and Shanyang District both came to inspect [the scene]. The coroner called out his report before completing his examination of our master's dead body, saying he had died from suicide by hanging. I was watching from the side. All he did was loosen his [Li Yuchang's] clothing in front and take off one stocking during his inspection. He didn't look closely at any other part of the body. But when we were undressing him to put him into his burial clothes, we took off his jacket, and I saw several streaks of blood on the front of it and bloodstains at the corners of his mouth as well. The coroner and others wiped those stains away. On the following day, as we were placing him into the coffin, a yin-yang master [*yinyang sheng*] took a spell made of paper and a small mirror and placed them on his chest.[3] I saw all of this myself.

"Why my master wanted to shorten his own life, I really don't know. It was just that on the third or fourth of the eleventh month, I heard Li Xiang say that the master had gone to the district *yamen* and had talked about inspecting the relief efforts with Magistrate Wang. He asked about the rosters of people to be accounted for, and they got into an argument. They couldn't agree. Master wanted to inspect four townships, and he had already finished more than two. Lord Wang wanted to have the jailer carry out the inspections for him and say that our master had done it, but my master wouldn't agree to give them up. Again, he asked the district clerk for the general population registers, but the clerk would not give them to him. They were only sent over on the fifth. The master said, 'He deceived me. Ever since I first took office, he has treated me as if I were a child, and I won't put up with it.' And on the sixth, when he went to the party, when Lord Wang returned to the *yamen*, I saw the commissioner named Lin talking secretively with him in the courtyard. I heard Commissioner Lin say, 'It's of utmost importance that you let me have a day or two before you go back.' Lord Wang said, 'I understand.' But I don't know what they were talking about; maybe it was something to do with this business. Beyond that, I couldn't make out what was said."

This felon's words were cunning, and his testimony very much seemed to have been crafted in advance with the intent to stall; it was not reliable. Allow me to examine him more rigorously, and when he has produced reliable testimony, I will prepare a MEMORIAL.[4]

Subsequently, on the twenty-sixth, Ma Liansheng testified about the prefect and the magistrate coming to the murdered man's house and demanding the keys to his chests. They removed all the contents—records Li Yuchang had kept during his inspection of the disaster area, his account books, and even two personal letters he had been writing, anything on which he had written. They ripped up the letters and took the rest with them, telling Ma Liansheng that if any official should ask about the victim's activities on the day that he died, he need not mention the drinking party at the district yamen.[5] On the twenty-seventh, according to a response to an edict from the emperor, an official of the Board of Punishments reported that Wang Shenhan had been removed from office as magistrate of Shanyang District and taken into custody along with the governor-general of Liang Jiang Tie Bao, Wang's servant Hu Tai, the coroner Li Biao, and the court clerk Zhu Xueli.[6]

In a memorial dated 14.6.27 (August 8) the following day, the governor-general of Zhili announced that, during interrogation, the inspector whom Ma Liansheng had identified only as Lin was in fact Lin Yongsheng; his secret conversation with Magistrate Wang Shenhan was the "key" (guanjian) to the whole case.[7]

On 14.6.28, a team of officials from the Board of Punishments questioned Wang Shenhan, the coroner, a clerk, and the monk of the abbey where the murdered man had been staying.

Your subjects again raised the question of how blood could flow from the mouth of a man who had hanged himself. And why this was not filled in on the coroner's report during the inquest. And why the drinking party at the district yamen on the sixth was not mentioned in [previous] testimony. . . .

The interrogators apparently cross-examined the cashiered magistrate relentlessly, but on this occasion, he did not admit to any lying. For his part, the coroner Li Biao admitted dereliction of duty in failing to examine the body thoroughly.[8] During his testimony later that day, Hu Tai, accountant for the cashiered magistrate Wang, admitted having seen dark blotches on the murdered man's face.

Hu Tai testified:

"On the eighth, when the body was being encoffined, I saw that Magistrate Li was wearing his long robe with an outer jacket. And the yin-yang master placed inside the coffin a small mirror and a talisman, which he said he had made to subdue the Official of the Day.[9] He told us to buy some incense and paper [sacrificial] money and to burn it as an offering in front of the coffin. Thereafter, my master told his servants that he wanted the keys to his chests, so that he could make an inventory of his clothing, and so on.

Hu Tai further testified that Magistrate Wang had taken all the dead man's chests with him, including one that contained thirty liang of silver. The monk Yuanfu testified in turn that he had been away chanting scriptures on the night of the murder and returned at midnight, when he immediately went to bed. The next morning, Li Yuchang's servant Li Xiang told him of the death; after the inquest, he, too, observed blood around the head of the murdered man's bed and suspected poison.

The coroner Li Biao testified:

"I am seventy-one sui in age, and I am the coroner for Shanyang District. On the seventh of the eleventh month of last year, about time for early tea, I went to the Virtuous Rewards Abbey to attend an inquest on the body of Li Yuchang. At that time, His Honor the prefect of Huai'an himself and [the district magistrate] Lord Wang were there to watch, along with their personal servants. . . .

Despite the cursory nature of his initial examination of the corpse, Magistrate Wang had told Li Biao that it was not necessary to go further. The coroner had noticed the bloodstains at the mouth of the corpse, but the local warden had brought a copper pan of water with which to wash them off—on the orders of the prefect.[10]

An undated memorial from either the twenty-eighth or the twenty-ninth records that, because Wang Shenhan continued to stonewall the interrogation, he was subjected to the form of torture reserved for officials: his ears were twisted, and he was forced to kneel on chains. Then he testified:

"Because I wanted to exaggerate the population figures and Li Yuchang would not agree, I conceived the idea of poisoning him."

Even after this, Wang would not reveal any of the details about how the poisoning was carried out. During testimony taken on the twenty-ninth by the governor-general of Liang Jiang and the provincial governor of Jiangsu, he admitted that the murdered man not only refused to inflate population figures in order to increase the relief payments to the area but was also planning to expose Wang. Li's servant Ma Liansheng finally provided the details. The emperor was so infuriated by this outrageous behavior that he wrote all over the memorial, harshly criticizing all of Wang's superiors who had failed to detect this fraud thus far.[11]

On the thirtieth, Wang Shenhan, now referred to as "the cashiered official," was questioned again, and again he prevaricated until subjected to further torture. Thereupon, he testified that he had plotted with Li Yuchang's servants Li Xiang and Bao Xiang, who in turn enlisted Ma Liansheng in the plot. Although the others confessed, Ma held out through hours of strenuous interrogation until finally, during the fourth watch of the night, he outlined the plot so that it was "as clear as a painting" (lili ruhua). Wang Shenhan provided more details:

"The reason for Li Yuchang's death was that Li Yuchang examined the population figures and came up with a little more than nine thousand households. I wanted him to add to it until it was more than ten thousand. I talked it over with Li's servant Li Xiang, and I told him to urge his master to compromise a bit and we all could benefit from it. But Li Xiang later told me that his master refused. Thereafter, when Li Yuchang came to the district court, I spoke to him about it directly, but he still refused. After that Li Xiang sent me a note saying that his master wanted to report me to the lieutenant governor [*fansi*] and that he had already completed a draft. I said, 'Not only will your master not go along, but he wants to turn me in instead! You go back and let me talk this over again.' After Li Xiang left, I told my gatekeeper Bao Xiang that Commissioner Li was going to turn me in, and he said, 'Why not talk over ways of doing him in with Li Xiang?' I said that would be taking the matter too far. 'You listen to hear whether in fact he is going to file a report and let me know.' That was on the fifth. On the sixth, I had planned on inviting the relief commissioners to come to the *yamen* to eat, but since the prefecture sent me out to investigate a murder case in Haizhou, it was late at night when I finally returned to the district, and the drinking party was all over. After I saw the guests off, I went to sleep.

"Early on the seventh, Bao Xiang said that he had already mentioned the subject we had been talking about the day before to Li Xiang, and he had promised him one hundred *liang* of silver to give to his local headman. Li had agreed to do it. But one person couldn't manage it all by himself, so he had talked it over with Ma Liansheng and had promised him one hundred *liang* of silver for his local headman as well. Ma had also agreed. That night, when Magistrate Li returned to his lodgings, Li Xiang made him a pot of tea and put the poison in it, so that he could serve it to him when Magistrate Li happened to ask for some. But then he was afraid that the poison was not strong enough to do the trick, and that's why he talked with Ma Liansheng about killing Magistrate Li by hanging him. This is why Li Xiang reported on the seventh that his master had hanged himself. At that time, Bao Xiang told me what he [Li] had privately agreed with him. And since this was already a done deal, I had no choice but to try to save the situation. In order to have a way of investigating the suicide of a commissioner, I filed a report with the prefecture, asking the prefect for direction, and his order was that he would go with me to investigate.

"When we got to the abbey, I saw that Li Yuchang's mouth had blood-stains, and so I ordered the coroner to wash them off first in order to facilitate the examination. At that time, the prefect took no pains in the examination; before the body had been taken down, he only took a look at him from outside the chamber door, and thereafter he remained in his official chair at some distance from the body. That is why he never discerned the marks of poisoning. . . .

For their part in the matter, Wang testified, Li's servants Li Xiang, Ma Liansheng, and his own servant Bao Xiang all received one hundred liang of silver, a princely amount.[12]

In another record of testimony taken that same day, Li Yuchang's servant Ma Lianshen added some fairly informal but very graphic details:

"On the sixth of the winter [twelfth] month of last year, Shanyang District invited Magistrate Li [Li Yuchang] over. Li Xiang and I went along. When it got to be the second watch, we came back to our lodgings. The magistrate was a little drunk, so he sat down and wanted some tea to drink. Li Xiang poured him a cup of tea in the room outside and brought it in and gave it to him. The magistrate drank it right down. Li Xiang poured him another cup and left it on the table. The magistrate sat around smoking for a while, talking about this and that, and he drank that cup of tea, too. I waited on him as he got undressed and went to bed. The rest of us all went to our room and took off our clothes and were sitting around rolled up in our quilts when we heard somebody calling at the door.

"Li Xiang went out, and somebody came in and stood and talked for a while in the dark. I asked Li Xiang who it was, and after I asked him a couple of times, he finally said it was Bao Xiang. Then Gu Xiang went out, and the three of them talked for a while. I said, 'Why don't you come sit in here where there's a light?' Li Xiang came in first; I asked him what Bao Xiang was doing here, and Bao Xiang said he wanted to ask our master to get up; there was something important he had to say to him. Then, Bao Xiang and Gu Xiang came in together. I said, 'If you have something to tell him, I'll go tell him for you. Why must you ask the master to get up?' Li Xiang said, 'The master took some medicine.' I said, 'The master's not sick. Why would he take medicine?' And Li Xiang said, 'The medicine the master took was poison!' I cried out, 'Why would you give the master poison?!' Li Xiang said that Bao Xiang had gotten some poison and had brought it over to give to him. He had put it into his tea and had given it to the master to drink. I wouldn't go along with Li Xiang and Bao Xiang. I asked them, 'Why did you want to hurt our master? I'm going to call for help!' Li Xiang and Bao Xiang said, 'It's no use to call for help; we already gave him the poison. If you call for help, it'll only involve you, and if you don't call, you can figure you will still be involved.' At that, I didn't dare say anything. After that, Bao Xiang promised me one hundred *liang* of silver.

"Bao Xiang told Li Xiang to go trick the Old Master into getting up. The Old Master asked what he had to say, and Li Xiang said that Bao Xiang had something important to say. At that, the Old Master got up, put on his clothes and socks, and stood in front of the bed. Li Xiang told Bao Xiang to go in, and Gu Xiang also went in. I stayed at the door looking in. Li Xiang and Gu Xiang squeezed in on him from both sides, and Bao Xiang went around behind him and grabbed him around the waist with his two hands, while Li and the other grabbed hold of his arms. The Old Master cried out, 'What's going on here?' Li Xiang kept hold of him by the arms, and Bao Xiang took advantage of the opportunity to take off his own sash [*dabao*] and wrap it several times around the Old Master's head and mouth.[13] Bao Xiang yelled out the door at me, 'Hurry up and get in here!' and he took off the Old Master's blue sash from around his waist, held it out to me, and told me to tie it up quick to the rafters of the room. Because I was scared of Bao Xiang and the others, all I could do was go into the room, get up on the bed, wrap the sash around the rafters a couple of times, and tie it up there. The three of them lifted up the master and hanged him from it. I went out at that point, but the three of them waited a while before they came out, too. I asked Bao Xiang and the rest why, after all, did they kill the master? And Bao Xiang said it was because our master had messed with [*jiao*] them on the business of inspecting the relief efforts and had gotten in their way and wanted to report them to the lieutenant governor. Not only would it be hard for them to get their silver, but they were afraid he'd get them into trouble. Originally, they planned just to poison him, but they were afraid that the poison wasn't strong enough to kill him, so they covered up what they had done by making it look like he had hanged himself. So when they had covered up all they had done there, he left. It was sometime after the third watch then. Then Li Xiang, Gu Xiang, and I all went to bed. I don't know what time it was when the monk Yuanfu came back.

From this point onward, his testimony matches that of other witnesses, with one final exception:

"A few days later, Li Xiang came back and said he was going to go ask Bao Xiang for his silver. But Bao Xiang wouldn't give him any and instead asked Li Xiang what he meant by asking him for silver. After that, Li Xiang didn't dare ask him again. And I don't dare ask him for the hundred *liang* of silver he promised me either. Everything I've said in testimony is the truth."[14]

In testimony taken either the first or the second of the following month (a day or two later), Wang Shenhan elaborated on his actions after the murder. After the inquest on Li Yuchang's body, the prefect left and Wang proceeded to ransack the dead man's chests for any official report on the embezzlement. He found what he was looking for, a complete draft of a report in which Li declared that the magistrate of Shanyang District wanted him to exaggerate the population in order to increase the amount of relief funds he could skim off for himself. Li also stated in the report that other inspectors were inflating the number of disaster victims for the same purpose and were attempting to circumvent his scrupulous accounting by preventing him from checking the census figures and having the jail warden check the figures instead. Wang admitted having sent Prefect Lin three hundred liang of silver with an additional one hundred for his assistant. He would gain around six hundred liang for every one thousand names added to the relief roster; and would share 30 percent of the spoils with the inspectors. The same day, Li's servant Ma Liansheng reiterated that he had not received any silver for his risks.[15]

On the sixth of the seventh month, Li's servant Li Xiang provided a few more details. He testified that when he relayed to his master the message via Bao Xiang that he should inflate the relief rosters for their own benefit,

". . . the master said that he most definitely would not dare overreport figures on his first time out as an official. And if Magistrate Wang insisted on overreporting, he would certainly file a complaint against him. And worse yet, he scolded us. I reported what he said to Bao Xiang, and because of that, the Shanyang magistrate hated him. . . ."

Li Xiang made the fateful pot of tea with the arsenic (xinmo) Bao Xiang gave him. On the night of the murder, he said the following to Bao Xiang, out of Ma Liansheng's hearing:

"At about midnight, Bao Xiang came over and called at the door. I opened the door for him, and he asked me, 'Have you given the master the poison yet?' I said that he'd taken it. He said, 'Has it taken effect yet?' And I said that it hadn't. Bao Xiang said, 'The only thing to do is to hang him to death.' He told me to ask the Old Master to get up, but by then he was already moaning that he had pains around his heart. Ma Liansheng tricked him into getting up, and the Old Master got dressed. Bao Xiang walked around behind him and grabbed him around the waist, I grabbed him by the wrists, and Gu Xiang held his feet firm. The Old Master cried out, 'What are you doing?' and I wrapped my kerchief around his mouth. . . ."[16]

Bao Xiang was not so forthcoming in admitting the particulars of his involvement in the murder, and so on the ninth of the seventh month, he was interrogated again.

The felon consistently prevaricated, until we added twisting of the ears and kneeling on chains; he was rigorously examined for six to eight hours, until finally he testified: ". . . My master gave me a 'red envelope' [packet of money] and told me to talk to Li Xiang about giving them three hundred *liang* of silver if they poisoned Magistrate Li. I then gave the envelope to Li Xiang, and he took it. . . . At the time of the second watch, my master told me to go find out whether Magistrate Li had taken the poison. I went over to the abbey, and Li Xiang said that he had already taken it, but the effect was really strong, and he didn't want anybody to hear him, so it would be better if we hanged him."[17]

On the tenth, the Grand Secretariat acknowledged receipt of an imperial instruction by noting that the victim's uncle, a military-degree holder from Shandong named Li Taiqing, had come to Beijing to file a complaint that his nephew had died under suspicious circumstances while on an inspection tour of relief efforts in Shanyang Dis-

trict. This text also records that the victim Li Yuchang had received his academic degree only the previous summer, and that the emperor had been impressed with him during the final examination and had appointed him to be a district magistrate in Jiangsu on the spot.[18] The emperor specifically lauded Li for upholding honesty in the face of intense pressure from his superiors to embezzle state funds. This is the first document to recommend that the victim's family should receive financial reward for his virtue and that the primary culprits be sent to Shandong to be executed at Li Yuchang's tomb. In addition, the emperor had penned a lengthy funerary poem to be inscribed on Li's tombstone. The uncle, Li Taiqing, was also to be rewarded for insisting on justice for his nephew.[19]

On that same day, Li Taiqing also testified about his nephew's return from the grave:

"In the second month of this year, I don't remember the date, Jing Chongfa, a person who had been my nephew's classmate in times past, was riding along on a donkey in the vicinity of a bean-curd shop in the district seat when he saw people carrying a sedan chair coming toward him from the west along the main road. It was an official, and so he immediately dismounted from his donkey. When the official descended from the sedan chair, he recognized that it was my nephew. He made inquiries of him, and my nephew said that he was on his way to take office as the City God of Qixia District.[20] Jing Chongfa was terrified, and he ran home to tell his wife about it. He also said that his head hurt severely, and he asked her to help him up onto the *kang* to lie down. Then he asked for tea to drink, but when he picked it up to drink, he cried out; 'Seeing this tea makes me think of that other time when I drank tea that was poisoned, and I died so bitterly!' Jing Chongfa's wife did not recognize that voice as her husband's, and she asked him who he was. He said, 'I am Li Yuchang. I was on my way to take office in Qixia District when I ran into my classmate Jing Chongfa, and I invited him to go with me to help in the administration.' And at that moment, Jing Chongfa died. Jing's wife told me this, and it is the truth."[21]

In testimony taken the following day, Li Taiqing related more information about himself:

"I am fifty-nine *sui* this year. In Qianlong 44 [1779], I entered the military school in my home district. There were three of us—an older brother and a younger brother, and I am the second. This Li Yuchang was the son of my elder brother Li Taiyun. He had no brothers or sisters, but he leaves a daughter. I live in the same house with our younger brother Li Taining and my niece by marriage, Ms. Lin. My brother Li Taining has two sons, and I have four, the second of whom has my grandson, whose name is Lingshuang. He's seven *sui* old.

"On the seventeenth of the tenth month of last year [December 4, 1808], I set out from our native place and arrived in Jiangning on the ninth of the eleventh month [December 25]. But my nephew Li Yuchang had already left for Shanyang to inspect the relief efforts. I proceeded there to see him, and on the eighteenth [January 3, 1809], I arrived in Shanyang. I went to the Virtuous Rewards Abbey to visit, but Li Xiang and the others were all wearing white sashes around their waists. When I made inquiries, Li Xiang and the others said that my nephew had already hanged himself to death. I wept bitterly and asked them why he had done that. They said that after he arrived in Shanyang, my nephew's mind became confused and his words all turned around, as if he had gone mad. He hanged himself because he was ill. Both the prefect and the magistrate had inspected the body, and he had been enshrouded. I took the story as true, and so I did not open the coffin to see for myself. Li Xiang said that all of the burial clothing and the boards for the coffin had been provided by Magistrate Wang.[22] The prefect had also come by to offer condolences, and so I should go thank them. When I met with Magistrate Wang, he said that he'd been on good terms with my nephew and that he would pay for all expenses of transporting the coffin back to our ancestral home. Later, he sent over 150 *liang* of fine silver [*yuansi yin*]. I set out on the sixth of the twelfth month [January 21], and on the sixteenth of the first month of this year [March 1], I arrived in Jimo District [in Shandong] and arranged the fifth of the seven memorial services for my nephew. I talked with his widow about removing the official robes [*mangpao*] he ordinarily wore and burning them.[23] We opened his clothing chest to take out new official robes. But when I inspected his clothing, there were bloodstains on the front of it, and everything from his chest down his lapels to the cuffs of his sleeves also had bloodstains, as if he had wiped his mouth with the backs of his hands. The lapel of his jacket [*magua*] had a big bloodstain on it. My nephew's wife and I were very doubtful in our hearts that he had died of hanging, and we wanted to open the coffin to look. We withdrew the nails and opened the coffin lid and noticed lime on my nephew's face: they had used lime to hide dark spots on his face. When we opened his clothing, his whole body was black. In accordance with *The Washing Away of Wrongs*, we used a silver needle, and when we inspected it, indeed it was black. Nor could it be washed clean with soap and water. Only then were we certain that he had been poisoned. Therefore, I came to Beijing to file a complaint. This is the truth."[24]

Events rapidly came to a head from this point onward. An imperial pronouncement of the next day, August 21, 1809, outlines the penalties for the perpetrators:

On Jiaqing 14.7.11, receipt of an EDICT that Li Xiang, Gu Xiang, and Ma Liansheng should be taken to the place of execution for death by dismemberment. Bao Xiang should be taken at once to the place of execution and beheaded. Li Xiang and the other three felons had all plotted to kill their master. Moreover, when his master Li Yuchang discovered the discrepancy in the relief records and was about to file a complaint at the lieutenant governor's office, Li Xiang went first to inform Bao Xiang secretly so that he in turn could inform Wang Shenhan, so that Bao Xiang and Wang Shenhan would plot to kill his master, having discussed it secretly beforehand with Li Xiang. This leading felon having agreed already, he discussed with Bao Xiang and Ma Liansheng that they should all act in concert.

This felon Li Xiang in particular being the chief criminal in this case, an official from the Board of Punishments will be deputed to escort the aforementioned felon to Shandong; along the route, local officials are to send troops and constables to guard him all the way there. Thereafter, custody is to be transferred to the prefect of Dengzhou, who will escort him to the tomb of Li Yuchang; there, he will be tortured by squeezing and then executed. Thereafter, his heart will be plucked out and offered as a sacrifice in order to alleviate the frustration and anger [of the murdered man].[25] Bao Xiang was the first to lay the plot; his viciousness is of the highest level. He should also be tortured by squeezing and then executed by beheading. The two felons Gu Xiang and Ma Liansheng, for their most serious offenses, will be beaten forty strokes each and then executed. Qin Ying, a senior official at the Board of Punishments, is deputed to go to the city prison to observe the punishment being carried out. As for the felon Wang Shenhan, because Li Yuchang upheld the right and refused to comply with him in the embezzlement of relief funds, and because he plotted along with Bao Xiang to poison him [Li], he should be sentenced to immediate beheading. However, he is to be granted temporary reprieve pending further interrogation. Let the others be punished as recommended. So be it.[26]

Subsequent communications on that same day stipulate penalties for any upper-level administrators who had failed to apprehend those who sought to profit from the relief *fforts and include a summary document clarifying all the evidence. The emperor concluded that this was a crime of "unprecedented" evil deserving the most severe punishments. The former magistrate Wang was sentenced to beheading with delay until the autumn assizes. Following the common practice of reducing sentences one degree, Wang's execution was commuted to one hundred blows with the heavy rod and exile three thousand li from his home, to Shuntian near Beijing in this case, in part because of his advanced age: Wang was more than seventy sui old, and the law stipulated reduced sentences for the very young and the very old.[27] In a later report from the same day, Wang Shenhan was questioned closely about his relations with all other administrators who had endeavored to cover up his scheme. Had he bribed them all? One had been an old friend whom he had presented with a gift of two hundred liang of silver when he was posted in the area, Wang testified. Being a person who does not forget kindnesses, the friend was willing to help him out without further reward. Even so, Wang sent him another one thousand liang soon after the murder and another similar amount at the New Year. Prefect Lin had not been a party to the murder, he declared. How would he dare to sacrifice a person of Lin's position to cover up his own misdeeds? He had sent Lin five hundred liang in gratitude for Lin's concern, however—with another hundred for his assistant. When asked where he had gotten all the silver that he had given away so liberally, Wang responded:

"By this time, I was a criminal who had committed a grave offense that could in no way be forgiven; it didn't matter how much I spent anymore. Even if it was not only this amount, why should I try to conceal it?"

Quoting the familiar aphorism about the truth of a major crime ultimately being revealed, the report concludes, "When the water falls, the rocks are exposed."[28]

The Jiaqing emperor's poem in Li Yuchang's memory is titled "Grieving for the Loyal" (Minzhong shi). Since he had met the man not long before he was murdered, the monarch's grief may have been heart-felt. The emperor was fifty that year, and such corruption within his administration surely must have been a great source of frustration.[29] Wang Gu, the prefect of Huai'an, testified that he had been negligent in his observation of Li Yuchang's corpse, but he had not been bribed to give a false report at the original inquest. He did receive a gift of silver from Wang Shenhan later, however, a total of two thousand liang.[30] Tie Bao, the member of the Grand Council whose correspondence began this case, was exiled to Urumqi in Xinjiang for ignoring the corruption going on beneath him in the hierarchy, as was the eldest son of Wang Shenhan, in accordance with the principle of punishing the families of the worst criminals. Wang's other three sons were pardoned.[31] By final tally, Wang Shenhan had apparently given away—or promised—twenty-three thousand liang of silver in connection with the case, although there was still some doubt about the accuracy of this figure.

NOTES

Source: *Shangyu dang* [Archive of imperial edicts], First Historical Archives, Beijing.

1. Joanna Waley-Cohen kindly provided a photocopy of these documents from the First Historical Archives, Beijing. Not all documents relating to the same case are grouped together; instead, they appear in the chronological order in which all such communications were received. For an analysis of this case and some of its ramifications, see Waley-Cohen, "Politics and the Supernatural." I am grateful for her assistance with the translation.

2. *Shangyu dang*, Jiaqing 14.6.21, 253–54.

3. The yin-yang master was presumably a Daoist priest of the informal Red Hat order.

4. *Shangyu dang*, Jiaqing 14.6.23, 277–80.

5. Ibid., Jiaqing 14.6.26, 317–18.

6. Ibid., Jiaqing 14.6.27, 325.

7. Ibid., Jiaqing 14.6.27, 327.

8. Ibid., Jiaqing 14.6.28, 339–40.

9. The talisman, made "to subdue the spirit of the day" (*fu rizi de benguan*), would serve to protect—or contain—the spirit of the dead, presumably because the priest suspected foul play.

10. *Shangyu dang*, Jiaqing 14.6.28, 343–45.

11. Ibid., Jiaqing 14.6.29, 351, 353–55.

12. Ibid., Jiaqing 14.6.30, 363, 365–67. By comparison, Naquin notes that in the 1810s, a soldier was paid 1.8 *liang* and two *dan* of rice per month, and in northern China, farmland sold for less than 2 to nearly 4 *liang* per *mou* (*Millenarian Rebellion*, 281).

13. The sash was a length of cloth worn around the waist and could be used for carrying things.

14. *Shangyu dang*, Jiaqing 14.6.30, 369–72.

15. Ibid., Jiaqing 14.7.1 (or 14.7.2), 11–13. On the same day, the coroner reiterated that he had just followed orders in identifying the cause of death and that he had received no payment at all for his interpretation. Ibid., 15.

16. Ibid., Jiaqing 14.7.6, 87–89. For Gu Xiang's identical account, see ibid., 91–92; and for Ma Liansheng's corroboration of these events, see ibid., 93–94. At the end of this third confession, it is recorded that all three servants were transferred to the Board of Punishments prison to await sentencing.

17. Ibid., Jiaqing 14.7.9, 161–62.

18. The highest academic degree, *jinshi*, was awarded to those few who passed an extensive series of examinations, the last of which was an oral examination administered ostensibly by the emperor himself. Apparently in this case, the Jiaqing emperor did administer that portion and remembered Li Yuchang clearly. This might explain the extreme penalties levied against the murderers.

19. *Shangyu dang*, Jiaqing 14.7.10, 181–83. For the memorial poem, see ibid., Jiaqing 14.7.11, 213–14.

20. The divine pantheon of late imperial China paralleled the hierarchy of the world of the living, with several administrative levels. District-level City Gods, literally, Lords of Walls and Moats (Chenghuang Daye), were regional deities, whose duties included making certain that justice prevailed. Even today, some Chinese file lawsuits with these deities at the same time that they take their opponents to court, in the hope that the administrators of the unseen world will enforce justice in this world as well. See Katz, "Indictment Rituals."

21. *Shangyu dang*, Jiaqing 14.7.10, 185–86. For another translation of this passage, see Waley-Cohen, "Politics and the Supernatural," 344–45.

22. Coffins were made from the most fragrant and sturdiest wood the family could afford, as a mark of respect for the dead; consequently, they could be quite expensive. Magistrate Wang's purchase of the boards for Li Yuchang's coffin was meant to be seen as his effort to console the family. Buddhist services for the dead might include chanting of scriptures for the first seven days afterward and on every seventh day thereafter until the forty-ninth day.

23. Presumably as a burnt sacrifice, so that he might have them to wear in the spirit world.

24. *Shangyu dang*, Jiaqing 14.7.11, 203–5. Sung Tz'u's *The Washing Away of Wrongs* was used from the thirteenth into the twentieth century as a reference guide for forensic examinations. Many educated households seem to have had their own copies. The guide notes that a silver needle inserted into the mouth of a person who has died of arsenic poisoning will come out black and cannot be washed clean.

25. Although not unique during the Qing period, such mutilation of a criminal and sacrifice to his victim were extremely rare. See Waley-Cohen, "Politics and the Supernatural," 337.

26. *Shangyu dang*, Jiaqing 14.7.11, 217–18.

27. Ibid., Jiaqing 14.7.11, 227–32. The law about reduced punishments for the young and the old is Article 22 of the Qing penal code; it specifically excludes redemption for those who commit death-penalty offenses. See Jones, *Great Qing Code*, 52.

28. *Shengyu dang*, Jiaqing 14.7.11, 237–40.

29. See the exchange between the Grand Secretariat and the emperor, in ibid., Jiaqing 14.7.12, 243.

30. Ibid., 14.7.12 (or 14.7.13), 257–59, 261. Wang Gu was so distraught over being implicated in this case that he attempted suicide by stabbing himself; he was later sentenced to immediate strangulation. Waley-Cohen, "Politics and the Supernatural," 337.

31. *Shengyu dang*, Jiaqing 14.7.22, 400. The law concerning the punishment of family members of the most serious offenders is very ancient; it appears in Articles 254 and 255 of the Qing penal code concerning crimes against the state. See Jones, *Great Qing Code*, 237–39.

Appendix 1

Banners and Other Social Organizations

E ven before the Manchus began their incursions into northern China, their primary social organization was composed of military units termed "banners"; each of the Eight Banners (Baqi) carried a distinctive flag. Apparently by around 1600, Manchu military might was divided among four nobles, designated by yellow, white, blue, and red banners; later, each banner was separated into two divisions, plain and bordered. Banners were divided into "companies" (*zuoling*), which were originally made up of Manchu lineage groups. Their original function was administrative, but these groupings were also used as a means of mobilizing the Manchus for military action. Originally, all bannermen were both farmers and soldiers. As the need for fighters increased, however, two out of every three Manchu men were pressed into service, and Han settlers on the agricultural lands of Manchuria (modern China's northeastern provinces) were organized into their own banner groups, which supplied the armies with food. In effect, these Chinese farmers served as agricultural slaves to Manchu commanders. Later, their Mongol and Han allies also organized into banners. Large stretches of land in the Beijing vicinity were expropriated as banner lands after the Qing conquest; Manchu nobles were encouraged to move south and take control of them. Banner organization remained extremely important during the decades in which imperial armies were wiping out all resistance throughout China. Likewise, Manchus were given a disproportionate allotment of both military and civilian government positions during the Qing period.[1] This is why many of the signatures on the final memorials to the emperor in the cases presented in this volume include several Manchu names. Article 9 of the Qing penal code also stipulated that bannermen offenders would be given reduced sentences for some crimes.[2]

HAN-MANCHU RELATIONS AND HAIRSTYLES

From the beginning of Manchu rule, difficult ethnic relations were further exacerbated by a rule dictating hairstyle for the newly subjected Chinese. The new rulers mandated that all Han men should shave their foreheads and wear the rest of their hair braided in back as a visible symbol of their submission to the Manchus. Thus, men who continued to wear their hair long (in the Ming period fashion) were immediately identified as rebels and could be executed. The only way a man could avoid this difficulty was by shaving his head completely and pretending to be a Buddhist monk.[3]

NOTES

1. For a general introduction to banner organization and the privileges that accrued to members of these groups, whether Manchus, Mongols, or Han, see Mote, *Imperial China*, 857–62, 787–88. A useful introduction to the Manchus as a cultural group is Crossley, *The Manchus*. For the relationships between nobles and Han farmers in Manchuria, see Reardon-Anderson, *Reluctant Pioneers*.

This is why many of the signatures on the final memorials to the emperor in the cases presented in this volume include several Manchu names. Article 9 of the Qing penal code also stipulated that bannermen offenders would be given reduced sentences for some crimes.[2]

2. Jones, *Great Qing Code*, 42; cf. Bodde and Morris, *Law in Imperial China*, 168, 170.

3. See Kuhn, *Soulstealers*, 12; and Mote, *Imperial China*, 828–29, 832–33.

Appendix 2

Popular Religious Movements

Probably the most detailed study of popular uprisings in China focuses on an earlier period, the Ming (1368–1644). Through a painstaking statistical analysis of all instances of banditry and rebellion in all of China's 1,097 counties, historian James Tong has demonstrated that the 630 uprisings that took place during the 277 years of Ming domination were generally the product of rational choice. When physical survival became uncertain and the chances of punishment were relatively low, desperate people frequently resorted to violence. Natural calamity was a major factor, but insufficient in itself: starving people do not necessarily have the strength to mount an armed assault on government outposts. Government weakness—in the form of poor leadership, inadequate military and police strength, and fiscal crisis—was another key factor in collective violence. So, too, were the antagonisms of class difference and the rapid social change experienced during that period. Most Ming period uprisings occurred in rural, sparsely populated areas away from centers of government strength. Violence was simply part of everyday life for large portions of the population during the Ming, however, and the same might be said of the Qing period, at least in general.[1]

What role did religious beliefs play in social unrest and rebellion? Scholars have pointed to the role of secret societies in organized violence on the local level; certainly, they were an ongoing concern for China's rulers for centuries. Their origin was not necessarily political, however. Historical records indicate that the notorious Heaven and Earth Society, supposedly devoted to the overthrow of the Qing court, "emerged as a mutual aid fraternity in response to the demographic and economic crises of the late eighteenth century, and that it was but one of several societies, or *hui*, to appear at this time."[2] Membership in these societies was generally cemented through a ritual involving an oath of devotion to the collective brotherhood, but it did not necessarily involve subscribing to a particular set of beliefs.[3]

Of particular concern to the authorities was the blood oath taken by new members: such activities seemingly copied famous scenes from two of the most popular story cycles of the time, known from the stage and from the novels *Romance of the Three Kingdoms* (Sanguo zhi yanyi), of 1522, and *Heroes of the Marshes* (Shuihu zhuan), or *Water Margin*, of around 1550 for earlier versions, with most common versions dating from 1610 and 1641. The former story narrates the rise and fall of a group that tries to restore the fallen Han dynasty early in the third century; the latter compiles the adventures of fictional knights-errant who make war on all authority, ostensibly to rid the state of corrupt leaders and protect the throne. Rebels could allude to either story. Membership in a secret society was generally considered a capital offense during the Qing.[4]

In the eyes of the Qing government, any religious belief or practice associated with secret organizations was threatening. Since the middle of the sixteenth century, based more on prejudice than on fact, almost all lay Buddhist and popular political groups were labeled heretical and assumed to be associated with the White Lotus Teachings. As a Fujian provincial director of education, Wang Run, wrote in 1816:

> These heterodox societies [*xiejiao*] make false claims about the world to come in order to cheat you. But let me ask: Which of you has seen a previous life or a future life? Of course Buddhism has always taught the doctrine of karma, which is nothing more than a means to encourage goodness; and chanting the scriptures and avoiding meat are only ways to calm the mind and approach the good. Respecting the gods is no more than not daring to do evil. Naturally, these gods and buddhas should be respected, but the "gods and buddhas" of the secret societies should be despised. . . . These buddhas are not true buddhas, and heaven will not accept them, just as the holy Son of Heaven will not accept greedy officials and evil underlings. . . . All of you must reflect, and not be seduced.[5]

Ultimately, widespread violent repression of all secret brotherhoods across China, regardless of their intentions, may well have contributed to anti-Qing sentiment.[6]

Yet, as the documents in this volume demonstrate, the White Lotus Teachings was not simply a religious movement; like many millenarian sects from the Han period onward, White Lotus groups posed a very real political threat to established authority over the next two thousand years. Although many groups were not well trained, they certainly had military organizations and large numbers of armed men. Destitute people tended to question the moral righteousness of their rulers, an attitude that fueled their aspirations to take control of local and regional governments. Emperors were expected to express paternalistic concern for the well-being of their citizens, and for every imperial house, such solicitous regard for the people was a major rationale for ruling. Extensive natural disasters, floods and droughts, during which central government aid was either slow in coming or lacking altogether could be seen as a sign of decadence on the part of the ruler and Heaven's wrath over his incompetence. These factors justified rebellion for the purpose of establishing a new regime.

Consequently, the Qing monarchy took these popular religious movements very seriously and treated their members generally as rebels—which meant with the utmost severity. Those taken into custody were regularly tortured to extract confessions, and all persons found to occupy positions of authority were executed. In marked contrast to regular perpetrators of major crimes whose fates ultimately were decided at the capital after several levels of judicial review, in the name of the emperor if not by the ruler himself, regional commanders had the legal right to execute rebels and traitors.[7] The same fate frequently awaited people of far less importance, as historians readily demonstrate.[8]

Consequently, officials were not necessarily interested in the teachings of these societies. Unlike their pursuit of the smallest bit of relevant information in murder cases, investigating officials asked for very little from religious practitioners. Usually, they sought only to ascertain that practitioners knew the doctrines and therefore deserved punishment as members of "heretical cults." Yet, many of the divinities and practices mentioned in testimony were held in common with popular religious groups throughout China during the late imperial period. Some are still prominent today. Divinities include the central gods of Daoism and several Buddhist figures, religious icons in the form of printed images and carved statues were important then as now, and charms that protect against disease and injury are still sought by visitors to China's temples. Among lay Buddhism's contributions to many secret societies of the Qing period are the chanting of mantras, the practice of vegetarianism, and a belief in Maitreya (Rulai), the Buddha of the Future. Even when such groups identified themselves otherwise, they were considered part of the White Lotus sect.[9] As a result, such teachings had to be practiced in secret and were often maintained by the most poorly educated people. Even ordained monks, who had to be literate so that they could read and recite the sutras that formed the core of their practice, were frequently objects of scorn in fiction written by the educated elite of the Qing. By the late eighteenth century, it was common for officials to identify all religious groups as "inherently rebellious."[10]

NOTES

1. For an introduction to traditional explanations for social disorder and the sources of the data, see Tong, *Disorder under Heaven*, chapters 1 and 8; alternative explanations and interpretive strategies are in ibid., chapters 2–7. For discussion of the prevalence of banditry (in contrast to the acts of rebellion traced by Tong) in the vicinity of the northern Ming capital Beijing, a major concern to the Ming government, see Robinson, *Bandits, Eunuchs*, esp. chapter 7; clearly, these highwaymen did not feel in any grave danger despite their proximity to the center of power. The contrasting conclusions advanced by these two studies may be traced in part to their different sources of information; both seek to dispel the older notion that somehow late imperial China experienced widespread social tranquility.

2. Murray and Qin, *Origins of the Tiandihui*, 1.

3. For a general overview of secret religious and political societies, see Ward, "Chinese Secret Societies." For a brief overview of both White Lotus and Eight Trigrams Teachings, see Chesneaux, *Secret Societies*, 36–40. See also Murray and Qin, *Origins of the Tiandihui*, 1–4.

4. See Murray and Qin, *Origins of the Tiandihui*, 12–16.

5. Ownby, *Brotherhoods*, 105, with slight modifications. The "Son of Heaven" referred to here is the Qing emperor.

6. On the resistance occasioned by official suppression, see ibid., 124–31.

7. Article 2 of the Qing penal code lists various degrees of rebellion as the first three among the Ten Great Wrongs; more specific laws outlining punishments for treason and rebellion are in Articles 254 and 255. See Jones, *Great Qing Code*, 34–35, 237–39.

8. For examples, see Naquin, *Shantung Rebellion*; and Naquin, *Millenarian Rebellion*.

9. See Ownby, *Brotherhoods*, 31–44. The fullest exploration of the White Lotus Teachings is ter Haar, *White Lotus Teachings*; see esp. chapters 4–6, on the development of the teachings and groups during the Ming period, and chapter 7, on Qing

persecution of White Lotus sectarians. For a brief introduction to this subject, see Dunstheimer, "Some Religious Aspects," 23–28. For antisocial elements in Chinese folk religious practices, see Shahar and Weller, *Unruly Gods*.

10. ter Haar, *White Lotus Teachings*, 261. The most detailed study in English is Naquin, *Millenarian Rebellion*. See also Ownby, *Brotherhoods*. For a listing of nearly two hundred individual societies formed under the name of the Heaven and Earth Society during the period 1728–1850, which provides a clear view of the prevalence of such groups, see Murray, *Origins of the Tiandihui*, 230–35.

Appendix 3

Cases Listed by Social Conflict

CRIMES OF PASSION

Case 1. Xu Si: A Scuffle over a Debt, 1702
Case 4. Li Cang: Blackmail and Arsenic, 1803
Case 5. Cao Ligong: Attempted Rape That Led to Murder, 1803
Case 18. Jin San: A Spurned Lover, 1728

CONFLICTS AMONG FAMILY MEMBERS

Case 2. Li Huaiyu: The Missing Brother, 1736
Case 6. Du Huailiang: Adultery That Brought Disaster, 1696
Case 11. Li Er and Li San: Two Pecks of Beans, 1737
Case 12. The Hong Brothers: A Quarrel Over Manure, 1738

DISPUTES AMONG IN-LAWS

Case 3. Ms. Guo: Accidental Homicide Concealed, 1794
Case 13. Ms. Wang: Incest and Violent Homicide, 1738
Case 14. Ms. Ma: Disguised Poisoning, 1795

VIOLENCE AMONG NEIGHBORS

Case 7. Rui Meisheng: Manslaughter over an Outhouse, 1722
Case 9. Luo Zhongyi: Kidnapping, 1728
Case 8. Jia Mingyuan: Accidental Homicide, 1796
Case 10. Wang Azhen: Murder for Extortion, 1779

RIVALRY OVER LAND

Case 15. A Village Vendetta and Han Intercession, 1728

ACTIVITIES THAT THREATENED THE STATE

Case 16. Rebellious Religious Sectarians, 1791–1814
Case 17. Ji Yanghua: Secret Society Member, 1814
Case 19. Luo Fenpeng: A Phony Scholar-Official, 1763

THE SUPERNATURAL AND JUSTICE

Case 20. Li Yuchang: A Magistrate Murdered for His Integrity, 1809

Chinese Character Glossary

Agui 阿桂 (1717–1797)

Aksu 阿克蘇 Akhsu

Anabu 阿那部

anchashi 按察使 (provincial) judicial review commissioner

badou 巴豆 croton seeds

bagu wen 八股文 eight-legged essay (for civil service examination)

Bagua 八卦 Eight Trigrams

Bagua Jiao 八卦教 Eight Trigrams Teachings (sect)

baibu 白布 plain (ordinary) clothing

Baidunuo 白都諾

Bailian Jiao 白蓮教 White Lotus Teachings

Baiyang Jiao 白洋教 White Ocean Teachings

Bao Gong 包公 Lord Bao

Bao Zheng 包拯

Baoding 保定府 Baoding Prefecture

baozhang 保長 local warden

Baqi 八旗 Eight Banners

Batai 巴泰

bazong 把總 squad commander

benshi 本事 talent

Bolin 伯麟

Bu Wenbin 步文斌

Bujun tongling yamen 步軍統領衛門 gendarmerie (Beijing)

buyuan 部院 senior vice president

can zhifu 參知府 vice prefect

Cao Fugui 曹幅貴

Cao Ligong 曹立功

Cao Wang 曹王氏 Mrs. Cao Wang

Cao Xueqin 曹雪芹

Cao Zhikang 曹之康

Caojiazhuang 曹家莊 Cao Family Manor

chan zhang 禪杖 meditation staff

Changde fu 常德府 Changde Prefecture

Changsha fu 長沙府 Changsha Prefecture

Chaozhou fu 潮州府 Chaozhou Prefecture

chen 臣 Your subject (first-person pronoun)

Chen Caiyu 陳彩玉

Chen Hongmou 陳宏謀

Chen Sanzi 陳三子

Chen Shaoyong 陳紹鏞

Chen Wenxian 陳文現

Chen Yuanjue 陳元爵

Chenggu xian 城固縣 Chenggu District

Chenghai xian 澄海縣 Chenghai District

Chenghuang Daye 城隍大爺 Lords of Walls and Moats (regional deities)

Chenjiazhuang 陳家莊 Chen Family Manor

chi 尺 unit of length

Chongming xian 崇明縣 Chongming District

Chuanshi 傳士 Pastoral Officer

Chunqiu 春秋 The "Spring and Autumn" Annals

cun 寸 unit of length

Da Qing lüli 大清律例 The Great Qing Penal Code

dabao 褡包 sash

Dacheng Jiao 大成教 Teachings of the Great Accomplishment

Dalisi 大理寺 Court of Judicial Review

Dalongtian xushang 大龍田墟上

Daming fu 大名府 Daming Prefecture

dan 石 unit of weight

Danglai Zhenren 擋來真人 Defender Perfected Man

Daokou 道口

Dashun 大順

Daxue 大學　The Great Learning

Defu 德福

Deming 德明

Dengzhou 鄧州　Deng Department

Deqing 德慶州　Deqing Depart
　ment

Desheng zhen 得勝鎮　Desheng
　Market

Di Qing 狄青

Dianhuo 點火　Igniter

diming 抵命　blood feud

Dong Sansheng 東三省

Dong Zhen Zhixing Kailu Zhenren
　東震至行開路真人　Path
　breaking Perfected Man of the
　Most Virtuous Conduct, Eastern
　Zhen Trigram

Dongchang fu 東昌府　Dongchang
　Prefecture

Dongguang xian 東光縣　Dong
　guang District

Dongyueguan 東岳觀　Eastern
　Peak Monastery

dou'ou lei 斗毆類　blows and
　affrays

dousha 鬥殺　homicide during an
　affray

Du Huailiang 杜懷亮

Du Kongxian 杜孔先

Du li cunyi 讀例存疑　Remaining
　Doubts after Reading the Sub
　statutes

Du li cunyi chongkanben 讀例存疑
　重刊本　A Typeset Edition of
　"Tu li ts'un i"

Du Xun 杜珣

Duan Wenjing 段文經

Duanwujie 端午節　Dragon Boat
　Festival

Duchayuan 都察院　Censorate

Duchayuan you fu duyushi 都察院
　右副都禦史　vice president of
　the Censorate

dudu 都督　governor general or
　military viceroy

dui trigram 兌卦

Ershierdu Ertu Lianbao 二十二
　都二圖練保　Twenty second
　Battalion, Second Section

falü 法律　judicial or legal (cate
　gory of documents)

Fang Yingyuan 方應元

fansi 藩司　lieutenant governor

fawang 法網　net of the law

Fengtian 奉天 (Shengjing 盛京)

Fengtian fu 奉天府 Fengtian Prefecture

fengying 風影 empty accusations

fu 府 prefecture

fu rizi de benguan 伏日子的本官 to subdue the spirit of the day

Fuhui quanshu 福惠全書 Complete Book concerning Happiness and Benevolence

Fuming 富明

fuming 父命 patricide

Fumomiao 伏魔廟 Quelling Monsters Temple

fumu guan 父母官 "parental" officials (local and regional)

fupian 附片 attachment

fuxing xiongyin 賦性兇淫 by nature violent and depraved

Fuzhou 復州 Fu Department

gai bai 該敗 deserved defeat

Gao Lai 高來

geng 更 watches of the night

Gengua Jiao 艮卦教 Gen Trigram School

gong'an xiaoshuo 公案小說 crime-case fiction

Gongchang 鞏昌

Gongzhongdang Qianlong chao zouzhe 宮中檔乾隆朝奏摺 Memorials from the Palace Collection, Qianlong Reign

Goujiashan 苟家山 Gou Family Mountain

guaigun 拐棍 kidnapper

Guan Gong 關公 Lord Guan

Guan Xiaoxian 關孝先

Guandong 關東 East of the Pass

guanggun 光棍 rogue rascals

Guangning xian 廣寧縣 Guangning District

Guangzhou fu 廣州府 Guangzhou Prefecture

guanhua 官話 standard Chinese (Mandarin) (lit., "the official language")

guanjian 關鍵 key

Guide fu 歸德府 Guide Prefecture

Guo Tingyi 郭庭議

guobian 過便 whenever convenient

Guoli Gugong Bowuyuan 國立故宮博物院 National Palace Museum

gusha 故殺 intentional homicide

gushao 故燒 intentional arson

Hanzu 漢族 Han ethnicity

Hanzhong fu 漢中府 Hanzhong Prefecture

haohan 好漢 real man

Hejian fu 河間府 Hejian Prefecture

Heshan xian 鶴山縣 Heshan District

Heshen 和珅

Heze xian 河澤縣 Heze District

Hong Kunwei 洪坤渭

Hong Xiuquan 洪秀全

Hong Yaozhang 洪堯章

Hongli 弘曆

Honglou meng 紅樓夢 *Dream of Red Mansions*

Hou Juguang 侯居廣

Hou Tian 後天 Later Heaven

Hsing-an hui-lan (Xing'an huilan) 刑案匯覽 *Conspectus of Penal Cases*

Huang Tsing-chia (Huang Jingjia) 黃靜嘉

hufang tiexie 戶房貼寫 financial section scribe

Huguang 湖廣

Hua xian 滑縣 Hua District

huandao 環刀 machete

Huang Liuhong 黃六鴻

Huizhou fu 惠州府 Huizhou Prefecture

Huolu xian 獲鹿縣 Huolu District

Ji Ba 季八

Ji Wensheng 季文升

Ji Xuezhu 吉學著

Ji Yanghua 吉仰花

Jia Lun 賈倫

Jia Mingkui 賈明魁

Jia Mingyuan 賈明遠

jia shen 夾審 interrogate using ankle-squeezing blocks

jiagun 夾棍 ankle-squeezing blocks (torture instruments)

jian 姦 illicit sex

Ji'an fu 吉安府

Jiang Lan 江蘭

Jiangzhou 絳州 Jiang Department

jiansheng 監生 student by purchase

jiao 㸽 messed with

Jiao Jinxian 焦進賢

Jiao Tingyan 焦廷彥

jiaohun 叫魂 soulstealing

Jiaqing 嘉慶

Jidang'a 吉黨阿

jie 節 (female) chastity

Jilin 吉林 Kirin

Jimo xian 即墨縣 Jimo District

jin 斤 unit of weight

Jin Hong 金鉷

Jin San 金三

Jin Yingdou 金應斗

Jing Chongfa 荊崇發

Jingde xian 旌德縣 Jingde District

Jingning zhou 靜寧州 Jingning Department

jingshi 經世 statecraft

jinshi 進士 presented scholar (the highest civil-service degree)

Jinzhou 錦州 Jin Department

Jishan xian 稷山縣 Jishan District

Jueluo (Gioro) Qishiwu 覺羅七十五

Jun xian 郡縣 Jun District

Junjichu 軍機處 Grand Council

Jurong xian 句容縣 Jurong District

Kailu Zhenren 開路真人 Path-breaking Perfected Man

kang 炕 brick platform

Kang Juncheng 康均城

Kangxi 康熙

Kejia zu 客家族 Hakka ethnicity

Keshenge'er 喀什噶爾 Kashgar

ketou 磕頭 full prostration (as sign of respect)

Kuche 庫車 Kucha

Lagao 喇稿 Lagao Village

Lan Dingyuan 藍鼎元

Lao Yezi 老爺子 Old Master (term of respect)

li 里 unit of distance

Li 禮 classical ritual texts

Li Bai 李白

Li Cang 李倉

Li Chenglong 李成龍

Li Chunguan 李春觀

Li Er 李二

Li Fu 李幅

Li Huaiming 李懷明

Li Huaiyin 李懷印

Li Huaiyu 李懷玉

Li Mao 李茂

Li San 李三

Li shi 李氏 Ms. Li

Li Shiguang 李世廣

Li Taining 李泰寧

Li Taiqing 李泰清

Li Taiyun 李泰運

Li Wencheng 李文成

Li Xuan 李煊

Li Yuchang 李毓昌

Li Ze 李澤

Li Zicheng 李自成

liang 兩 unit of weight

Liang Dun 梁敦

Liang Kentang 梁肯堂

Liangguang 兩廣

Liangjiang 兩江

liangxin nanmei 良心難昧 hard to ignore one's conscience

Liaocheng xian 聊城縣 Liaocheng
District

lili ruhua 歷歷如畫 as clear as a
painting

lili ruhui 歷歷如繪 as clear as a
picture

lilun 理論 discuss

Lin Qing 林清

Lin Sheng 林盛

lingchi 凌遲 execution by dismemberment

Linjin xian 臨晉縣 Linjin District

linsheng 廩生 stipend student

Liu Fushan 劉復善

Liu Jingting 劉敬廷

Liu Tiangui 劉天貴

Liu Wuxun 劉五訓

Liu Xinglong 柳興隆

Liu Zhaokui 劉照魁

Liushui 流水 Navigator

Liuyanji 柳堰集 Willow Slope
Village

Longyang xian 龍陽縣 Longyang
District

Lu Ayu 盧阿愚

lufu zouzhe 錄副奏摺 depositions
appended to memorials

Lugousi 盧溝司 Lugou Subdis-
trict

Luling xian 盧陵縣 Luling District

Lunyu 論語 *The Analects of Confucius*

Luo Fenpeng 羅奮鵬

Luo Yaosheng 羅耀生

Luo Yunpeng 羅雲鵬

Luo Zongyi 羅宗義

Luzhou gong'an 鹿洲公案 *Legal
Cases from Luzhou*

Ma Liansheng 馬連升

Macunbao 馬村堡 Ma Village

magua 馬掛 jacket worn over official robes

mangpao 蟒袍 official robes

Man 蠻族 Man ("barbarian")
peoples

Mayitun 螞蟻屯 Ant Farm Station

meilai meiqu 眉來眉去 made eyes
at each other

Meng Jian 孟楗

Mengshancha 蒙山岔 Mount
Meng Fork

Mengzi 孟子 *The Works of Mencius*

Miao Zhuang *yexing* 苗獐野性
violent nature of the Miao and
the Zhuang

min 民 common subject

ming'an 命案 homicide case

Minggong shupan qingming ji 名公書判清明集 *The Enlightened Judgments of Famous Judges*

Minzhe 閩浙

"Minzhong shi" 憫忠詩 "Grieving for the Loyal"

mousha 謀殺 premeditated homicide

mu 畝 unit of area

Mukden (Manchu name for Fengtian 奉天, or Shengjing 盛京)

muyou 幕友 friends at court (legal secretaries)

na xinbian 納新編 file a new registration

nan kuanyou 難寬宥 cannot be pardoned

Nanling xian 南陵縣 Nanling District

nanren 男人 male

Neige 內閣 Grand Secretariat

Neige tiben Xingfa lei 內閣題本刑罰類 Grand Secretariat routine memorials, Crimes and Punishments

Ningguo fu 寧國府 Ningguo Prefecture

Ninguta 寧古塔

Ningxiang xian 寧鄉縣 Ningxiang District

Ningyuan zhou 寧遠州 Ningyuan Department

Niu Bing 牛炳

nongmin qiyi 農民起義 peasant uprising

Nu'erhachi 努爾哈赤 Nurhaci

Ouyang Zhang 歐陽璋

paijia 牌甲 local warden

paipiao 牌票 deed

paitou 牌頭 constable

Pei xian 沛縣 Pei District

Pingxin zhen 憑信鎮 Pingxin Market

pinku nandu 貧苦難度 hard to bear being poor

pixinmo 砒信末 arsenic powder

pohan 潑悍 shrewish woman

Putai xian 蒲臺縣 Putai District

Puzhou fu 蒲州府 Puzhou Prefecture

qi 氣 breath, spiritual essence

Qian Rubi 錢汝馼

Qianlong 乾隆

Qin Li 秦理

Qin Shihuangdi 秦始皇帝

Qin Xuezeng 秦學曾

Qin Ying 秦瀛

qing mi 情密 a close relationship

qing re 情熱 a hot relationship

Qing xian 青縣 Qing District

Qing Zhang 慶章

qingji 情急 in the heat of the moment

Qingshui xian 清水縣 Qingshui District

qiongzhe de ji de 窮着的急的 desperately poor

Qiqihaer 齊齊哈爾 Tsitsihar

qiren 旗人 bannermen

Qiu Yunheng 邱運亨

qiushen 秋審 autumn assizes

"Qiusheng" 求生 Seek to Preserve Life

Qixia xian 棲霞縣 Qixia District

Qu Yuan 屈原

Quanshi 全士 Officer of Totality

renzu guigen 認祖歸根 acknowledging the ancestor and returning to the root

ru hui 如繪 like a picture

Rui Jiu 芮九

Rui Meisheng 芮梅生

Rui Mian 芮冕

Rulai Fo 如來佛 Maitreya, the Buddha of the Future

runyue 閏月 intercalary month

San Fo ying jie 三佛應劫 The Three Buddhas' Response to Calamities

Sanfasi 三法司 Three Judicial Offices

Sanguo zhi yanyi 三國志演義 Romance of the Three Kingdoms

sapo kunao 撒潑哭鬧 crying and screaming

Shaangan 陝甘

Shahukou 殺虎口 "Killing Tigers" Pass

Shan xian 單縣 Shan District

Shangyu Dang 上諭檔 Archive of Imperial Edicts

Shanyang xian 山陽縣 Shanyang District

Shen Mengjian 沈孟堅

sheng 省 province

Sheng Dao 聖道 The Sagely Way (Confucianism)

sheng Qing 盛清 "high" Qing

shengyuan 生員 licentiate (lowest degree holder)

shenyuan 伸冤 relieve an injustice

shi 氏 Ms.

Shi 詩 or Shijing 詩經 Book of Poetry

Shi Wenzhuo 石文焯

Shitou ji 石頭記 Story of the Stone

shiwen 時文 contemporary essay (for civil service examinations)

Shu 書 or *Shujing* 書經 *Book of Documents*

Shuihu zhuan 水滸傳 *Outlaws of the Marsh*

Shunde fu 順德府 Shunde Prefecture

Si'en fu 思恩府 Si'en Prefecture

Sige Guanling 四格管領 *Fourth Prince of the Blood*

Siku jinshu 四庫禁書 *Proscribed Books in All Categories*

Sishu 四書 Four Books

Song Ci 宋慈 (Sung Tz'u)

Song Fu 宋幅

Song Luo 宋犖

Song Shichen 宋世臣

Song Shizhong 宋世忠

Song Tingzuo 宋廷佐

Songjiazhuang 宋家莊 Song Family Manor

songshi 訟師 litigation master

Su Changchen 蘇昌臣

sui 歲 years of age

Suining xian 遂寧縣 Suining District

Sun Guozhu 孫國柱

Suonuomu Zhamuchu 索諾木扎木楚

Taibai miao 太白廟 Taibai Temple

Taijian 太監 Grand Eunuch

Taiping Tianguo 太平天國 Taiping Heavenly Kingdom

taiye 太爺 master, or magistrate

Tan Hongfa 譚弘發

Tan Hongren 譚弘仁

Tan Mingquan 譚明權

Tang Pin 湯聘

Tanzhe si 檀柘寺 Tanzhe Monastery

Tian Di ziran, Yuqi fen san; Zhongzhong xuanxu, Huang lang Taixuan 天地自然，玉氣分散，種種玄虛，黃朗太玄 Heaven and Earth are as they are, The Jade Vapor has spread around; So many kinds of Mysterious Space, Brown [Earth] and Bright [Heaven] are the Great Mystery.

Tiandi Hui 天地會 Heaven and Earth Society

Tianli Hui 天理會 Heavenly Principle Society

Tianping Dawang 天平大王 Great King of Heavenly Peace

Tianzi 天子 Son of Heaven

tiaoxi 調戲 flirt

tiben 題本 routine memorials

tidu junwu 提督軍務 provincial commander in chief of military affairs

Tong Yuxiu 佟毓秀

Tongzhou 通州 Tong Department

tu zao xiong e 突造兇惡 sudden fit of malice

tucai haiming 圖財害命 murder for personal gain

Tuna 圖納

tuntian 屯田 military-agricultural colonies

waichao 外朝 outer court

waisheng nüxu 外甥女婿 husband of sister's child

Wang A'ang 王阿昂

Wang Azhen 王阿鎮

Wang Chengxian 王承先

Wang Daolong 王道瀧

Wang Gu 王轂

Wang Huizu 汪輝祖

Wang Manchuan 王滿川

Wang Shenhan 王伸漢

Wang Shiqing 王世清

Wang Wenyu 汪文煜

Wang You 王有

Wang Zizhong 王子重

Wangjiazhuang 王家莊 Wang Family Manor

wangzhi faji 罔知法紀 utterly lawless

Wei Fu'e 韋付額

Wei Fuge 韋扶割

Wei Fujuan 韋付卷

Wei Fuyan 韋扶眼

Wei Guangding 韋光定

Wei Yingjuan 韋應眷

Weinan xian 渭南縣 Weinan District

wen 文 unit of currency

Wen Duxun 文都遜

wo 我 first-person pronoun

wu lianchi 無廉恥 have no sense of shame

Wu Yingfen 吳應棻

Wuchang 武昌 capital of Huguang

Wuding fu 武定府 Wuding Prefecture

Wulangting 五郎廳 Wulang Subprefecture

wuzuo 仵作 coroner

Xia Wenjiong 夏文炯

xian huan jie cao 啣環結草 "eternally grateful for your favor"

Xian Tian Jiao nei Zhenzi yigua 先天教內震子一卦 Zhen Trigram of the Teachings of the Former Heaven *xiancheng* 縣丞 assistant magistrate

Xiande 憲德

Xianglin 祥林

Xiangyang fu 襄陽府 Xiangyang Prefecture

Xiangyang xian 襄陽縣 Xiangyang District

xiangye yumin 鄉野愚民 country bumpkin

Xianyang xian 咸陽縣 Xianyang District

xiao furen 小婦人 first-person pronoun used by women

xiaode 小的 first-person pronoun used by men ([my] humble [self])

Xiaojing 孝經 *Classic of Filial Piety*

Xideshen 希德慎

Xie Tao 解韜

xiejiao 邪教 heterodox societies

xifa 戲法 sleight of hand

Xilabu 西拉布

Xilu ting 西路廳 Xilu Subprefecture

Xin Kaihe zhen 新開河鎮 New Kaihe Market

xing 性 basic nature

xing 姓 surname

xing fang 行房 have marital (sexual) relations

Xing *shi* 邢氏 Ms. Xing

Xing'an huilan 刑案匯覽 *Conspectus of Penal Cases*

Xingbu 刑部 Board of Punishments

Xingbu shangshu 刑部尚書 secretary of the Board of Punishments

xingfa 刑罰 crime and punishment

xingjian 行姦 have illicit sex

Xingke 刑科 Office of Scrutiny (of the Board of Punishments)

xingming 刑名 specialists in penal law (legal secretaries)

Xingning xian 興寧縣 Xingning District

xinmo 信末 arsenic

xiong'e 兇惡 evil act

xiongfan 兇犯 vicious criminal

xiongming 兄命 fratricide

Xiyuan jilu 洗冤集錄 *The Washing Away of Wrongs*

Xu Anguo 徐安幗

Xu Ren 徐任

Xu Si 徐四

Xu Xian 許憲

Xuanye 玄燁

Xue Yunsheng (Hsüeh Yun-sheng) 薛允升

xun 旬 ten-day period

xunfu 巡撫 (provincial) governor

xunjian 巡檢 subdistrict magistrate

Xuyi xian 盱眙縣 Xuyi District

yamen 衙門 administrative compound, court

yan 煙 tobacco or opium

Yan Jian 顏檢

Yan Ruilong 嚴瑞龍

Yan Xishen 顏希深

Yang Junwen 楊濬文

Yang Wenqian 楊文乾

Yangli zhou 養利州 Yangli Department

yanxun 嚴訊 interrogate strenuously

Yao Liang 姚梁

Yaozhou 耀州 Yao Department

Ye Ruzhi 葉汝芝

Yedao Hui 掖刀會 Sword-Carrying Society

Ye'erqiang 葉爾羌

yexing xiongcan 野性兇慘 violent nature

Yi 易 or *Yijing* 易經 *Book of Changes*

yi 蟻 I (lit., "ant[like in insignificance]")

Yihemen 義和門 Righteous Harmony Sect (the "Boxers")

Yinghe 英和 (1771–1839)

Yingshou 英綬

Yinjishan 尹繼善 (1696–1771)

yinyang sheng 陰陽生 yin-yang master (Daoist priest)

Yinzhen 胤禎 (1678–1735)

Yishan xian 宜山縣 Yishan District

yishi dongle xienian 時動了邪念 all of a sudden moved by an evil thought

yishi qifen 時氣憤 (or 忿) momentarily lost my temper

yishi qimi le 時氣迷了 momentarily went berserk

yishi qingji 時情急 in the heat of the moment

Yiyang xian 伊陽縣 Yiyang District

Yonghegong 雍和宮 Yonghe Palace

Yongji xian 永濟縣 Yongji District

Yongle zhen 永樂鎮 Yongle Market

Yongshun 永順司 Yongshun Subdistrict

Yongtaili 永太里 Yongtai Hamlet

Yongzheng 雍正

You Qing 尤清

Yu Tingfu 于廷輔

yuan 冤 luck

Yuan Chenglong 袁承寵

Yuan Zhancheng 元展成 (d. 1744)

Yuanfu 元福

yuansi yin 元絲銀 fine (high-grade) silver

Yungui 雲貴

Yunli 允禮

zan shen 拶審 interrogate with finger-squeezers

Zaoyang xian 棗陽縣 Zaoyang District

Zhaijiucun 寨舊村 Old Stockade Village

zhaishi 摘釋 to be held accountable

Zhan Qingzhen 詹清真

Zhang Mengbai 張夢白

Zhang Qu 張渠

Zhang *shi* 張氏 Ms. Zhang

Zhang Mingfu 張明甫

Zhang Xiangqian 張象乾

Zhang Xun 張巡

Zhang Zhisheng 張至聲

Zhang Zhongxiu 張鍾秀

Zhangde fu 彰德府 Zhangde Prefecture

Zhangzhou fu 漳州府 Zhangzhou Prefecture

Zhao Lun 趙綸

Zheng Dao 正道 Proper (Confucian) Way

Zhengding fu 正定府 Zhengding Prefecture

Zhengua Jiao 震卦教 Zhen Trigram School

zhengzhan wuchang, chousha buyi 爭佔無常,雛殺不已 struggled constantly for control, with unending blood feuds

Zhenkong Jiaxiang Wusheng Fumu 真空家鄉無生父母 Primordial Father and Mother of the True Vacuity Land

Zhili 直隸 Zhili Province

Zhilu Zhenren 指路真人 Trailblazing Perfected Man

zhixian 知縣 district magistrate

zhiyuan 職員 term for lower-level degree holders, could be used as first-person pronoun

zhong 忠 loyalty (to the emperor)

Zhongxiao Wang 忠孝王 Loyal and Filial King

Zhongyong 中庸 *The Doctrine of the Mean*

Zhou Bangyuan 周邦元

Zhou Fengyang 周奉揚

Zhou Fuquan 周扶全

Zhou Guizheng 周貴正

Zhou Sanming 周三明

Zhou Wenqiang 周文強

Zhou Yongtai 周永泰

Zhou Yuren 周于人

Zhu Bingren 祝秉仁

Zhu Jia Xinzhuang 朱家新莊 New Zhu Family Manor

Zhu Shaozeng 朱紹曾

Zhu Xian 祝現 (祝顯)

Zhu Zhaolong 竺兆隴

Zhu Zuoding 朱作鼎

Zhuang Man 僮蠻 Zhuang "barbarians"

zhuangding 莊丁 farmworker

zhuangtou 莊頭 manor head

Zhuangzu 僮族 Zhuang people

zhuofu 拙婦 first-person pronoun used by women

Zong Liushui 總流水 General Navigator

Zongli liangchu 總理糧儲

zu 祖 clan, lineage

Zuo Fengxian 左奉先

Zuo Zhuan 左傳 Zuo Commentary (to *Chunqiu*)

zuoling 佐領 companies

zuozao 做棗 preserving jujubes

Zuozhi yaoyan 佐治藥言 *Admonitions on Assisting with Governance*

Bibliography of Studies in English

Allee, Mark A. *Law and Local Society in Late Imperial China: Northern Taiwan in the Nineteenth Century.* Stanford, Calif.: Stanford University Press, 1994.

Antony, Robert J. "Scourges on the People: Perceptions of Robbery, Snatching, and Theft in the Mid-Qing Period." *Late Imperial China* 16.2 (1995): 98–132.

Bartlett, Beatrice S. *Monarchs and Ministers: The Grand Council in Mid-Ch'ing China, 1723–1820.* Berkeley: University of California Press, 1991.

Bernhard, Kathryn, and Philip C. C. Huang, eds. *Civil Law in Qing and Republican China.* Stanford, Calif.: Stanford University Press, 1994.

Bodde, Derk. "Prison Life in Eighteenth-Century Peking." *Journal of the American Oriental Society* 89.2 (1969): 311–33.

Bodde, Derk, and Clarence Morris. *Law in Imperial China: Exemplified by 190 Ch'ing Dynasty Cases (Translated from the* Hsing-an hui-lan) *with Historical, Social, and Juridical Commentaries.* Cambridge, Mass.: Harvard University Press, 1967.

Brokaw, Cynthia. *Commerce in Culture: The Sibao Book Trade in the Qing and Republican Periods.* Cambridge, Mass.: Harvard University Asia Center, 2007.

———. "Supernatural Retribution and Human Destiny." In *Religions of China in Practice*, edited by Donald S. Lopez, Jr., 423–36. Princeton, N.J.: Princeton University Press, 1996.

Brook, Timothy, Jérôme Bourgon, and Gregory Blue. *Death by a Thousand Cuts.* Cambridge, Mass.: Harvard University Press, 2008.

Brunnert, H. S., and V. V. Hagelstrom. *Present Day Political Organization of China.*

Revised by N. Th. Kolessoff. Translated by A. Beltchenko and E. E. Moran. Shanghai: Kelly and Walsh, 1912.

Buoye, Thomas. "Economic Change and Rural Violence: Homicides Related to Disputes over Property Rights in Guangdong during the Eighteenth Century." *Peasant Studies* 17.4 (1990): 233–59.

———. *Manslaughter, Markets, and Moral Economy: Violent Disputes over Property Rights in 18th-Century China*. New York: Cambridge University Press, 2000.

———. "Suddenly a Murderous Intent Arose: Bureaucratization and Benevolence in Eighteenth-Century Homicide Reports." *Late Imperial China* 16.2 (1995): 62–97.

Capote, Truman. *In Cold Blood: A True Account of a Multiple Murder and Its Consequences*. 1965. New York: Vintage Books, 1993.

Carlitz, Katherine. "Genre and Justice in Late Qing China: Wu Woyao's *Strange Case of Nine Murders* and Its Antecedents." In Hegel and Carlitz, *Writing and Law*, 234–57.

Cheng, Pei-kai, and Michael Lestz, with Jonathan D. Spence, eds. *The Search for Modern China: A Documentary Collection*. New York: Norton, 1999.

Chesneaux, Jean. *Secret Societies in China in the Nineteenth and Twentieth Centuries*. Translated by Gillian Nettle. Ann Arbor: University of Michigan Press, 1971.

Ch'ü T'ung-tsu. *Law and Society in Traditional China*. Paris: Mouton, 1961.

———. *Local Government in China under the Ch'ing*. 1962. Reprint, Cambridge, Mass.: Harvard University Council on East Asian Studies, 1988.

Conner, Allison W. "Chinese Confessions and the Use of Torture." In *La Torture judiciare: Approches historiques et juridiques*, edited by Bernard Durand, 63–91. Lille, France: Centre d'histoire judiciare éditeur, 2002.

Crossley, Pamela Kyle. *The Manchus*. Cambridge, Mass.: Blackwell Publishers, 1997.

Curwen, Charles A. *Taiping Rebel: The Deposition of Li Hsiu-ch'eng*. Cambridge: Cambridge University Press, 1977.

de Grazia, Margreta. "Sanctioning Voice: Quotation Marks, the Abolition of Torture, and the Fifth Amendment." In *The Construction of Authorship: Textual Appropriation in Law and Literature*, edited by Martha Woodmansee and Peter Jaszi, 281–302. Durham, N.C.: Duke University Press, 1994.

Dunstheimer, Guillaume. "Some Religious Aspects of Secret Societies." In *Popular Movements and Secret Societies in China 1840–1950*, edited by Jean Chesneaux, 23–28. Stanford, Calif.: Stanford University Press, 1972.

Ebrey, Patricia Buckley. *Cambridge Illustrated History of China*. New York: Cambridge University Press, 1996.

———, ed. *Chinese Civilization: A Sourcebook*. 2nd ed. New York: The Free Press, 1993.

Elman, Benjamin A. *A Cultural History of Civil Examinations in Late Imperial China.* Berkeley: University of California Press, 2000.

Friedman, Lawrence M. *Crime and Punishment in American History.* New York: Basic Books, 1993.

Giles, Herbert A. *Historic China and Other Sketches.* London: Thomas de la Rue, 1882.

Gulik, Robert H. van, trans. *T'ang-yin-pi-shih, "Parallel Cases from 'Under the Pear Tree,'" a 13th-century Manual of Jurisprudence and Detection.* Leiden: E. J. Brill, 1956.

Guy, Kent. *The Emperor's Four Treasuries: Scholars and the State in the Late Ch'ien-lung Era.* Cambridge, Mass.: Harvard University Council on East Asian Studies, 1987.

Harrell, Stevan, ed. *Cultural Encounters on China's Ethnic Frontiers.* Seattle: University of Washington Press, 1995.

Harrison, Judy Feldman. "Wrongful Treatment of Prisoners: A Case Study of Ch'ing Legal Practice." *Journal of Asian Studies* 23 (1964): 227–44.

Hayden, George A. *Crime and Punishment in Medieval Chinese Drama: Three Judge Pao Plays.* Cambridge, Mass.: Harvard University Press, 1978.

Hegel, Robert E. "Distinguishing Levels of Audiences for Ming-Ch'ing Vernacular Literature: A Case Study." In *Popular Culture in Late Imperial China,* edited by David Johnson, Andrew J. Nathan, and Evelyn S. Rawski, 112–42. Berkeley: University of California Press, 1985.

———. "Images in Legal and Fictional Texts from Qing China." *Bulletin de l'Ecole français d'Extrême-Orient* 89 (2002): 271–83.

Hegel, Robert E., and Katherine Carlitz, eds. *Writing and Law in Late Imperial China: Crime, Conflict, and Judgment.* Seattle: University of Washington Press, 2007.

Herman, John E. "Empire in the Southwest: Early Qing Reforms to the Native Chieftain System." *Journal of Asian Studies* 56.1 (1997): 47–74.

Ho Ping-ti (He Bingdi). *The Ladder of Success in Imperial China: Aspects of Social Mobility, 1368–1911.* New York: Columbia University Press, 1962.

———. "The Significance of the Ch'ing Period in Chinese History." *Journal of Asian Studies* 26.2 (1967): 189–95.

Huang Liu-hung (Huang Liuhong). *A Complete Book concerning Happiness and Benevolence: A Manual for Local Magistrates in Seventeenth-Century China.* Translated and edited by Djang Chu. Tucson: University of Arizona Press, 1984.

Huang, Philip C. C. *Civil Justice in China: Representation and Practice in the Qing.* Stanford, Calif.: Stanford University Press, 1996.

Huang, Ray. *China: A Macro History.* Armonk, N.Y.: M. E. Sharpe, 1997.

Hucker, Charles O. *A Dictionary of Official Titles in Imperial China.* Stanford, Calif.: Stanford University Press, 1985.

Hummel, Arthur W., ed. *Eminent Chinese of the Ch'ing Period (1644–1912)*. Washington, D.C.: Government Printing Office, 1943.

Jones, William C., trans. *The Great Qing Code*. New York: Oxford University Press, 1994.

Kahn, Harold L. *Monarchy in the Emperor's Eyes: Image and Reality in the Ch'ien-lung Reign*. Cambridge, Mass.: Harvard University Press, 1971.

Katz, Paul R. "Indictment Rituals and the Judicial Continuum in Late Imperial China." In Hegel and Carlitz, *Writing and Law*, 161–85.

King, Peter. *Crime and Law in England, 1750–1840: Remaking Justice from the Margins*. New York: Cambridge University Press, 2006.

Kuhn, Philip A. *Soulstealers: The Chinese Sorcery Scare of 1768*. Cambridge, Mass.: Harvard University Press, 1990.

Lamley, Harry J. "Lineage Feuding in Southern Fujian and Eastern Guangdong under Qing Rule." In *Violence in China: Essays in Culture and Counterculture*, edited by Jonathan N. Lipman and Stevan Harrell, 27–64. Albany: State University of New York Press, 1990.

Lan Dingyuan. "Lan Dingyuan's Casebook." Translated by Lai Jeh-hang and Lily Hwa. In *Chinese Civilization and Society: A Sourcebook*, edited by Patricia Buckley Ebrey, 292–96. 2nd ed. New York: Free Press, 1993.

Lan Ting-yüan (Lan Dingyuan). "Lan Lu-chow's Criminal Cases." In *Historic China*, by Herbert A. Giles, 141–232.

Liu, Yongping. *Origins of Chinese Law: Penal and Administrative Law in Its Early Development*. New York: Oxford University Press, 1998.

Macauley, Melissa. *Social Power and Legal Culture: Litigation Masters in Late Imperial China*. Stanford, Calif.: Stanford University Press, 1998.

MacCormack, Geoffrey. "Cause, Status and Fault in the Traditional Chinese Law of Homicide." In *Critical Studies in Ancient Law, Comparative Law and Legal History*, edited by John W. Cairns, O. F. Robinson, and Alan Watson, 173–82. Portland, Ore.: Hart Publishing, 2001.

———. *Traditional Chinese Penal Law*. Edinburgh: University of Edinburgh Press, 1991.

Mair, Victor H. "Language and Ideology in the Written Popularizations of the *Sacred Edict*." In *Popular Culture in Late Imperial China*, edited by David Johnson et al., 325–59. Berkeley: University of California Press, 1985.

McKnight, Brian, and James T. C. Liu, eds. and trans. *The Enlightened Judgments: Ch'ing Ming chi, The Sung Dynasty Collection*. Albany: State University of New York Press, 1999.

McLeod, Katrina C. D., and Robin D. S. Yates. "Forms of Ch'in Law: An Annotated

Translation of the *Feng-chen shih*." *Harvard Journal of Asiatic Studies* 41:1 (1981): 111–63.

Meijer, Marinus Johan. "The Autumn Assizes in Ch'ing Law." *T'oung Pao* 70 (1984): 1–17.

———. *Murder and Adultery in Late Imperial China: A Study of Law and Morality*. Leiden: E. J. Brill, 1991.

Min, Tu-ki (Min Douji). "The Theory of Political Feudalism in the Ch'ing Period." In *National Polity and Local Power: The Transformation of Late Imperial China*, edited by Philip A. Kuhn and Timothy Brook, 89–136. Cambridge, Mass.: Harvard University Press, 1989.

Mote, Frederick W. *Imperial China 900–1800*. Cambridge, Mass.: Harvard University Press, 1999.

Murray, Dian H. *Pirates of the South China Coast 1790–1810*. Stanford, Calif.: Stanford University Press, 1987.

Murray, Dian H., in collaboration with Qin Baoqi. *The Origins of the Tiandihui: The Chinese Triads in Legend and History*. Stanford, Calif.: Stanford University Press, 1994.

Naquin, Susan. *Millenarian Rebellion in China: The Eight Trigrams Uprising of 1813*. New Haven, Conn.: Yale University Press, 1976.

———. *Shantung Rebellion: The Wang Lun Uprising of 1774*. New Haven, Conn.: Yale University Press, 1981.

———. "The Transmission of White Lotus Sectarianism in Late Imperial China." In *Popular Culture in Late Imperial China*, edited by David Johnson et al., 255–90. Berkeley: University of California Press, 1985.

———. "True Confessions: Criminal Interrogations as Sources for Ch'ing History." *National Palace Museum Bulletin* 11.1 (1976): 1–17.

Naquin, Susan, and Evelyn S. Rawski. *Chinese Society in the Eighteenth Century*. New Haven, Conn.: Yale University Press, 1987.

Ownby, David. *Brotherhoods and Secret Societies in Early and Mid-Qing China: The Formation of a Tradition*. Stanford, Calif.: Stanford University Press, 1996.

Park, Nancy E. "Corruption in Eighteenth-Century China." *Journal of Asian Studies* 56.4 (1997): 967–1005.

Park, Nancy, and Robert Antony. "Archival Research in Qing Legal History." *Late Imperial China* 14.1 (1993): 93–137.

Reardon-Anderson, James. *Reluctant Pioneers: China's Expansion Northward, 1644–1937*. Stanford, Calif.: Stanford University Press, 2005.

Reed, Bradly W. *Talons and Teeth: District Clerks and Runners in the Qing Dynasty*. Stanford, Calif.: Stanford University Press, 2000.

Robinson, David. *Bandits, Eunuchs, and the Son of Heaven: Rebellion and the Economy of Violence in Mid-Ming China*. Honolulu: University of Hawai'i Press, 2001.

Rowe, William T. *Saving the World: Chen Hongmou and Elite Consciousness in Eighteenth-Century China*. Stanford, Calif.: Stanford University Press, 2001.

Shahar, Meir, and Robert P. Weller, eds. *Unruly Gods: Divinity and Society in China*. Honolulu: University of Hawai'i Press, 1996.

Sharpe, J. A. *Crime in Early Modern England, 1550–1750*. London and New York: Longman, 1984.

Sommer, Matthew H. *Sex, Law, and Society in Late Imperial China*. Stanford, Calif.: Stanford University Press, 2000.

Spence, Jonathan D. *The Death of Woman Wang*. New York: Viking Press, 1978.

———. *Emperor of China: Self-Portrait of K'ang-hsi*. New York: Vintage, 1975.

———. *God's Chinese Son: The Taiping Heavenly Kingdom of Hong Xiuquan*. New York: Norton, 1996.

———. *The Search for Modern China*. 2nd ed. New York: Norton, 1999.

———. *Treason by the Book*. New York: Viking, 2001.

———. *Ts'ao Yin and the K'ang-hsi Emperor: Bondservant and Master*. New Haven, Conn.: Yale University Press, 1966.

St. André, James. "Reading Court Cases from the Song to the Ming: Fact and Fiction, Law and Literature." In Hegel and Carlitz, *Writing and Law*, 189–214.

Stary, Giovanni. *A Dictionary of Manchu Names: A Name-Index to the Manchu Version of the "Complete Genealogies of the Manchu Clans and Families of the Eight Banners," Jakūn gūsai Manjusai mukūn hala be uheri ejehe bithe/Baqi Manzhou shizu tongpu*. Wiesbaden, Germany: Harrassowitz, 2000.

Stone, Lawrence. "Interpersonal Violence in English Society 1300–1980." *Past and Present* 101 (1983): 22–33.

Sung Tz'u (Song Ci). *The Washing Away of Wrongs*. Translated by Brian McKnight. Ann Arbor: University of Michigan Center for Chinese Studies, 1981.

ter Haar, Barend J. *The White Lotus Teachings in Chinese Religious History*. Leiden: Brill, 1992. Reprint, Honolulu: University of Hawai'i Press, 1999.

Theiss, Janet. *Disgraceful Matters: The Politics of Chastity in Eighteenth-Century China*. Berkeley: University of California Press, 2005.

Tong, James W. *Disorder under Heaven: Collective Violence in the Ming Dynasty*. Stanford, Calif.: Stanford University Press, 1991.

van der Sprenkel, Sybille. *Legal Institutions in Manchu China: A Sociological Analysis*. London: University of London Athlone Press, 1962.

Wakefield, David. *Fenjia: Household Division and Inheritance in Qing and Republican China*. Honolulu: University of Hawai'i Press, 1998.

Wakeman, Frederic, Jr. *The Great Enterprise: The Manchu Reconstruction of Imperial Order in Seventeenth-Century China*. Berkeley: University of California Press, 1985.

Waley-Cohen, Joanna. "Politics and the Supernatural in Mid-Qing Legal Culture." *Modern China* 19.3 (1993): 330–53.

Ward, Barbara. "Chinese Secret Societies." In *Secret Societies*, edited by Norman MacKenzie, 210–41. New York: Holt, Rinehart, Winston, 1968.

Watt, John R. *The District Magistrate in Late Imperial China*. New York: Columbia University Press, 1972.

Weisberg, Richard, and Jean-Pierre Barricelli. "Literature and the Law." In *Interrelationships of Literature*, edited by Jean-Pierre Barricelli and Joseph Gibaldi, 150–75. New York: Modern Language Association, 1982.

Will, Pierre-Etienne. *Bureaucracy and Famine in Eighteenth-Century China*. Translated by Elborg Forster. Stanford, Calif.: Stanford University Press, 1990.

Yang, C. K. *Religion in Chinese Society*. Berkeley: University of California Press, 1961.

Ye, Wa, and Joseph W. Esherick, comps. *Chinese Archives: An Introductory Guide*. Berkeley: Center for Chinese Studies, Institute of East Asian Studies, University of California, 1996.

Youd, Daniel. "Beyond *Bao*: Moral Ambiguity and the Law in Late Imperial Chinese Narrative Literature." In Hegel and Carlitz, *Writing and Law*, 215–33.

Zehr, Howard. *Crime and the Development of Modern Society: Patterns of Criminality in Nineteenth Century Germany and France*. London: Croom Helm; Totowa, N.J.: Rowman and Littlefield, 1976.

Zhou, Guangyuan. "Illusion and Reality in the Law of the Late Qing: A Sichuan Case Study." *Modern China* 19.4 (1993): 427–56.

Index

brotherhood, in religious groups, 248. *See also* religious communities; secret societies

brothers, relations between, 37–51, 122–27, 128–33, 201

Buddhism, 6, 175, 248–49

Buddhist monks, ix, 202–4, 223, 231, 242n22, 246, 250

bureaucratic structures, 9, 10, 12,

burial clothing, 229, 238

butchers, 120, 183

caning, as punishment, 101, 102n2

cattle, 151, 156, 158, 165, 173. *See also* water buffalo

Cedan, 143

censorate, 31–32, 76, 132, 206

charms, healing, 202, 241n9, 249

chastity, 9, 73, 78n7

Chen Shaoyong, 190

children, 10, 125, 206–7, 211–12, 214, 237–38; as occasion for argument, 81; position in family, 86–87, 89, 189; in religious institutions, 202; sale of, 39, 45, 107–15; testimony by, 114–15, 130, 214; as victims of violence, 151, 154, 209. *See also* kidnapping

civil lawsuits, 10, 12, 122

clerks, government, 183, 226–41

clothing, 40–41, 54, 57, 66–74, 85, 108, 115, 177, 208, 223, 229, 231, 241n13. *See also* burial clothing; dress, style of

collective violence, 247–50. *See also* rebellion; religious communities

commitments, personal, 177, 186, 197, 248

compensation, financial, 51, 102, 148, 171–73

complaints, written, 14–15; examples of, 31, 38–39, 53, 65, 80, 87, 91–92, 105, 149–53, 166, 206, 236, 239

confessions, 58, 80, 140, 228–40; in accidental homicide, 95, 99–101, 124–25, 131–32; forced, 10; legal means to obtain, 16; of perpetrators, 40, 48–51, 56–57, 69–72, 83–89, 107–8, 110–15, 119–20, 135–38, 144–45, 158–67, 201–4, 207–8, 214–16, 219–21, 233–36; requirement to obtain, 16, 22, 60–

62; under torture, 160–65. *See also* depositions, witness; testimony

conflict resolution, 10, 12, 140–42, 173–74

"Confucian" values, 8–10, 12, 13, 23, 24n13, 27n45, 37, 122–45, 248–50. *See also* education system; family: relationships

conscience, 39, 46. *See also* shame

contracts, legal, 44, 122

corporal punishments. *See* beating, as punishment; beheading; dismemberment; punishments; strangulation

coroners (*zuowu*), 15, 31, 42, 53, 59, 66, 92, 105–6, 117, 129, 134, 143, 151, 208–9, 229–31, 241n16

corpses, 15, 31, 41, 43, 47, 53, 65–66, 73, 75, 78n3, 85, 87, 105, 117–19, 123, 129, 134–35, 138, 143, 151, 208–10, 229, 240

corvée labor, 191, 200n14

counter complaint, 152–53

courtroom, 15–16

crime case fiction (*gong'an xiaoshuo*), 20, 26n41

culpability for crimes, 10, 11, 12, 13, 19, 95

Da Qing lüli, 13, 36

dates, and dating, xv–xvi, 127n5

Daoist priests, 220, 229, 241n3. *See also* religious communities

debt collection, 104–10

debts, and indebtedness, 31, 32–36, 108, 210–11, 214–15, 219, 223

decapitation. *See* beheading

degrees, academic, 117–18, 121n1, 219, 221, 226, 242n18. *See also* education system

deities, 242n20

Deming, 104

depositions, witness, 15; examples of, 32–33, 35, 39–41, 43–47, 54–56, 67–68, 81–83, 93–95, 97–101, 108–10, 118–19, 123–24, 130–31, 137–38, 140, 143–45, 155–57, 168–70, 207, 209–14, 228–30, 237–39. *See also* confessions; testimony

destruction of property, 90–96, 148–74

Deyu, 117

disability, physical, 82, 84

ASIAN LAW SERIES

CPSIA information can be obtained
at www.ICGtesting.com
Printed in the USA
JSHW081218260223
38226JS00002B/26